The Interpretation of
BACH's Keyboard Works

The Interpretation of
BACH's Keyboard Works

Erwin Bodky

PROFESSOR OF MUSIC
BRANDEIS UNIVERSITY

HARVARD UNIVERSITY PRESS
Cambridge, Massachusetts   1960

Library of Congress Catalog Card Number 58–10396
Printed at the Pitman Press, Bath, England

Preface

The nucleus of the research work on the instrument problem, which forms the first part of this book, was first published some twenty-eight years ago in my *Der Vortrag alter Klaviermusik* (Berlin: Max Hesse Verlag, 1932). It was largely through the recommendation of the late Alfred Einstein that this youthful book was honored with a place in the distinguished series of Hesse's *Musik-Handbücher*. During the time since then, I have consolidated my findings and, in the present book, expound the theses on a much broader basis than I was able to furnish in the first "essay."

Meanwhile, I have learned that in regard to all the other problems of Bach interpretation we achieve much better results when we do not try to confine the master's works to the traditional rules of the baroque era, which were derived from works of much smaller scope. These rules should be accepted as a basis for Bach performance only insofar as they are verified by unambiguous facts from Bach's writing methods. The large quantity of fact-finding material which is presented here for the first time may speak for itself.

Although I know only too well and have outlined over and over again how much of Bach's language is still a secret, I hope that the principle of my approach to the problem of the interpretation of Bach's keyboard works may prove to be a spring-board to further investigations.

For detailed and helpful suggestions I am deeply indebted to Professors Putnam Aldrich, Kenneth Levy, Eduard Lowinsky, and Alfred Mann, and to Frank Hubbard and Hugo Kauder. I regret that I cannot now express my thanks to my revered friends, the late Alfred Einstein, indefatigable and benevolent adviser of an entire generation of scholars, and the late Herman de Grab, fine connoisseur of early music, who watched the growth of this study with friendliest encouragement.

To the following publishers I express my appreciation for permission to include material from their books: to the Harvard University Press for quotations from Paul Hindemith, *A Composer's World*; to W. W. Norton and Co., Inc., New York, for quotations from their translation of C. P. E. Bach, *Essay on the True Art of Playing Keyboard Instruments*, by William Mitchell, and from Curt Sachs, *The Commonwealth of Art*; to Köhler and Amelang, Leipzig, for quotations from Arnold Schering, *Das Symbol in der Musik*. (I should mention that translations are mine unless otherwise stated.) The pictures of the harpsichord on the jacket and the clavichord on the jacket and in the book are reproduced with permission from Donald Boalch, M.A., *Makers of the Harpsichord and Clavichord, 1440–1840* (London: George Ronald; New York: The Macmillan Co.)—the harpsichord by courtesy of Mr. R. Russell, the clavichord by courtesy of Mr. J. M. Taphouse and Professor J. A. Westrup. The pictures of the harpsichord and the clavichord actions are reprinted with permission from Hanns Neupert, *Vom Musikstab zum Modernen Klavier* (Bamberg: J. C. Neupert); the Hass harpsichord from the catalogue of the Musikhistorisk Museum, Copenhagen. The picture of the Bach Flügel is reprinted from Hanns Neupert, *Das Cembalo*; Bach's Table of Ornaments from Ludwig Landshoff's edition of Bach's Inventions and Sinfonias, C. Peters, Leipzig; the "gebunden" clavichord from Bertha van Beijnum-von Essen, *Bouwengeschiedenis van het Klavier* (Rotterdam: W. L. and J. Busse's).

Professor Putnam Aldrich kindly permitted extensive quotations from his unpublished Harvard dissertation, "The Principal Agréments of the Seventeenth and Eighteenth Centuries." Invaluable help was given by Janice Richmond Lourie and Sandra Rosenblum in the preparation of my manuscript. Mr. Ernst Vogel, Basel, copied the music samples in Appendix B in the most painstaking way, and the editorial staff of the Harvard University Press cannot be thanked enough for their co-operation in the production of this book. Finally, I want to express my deep gratitude to Mrs. Adolph Ullman and Mrs. Helen S. Slosberg, and especially to Brandeis University for grants which helped make publication of this book possible.

Erwin Bodky

Publisher's Note: At the time of his death in December 1958, Professor Bodky had completed his work on the manuscript of this book and was giving it a final reading preparatory to checking proof. The Press, with the co-operation of the Eda K. Loeb Music Library of Harvard University, has handled the proofreading and indexing, and so far as was possible made the corrections that Professor Bodky would normally have made himself.

Contents

List of Illustrations

The Interpretation of
BACH's Keyboard Works

Introduction

Whoever sets out to study the so-called "piano works" of Johann Sebastian Bach with the earnest desire to play them as Bach expected them to be rendered finds himself caught in a most puzzling situation. He discovers complete disagreement among all those whom he consults for guidance in the correct style of performance—a confusion of opinions such as cannot be found in any other field of interpretation of great music. No two pianists, no two harpsichordists, ever give approximately similar performances of the same piece; no two editions of the "piano" works agree even about such basic elements of interpretation as tempo, dynamics, and articulation. Some teachers think that they achieve the true Bach style by banning all crescendos and diminuendos, by not using the pedal at all, and by keeping time in the strictest metronomical way. Other teachers advise just the opposite and anxiously look for the smallest opportunity for the display of romantic sentimentality. Musicologists themselves have not been able to agree upon what might have been Bach's own artistic intentions, although the problems inherent in the keyboard works have certainly not been neglected.

This deplorable confusion was created—alas—by Johann Sebastian Bach himself. When he wrote for keyboard instruments, he put down very little beyond the naked notes, and thus gave almost no direct information about tempo, dynamics, and articulation. It was neither laziness nor carelessness that caused Bach to omit all guiding marks in his keyboard music. He merely shared the habits of the other composers of his period, and, since all these men displayed this same deficiency in their manuscripts, only two conclusions are possible: these musicians felt certain that whoever of their contemporaries played a keyboard instrument had a general knowledge of how to treat these problems; and the compositions themselves contained some secret guiding marks that imparted to connoisseurs the correct manner of performance.

The first of these conclusions is not a new one. The scarcity of material on performance practice in musical treatises of this period makes

1

it evident that there existed a kind of unwritten code which had been transferred from generation to generation as an oral tradition. Unfortunately, the eighty years from Bach's death in 1750 to the beginning of the Bach renaissance after 1829, the year of Mendelssohn's revival of the *St. Matthew Passion*, were sufficient to destroy all knowledge of baroque music and its principles of interpretation. Since 1829, legions of historians, musicologists, and artists have tried to restore this lost knowledge bit by bit, a labor which may be justifiably compared with the efforts to regain information on Roman and Grecian culture with the help of the excavations at Pompeii and Mycenae. Yet the confusion that still governs our contemporary dealings with the problems of Bach interpretation proves that the material provided by several generations of research workers has not yet brought sufficient results to re-establish the basic laws according to which Bach's keyboard music was and should be performed.

What can be said about the second of our conclusions, that the keyboard compositions by Bach contain some secret guiding marks, characteristic signs which were known in his time to everybody who played a keyboard instrument and which contained the basic information needed for a good rendition? We will show that this conclusion is correct too, and that only a gap in research work has prevented us from becoming aware of this all-important fact. Bach certainly did not—and could not —foresee that a few decades later his keyboard music would no longer be played on the harpsichord and clavichord, for which he had written it, but on an entirely new instrument, the pianoforte. It seems almost unbelievable that we have accepted the legitimacy of the piano as the successor of the harpsichord and clavichord with such lightheartedness. This belief is still so prevalent in the musical world that many thousands of music lovers, including professionals, do not know that Bach never wrote a single note for the modern piano, which was still rather poor, mechanically, during his lifetime. Would it not, therefore, have been only logical that, before one dared to play compositions written for harpsichord and clavichord on the piano, a painstaking and systematic examination of the mechanisms, techniques, possibilities, and limitations of the old instruments should have been undertaken? Strangely enough, such a thorough investigation has never been made heretofore.

In the pages to follow we present the far-reaching results which could be obtained from the exploration of this so badly neglected subject. We will show that one needs to familiarize oneself with only a few basic technical principles of the old instruments in order to reach some startling conclusions. It will become obvious that the generally established belief —that the composers of the baroque period did not care whether one played their keyboard music on the harpsichord, on the clavichord, or even on the organ—can, at least for the keyboard works of Johann Sebastian Bach, no longer be maintained. We will see that Bach's methods of composition are much more refined than those of his predecessors, and we will seek out the secret guiding marks, the beacons that he built into his keyboard compositions to direct their interpretation. Only the thoughtless and entirely mechanical transfer of the compositions from harpsichord and clavichord to the piano has prevented discovery of these marks at an earlier time. In addition, we will show that knowledge of the instrument for which an individual keyboard composition was designed is indispensable for a true understanding of the meaning of the piece, and that this knowledge is sufficient to disperse most of the difficulties that have so far prevented us from finding a unified and historically and aesthetically justified way of interpreting the works of Bach on the piano.

Yet the instrument problem is not the only one that puzzles an interpreter of Bach's music who takes his task seriously. Although problems of dynamics disappear with the solution of the instrument question, those of tempo, ornamentation, and articulation still remain, and the nature of the issues involved makes it impossible that valid solutions for all aspects of them can and will ever be found. In our discussions of these problems it seems to us most imperative to separate as clearly as possible what we know to be fact from what is based only on personal interpretation and evaluation. In too many cases such interpretations have been offered to the Bach student in a way that has led him to believe they were authoritative ones.

Unfortunately, in the case of Bach, even the authentic rules (those which, according to the contemporary texts, were part of the common practice of the period) will not give us over-all solutions. Bach's artistic imagination was so great that scarcely a rule exists which he did not gladly break if he found it appropriate to do so. However, it is exactly these cases of rule-breaking which we found extremely fruitful for gaining insight into Bach's artistic goals, and good luck and incessant searching have enabled us to present a considerable amount of hitherto undiscussed material pertaining to these problems. It may be disappointing that the formidable weight of the cases of rule-breaking forces us to abstain from making dangerous generalizations and sweeping rules, especially for the problems of ornamentation and articulation. Yet a careful study of them will make it clear how much a composer of this period could dare to leave to the creative imagination of the "connoisseurs and amateurs of music" for whom he wrote "to refresh their spirits" (the formula so frequently found on title pages of baroque music).

To restudy the basic language of Bach's time will certainly be much more profitable than to meditate about which part of Bach's music is outmoded (especially in regard to his ornaments) and about what has to be done to save the timeless values in his music from being overshadowed by those places in which he "paid tribute to his bourgeois surroundings." These eternal values will become our own far more easily if we approach the work of the great composer with that spirit of humility we owe to its greatness, instead of debating how to adapt his music to the idiom of our contemporary musical conceptions. In such a spirit of humility this book tries to bring us at least somewhat closer to a kind of Bach interpretation that is worthy of its great subject.

CHAPTER 1

Historical Review

In order to understand the comparative features of the harpsichord and clavichord, the instruments for which Bach wrote, it will be necessary to give a brief description of the historical development and the principles of construction of these instruments.[1] The earliest history, especially that of the clavichord, is still somewhat obscure.[2] One finds both instruments mentioned for the first time in Johannes de Muris' *Musica Speculativa* (1323); the earliest pictures seem to be those of the *Weimarer Wunderbuch* (1440),[3] which are preceded only by a miniature depicting a harpsichord from the year 1409.[4] The oldest harpsichord that has come down to us is in the Victoria and Albert Museum in London; it was made by Hieronymus Bononiensis[5] and is dated Rome, 1521. The clavichords that have been preserved are of somewhat later date, but by 1550 quite a few "clavichordiemakers" were registered in the city of Antwerp.[6]

---

[1] For a more comprehensive report see Curt Sachs, *The History of Musical Instruments* (New York, 1940).

[2] We do not yet know the exact date when the Greek "testing instrument," the "monochord," became a keyed, "polychordic" instrument. Around A.D. 1100, it had evidently become a musical instrument played by acrobats and minnesingers. The names "monochord" and "clavichord" were used interchangeably for quite a while.

[3] These are frequently reproduced. See Hanns Neupert, *Das Cembalo* (Kassel, 1933), p. 26. In the *Archiv für Musikforschung*, Jahrgang 1 (1936), Heft 1, p. 42, Georg Schünemann published in an article, "Die Musikinstrumente der 24 Alten," an unusually beautiful picture of a clavichord, found in Cod. 8789, Bl. 3, Coburg, Gymnasium Casimirianum, dated 1448.

[4] See Sachs, p. 337.

[5] See Donald Boalch, *Makers of the Harpsichord and Clavichord, 1440–1840* (New York, 1956).

[6] Dr. J. A. Stellfeld, "Bronnen tot de Geschiedenis der Antwerpsche clavecymbel- en orgelbouwers in de XVIe en XVIIe eeuwen," *Vlaamsch Jaarboek voor Muziekgeschiedenis* (Antwerp, 1942), pp. 3ff. Especially interesting is a remark (p. 66) on Joost Kareest, born in 1500; originally a clavichord maker, he later became a harpsichord maker.

The chief difference between the two instruments is in the manner of tone production. All instruments belonging to the harpsichord family —virginals, spinets, and cembali—produce their tone with the help of a plectrum that plucks the strings. This plectrum, made from a crow quill or, later, from leather, is attached to the upper end of a jack, a piece of wood set into vertical motion by pressing down a key. If the finger is lifted from the key, the jack falls back and an escape spring makes it ready for the next plucking. The tone produced in this way is of metallic brilliancy but not unpleasantly sharp, so that old writers talk frequently of the "silvery sound" of the harpsichord. This tone, however, always has the same volume and cannot be directly influenced by touch. In other words, crescendo and diminuendo cannot be produced on a harpsichord.

The boredom created by such a deficiency was early recognized, and since no change in the tone volume could be achieved by mechanical devices, the only way to give the instrument any variety of sound was to add more sets of strings that either produced the same tone once more in a slightly different tone color, or that sounded one octave higher or lower. The official names of these sets of strings are "eight-foot" register for normal pitch, "four-foot" for the octave higher, and "sixteen-foot" for the octave lower.[7] The tone volumes of these sets of strings do not differ much in intensity, but the difference in tone color is very great, so that one speaks of the "light" or "bright" character of the four-foot and the "dark" character of the sixteen-foot set. The various registers will be represented hereafter by the symbols 8', 4', 16'.

Soon it became necessary to add a second keyboard for handling one or two sets of strings individually, and here and there harpsichords with three keyboards can be found.[8] Hand stops—little buttons within reach of the player's hand above the keyboard—regulate the "putting in" or "taking out" of these series of strings by placing the plectra either in a position to be ready for plucking or in a neutral spot to one side of the strings. By putting all plectra in a neutral spot, the player can make the harpsichord entirely "mute."

In addition to the basic registers, most harpsichords are equipped with a lute stop, a damping device that prevents the strings from prolonged vibration, making the tone similar to that of a lute. Instruments with two keyboards are also provided with a coupler, which allows the strings of the upper keyboard to be played on the lower one too, so that all sets of strings can be played at the same time. This is called the "full work" of

---

[7] These terms were adopted from organ usage, where they are more applicable since they describe the actual length of the organ pipes.

[8] First evidence of a harpsichord with two keyboards appears in the middle of the sixteenth century. See Sachs, p. 341.

the instrument. The coupler works in such a way that two handles, one at each end of the lower keyboard, make it possible to push the entire keyboard one inch backward; this manipulation places all jacks in position for simultaneous attack. Note that two hands are necessary for handling the coupler, so that this device can be used only if the composer has given a brief rest to both hands at the same time. Any change in registration through the use of hand stops is possible only if one hand has a rest sufficiently long to move the stop. Both these facts should be kept in mind, since they will prove to be of greatest importance when we try to retrace the playing methods used on the harpsichord.

Great variety can be found in the types of harpsichords. The names "virginal," "spinet," and "spinettino" were reserved for instruments with only one set of strings. They were built in rectangular or pentagonal forms, while harpsichords were constructed in the form of a harp placed in a horizontal position, similar to the modern grand piano. Harpsichords with one keyboard were most often provided with two sets of strings, two 8' (each of slightly different tone color) or one 8' and one 4'. Instruments with only one 8' set were sometimes supplemented by a spinettino with 4' strings placed above, thus effecting an additional tone color. Harpsichords with two keyboards were generally equipped with three sets of strings, 8' and 4' on the lower keyboard, and another 8' on the upper.[9] Coupler and lute stop were often added to this arrangement.

The finest type of harpsichord was probably the so-called "Bach harpsichord" of the Berlin State Collection of Early Music Instruments. This wonderful instrument, which was originally, but erroneously, believed to have belonged to Johann Sebastian Bach himself,[10] has the following disposition: upper keyboard—8", 4", and lute; lower keyboard—8', 16', with coupler. On such an instrument, one can play every note written in a composition from four different positions on the keyboard: on the two 8' registers at the given pitch, on the 4" register by playing the key one octave lower, and on the 16' register by playing one octave higher than notated. (The two latter versions will sometimes have to be excluded if the range of

---

[9] See below, Chapter 2, p. 52.

[10] The puzzle about the origin and date of this celebrated instrument has been greatly increased by a recent publication by Mr. Friedrich Ernst, the well-known and very able restorer of the Berlin State Collection: *Der Flügel Johann Sebastian Bachs* (Frankfurt, 1955). In the course of his restoration work, Mr. Ernst came to the startling conclusion that when this harpsichord was built around 1730, it did not have a 16' register (p. 60), but that this register, together with new keyboards, was added around 1850 (pp. 29 and 75). Space forbids our going into detail about the complex technical problems involved, which will certainly be widely discussed among experts. One cannot refrain from wondering, however, who that rare person was who wanted an old harpsichord rebuilt at this time and was interested in the addition of a 16' register. Equally puzzling is the question of how it was possible around 1850 to find restorers whose skill was so extraordinary that out of their hands came one of the most beautiful harpsichords of the entire world.

the melodic line goes beyond the range of these registers.) The variety of tone colors that can be achieved by means of registration is surprisingly large, as one can see from Chart 1.

CHART 1[a]

Without coupler		With coupler	
Lower keyboard	Upper keyboard	Lower keyboard	Upper keyboard
8'	8"	8', 8"	8"
8'	8", L	8', 8", L	8", L
8'	4"	8', 16', 8"	8"
8'	8", 4"	8', 16', 8", L	8", L
16'	8"	8', 4"	4"
		8', 8", 4"	8", 4"
16'	8", L	8', 16', 4"	4"
16'	4"	16', 8"	8"
16'	8", 4"	16', 8", L	8", L
16'	8", L, 4"		
8', 16	8"	16', 4"	4"
8', 16'	8", L	8', 16', 8", 4"	8", 4" (full work)
8', 16'	4"		
8', 16'	8", 4"		
8', 16'	8", 4", L		

[a] A single prime refers to the lower keyboard, a double prime refers to the upper keyboard, and L refers to lute. These abbreviations will be used hereafter when the keyboards are distinguished.

The range of this instrument is five octaves on both keyboards, from F_1 to f''', but seven octaves in the strings. Compared with the modern piano, this harpsichord has four more keys on the low side and seven less in the high octaves.

As far as can be concluded from the instruments now in museums, the very large type of harpsichord was quite rare. Only about half a dozen such instruments seem to have survived at all.[11] Certainly harpsichords of this size were rather expensive and therefore much less popular than the smaller types. It is remarkable that there exist several harpsichords which show the greatest luxury in the woodwork, having ivory and precious stones inlaid for ornamental purposes, but which do not have the 16' register. This makes it evident that the owners of these instruments were

[11] One of the finest is the huge harpsichord built in Hamburg in 1710 by J. A. Hass, now in the Belle Skinner Collection of Old Musical Instruments, Holyoke, Mass. This superb instrument is equipped with five sets of strings, including a 2' tone in addition to the traditional 8' and 16' on the lower keyboard, and 8" and 4" on the upper keyboard. For a description and picture, see *The Belle Skinner Collection of Old Musical Instruments* (Holyoke, 1933), a descriptive catalogue compiled under the direction of William Skinner, pp. 62–63.

less concerned with having a 16′ register than with having a beautiful piece of furniture. However, to conclude from the rarity of the 16′ register that it should not be used at all, even in Bach's largest keyboard works, does not seem justifiable. We know only too well how big a role mere chance played in permitting the survival of the instruments that we now find in the museums of the world; furthermore, it is obvious that small pieces of furniture were more likely to be kept from generation to generation than large ones.

Another circumstance must be considered in explaining the rarity of large harpsichords. When the piano started to replace the harpsichord, toward the end of the eighteenth century, many harpsichords were rebuilt as pianos by placing the new mechanism in the old frame. Since it was cheaper to remodel the old instrument than to order a brand new piano, and since the frames of only the largest harpsichords were big enough for this purpose, it seems rather probable that the majority of the large harpsichords disappeared this way, and that the actual ratio between the numbers of large and small harpsichords was quite different from what the museum figures tell us.[12] Most of the major museums of the world have specimens of these rebuilt pianos.

Still larger harpsichords with three keyboards are so extremely rare that we need merely mention their existence. Not a single composition demands this type, whereas we shall see later on that some of the most important works of the literature for harpsichord are written specifically "for a harpsichord with two keyboards."

While the smallest and largest types of harpsichords differ considerably, not only in size but also in mechanical details, clavichords[13] show much less variety in design. The tone is produced with utmost simplicity; a small brass wedge, called a tangent, which is attached to the rear end

---

[12] For these reasons we cannot agree with Mr. Ernst that the 16′ register "is foreign to the idiom of baroque music" and that "it would be difficult to find any German musician who might have had any special interest in it" (*Der Flügel Johann Sebastian Bachs*, pp. 61, 63). Although one will later see how sparingly we ourselves will use this register for Bach interpretation—much more sparingly than most of the harpsichord players of our time—we do not think that it is permissible to draw conclusions of such importance from the very few instruments preserved. The fact that Bach sometimes makes use of the "pedal installation," which is an 8′ plus 16′ affair, proves that he cannot have disliked 16′ effects. We also cannot agree with Mr. Ernst about the basically conservative attitude of the "harpsichord makers' guild," which allegedly abhorred new experiments (p. 53). On the contrary, there existed hardly any field of handicraft in which so much independent experimentation was constantly done by so many individually minded artisans, and Mr. Ernst acknowledges that around 1730 there existed "a spirit of joy in experiments among the instrument makers" (p. 51). See also note 31 below.

[13] Other names frequently used are monochord, manichordium, instrument, and clavier. This last name has caused considerable confusion because around 1790 the modern piano also began to be called "clavir" or "clavier." Later the piano was called "klavier," the name by which it is known today in German.

of the key, hits the string from below and presses against the string as long as the finger remains on the key. These tangents divide the strings, which are always parallel to the long side of the rectangular box, into two parts. Only one of them is allowed to vibrate, while the other is damped by a small piece of cloth woven through the strings. The pitch of the tone, which is produced by the tangent on the "sounding side" of the string, depends entirely on the place where the string is hit, and the older clavichords made good use of this possibility by producing two or even more tones on the same string. Of course, these tones could never be used simultaneously. Such clavichords were called *gebunden* in German, which may be translated as "fretted." They had considerably fewer strings than keys, a factor which contributed to their moderate price.

Toward the end of the first decade of the eighteenth century (the date cannot yet be clearly fixed[14]), a key was assigned to each individual string, thus making the instrument *bundfrei* (unfretted). That the richer use of chromatic modulation, which was made possible through the advancing of equal temperament by Andreas Werckmeister's writings, had much to do with this development in the principles of clavichord building, seems to be clear beyond doubt. Bach's preludes and fugues, using all the major and minor keys, could never have been written for a *gebunden* clavichord.

A special effect of the instrument is the *Bebung*, a vibrato, indicated by a row of dots above a note ( ), used here and there, especially in C. P. E. Bach's works. This peculiar and charming effect is achieved by increasing and decreasing the pressure of the finger on a key, which makes the pitch of the tone go up and down. Yet the importance of the *Bebung* should not be overrated, as we see clearly from a warning in Daniel G. Türk's *Klavierschule* (Leipzig, 1789), one of the most popular manuals of the late eighteenth century: "The *Bebung* should properly be applied only in pieces of mournful character. One should not use it too frequently and should avoid exaggeration caused by too heavy pressure."

In contrast to the harpsichord, crescendo and diminuendo can be achieved on the clavichord by modification of touch. Yet this instrument is seriously handicapped by its inability to produce loud sonorities. In the language of today's dynamic marks, its range extends from *ppp* to *mf*. Within these limits, however, the tone of the clavichord is of an almost unearthly beauty and tenderness. Unfortunately, the production of this beautiful tone is surprisingly difficult. Since the lever, which the key of the clavichord represents, is very short, one must always play at the edge of the keys to get the utmost sonority. Whoever works for a long time with a clavichord will soon discover that the strange statement sometimes

---

[14] For a closer approximation of this date, see Chapter 2, footnote 2.

found in old documents, that more than ten years seem to be necessary to learn how to master this technique, is not such a terrible exaggeration.[15]

It is obvious that playing at the edge of the keys makes the thumb a very awkward finger when used in passages, since there is always the danger that it will glide off the key. So we discover that the rules for fingering by the old composers, who tried to exclude the thumb, are not at all as backward and as stupid as they have appeared to later generations. If Bach was one of the first to give the thumb greater activity, he could do so only because the construction of the *bundfrei* clavichord was paralleled by an enlargement of the clavichord keys. While the oldest and smallest clavichords were not much longer than two feet and had no legs, so that one simply put them on a table, the *bundfrei* clavichords reached a length of five feet or more and had four legs. To help increase the tone volume, two or sometimes three strings were given to a single tone. Yet even then the tone of the clavichord remained so soft that, in general, it could be played only as a solo instrument and was unfit for use in any ensemble music. To the player himself, the possibility of making shadings of a delicacy unheard of on any other musical instrument gives an aesthetic pleasure beyond comparison. The fact, almost completely forgotten, that music of this period was intended for the enjoyment of the players rather than the listeners—a fact that is so clearly evident in the standard dedication formula, "For connoisseurs and amateurs"—becomes more convincing than ever here.

This short description of the two instruments is certainly sufficient to show how different a composition will sound when played on one or the other. On a clavichord each composition can be played "as written," within the limits of expression between *ppp* and *mf*. If we play the same composition on a harpsichord, however, what we will hear depends entirely on the type of instrument that we select for our interpretation. On a harpsichord with one keyboard and no register stops, the composition will still sound "as written," but, in contrast to the performance on the clavichord, all possibilities of dynamic shadings are gone. We will hear the entire composition on the same tonal level from beginning to end, a prospect not too pleasing if the composer has not taken the precaution

---

[15] See the charming letter written around 1529 by Pietro Bembo, famous poet and scientist, to his daughter Elena, as published in Max Seiffert's *Geschichte der Klaviermusik: Umarbeitung der Geschichte des Klavierspiels und der Klavierliteratur von C. F. Weitzmann* (Leipzig, 1899; hereafter cited as Seiffert-Weitzmann), p. 25. "In regard to your request to learn how to play the monochord, I must tell you that since you are so young, you cannot yet know that playing is only good for lighthearted and idle women. It would give you little pleasure and fame if you were to play badly. But to play well you would have to spend ten to twelve years without thinking about anything else. If your friends want you to learn to play for their pleasure, tell them that you do not want to become ridiculous, and better remain satisfied with science and needlework."

of using sufficient variety in his setting so that we forget the monotony caused by the lack of any change in expression. However, if we take a harpsichord with several registers on one or two keyboards and try the same composition again, the piece will no longer sound exactly "as written." Those parts of it that are played with the combined 8' and 4' registers will produce not only the original notes, but also their higher octave. If we add the 16' register, the lower octave will also be heard. The same composition that we played at first intimately and *cantabile* in the limits between *ppp* and *mf* on the clavichord, then monotonously and dryly on a harpsichord without register stops, will now have the advantage of the colors of the harpsichord registration; it will show itself clearly cut into sections of different tone volume which provide the piece with the most characteristic feature of harpsichord playing, the so-called "terrace dynamics" (sound levels of different intensity).

How is one to find out which of the two instruments is the right one to be used if the composer has not informed us of his own preference? It certainly seems improbable that he should have felt indifferent to such heterogeneous acoustical results. Some important questions arise immediately. How and where should one apply changes in registration if the harpsichord is used? How can one know whether one is playing them correctly, if the composer has given no obvious indications along these lines?

At the moment we are not yet sufficiently equipped with knowledge to give adequate answers to these all-important questions. All we can see at the outset is that the harpsichord and clavichord have very little in common and that both instruments are different from the modern piano. Whereas the clavichord has some kinship with the piano, the harpsichord obviously has none; it is much closer to the organ, with which it shares the "terrace dynamics" and the impossibility of making crescendos and diminuendos by touch alone.

At any rate, it occurs to us for the first time that it is rather a major operation to transfer Bach's keyboard works from the atmosphere of harpsichord and clavichord to the entirely different acoustical conditions of the piano, and to make them sound on this instrument exactly as they were intended to be heard. Who would ever dare to do the same with an organ composition? Luckily, Bach's organ works have been spared such treatment, perhaps because of their three-staved notation (the third staff is reserved for the pedal part), which makes a literal playing of the written notes with only ten fingers impossible. Also, in the case of the organ, even the layman knows that we hear many more notes on that "royal instrument" than the composer writes down, since a multitude of register stops adds octaves and even other additional tones, the so-called "mixtures." A literal playing of the original notes on the piano would obviously make little sense, and transcriptions, such as those by Liszt, Tausig, Reger, and Busoni, must be made to give the piano player an approximate idea of the true meaning of an organ work. Do not the registers of the harpsichord suggest a similar treatment: do they not also ask for a transcription?

Certainly we do not have the right to blame the generation of 1830 for not knowing what to do with Bach's keyboard music when the general interest in this long-forgotten composer began, all of a sudden, to rise again. This generation was not only mentally unprepared for meeting a problem of such magnitude, but, in this particular case, was even unaware of the existence of a problem. A brief excursion into the early history of the piano will quickly explain the peculiar circumstances under which the Bach renaissance made its start.

The piano had been invented in 1709 by Bartolommeo Cristofori, who lived in Florence. The hammer mechanism of the new instrument was a revolutionary step away from the method of tone production used in the clavichord; acoustically, however, the immediate result was in the nature of a setback, since the dull tone produced by the hammer could by no means compete with the unearthly sweetness of the clavichord tone. So slowly did the tonal quality of the piano improve that Bach, who became acquainted with the instrument in the last decade of his life through his friend Gottfried Silbermann,[16] seems to have given it a very hesitant approval. At least that is what a contemporary report tells us.[17] Accordingly, Bach did not find the piano a worthwhile medium for any composition. It might be correct to state that not before 1770 was the mechanical construction of the piano advanced enough to please players and composers, and it is noteworthy that just during this period of growing competition from the piano, the clavichord enjoyed its final flowering: the period of *Empfindsamkeit* (sensibility).

C. P. E. Bach was the spiritual leader of this movement, which may be dated from 1750 to 1780. Around 1800, however, the defeat of the harpsichord and clavichord became final, and both instruments went into the attics with amazing speed. Yet it would be wrong to attribute this quick and easy abandonment of the instruments and the playing traditions of three centuries merely to the greater technical perfection of the new instrument. Although there exist many documents from the eighteenth century that complain of the mechanical deficiencies of harpsichord and

---

[16] Gottfried Silbermann was a famous builder of organs, harpsichords, and clavichords, and also a pioneer in the building of pianos.

[17] Jacob Adlung, *Musica mechanica organoedi* (Berlin, [1768]; reprint, Kassel, 1931), II, 116.

clavichord—blaming the harpsichord especially for its lack of tone shading and the clavichord for the smallness of its tone—Bach, Handel, and all the other composers would never have written so many important works for these instruments had they not believed them to be at least tolerably well suited to expressing their musical ideas. The true reason for the defeat of the old instruments was, of course, the gigantic change in style and taste that shocked the musical world at the time of Bach's death. Had the new style left any elements in the musical language for which harpsichord and clavichord could have been appropriate media, the piano would not have become victorious so easily, and both old instruments might perhaps have survived in use, even to our time.

However, such was not the case. The generation of 1830 had not only lost all contact with the musical style of the eighteenth century and with the instruments most typical of that period, but also had every good reason to be tremendously proud of the conquest of the many new possibilities in musical expression achieved by the great Viennese masters. Is it any wonder that musicians in such a position did not for a moment perceive the necessity of reviving the harpsichord and clavichord in order to do justice to Bach's keyboard compositions? They simply started playing these works on the piano. Without any thought about the problem of whether his music was really fit for an exact transfer, these musicians were fully convinced that old Bach could only have been very happy if he had been able to hear how wonderful his compositions now sounded on the piano. The most extreme document of this attitude is the first complete edition of Bach's keyboard works, by Carl Czerny, Beethoven's pupil. Here the editor put a strange classic-romantic gown upon these compositions, as if Bach had been a contemporary of the great Viennese composers. In Czerny's preface one reads: "It has been my endeavor to indicate tempo and interpretation according to the impression, which I remember clearly, that was made on me by Beethoven's rendering of a great number of these pieces." Respect for authority prevents one from questioning the authenticity of this edition. However, as we shall see later, it is precisely Czerny's version, the most popular even now, that most often misinterprets Bach's works to the greatest degree.

A linguistic misunderstanding added more confusion to the peculiar problem that Bach's keyboard music offered. In Germany the modern piano, which had first been called "pianoforte," was now called "Klavier." No wonder that whoever saw only the title of Bach's great collection of preludes and fugues, *Das Wohltemperierte Klavier* (which was among the first of his works to regain popularity), immediately thought that these pieces were written for the "Klavier": namely, the piano. Since the knowledge of "Old Music" had gone so completely into oblivion, and since, which was even more important, the general musical culture of this generation was far below the high standard that had distinguished the eighteenth century, very few people of this period knew that in the former century the word "Klavier" had a completely different meaning, that of "keyboard." A composition for "Klavier" actually meant, therefore, a composition written for any instrument with keys; even the organ belonged to this category, along with the harpsichord and clavichord. For proof of this fact one needs only to see the title *Klavier-übung*, given by Bach to selected keyboard compositions that he published himself. The third part of this *Klavierübung* consists of organ pieces.

A small organ, the so-called "Hausorgel" (home organ—not to be confused with the modern harmonium or "American organ" but a real little "church organ"), was a popular instrument during the time of Bach and was found in the homes of multitudes of music lovers. The title *Wohltemperierte Klavier* indicates, therefore, that the forty-eight preludes and fugues form a collection of pieces for harpsichord, clavichord, and organ. The correct translation of Bach's title should be "The Welltempered Keyboard," and from now on we will refer to the collection in this more appropriate manner.

From the translations of this title into other languages, one can see how great the confusion about it and the meaning of the word "Klavier" was in countries other than Germany. The traditional English title is *The Welltempered Clavichord*,[18] while the French one is *Le Clavecin bien tempéré*. Contrary to popular belief, the French word "clavecin," like the Italian "cembalo," not only designates the harpsichord but also means "keyboard," exactly as does the German word "Klavier." Therefore, titles like "per il cembalo" or "pour le clavecin," both frequently found in the eighteenth century, do not safely indicate compositions for the harpsichord. To give some evidence for this little-known fact, let us mention the subtitle "Pieces de Clavecin" found on the title page of Johann Kaspar Ferdinand Fischer's *Das Musikalisches Blumenbüschlein*

---

[18] Merely as a curiosity I add "The Welltempered Pianoforte" found in the English translation of Robert Schumann's *On Music and Musicians* (tr. F. R. Ritter, London, 1891), p. 413. I also cannot abstain from reprinting a criticism from the Portland *Daily Oregonian* (1944) on a recital of sonatas for violin and harpsichord by Bach and Mozart. "Bach was played with an equal meticulousness and with an especially fine sense of the spirituality of his slow movements. But to this listener the instrumental timbres were less harmonious than in the Mozart compositions. This may be due to individual preferences. Bach liked the clavier, Mozart the harpsichord. There is never a moment's question of the rightness of the instrument for the latter's works." This critic evidently had the idea that the word "clavier" used by Bach meant "modern piano." This confusion reveals how detrimental it is for the better understanding of harpsichord music to extend the range of its literature unnecessarily to areas where all historic evidence is against it. The good cause of the harpsichord does not need to be defended by any composition of Mozart's, be it a violin sonata or a *rondo alla turca*.

(1699); in the preface, the author states that this work is exclusively meant for the clavichord (see p. 21 below). Furthermore, Gottfried Silbermann called a clavichord of his own invention—an instrument where every tangent hit its string exactly in the middle, so that both sides of the vibrating string could be used for tone production—by the name "clavecin d'amour."[19] The word "cembalo" was even used to designate the modern piano, as can be seen from Beethoven's remark in the Piano Sonata, Op. 101 (a few bars before the beginning of the last movement), *"Tutto il cembalo ma piano."* In regard to the inclusion of the organ in the list of keyboard instruments, it is interesting to see that Czerny still remembered this fact. He says in the preface to the *Welltempered Keyboard* that extremely rapid tempi have to be moderated very decidedly "when playing these pieces on the organ," finding it obviously quite natural that people might do so. This remark, however, and the doublings of the bass line in the C minor and D major fugues are the only remnants in this edition of a vague knowledge of the "Old Style."

Considering all these aspects of early nineteenth-century musical culture and the fact that by 1830 the piano was the only surviving keyboard instrument (the "home organ" had disappeared from use along with the harpsichord and clavichord), we really have no right to lay too much blame on this generation for feeling perfectly content with their solution: piano = harpsichord = clavichord = home organ. Much less understandable, however, is the bizarre fact that, in spite of all the research work which has meanwhile been dedicated to a better understanding of the stylistic problems in Bach's art, our present-day treatment of the keyboard works is, in most respects, identical with the methods of one hundred years ago. The Czerny edition is still very widely used, and everybody still plays Bach on the piano without making any adjustments for the change in instrument. Our first experiments with playing the same piece successively on a clavichord and a harpsichord taught us immediately how different the acoustical results are in each case, and we can easily perceive new differences when we play the same piece on the piano. It is therefore inevitable that the question must arise again: did the difference between harpsichord and clavichord mean something to Bach, and if it did, what did Bach do to help us find the right instrument on which to perform each keyboard composition? We cannot approach the problem of how to treat these pieces on the piano before this problem is solved.

---

[19] The mechanism of the clavecin d'amour is described in Johann Nikolaus Forkel's *Musikalischer Almanach* (1782), p. 18, and in Adlung, II, 125. Carl Georg Parrish in "The Early Piano and Its Influence on Keyboard Technique and Composition in the Eighteenth Century" (unpublished dissertation, Harvard University, 1939), says, "A harpsichord was called clavichordio in Italy, a clavichord was called dumb spinet in England and sometimes a clavecin d'amour" (p. VIII), without reference to his sources.

It is strange that musicology has never made a serious attempt to determine the relative positions that both these old instruments held in their time. No doubt any possible research in the field of old keyboard music must start here. Such a neglect of so obvious a source of information could not have occurred without reason, and, indeed, it looks as if in this particular case musicology has become the victim of preconceived notions generally considered too well established to need re-examination.

The factor most responsible must have been the apparently wide-spread belief that the indifference which the sixteenth and seventeenth centuries displayed toward any significant differentiation between harpsichord, clavichord, and organ compositions also survived in the eighteenth century. Numerous titles verify beyond doubt that during the first 250 years of keyboard music (1450–1700)[20] a clear distinction between music for organ, harpsichord, and clavichord was not aimed for.[21] In the sixteenth century these instruments had almost no literature of their own, but borrowed from vocal literature. That indifference to the choice of instrument continued throughout the entire seventeenth century. Except for the English virginal music, which is inseparably linked with this instrument and cannot be transplanted to any other medium (see p. 24 below), the keyboard music by Sweelinck and Scheidt, and even that by Pachelbel and Boehm, rarely shows a setting that would exclude one of the three keyboard instruments completely.

One must not forget that a pedal installation on harpsichords and clavichords made it possible to play a considerable amount of organ music on them.[22] The habit of attributing variations on church melodies to the organ, and variations on secular songs to harpsichord and clavichord, has no justification in fact. It is reported that Sweelinck once improvised on his organ in Amsterdam on the popular song "Der lustige Mai."[23] On the other hand, many choral variations by Boehm and Pachelbel are written only *manualiter* (without pedal part) and show in the unusual

---

[20] The gap in our knowledge of early keyboard music, which extends from the pieces in the Robertsbridge Codex (around 1325), the earliest known document, to 1450, has only recently been narrowed by the discovery of pieces for the late fourteenth century in Codex Faenza 117 (see Dragan Plamenac, "Keyboard Music of the Fourteenth Century," *JAMS*, vol. IV, no. 3, 1951, p. 179).

[21] See, for example, Andrea and Giovanni Gabrieli, *Ricercari composti et tabulati per ogni sorte di stromenti da tasti* (Venice, 1585); Froberger, *Partitas, Toccatas, Canzonas per Cimbali, Organi et instrumenti* (c. 1650). The word "instrument" is often used as another name for "clavichord" in the sixteenth and seventeenth centuries. In the eighteenth century, however, the name "instrument" was used for the square type of harpsichord (see Adlung, II, 123).

[22] Such pedal installations correspond with the pedal on an organ in shape and size. In primitive types the pedal has no strings of its own, but its keys are tied to the corresponding keys of the keyboard by tiny ropes; larger types have their own strings (mostly 8' and 16') in a box placed underneath the pedal.

[23] Seiffert-Weitzmann, p. 75.

intimacy of their character that they might easily have had a place in the "home service" that united the entire family around their keyboard instrument, whichever it was. Even as late as 1700, the title of Kuhnau's famous "Biblical Sonatas," *Sei Sonate da suonare sul Organo, Clavicembalo ed altri Stromenti famiglianti* (Six sonatas to be played on the organ, the harpsichord, or similar instruments), shows the composer still leaving the selection of the proper instrument open to choice, although at least two of these sonatas prove in technical details that the composer must have had the clavichord in mind when he wrote them.[24] Therefore, it might not be impossible that commercial practicality, the wish to interest the greatest possible number of players, had something to do with such a title. Indeed, many pieces of this period, written for one solo instrument with thorough bass, were advertised "for violin, flute, or oboe."

It is this rather generally acknowledged indifference to the selection of one particular instrument during the seventeenth century which must have kept the musicologists away from a closer investigation of this problem in the music of Johann Sebastian Bach. One of the recent publications in this field, Cornelia Auerbach's essay *Die deutsche Clavichordkunst des 18. Jahrhunderts*,[25] states categorically: "For the keyboard work of J. S. Bach the question of the proper instrument is without significance. . . . Even if we were to succeed in finding which of his pieces might have been meant for the clavichord, I do not think that this would contribute to the understanding of Bach's art in view of the fact that the very little evidence which might be found would leave the way open only to personal conjecture." In the technical analysis that we will undertake later, we will be able to prove how infinitely more refined Bach's keyboard style is than that of all his predecessors, making the differentiation between harpsichord and clavichord works so obvious that it simply cannot be overlooked.

Yet even for the seventeenth century, we are not completely convinced that the alleged indifference toward the keyboard instrument in question was quite so general as the titles from that period suggest. In the vast majority of cases, the same composers who left the selection of the instrument to the player also failed to tell him in what tempi their compositions should be played; indications of dynamics and articulation,

---

[24] The separation of the *cantus firmus* from the accompaniment, in the sonata "The Fight between David and Goliath," can be made audible only on a clavichord. The prescriptions *più piano*, *forte*, and *piano*, in the sonata "Jacob's Marriage," also cannot be fulfilled on any other instrument. It is interesting in this respect to note that Kuhnau seems to have had a kind of predilection for the clavichord. Johann Mattheson gives a report of a letter by Kuhnau, in which the latter says that during a contest on several instruments he preferred to play on the clavichord. Mattheson finds this remark so important that he adds: "Whoever wants to give preference to the harpsichord over the clavichord may well notice this!" (*Critica Musica*, Hamburg, 1722–1725, p. VII).

[25] (Kassel, 1930), p. 24.

which are so essential for a lively interpretation, are completely lacking as well. Should this logically mean that the composers were also indifferent to whether one played the same work slow or fast, loud or soft, legato or staccato, not to speak of the various possibilities of the articulation and phrasing of the melodic line? No one would dare answer such an absurd question with a "yes," and therefore, only one conclusion, already mentioned in the introduction, is possible. Since a composer of this period could take the risk of writing down only the naked notes, foregoing almost any indication about how his music should be interpreted, and since books of the same period dealing with musical matters do not answer a single one of these questions, it becomes apparent that there must have existed a great quantity of traditional rules known to the entire musical world.

A brief glance at the musical life of this period will be sufficient to prove this assumption. The "concert hall" and the "concert public" did not yet exist. Aside from the professional players, who served the musical needs of the churches, the courts, and less frequently the cities (town musicians, *Stadtpfeifer*), there was only the small group of "connoisseurs and amateurs" (*Kenner und Liebhaber*) for whose enjoyment (*Gemütsergötzung*) a composer could and would write. The standard of the musical knowledge of these amateurs was infinitely higher than that which we have a right to expect from a music lover of our day. The art of improvisation of the thorough bass, the right—almost the duty—to add "graces" to the melodic lines, the understanding of the contrapuntal forms, the experienced ear that is needed for the full enjoyment of the imaginary harmonic background of compositions like Bach's sonatas and suites for unaccompanied violin or cello—all these disciplines belonged to the mental equipment not only of the professionals, but also of the amateurs, and were acquired only by instruction from person to person. The help of books was rarely needed and could never give more than some elementary knowledge in a very limited field. Bach himself, who once dictated the rules for improvising a thorough bass to a pupil, broke off suddenly after having explained only the most conventional basic facts and burst out: "The rest may better be explained by oral instruction."[26]

How prevalent this oral tradition was, even as late as 1776, is confirmed by a most interesting remark in the preface to Johann Wilhelm Haessler's *Sechs neue Sonaten für Clavier oder Piano*. The author says therein that his sonatas are partially meant for the clavichord, partially for the piano, and that "connoisseurs will easily find the difference without my help." Such a casual remark, preserved only by good luck,

---

[26] Philipp Spitta, *Johann Sebastian Bach* (Leipzig, 1873–1880), vol. II, Appendix, p. 952.

makes it highly doubtful that the old keyboard instruments were really used as interchangeably as we have all been led to believe.

There is, however, a second basic conception that has contributed to preventing musicologists from penetrating more deeply into the problems of harpsichord and clavichord. It is the widespread belief that the clavichord was so negligible a musical instrument that it had no practical importance, no literature of its own,[27] and only one *raison d'être*: it represented the cheapest form of a not entirely mute keyboard that a poor organist could afford to buy for practicing purposes, since practicing in winter in the ice-cold churches was impossible. If it ever had any importance at all, its use was entirely restricted to Germany. Wanda Landowska has persistently pointed out that in her opinion the clavichord never played any influential role in music. In her book *La musique ancienne* we find the following passages: "In France and Italy it [the clavichord] was hardly known at all. . . . The clavichord had a very limited influence upon the musical art and was never generally accepted, since there were never professional clavichordists. Germany is the only country where it played a certain role, but not that which one attributes to it now. Excluded from the important music it served only to accompany a little voice, or as an instrument for beginners."[28]

The numerous titles in early Italian publications of keyboard music; the many documents produced by Otto Kinkeldey in his monumental book on sixteenth-century keyboard music,[29] which mention nobility at the courts in Italy and Spain playing the clavichord; together with the famous letter of Pietro Bembo in Florence (see note 15 above), are sufficient proof that at least in the earlier periods the clavichord must have been well known in countries other than Germany.[30] Yet to do Wanda

---

[27] With the obvious exception of the brief period from 1750–1780, when the instrument went through its final flowering.

[28] "En France et en Italie on ne l'a presque pas connu. . . . Le clavichord eut une influence bien limitée sur l'art musical et ne fit jamais école, car il n'y eut jamais des clavichordistes. L'Allemagne est le seul pays, ou cet instrument ait joué un certain rôle mais pas celui qu'on lui attribue aujourd'hui. Exclu de la grande musique il servait pour accompagner une petite voix ou comme instrument pour commençants" (Paris, 1909, pp. 196–197). See also her article "En vue de quel instrument Bach a-t-il composé son Wohltemperiertes Klavier?" in *La Revue musicale*, vol. IX, no. 2 (December 1, 1927).

[29] *Orgel und Klavier in der Musik des 16. Jahrhunderts* (Leipzig, 1910).

[30] See also Stellfeld, "Bronnen tot de Geschiedenis der Antwerpsche," on the many clavichord makers listed in the sixteenth century as members of the guild of St. Lukas in Antwerp. In his article "Portugiesische und spanische Clavichorde des 18. Jahrhunderts," Macario Santiago Kastner of Lisbon presents ample evidence for the widespread use of the clavichord in Spain and Portugal at a period during which the reservation of it for Germany, as the only country in which it blossomed, had hitherto remained uncontested (*Acta musicologica*, vol. XXIV, fasc. I–II, 1952, p. 52). In my publication *Der Vortrag alter Klaviermusik* I have already expressed my expectation that later research will produce evidence for use of the clavichord in France. This has now actually happened. In an article, "La Facture instrumentale à Paris au seizième siècle" (Galpin Society *Journal*, VII, April 1954, p. 11), François

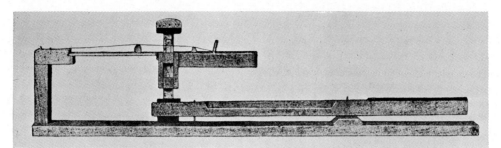

I. THE ACTION OF THE HARPSICHORD
(from Hanns Neupert, *Vom Musikstab zum modernen Klavier*, J. C. Neupert, Bamberg, 1926)

II. HARPSICHORD MADE IN HAMBURG, 1723, BY H. A. HASS
(from *Das Musik-Historische Museum Copenhagen*, Copenhagen, 1911)

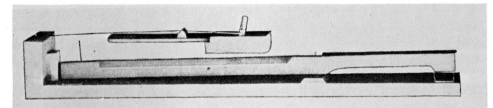

III. THE ACTION OF THE CLAVICHORD
(from Hanns Neupert, *Vom Musikstab zum modernen Klavier*, J. C. Neupert, Bamberg, 1926)

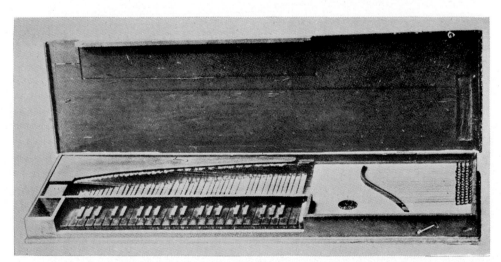

IV. "GEBUNDEN" CLAVICHORD MADE ABOUT 1600
(from Bertha van Beijnum-von Essen, *Bouwengeschiedenis van het Klavier*, W. L. and J. Busse, Rotterdam, 1932)

Landowska justice, we have to acknowledge that at least some belief that the clavichord was a typically German instrument must already have existed in the eighteenth century. Mattheson in his *Critica Musica* mentioned such a presumption but rebuked it with the following words: "Clavichords must be found in England, at least among the many Germans there. Here in Hamburg there are people who annually send as many clavichords as they can manufacture to England, Spain, and Holland. Where are they indeed?"[31] That no "clavichordists" are mentioned need not surprise us. Titles like "organists" and "harpsichordists" are not names for describing concertizing artists but only describe people in salaried positions; since the clavichord is outspokenly a solo instrument, playing it could never be a money-making business.

That the clavichord was mechanically too poor an instrument ever to be used for anything more than the first attempts of beginners is strongly contradicted by the fact that it is mentioned in titles which have nothing to do with a beginner's situation. Johann Krieger's *Sechs musikalische Partien* (1697) were written for "spinet or clavichord," a prescription linking the smallest type of harpsichord with the clavichord. The most interesting document is, however, Johann Kaspar Ferdinand Fischer's *Das musikalische Blumenbüschlein* (1699). This work was presented by Fischer to Franziska Sybilla Augusta, wife of his patron, the Markgraf Ludwig von Baden, in honor of the birth of a prince. In the preface Fischer says, "I do not want to hurt the tender ears of the newly born prince with the sound of trumpets and strings but present herewith some quieter music designated *exclusively* [*allein*; italics mine] for the clavichordium or instrument." The full significance of this remark becomes evident from the fact that Bach was deeply influenced by this and other works of Fischer's. He not only literally took over from Fischer the theme of the E major Fugue, *W.K.* II, but imitated him stylistically in the most drastic way.[32]

It cannot be denied, however, and seems almost to be fated that anybody who only casually approaches a clavichord must inevitably

---

Lesure presents the inventories of a series of French harpsichord makers from 1556 on, in which quite a few clavichords are mentioned as being in their possession. Mr. Frank Hubbard of Boston, to whom I am indebted for having drawn my attention to this article, has been able to find similar documentary evidence of clavichords in France reaching to the year 1661, in the *Minutier Centrale* of the Archives Nationales.

[31] Vol. II, part 6, p. 150. This remark throws an interesting sidelight upon our thesis that many more large harpsichords existed than the very small number of survivals would indicate. How very few old clavichords can now be found in England, although their smallness gave them a much better chance of being preserved!

[32] Compare the Prelude in B flat minor, *W.K.* I, with Prelude 2 from Fischer's *Blumenbüschlein* (in Johann Kaspar Ferdinand Fischer, *Sämtliche Werke für Klavier und Orgel*, Leipzig, 1901, p. 9); or the Prelude in C major, *W.K.* I, with Fischer's "Praeludium harpeggiato," No. 1 of the *Musikalischer Parnassus*, in *Sämtliche Werke*, p. 35 (see p. 125 below).

3

come to the conclusion that one can hardly call it a musical instrument at all. We have mentioned already, in the description of its mechanism, how difficult it is to produce a clean and well-projected tone on it. Because no other keyboard instrument offers any problems of tone production, it is hardly surprising that a player who tries a clavichord for the first time does not think it his own fault when the instrument produces only a miserable and doleful sound. Convinced that this poor tone is all that the instrument can offer, almost everybody gives up playing the clavichord after a brief attempt, and the legend that it is no real musical instrument spreads.[33] Nevertheless, it is somewhat surprising that the discovery of the important role which the clavichord plays in the works of Bach was not made by those who did the first pioneering for the revival of the harpsichord. It may be that the first harpsichordists, who were all "concertizing artists," looked upon old keyboard music and old keyboard instruments so completely from the viewpoint of their usefulness for the concert hall that they saw no reason to give attention to the clavichord, whose intimate tone made public demonstration impossible.[34]

In all probability, however, one detail of construction in modern harpsichord building has played the most decisive role in leading the first harpsichordists, as well as others, to believe that the clavichord played a negligible role in its time. It goes without saying that a modern harpsichord player who is a "traveling artist" cannot use an old harpsichord for concertizing purposes. Harpsichords constructed in former centuries were built to be "stationary instruments," never to be moved from city to city. Their fragile frames were of wood, and the strings were very thin. A harpsichordist of this period who wanted to appear in a

---

[33] From Professor Oskar Fleischer, late director of the State Collection of Early Music Instruments in Berlin, I once heard the charming and very typical story of what happened when he guided Anton Rubinstein, the famous pianist, through the museum. Rubinstein saw a clavichord for the first time. Standing before one of the smallest instruments of this type, the giant of colossal piano tone put his hands upon the miniature keyboard and started to play the first measures of the Prelude to *Die Meistersinger*. The result must have been terrifying. With a broad laugh the pianist turned away to other instruments, and his acquaintance with the clavichord was finished.

[34] I am certainly the last one to advocate the use of the clavichord in concert halls, because the chief purpose of the instrument is clearly to bring enjoyment to the player. Yet, in order to spread knowledge about this little-known instrument, I have frequently had to demonstrate it in large halls. The acoustical results were in marked contrast to all expectations, and always the same. The tone of the clavichord was weakest at short distances. At about twenty to thirty feet, however, the tone became clearer and clearer, and halls of a capacity of four hundred to six hundred listeners seemed to be the ideal size. Even an audience of two thousand could hear the instrument without difficulty if two precautions were taken. The instrument had to be placed in the center of the hall, with the public sitting in horseshoe form, and no window or door could be open. A single open window is sufficient to destroy the tone volume of the clavichord. Played in the open air, the instrument is inaudible at a distance of only ten feet. However, no document that testifies to any use of the clavichord for concertizing purposes has come down to us.

foreign city could be certain to find a harpsichord ready for use wherever he wanted to show his craftsmanship, be it in the palace of a nobleman or in the house of a wealthy citizen. But since the modern harpsichordist will very seldom find a harpsichord at the place where he is going to concertize, he needs a much more robust instrument that can withstand all the hazards of traveling. Therefore, modern harpsichords show a wide departure from the old models, particularly in the use of iron frames, much stronger strings, and—most important—in the change from "hand-stop registration" to "pedal registration."

At first glance, this last device looks like a very harmless, convenient improvement. Whereas on the old instruments changes in registration had to be planned in accordance with the rests that existed for one or both hands, the pedal registration makes the change of tone colors independent of this restriction. However, the results of this change in construction have been nothing short of devastating to the true understanding of the entire repertoire of keyboard music of Bach's time.[35] Not only do the players of the modern instrument make many more changes of registration than the composers desired, thus destroying the inseparable link between registration and musical architecture, but at the same time

---

[35] Attempts have been made to defend the modern pedal registration by reference to the fact that the pedal had already been invented in the seventeenth century. Thomas Mace in his *Musick's Monument* (London, 1676), reports on "an Instrument of a Late Invention, contriv'd by one Mr John Hayward of London, a most excellent Kind of Instrument for a Consort, and far beyond all Harpsions or Organs. *The player had* several Various Stops at Pleasure; and all Quick and Nimble, by the Ready Turn of the Foot. . . . There being right underneath his Toes four little Pummels of Wood, under each Foot two, any one of those four he may Tread upon at his Pleasure; which by the Weight of his Foot drives a Spring, and so Causeth the whole Instrument to Sound, either Soft or Loud, accompanying as he shall chuse to Tread any of them down" (quoted in Sachs, p. 377). Eta Harich-Schneider, also quoting Mace in *Die Kunst des Cembalospiels* (Kassel, 1939), adds to the description: "This description is the more interesting, since it proves that the modern fashion of pedal registration is not, per se, out of style as is pretended by many musicians who approach Early Music in too puristic and narrow-minded a way" (p. 8). We are afraid that here narrow-mindedness belongs less to the "puristic" musicians than to this statement, which is rather well characterized by the title of an article from the same author: "Performance in Style with Little Errors" ("Stilaufführungen mit kleinen Fehlern," *Die Musik*, XXXI, vol. 7, April 1939, p. 441. This very controversial article received a strong rebuff from the venerable professor Gustav Scheck in "Ein Beitrag zur Aufführungspraxis alter Musik," *Die Musik*, XXXI, vol. 8, May 1939, p. 530).

More to the point are the conclusions which Curt Sachs draws from the fate which the invention, reported by Mace, met with: "In spite of this marvelous quality, the pedal had no success; not one source besides Mace mentions it. If the failure had been in the mechanical field, then cleverer hands would have improved the contrivance. It rather must be looked for in the musical field. 'Several various stops at pleasure, and all quick and nimble'—this was certainly not to the taste of the seventeenth century. Music in that time was much less motley and variegated than we like to imagine, and we had better modify our ideas than force an inappropriate style upon ancient music" (pp. 377–378). Schneider's reference to English harpsichords of the eighteenth century which were equipped with pedals is equally wrong. All these instruments were built from about 1755 on, after Bach's death, and therefore could not influence the writing methods of a composer of the time of Bach. No doubt Curt Sachs is right again when he states that "the competition of the piano caused the harpsichord makers to think of all possible accommodations in order to keep up with the newcomer" (p. 378).

the pedal construction has prevented these players from making a very important discovery concerning Bach's works, namely, that in addition to the multitude of pieces in which the composer handles the sound possibilities of the harpsichord with incredible brilliancy and finesse, there exist many pieces that not only contain no rests applicable to the changing of registration, but that are architecturally constructed in such a way that any effects of *terrace dynamics were obviously and intentionally avoided*. Such pieces allow, therefore, only one type of interpretation: they must be played from beginning to end in *one* registration, and any change of tone color must be renounced. Since pieces that do not follow the traditional pattern of terrace dynamics comprise close to half of Bach's entire keyboard music, a question of cardinal importance arises. Is it thinkable that the same composer who, in his major compositions for the harpsichord, shows the keenest feeling for tone color and outspoken dynamic contrasts and makes the most intelligent use of the effects of registration of this instrument should have written so many compositions that look wonderful on paper but can only sound dry and monotonous when played on the harpsichord?

In our previous description of a small harpsichord with one keyboard and one set of strings, we remarked that a composer would have to use sufficient variety in his setting that the audience would forget the monotony caused by the total lack of change in sound on his instrument. It is amazing to see that even the first composers who wrote for this type of instrument, the English virginalists (around 1600), were not only fully aware of this problem but solved it in an unsurpassable manner. The ways in which William Byrd, Giles Farnaby, John Bull, and the other composers of this school were able, at every turn, to draw new sound combinations from their single keyboard, and their methods of alternating between a "thin setting" in two-part writing to make the instrument sound *piano*, and a "full setting," using big chords or rolling figures to make the instrument sound *forte*, are simply extraordinary; they fill us over and over again with profound admiration.

We have no documentary evidence that Bach knew any compositions of this great period, although there are some well-known links between the virginalists and the continental composers, for example, the Bull–Sweelinck–Scheidt line, which leads directly to the geographical vicinity of the Bach family. Yet, in spite of the fact that Bach never applied a similar technique systematically in any of his compositions, this method of utilizing a single keyboard was well known to him and his contemporaries, inasmuch as this was the normal way of improvising a thorough bass if one did not have a larger instrument at one's disposal. This is proved by Johann Joachim Quantz's famous description of thorough-bass improvisation: "On a harpsichord with one keyboard, '*piano*' can be produced by using a light touch and by reducing the number of parts; '*mezzo forte*' by doubling the parts in the left hand; '*forte*' by adding consonances in the bass; '*fortissimo*' by playing these notes rapidly in 'broken' form, combined with a heavy touch."[36]

One might almost be reading a description of compositions for the virginal, so close are the artistic devices described here to the writing techniques of the old English composers. Bach, however, never used a similar technique in those of his keyboard works that do not allow any contrast of registration when played on a harpsichord, and this fact alone would suffice to prove that such pieces have nothing at all to do with the harpsichord. If the owners of modern harpsichords had been forced to abandon all registration effects for the very large quantity of Bach's works that are involved in this problem, they would have been the first ones to discover that there exists only one remedy for such pieces: they must be played on a clavichord, the only instrument with one keyboard that makes possible a performance of such refinement as the complicated texture of these pieces requires.

The discovery that the writing technique of the virginalists, at least in the field of the improvisation of the thorough bass, was generally known to musicians up to the eighteenth century is of still greater consequence. It inevitably makes the alleged indifference of the seventeenth-century composers to the instrument on which their keyboard compositions were to be played more open to doubt. Although it seems improbable that full stylistic evidence of a differentiation between harpsichord and clavichord style at this period will ever be found,[37] the disappearance of the "virginal technique" during the course of the seventeenth century makes it rather evident that the harpsichord with which seventeenth-century composers reckoned was no longer the instrument with one keyboard and one set of strings. The ever-increasing demand for stronger dynamic contrasts during this period is evidenced in instrumental music by Giovanni Gabrieli's *Sonata pian' e forte*, and in organ music by Sweelinck's *Fantasies "op de manier van een echo"* (in the manner of an echo), which required two keyboards for proper execution. This trend probably was influential in putting higher demands for increased tonal flexibility upon the harpsichord. Since harpsichords with two keyboards were built from 1538 on (see p. 6), and since nearly the entire keyboard music of this

---

[36] Johann Joachim Quantz, *Versuch einer Anweisung die Flöte traversière zu spielen* (Berlin, 1752; reprint, ed. Arnold Schering, Leipzig, 1906), Book XVII, part 6, paragraph 17.

[37] Max F. Schneider, in his *Beitrage zu einer Anleitung Clavichord und Cembalo zu spielen*, Sammlung musikwissenschaftlicher Abhandlungen unter Leitung von Karl Nef, vol. XVI (Strasbourg, 1934), undertook such an attempt, basing his research entirely on the method of analysis that I applied in my book *Der Vortrag alter Klaviermusik*.

time consisted of toccatas and variation works—compositions built in
sections allowing, or rather asking for, the application of varieties of
dynamics—it seems only natural to assume that such works were meant
to be played on harpsichords equipped with possibilities for color modification at least on one, preferably on two keyboards. Logically, "virginal
technique" was then no longer necessary. That Bach, in addition to
writing most brilliantly for a harpsichord with two keyboards, starts
writing compositions in which terrace dynamics are not applied and
virginalistic technique is not used as a means to give satisfaction to the
ear is of tremendous significance.

We hardly need more evidence to come to the inevitable conclusion
that it can only have been the clavichord that was in Bach's mind when
he wrote in such a totally new style. In the course of our study we are
going to show that substantial proof for the role of the clavichord in
Bach's creative output can indeed be found, by examining Bach's keyboard
works from the viewpoint of their playability on harpsichord and clavichord. With amazement we will see that the neglect of taking the clavichord
seriously has up to now prevented us from getting a complete and true
picture of the real problems in the interpretation of Bach's keyboard
works. We will find that the range of influence of the clavichord is far
greater than one ever expected it to be, and that Bach did not need to
indicate which piece was meant for the harpsichord and which for the
clavichord, because he almost always conveyed this message to the
experienced player with "invisible ink." So he too could have said, as
Johann Haessler did, "Connoisseurs will easily find the difference."

Only one little task has to be completed before we are ready for this
undertaking. Although, as we have seen, the documents from the seventeenth century reveal almost nothing in regard to choice of instruments,
we must still find out whether we are luckier in regard to the documents
from Bach's own time. The first question is, of course, whether there exist
titles of compositions in Bach's own hand that might indicate his intentions.

Immediately we see one interesting fact: titles like "for all keyboard
instruments" cannot be found any more. Almost all Bach's organ compositions are clearly reserved for the "royal instrument," which owes this
distinguishing name mostly to the majesty of his works for it. The only
"general" title used by Bach is the word "Klavier," which we find in
Das Wohltemperierte Klavier and in the *Klavierübung in vier Teilen*
(Keyboard Exercise[38] in Four Parts). We have already shown that during
Bach's lifetime the meaning of "Klavier" was "keyboard instrument":
that is, harpsichord, clavichord, and organ. At first glance one might

---

[38] Albert Schweitzer says rightly that a better translation, although not so literal, would
be "Keyboard Entertainment" (*Johann Seb. Bach, le musicien-poète*, Leipzig, 1908, p. 297).

think that, with the use of this word, the title "for all keyboard instruments" returns through the back door. Yet there is a fundamental difference between the prescriptions "for all keyboard instruments" and Bach's use of the word "Klavier." Whereas the first phrase allows an indiscriminate exchange between all three instruments, Bach's "Klavier" means one keyboard instrument for some pieces, another for other pieces, as we can clearly see from the compositions united under the title *Klavierübung*. For the Italian Concerto, the French Overture, and the *Goldberg Variations*, in the second and fourth parts of the collection, Bach explicitly requested that a harpsichord with two keyboards be used. These are the only titles in the entire keyboard works that make this special reservation. The third part of the *Klavierübung* consists exclusively of organ pieces, the famous so-called "Organ Mass." We see, therefore, that the title *Klavierübung* does not mean "for organ or harpsichord," but "here organ and there harpsichord," proving the correctness of our interpretation of the title *Das Wohltemperierte Klavier* as a collection of harpsichord, clavichord, and organ pieces. These are the only precise titles that have come down to us from Bach's own hand. Titles like *Six Suites per il cembalo*, as we find them frequently on contemporary copies, are of no help, since the word "cembalo" also means only "keyboard."[39]

Surprisingly enough, not a single testimonial about Bach's harpsichord or clavichord playing has come down to us from his contemporaries. Organ playing was the only branch of his musical activities that brought him fame during his lifetime. One remark, however, in the oldest of all Bach biographies, Johann Nikolaus Forkel's famous book *Über Johann Sebastian Bach's Leben, Kunst und Kunstwerke*, asks for our special attention, because it offers the only existing report on Bach's opinion concerning the keyboard instruments at his disposal: "The clavichord was his favorite and he used it for private musical entertainment and for

---

[39] Some mystery darkens the title of the Inventions, dedicated by Bach to the "lovers of the clavier" (*den Liebhabern des Clavires*). Had Bach meant here with the word "Clavir" the same as he meant in the title of the *Welltempered Keyboard*, namely, to select for each piece one of the three keyboard instruments, he would have said more correctly "lovers of the keyboards" (*den Liebhabern der Clavir*). Since all the Inventions show stylistically that they seem to be meant only for the clavichord, one would have to assume that in this instance Bach called the clavichord by the name "Clavir." As far as our knowledge goes, this term seems hardly to have been in general use before 1750 to designate the clavichord exclusively. In addition, the words that these pieces should be used "to achieve a singing touch" (*um eine cantabile Art im Spielen zu erlangen*), which Bach wrote in the preface, make the reservation of them for the clavichord almost one hundred per cent evident. Yet Wanda Landowska ascribes even these Inventions to the harpsichord alone, stating that "since the clavichord is a singing instrument by nature, *long studies were not necessary* [italics mine] to achieve expressive effects on it; therefore Bach must have had the harpsichord in mind, on which it is very difficult to play 'cantabile'" ("Bericht uber die Tagung der Neuen Bach-Gesellschaft in Duisburg," *Bach-Jahrbuch*, 1910, p. 181). However, I refer the reader to the previously cited statements concerning the difficulty of clavichord touch.

practice. He found it most apt for the expression of his finest thoughts and did not believe that such variety of nuance in tone could be achieved on any *Flügel* [another German name for harpsichord] or pianoforte as on the clavichord, which was indeed poor in volume but extraordinarily flexible in detail."[40]

There has been much discussion in regard to the trustworthiness of these lines, which, if they present a valid picture of Bach's ideas, require us to give primary attention to all possible clues pointing toward the clavichord in Bach's keyboard works. It is now very interesting to see the great discrepancy in reaction to these lines between the two leading Bach authorities. Both Spitta and Schweitzer repeat them, not doubting their correctness at all. But, says Spitta, "the gravity of Bach's musical ideas, which stem from the sublime Alpinesque summits of the organ, are too much for the tender instrument."[41] He concludes that Bach must have had an ideal future instrument in mind when writing his keyboard works, which could be no other than the modern piano! Schweitzer also finds the clavichord completely inadequate for Bach's works. In numerous attempts to discover the dynamic plans of some of his works, Schweitzer tries by every means to provide each piece with the terrace dynamics of the harpsichord. However, he must admit that "with many preludes and fugues our efforts are in vain; we can discover in them no dynamic plan that could not be replaced equally well by another."[42] In regard to registration he confesses that "we have to be satisfied with a certain amount of probability" (*mit einer gewissen vertrauenerweckenden Wahrscheinlichkeit*). He doubts that Bach would have admired the modern piano, for he writes: "Compared with the delicacy of the clavichord tone, he probably would have considered the tone of the piano to be rather dull and not fit for polyphonic playing."[43]

It does not lessen our deep and thankful admiration for the two great Bach biographers if we simply state that on this occasion both of them came to erroneous conclusions. In the case of Schweitzer, it is apparent that he himself did not feel quite happy with his all-harpsichord recipe. Spitta's enthusiasm for the modern piano is understandable, in the light of the general atmosphere of the nineteenth century, but his idea that Bach's ideal instrument would have been precisely the piano needs, of course, no discussion. Although it is a vain enterprise to speculate on Bach's dream-fantasies, there cannot be any doubt about how different such an instrument would have been from that which is realized by the

---

[40] (Leipzig, 1802), p. 17.
[41] Vol. I, pp. 665ff.
[42] *Bach*, p. 334.
[43] *Bach*, p. 326.

modern piano. It might perhaps have been a sort of combination of the best qualities of harpsichord and clavichord: a harpsichord with flexible tone, but hardly an instrument without the registers to give contrast in tone color.

During the years 1903–1910 there was much public discussion among Karl Nef, Richard Buchmayer, and Wanda Landowska about the harpsichord–clavichord–piano problem, with Buchmayer taking the stand for the clavichord and Nef and Landowska defending the harpsichord not only against the piano, but even against the clavichord.[44] In my book *Der Vortrag alter Klaviermusik* I gave close attention to the viewpoints of both parties, and the reader interested in the rather telling details of the pros and cons of this question is referred to that book.[45] Here it will be sufficient to say that Nef was the first one to question the trustworthiness of Forkel's report. He believed that Forkel, who wrote his biography fifty years after Bach's death and who was an intimate friend of C. P. E. Bach, might have mistakenly mixed up the son's famous predilection for the clavichord with the opinion of his father.

These long-lasting discussions, which were waged with considerable heat and not always with the noblest of weapons, ended abruptly after the Bach Festival of 1910 in Duisburg, when it became apparent that no party was able to convince the other.[46] Since then the *status quo* has been

---

[44] *Jahrbuch der Musikbibliothek Peters*, 1903; *Bach-Jahrbuch*, 1908, 1909, 1910. For specific references, see Bibliography under authors.

[45] Pages 98ff. Only one argument perhaps needs special mention, as it has frequently been used to minimize the role of the clavichord in Bach's keyboard works. It is a fact that in the specification of musical instruments in Bach's household at the moment of his death, no clavichord is mentioned. The official list read: "One veneered Clavecin, one Clavesin [*sic*] one ditto, one ditto, one ditto smaller, one Spinettgen." It should not be forgotten, however, that it is impossible, without opening the cover of a keyboard instrument built in rectangular form, to know with unfailing certainty whether it is a spinet or a clavichord. Only in Italy did spinets mostly have five sides; in Germany they were often built rectangularly. It is therefore entirely possible that the officer of the "Archivgericht" in Leipzig simply stated what he saw of the instruments without going into detailed examination. Hans T. David mentions the well-known statement from the Appendix of the *Specificatio* that Christian Bach had received three claviers with a set of pedals from the late departed during his lifetime, and concludes that "the term *claviers* is here presumably used, in contrast to the *clavecins* listed in the *Specificatio*, to mean clavichords rather than keyboards" (Hans T. David and Arthur Mendel, *The Bach Reader*, New York, 1945, p. 197). Some people have used this statement to explain the absence of clavichords in Bach's household at the time of his death. Yet it is highly improbable that Christian should have received three clavichords. Such a gift does not make any sense: two clavichords put above a "sounding pedal" are enough to be used as a substitute for practicing on an organ; the third instrument would probably have been a clavecin. At any rate, no conclusions can be drawn from such confused bits of information.

[46] From the report on the meeting of the members of the Bach Society at this festival we may cite only the following excerpt: Mme. Landowska, who had brought a Silbermann clavichord with her, asked those present to try the Italian Concerto, the Chromatic Phantasy, and a toccata on it. No wonder that because of the selection of these pieces, which Mme. Landowska could hardly have chosen in earnestness, the report states that "this practical experiment convinced the members more of the superiority of the harpsichord than all theoretic discussions could ever have achieved" ("Bericht über die Tagung der Neuen Bach-Gesellschaft in Duisburg," p. 181).

maintained: one continues to play Bach on the piano following one's own taste, either constructing a sort of "pseudo-historical version" (no expression allowed, no pedal to be used, strictest adherence to metronomical regular tempi) or, worse, taking Bach's compositions as a medium for expressing one's "modern feelings," while pitying the old Master because he could not anticipate the richness of the modern soul.[47] Since musicological research has not been able to produce more evidence about the harpsichord-clavichord problem beyond the few documents just reported, we have to admit that we shall be unable to use these documents to any degree in our quest, although indirect evidence for the existence of tendencies toward differentiating the instruments has doubtless been unveiled. Let us stress once more, despite the danger of becoming repetitious, that the "earmindedness" which the virginalists proved to have possessed to such an unusually high degree cannot have completely faded out in subsequent generations of musicians, who still applied virginalistic technique in their improvisations of the thorough bass, and who also knew very well how to exploit a harpsichord with two keyboards for the application of terrace dynamics in toccatas, variations, and concertos. It is equally unthinkable that a master like Johann Sebastian Bach should show evidence for earmindedness in only about half of his keyboard works, especially in the light of his alleged preference for the clavichord reported by Forkel—a preference which, although it has been debated, cannot be totally disregarded. Yet since all these facts have been insufficient to influence decisively our conception of Bach interpretation, the only method that gives us a chance to clarify the problems offered by Bach's keyboard works is that which we are going to undertake now: to examine the keyboard works most carefully and without any preconceived opinions, in order to see how they lend themselves for performance on harpsichord and clavichord under the mechanical conditions offered by these instruments.

---

[47] See the memorable involuntary comedy in Eugen D'Albert's preface to his edition of the *Welltempered Keyboard*: "Much in his music can no longer appeal to the feelings of our time. Bach did not know about the innumerable stages of passion, sorrow and love, and never thought that one could reproduce them in music."

CHAPTER 2

The Instrument Question

THE INSTRUMENTS USED IN THE INQUIRY

If we are to examine Bach's keyboard works to determine how and on which instrument they should be played, our success will depend entirely on the correct selection of the type of instrument that we use for such an experiment. We have already described the immense change in the technique of playing the harpsichord that takes place when registration by hand stops is replaced by pedal registration. Therefore, only an instrument with hand stops can be used for our purposes. For the largest compositions we may take the so-called "Bach Flügel" (described on p. 7) as a model. This instrument has 8', 4', and lute register on the upper keyboard and another 8' and 16' plus coupler on the lower.[1] To facilitate reference to its individual registers, we will use the symbols 8″, 4″ for the registers of the upper keyboard, and 8', 16' for those of the lower, as we did on Chart 1 above.

For smaller compositions, we may choose an instrument with only eight-foot strings on the upper keyboard and eight-foot and four-foot

---

[1] It may seem strange that we dare to take this extremely rare type of harpsichord as a model for our inquiry, especially in view of Mr. Friedrich Ernst's arguments against its authenticity (Chapter 1, note 10). Yet, for the reasons outlined in Chapter 1, we want once more to stress our strong conviction that the handful of large harpsichords preserved in our museums do in no way testify to a similar scarcity in the Bach period. None of their dispositions, which also differ widely among each other, can with any justification be called the only right and historical one. Although the "Bach disposition" seems to appear only once among them (Ernst, *Der Flügel Johann Sebastian Bachs*, p. 65), it is impossible to deny (and one does not need to be a mathematician to realize this) that this disposition provides for the greatest variety of tone colors of all possible arrangements. Why should we not trust that the harpsichord makers showed the same amount of thoughtfulness and skill which contemporary organ builders so clearly possessed? As long as we use the 16' register with utter caution and include it in our plans for registration only where architectural considerations justify it, nothing can go wrong.

strings (with coupler) on the lower. For this harpsichord, 8″, 4″ will indicate the *lower* keyboard and 8′ the *upper*. Now and then a harpsichord with only one keyboard but with 8′ and 4′ sets of strings, or with two different 8′ series, will have to be considered.

Let it also be remembered that on an instrument with hand-stop registration, a change of registers during playing can be achieved only if a rest in one hand allows time for this manipulation. Furthermore, the coupler can be handled only if both hands are free at the same time. Yet it would be wrong to insist blindly and pedantically that changes in registration are allowed only and without exception at places where rests provide an opportunity. We know that organ players often relied upon "helpers" for drawing registers. These helpers were actually indispensable when the register stops were placed too far away from the organ bench, as was frequently the case. It would not have been unusual if such helpers were occasionally used by harpsichordists in order to make sudden changes in registration possible. Although it would be ridiculous to suppose that Bach reckoned with a helper when he composed his forty-eight preludes and fugues, which in his own estimation belonged to the category of pedagogic works, nevertheless, for some of his most brilliant compositions, the role of a helper should be considered if the style of a composition seems to ask for it.

The clavichord that we use for our experiments should be a *bundfrei* (unfretted) clavichord, which means that every key has its individual string. Since these *bundfrei* instruments began to appear in the second decade of the eighteenth century, it is unthinkable that Bach would not have been familiar with this improvement of the clavichord by 1720 when he began to write the Inventions and the first volume of the *Well-tempered Keyboard*.[2] We know well what a keen observer of all advances in the construction of musical instruments Bach was; indeed, it is reported that he consulted with instrument makers on problems of the viola pomposa and the lute-clavecymbal.

Our examination of Bach's keyboard compositions must logically begin with the three pieces that Bach specifically designated for "a

---

[2] For a long time it was the general belief that Tobias Faber of Crailsheim (Württemberg) had been the first one to construct a *bundfrei* clavichord, in 1736. This date was one of the chief arguments used by Wanda Landowska to deny any possibility of the connection of a clavichord with Bach's *Welltempered Keyboard*, because the complicated chromatic progressions in this work could not be played on a "fretted" instrument. However, Francis W. Galpin reports that he saw a *bundfrei* clavichord, made by W. Gruneberg of Alt Brandenburg and dated 1700 (!), in Dr. Henry Watson's collection (Galpin, *Old English Instruments of Music*, Chicago, 1911, p. 115). The recent discovery of a *bundfrei* clavichord made by Gottfried Silbermann in 1723 (now in the Stadt Museum at Markneukirchen) brings an instrument constructed by Bach's intimate friend into closest connection with the date of the first volume of the *Welltempered Keyboard*, which was written in 1722 (see Joseph Wörsching, *Die historischen Saiten-Klaviere und der moderne Clavichord und Cembalo Bau*, Mainz, 1946, p. 21).

harpsichord with two keyboards." Since here we will not have to ponder whether we have the right or wrong instrument under our fingers, we can devote our study to discovering how Bach intended the harpsichord to be used. With this knowledge we will have some bases on which to choose the correct instrument and method of interpretation for other pieces. Let the Italian Concerto, or more correctly, the Concerto in the Italian Manner (*Concerto nach Italienischem Gusto*) be our first test piece.

THE ITALIAN CONCERTO

The title itself gives the first clue to the architecture of the piece. It is meant to be an imitation of a concerto grosso, the well-known type of composition for orchestra that had been developed in Italy around 1650 and that found its first climax in Corelli's concerti grossi, written in 1712. The most characteristic feature of such a concerto is the constant alternation between the full orchestra or *grosso* and a small group of solo players, the *concertino*. This smaller ensemble, traditionally two violins and continuo (harpsichord with violoncello), is identical with that used for the so-called "trio sonata," equally popular during the same period. The Italian Concerto by Bach is, then, the "harpsichord score" of an imaginary concerto grosso.[3]

Bach has been praised for the originality of this idea. Yet, when Johann Kuhnau wrote his famous Sonata in B flat major in 1692, which he proudly announced as the first sonata written for a keyboard instrument, he consciously imitated the form of the trio sonata. The idea of transcribing for the harpsichord a musical form hitherto used only in another branch of instrumental music was, therefore, no novelty. However, Bach was not even the first to imitate concerto-grosso style on the harpsichord. Johann Mattheson's "Sonata pour le clavecin," written in 1713, and dedicated to the "person who will play it best," is a clear forerunner,[4] even though the title "concerto" is not used. Bach must have known this composition because an undeniable stylistic relation exists between it and his Italian Concerto.

The legend spread by the admirers of the composer, that on the organ he used the strangest, most unusual and unheard-of register combinations, is sufficient to make us feel very uneasy when it comes to any

---

[3] Looking at the ever-increasing number of Bach's compositions for single instruments that have been more or less (mostly less) successfully transcribed for modern orchestra, one wonders why nobody has ever "orchestrated" the Italian Concerto, which would at least make some sense if done "in style."

[4] As a later outgrowth of a related idea, I would like to mention Chopin's Allegro de Concert in A major, Op. 46, which represents a piano piece written in the style of a first movement of a piano concerto. One may also notice similar features which are characteristic of this type of treatment in the first movement of Beethoven's Sonata in C major, Op. 2, No. 3.

discussion of registration problems. However, the print of the Italian Concerto does contain some information about its registration, a circumstance for which we must be very grateful. Yet our peace of mind is soon dispelled when we see that all Bach did was to add, in a few places, the words *forte* and *piano* which, in terms of the harpsichord, do not mean loud and soft as such, because loud and soft do not exist as single registers on this instrument. The true meaning of these words is *octave doubling* for *forte* and *single tone* for *piano*. If these words are printed between the staves they are meant for both hands, otherwise they are placed above or below the part to which they belong.

Why Bach made use of these instructions for dynamics only in this piece and in the French Overture will never be explained. At first, one might think he did it because these pieces are among the few that he himself published; but then one wonders why the six Partitas, which he had published even earlier, have no register indications. That the seeming novelty of the musical forms of the concerto or the overture prompted Bach to explain the inner organization of these pieces by the registration marks does not hold either, since by this time he had already written other "concertos" for harpsichord (e.g., the Prelude of the English Suite in G minor), without believing such information to be necessary. Also unexplainable is the fact that the register marks given by Bach in the Italian Concerto are incomplete, as they are missing in more places than could be accounted for by printer's negligence. Fortunately, enough register marks remain to make clear Bach's artistic intentions.

When one begins to examine the first movement in detail, one sees immediately that the piece is carefully divided into *forte* sections, representing the orchestral *tutti*, and other sections in which either the right hand remains *forte* while the left hand plays *piano*, or, as in two cases, both hands are marked *piano* (bars 67–68 and 129–138[5]). These sections represent the concertino parts of the movement. Only once (bar 103) is a *forte* sign missing at a place where it is obviously necessary. Happily, this place is so clearly the point at which a *tutti* section returns that we have here the evidence of a printer's mistake rather than a planned omission.[6] In its entirety the piece is a model of terrace dynamics, and since the end of every section is most clearly marked by a strong cadence, the change from one keyboard to the other is technically very simple.

The choice of registers for the performance of this music depends on

---

[5] It is not absolutely certain whether the *piano* in bars 129–138 might not be meant for the left hand only. In this case the "echo bars," 67–68, would be the only ones in the entire piece in which both hands are *piano*.

[6] In this very bar the Bülow edition commits the serious mistake of indicating a *pianissimo*, which contradicts the basic architecture of this movement.

what type of harpsichord we select. The prescription "for a harpsichord with two keyboards" does not tell us whether Bach had in mind the largest type of harpsichord (8′, 16′, and coupler on the lower keyboard; 8″, 4″, and lute on the upper), or an instrument with only 8″, 4″, and coupler contrasting with 8′ on the other keyboard. To our surprise, we will soon see that the composition itself will clarify the instrument question to a greater degree than we might have dared to expect.

A performance on the smaller instrument without the 16′ register offers no problems at all. The *forte* parts are played on the keyboard with 8″ and 4″ registers, the *piano* parts on the keyboard with 8′ alone. If we have a large instrument at our disposal, however, on which the 16′ register is placed on the opposite keyboard from the 4′ register, matters become more complicated. The first thought of every harpsichord player would, of course, be to give the opening *tutti* the splendor of the full work of the instrument, the wonderful sonority achieved by coupling both keyboards. What is to be done, however, in bar 30 (Ex. 1)?

Ex. 1. Italian Concerto, Movement 1, bar 30

Here Bach asks that the left hand start playing *piano*. The instrument has, at this moment, 8″ and 4″ on the upper keyboard, which could serve as *piano*, in contrast to the *forte* of the lower keyboard, which still has all the registers combined for the full work. Therefore we could simply play the left-hand part on the upper keyboard while the right hand stays on the lower one. However, we immediately discover that this will not do: because of the 16′ register the right-hand part also sounds one octave lower than written and thus goes below the bass part of the left hand. This ruins the clarity of the voice leading so completely that this version must be given up. It is true that the cause of the trouble, the 16′ register, could easily be removed during the rest in measure 30, which is long enough for this action. Then the left hand would play 8″ and 4″ on the upper keyboard, and the right hand 8′, 8″, and 4″ on the lower. (We could not give up the coupler, owing to the lack of a simultaneous rest in both hands.) But the very small difference in sound volume that we would now get from the two keyboards would be insufficient to give us the feeling of contrast between *forte* and *piano*, so this registration must also be rejected.

The idea of using the coupler in the *tutti* must therefore be dismissed, and our next attempt could begin with the right hand playing 8″ and 4″, the left playing 8′ and 16′. But a new disappointment awaits us: the wonderful sonority of the *tutti* with coupler is gone. The right hand sounds light, the left hand dark, and these two tone colors do not mix in a way that one can call a balanced *forte* for both hands. However, there does exist a remedy for this unpleasant accoustical result: we could play the part of the left hand one octave higher than written, and thus restore the sonority of the *tutti* sound. If this sounds like an odd solution, it would nevertheless seem to be in accord with the reports about the eccentricities of Bach's registration practices, and we might feel proud to be so close to Bach's own ways. Of course, the 16′ has to be disengaged in measure 30 and can only be drawn again in measure 163 where the last *tutti* starts. Acceptable as this plan might be, it cannot be fully defended: since the intermediate *tuttis* do not allow a similar treatment, the first and last would receive undue extra color. The only conclusion which we can reach after all these experiments is that the 16′ register cannot be used in this movement and that the movement was clearly written for the average type of harpsichord that has 8″ plus 4″ and coupler on one keyboard and 8′ alone on the other. It hardly needs to be mentioned that had we used a harpsichord with the disposition 8′, 4′, 16′, 8″, which is so popular nowadays, the same results would appear; for the reasons given, the 16′ cannot be used.[7]

---

[7] Since only very few descriptions of registration suggestions have so far been published, readers who are interested in another description of how to register this movement are referred to Eta Harich-Schneider, *The Harpsichord* (Kassel, St. Louis, 1954). We cannot, however, pass over her recommendations without serious reservations. On p. 53, she says: "For many years I had the privilege of performing Bach's music regularly on the (*presumably genuine*) [italics mine; see pp. 7ff.] 'Bach-harpsichord' of the famous Berlin collection . . . and I became familiar with the sonorous, dynamic and technical practicabilities of this beautiful instrument. . . . The first '*tutti*' comprises the measures 1–30; it does not bear a dynamic indication, but it is clear from the form of the whole movement, that this fully scored introductory section must be played forte, at least with coupled eight-foot and four-foot (8′ + 4′). The Berlin Bach-harpsichord had a sixteen-foot (16′) and I used to play the first and the last '*tutti*' of this movement with *all* [italics mine] the registers: 8′, 8′, 4′, 16′.—From bar 31 to bar 52 the bass accompaniment is indicated *piano*, the treble part *forte*. I interpret the *forte* as 8′ + 4′ on the stronger manual, the *piano* as 8′ on the softer manual." This can be done, however, on the Berlin instrument only by removing in bar 30 the 16′ register as well as the coupler. The brief rest in the right hand in this bar allows only the removal of the 16′, and this not too easily; there is no possibility for taking out the coupler, a manipulation which, as one will recall from our description, requires *two hands*. The author must somehow have felt this impossibility, for she continues on p. 54: "At bar 52 both parts are marked *forte*, so the hands join on the stronger manual: 8′ + 4′ (or 8′, 8′, 4′)." For the reasons just mentioned, only the latter of these two suggestions is possible. But now a serious dilemma follows: when the 16′ register is taken out, the two keyboards of the Berlin instrument offer only two possibilities for contrasting tone volumes that could be used here:

V. CLAVICHORD BY H. A. HASS, DATED 1743

(from Donald Boalch, M.A., *Makers of the Harpsichord and Clavichord, 1440–1840*, George Ronald, London, plate XV; by courtesy of Mr. J. M. Taphouse and Prof. J. A. Westrup)

VI. THE "BACH FLÜGEL," TWO MANUALS; IN THE BERLIN STATE COLLECTION OF EARLY MUSIC INSTRUMENTS

(from Hanns Neupert, *Das Cembalo*, Kassel, 1933)

VII. BACH'S TABLE OF ORNAMENTS

(from Ludwig Landshoff, *Inventionen und Sinfonien*, C. Peters Edition, Leipzig, 1933)

For the second movement Bach's only prescriptions are *forte* for the right hand, *piano* for the left hand, at the beginning. Although this looks as if we should simply continue with the same registration that we applied for the first movement, it goes without saying that such a procedure could produce only the most boring effect. The situation calls for new tone colors, and fortunately, more solutions for the juxtaposition of *forte* and *piano* are available even without the 16' register.

The first information about what to do can be deduced immediately from the principles of form applied by Bach. It is apparent that the right hand is written in the style of a "violin solo" while the left hand provides a sort of accompaniment in two parts. This proves that Bach continued to think in terms of the concerto-grosso idea in this movement also. In orchestral compositions of this type, it was customary for the second movement to be played only by the concertino instruments. Bach himself has given us wonderful examples of this type of setting in his Fifth Brandenburg Concerto, in the A minor Triple Concerto, and in the Concerto in C major for Two Harpsichords. The imaginary concertino instruments that might perform the second movement of the Italian Concerto could be one violin and two violas da gamba for the accompaniment. The violas could even produce the contra-A, the lowest tone of the piece, which would be impossible for a cello. This second movement is precisely the one that has always been used by the adversaries of the harpsichord for triumphantly pointing out the merits of the modern piano. Only on the piano, they have said, can one do justice to this magnificent unending melody, for the performance of which the harpsichord seems to be entirely unfit. We must therefore look for a registration interesting enough to silence the voices of those who take this movement as the ultimate proof of the inferiority of the harpsichord to the piano.

Lower keyboard		Upper keyboard
8'		8', 4'
	or	
8', 8', 4' (coupled)		8', 4'

It is obvious that of these possibilities only the first makes sense. The dynamic difference between 8', 8', 4', and 8', 4' is much too small to be interpreted as standing for *forte* and *piano*.

From now on, however, the recommendations of Mme. Harich-Schneider become totally incomprehensible. After suggesting that bars 65–66 be played in 8' + 4' registration (upper keyboard, of course), and bars 67–68, their "figurated echo," with 8' only (lower keyboard), she says (p. 54) that "from bar 69 to the first beat of bar 90 the registration stays 8', 8', 4'." This can be done only on the lower keyboard *coupled*. After this, she recommends 8' + 4' for the treble part and 8' for the bass part—a recommendation that requires uncoupling again. One sees at first glance that the Berlin instrument does not allow such constant coupling and uncoupling, which must be done every time by hand. Only on an instrument with pedal registration can such manipulations be made, and it is up to the artistic conscience of a harpsichord player whether he wants to deviate so far from what could be done on historic instruments. The Bach harpsichord, however, cannot be called in as a crown witness for this procedure.

4

Because of the difference in form between the first and second movements, the meanings of *forte* and *piano* also differ. While in the first movement the *tutti* parts had to be separated from the concertino, here it is necessary only that the "solo instrument" be louder than its accompaniment. Although in general *forte* and *piano* mean tone with octave and single tone, there also exists a finer differentiation in intimate cases. On almost all historic harpsichords (unfortunately not on all modern ones) the tone of the 4' register is outspokenly "sharp" compared with the "normal" sound of an 8' register. Therefore, playing with the right hand on the 4' register only, but one octave lower than the notation indicates, would in itself give a beautiful contrast to the tone color of the left hand playing on the other keyboard with the normal 8' register. We can further increase this differentiation if we make the 8' accompaniment softer than usual by applying a simple trick: we must merely watch that we do not draw the register stop of the 8' completely but only partially, so that just a small part of the leather tongues pluck the strings. The tone produced this way is most delicate and forms a happy contrast with the 4' *low* register for the leading part. This sound effect is by no means unjustified historically, since one can very easily produce it on every instrument with hand stops. On the modern harpsichords with pedal registration one can do the same by putting the pedal only halfway down. Many instruments even have a "catching device" to retain the pedal in halfway position. Unfortunately this possibility of giving every register another shading is too often abused by owners of harpsichords with pedal registration. By changing the position of the pedal gradually, the tone acquires small crescendos and diminuendos, thus producing clavichord effects on the harpsichord (see also p. 63).

For the second movement, then, the registration using the 4" played one octave lower against 8' *piano* gives a very dignified setting. It would, however, be wrong to assume that this registration must be strictly maintained throughout the entire movement, as most players believe to be their duty. Architecturally considered, this movement is clearly divided into two "verses," of which the second one is much more excited. (See the syncopations that come increasingly to the foreground.) Since the two verses are separated by a measure, bar 27, in which the right hand has a rest (Ex. 2), this bar provides an excellent opportunity to give a new meaning to the *forte-piano* relation: on the fourth eighth note of the bar we can restore the normal 8' tone volume by putting the register back into its normal position. After having done this, enough time remains to add the 8" register to the 4" already drawn. The second part of the piece can now be played with 8" plus 4" against 8', but we would advise the player to keep the right hand one octave lower than written, in order to avoid returning to the tone color of the first movement, which, as we shall soon see, will be needed again for the last movement.

Ex. 2. Italian Concerto, Movement 2, bar 27

Playing one octave lower is not an offense against the original notes that Bach wrote because these notes are still audible in the 4' register. Although crossings with the higher notes of the left hand take place frequently, the low bass notes prevent the harmony from ever becoming obscured. The added notes of the lower octave now give the melody a most charming dark color that will certainly compensate for any memories we may have of how this movement *could* sound on the modern piano.

All these suggestions have been given for the simpler harpsichord. If we want to consider using the 16' register of the larger instrument, which is not unjustified here even though it is inapplicable in the first movement, we can make our interpretation of this movement still more "exotic." The first verse could be played with 4" *low* (notes played one octave lower than written) for the melody, against 16' *high* (notes played one octave higher than written) for the accompaniment; the second verse would be 8" and 4" *low* against 8' and 16' *high*. This version is one of fascinating power, but asks for complete concentration on the part of the player. Well done, it will make us quickly forget any prejudiced idea that this movement surmounts the possibilities of the harpsichord.[8]

The last movement offers no new problems. It shows the same juxtaposition of *tutti* and solo parts as the first *Allegro*, and again, the individual sections are clearly separated by strong cadences. Only one new use of registration is noteworthy: just after the first *tutti*, Bach asks for continuous changes between *forte* and *piano* for both hands, obviously enjoying the sudden and unexpected alternation of tone colors and the

---

[8] By recommending for the second verse a registration in which octaves are used for the melodic line, I am well aware of the objection, easily made, that at this moment the imitation of a "violin solo" is given up. However, we must remember that the Italian Concerto is meant to be a real "concerto" for the harpsichord, a composition written to show off the sound possibilities and virtuosity that this instrument can display. The inability to imitate the nuances of violin tone would become very apparent and would lead to undeniable boredom if one played the entire movement in a single tone color. Bach himself, when he was making arrangements of pieces for violin, did not necessarily preserve the original violin character, as may be seen, among other places, in his transcription of the famous Prelude in E major (a violin solo) for organ with orchestra in Cantata 29.

display of virtuosity. Whereas in the first movement only one *forte* sign was lacking, however, the entire middle section of this movement is left completely unregistered. Nevertheless, the structure of the piece makes it unthinkable to leave it in one color, and I sincerely believe that the additional changes in registration which I would like to suggest correspond so logically to the structure of the piece that explanation of their justification may be spared. Using the lessons that we will draw later from the French Overture (below), it seems that the following *forte* and *piano* marks should be added: Right hand—*piano*, bar 104; *forte*, bar 113; *piano*, bar 117 from the second eighth; *forte*, bar 123 from second eighth; *forte*, bar 140. Left hand—*piano*, bar 104, second quarter note; *forte*, bar 115 from second eighth; *piano*, bar 117; *forte*, bar 124.[9] In regard to the possibility of a more varied registration than 8″ and 4″ against 8′, the 16′ register and coupler cannot be used for the same reasons as in the first movement. Because there is also no urgent reason for using these devices in the second movement, it becomes fully apparent that a harpsichord built without the 16′ register is sufficient to bring out the full inner meaning of the Italian Concerto.

Let us summarize the results of this experiment. We have seen that a careful examination of the playing possibilities of this piece clarified the question of what type of harpsichord Bach must have had in his mind for its performance. We have also found out that the terrace dynamics are unmistakably underlined by cadences, that only in the second movement can good reasons be seen for a change of registration within a piece, and that in general, all the demands for proper registration are fulfilled through the distribution of "light and shadow" (*forte* and *piano*).

THE FRENCH OVERTURE

We will now turn to the second piece in which Bach designated the way to use the registration of the harpsichord, the French Overture. The title again gives us the basic information about its structure. Whereas we found that the Italian Concerto is a kind of harpsichord score for an imaginary concerto grosso, the French Overture is the imitation of another type of piece for orchestra, the so-called "orchestra suite."

Three special requirements distinguish an orchestra suite from a suite for a solo instrument. The first piece in an orchestra suite has to be an overture in "French style," a piece in three parts, slow–fast–slow, making ample use of dotted notes in the slow sections. Instead of an

---

[9] That there is something wrong with the printed dynamic marks is proved by the fact that the *piano* in bar 127 is followed by another *piano* in bar 155.

allemande, which is omitted in an orchestra suite, the first dance is a courante. Finally, although not without exceptions, the last piece, which in solo suites is always a gigue, can be a piece in "free style," while the gigue takes the next to the last place. Two of the four orchestra suites by Bach show all these typical features. The titles for the last movements are "Badinerie" and "Rejouissance." In the French Overture we also find Bach faithfully adhering to all the special features. The first piece is an overture, there is no allemande, and the last piece, which is preceded by a gigue, is called "Echo." Almost all the necessary registration marks are in Bach's own hand. Since the very few places where they are missing leave no doubt about what should be done, the French Overture is indeed the most precisely registered piece of the entire harpsichord literature.

In the *Allegro* section of the Overture, we find the same *piano* and *forte* marks as in the first and last movements of the Italian Concerto. Not only are the sections separated by strong cadences, but the contrasts between them are even more outspoken than in the other compositions because the *forte* sections are followed by *piano* sections for both hands. (As we will remember, in the Italian Concerto the right hand almost always remained on the *forte* keyboard, and it was only the left hand that provided the alternation of grosso and concertino.) In the middle of the *Allegro* movement, in a kind of development section, Bach carefully indicates the entrances of the leading subject with *forte*, while the accompanying voices are kept *piano*. As we progress this will become a very important piece of information for analogous places in other pieces.

It is obvious that the opening and closing sections of the Overture require a stronger registration than the middle part, which is as clearly a piece for 8″ and 4″ (*forte*) against 8′ (*piano*), as are the quick movements of the Italian Concerto. These sections must, therefore, be played with coupler, and certainly no objection to the use of a 16′ register could be found. The coupler can easily be taken out after the last chord of the first section and put back again after a momentary interruption before the "recapitulation" begins. Such a short interruption cannot be called inartistic. On the organ such situations arise very often, and if one prepares for the approach of the "recapitulation" by a small ritardando,[10] this interruption will pass almost unnoticed by the listener.

---

[10] This might perhaps be the proper place to talk about the widely discussed problem of the ritardando. The opinions of eminent musicians clash here with unusual violence. There can be no doubt, however, that a ritardando at the end of a piece was common practice. One needs only to look into vocal scores by Handel and Bach to discover a very remarkable feature found in almost all arias accompanied by obbligato instruments: in the penultimate measure both composers usually give these instruments a rest, breaking off their parts rather abruptly, while only harpsichord and the continuo violoncello continue to accompany the singer. This could have served no other purpose than to give the singer an opportunity for free interpretation, and it was simply a wise precaution on the part of the composer to leave the *colla parte*

The Overture is followed by a Courante, two Gavottes, two Passe-pieds, a Sarabande, two Bourrées, a Gigue, and an "Echo." The next indication of registration occurs in the second Gavotte, which is marked *piano*. As the second Passepied and the second Bourrée are also marked *piano*, it goes without saying that the first Gavotte, the first Passepied, and the first Bourrée are meant to be played *forte*. The Courante stands between *forte* pieces, the Overture and the first Gavotte, and should logically be played *piano*, which fits perfectly with its unusually intimate character. Only the Sarabande and the Gigue puzzle us. In principle the Sarabande leans more to a *piano* setting, the Gigue to a *forte*. If we try to prove this, however, by striving to maintain the alternation between loud and soft, we meet with another problem. We cannot say authoritatively whether in the case of dances that have a twofold appearance, which we find here more often than in other keyboard compositions by Bach, the first should be played again after the second, as we do nowadays with the return of the Minuet after the Trio. Factually this problem seems unsolvable because of the lack of contemporary information. Only in the Second and Third English Suites, which have come to us only in contemporary copies, do we find the word "alternativemente" over the first dance, but there is no evidence that the first dance should be repeated in every case, as almost all editors of pedagogical editions would make us believe. If we do not believe in this repetition, the Sarabande of the French Overture creates a dilemma by standing between a soft and a loud piece, so that the regular alternation is interrupted.

In any case, if we have a 16′ register at our disposal we can give the Sarabande some degree of special treatment. The combination of 4″ and 16′ registers, achieved with the help of the coupler, gives one of the most beautiful tone colors that the harpsichord can produce. The solemn, almost organ-like character of this combination lends itself best to the treatment of this most aristocratic of all Bach's dance movements. If no 16′ register is available, we can give the Sarabande some distinction by

---

accompanying to the *maestro al cembalo*, rather than to involve the entire orchestra in so risky a task. Since the continuo cello player almost never had a part of his own, but was accustomed to play from the harpsichordist's part, sitting at his left side, there was no danger that he would not be able to follow the liberties taken by the singer.

How much one should slow down, unfortunately, cannot be defined exactly. C. P. E. Bach says that the listeners should feel that the piece is over. (*Versuch über die wahre Art, das Klavier zu spielen*, Berlin, 1759, 1762, vol. II, p. 254; Eng. ed., *Essay on the True Art of Playing Keyboard Instruments*, trans. William J. Mitchell, New York, 1949, p. 375. All page references hereafter are to this edition.) In general we may have the right to say that many modern performers, especially orchestra conductors, overdo the ritardandos considerably. Slowing down with every cadence is one of the worst but most widespread habits. Nothing justifies such procedure. It can only be called a display of bad taste because it brings the music to almost half a dozen complete standstills and reminds one of the traffic rule, "Slow down at each intersection."

playing the repetitions of both parts on the softer 8', as opposed to the other dances in which no change in tone color is justified because the "second dance" provides the contrast. The Gigue is, of course, a loud piece for which even the application of the full work is permissible. Finally, the last piece of the Overture, the famous "Echo," gives us the most elaborate report in the entire keyboard music of methods of harpsichord registration. Here Bach tells us about his intentions to the most minute detail, and we do not know what to admire most in this admirable piece: the appealing yet so dignified melodic line, the virtuosity of the setting, or the spark of genius that lets the "Echo" answer not literally, as everybody else would have done, but in a stylized way.

Let us again examine what general conclusions can be drawn from our newly gained experiences. We have seen that the terrace dynamics can be traced with the same clarity as in the Italian Concerto. Furthermore, in the middle of the first movement Bach distinguished between entrances of the theme and accompanying voices in his dynamic plan. We have also learned that short dance pieces have to be played in one tone color without any more intricate variety, but that in special cases, as in the "Echo," it may happen that the registration is meant to be changed after every few bars.

THE *GOLDBERG VARIATIONS*

Before we start a survey of how to apply these experiences most effectively to those works that do not contain Bach's own directions, we must examine the third work in which the composer provided special marks for registration, the *Goldberg Variations*. To our surprise, we find that this time Bach used a different system for communicating his intentions. No *forte* and *piano* marks appear, but for each variation Bach specified whether it should be played on one or two keyboards. At first glance this seems to give us less information than we could get by the other system, and we ask ourselves why Bach gave up the old method. The most appropriate answer seems to be linked to the fact that it was customary in Bach's time to give every variation *one* registration and not more. Bach might have thought that the character of each variation revealed the proper registration and that he did not need to state such obvious facts. Soon we will observe that the information we receive from the new system goes much deeper than we could anticipate, and into unexpected directions.

In the first variation Bach prescribed "one keyboard" even though the piece makes use of crossing of the hands, a device that is very characteristic of this work and is generally considered one of the most typical features of brilliant harpsichord style in which the mechanical possibilities offered by two keyboards are most effectively exploited. Even in the fifth variation, where the hands cross continually, Bach wrote "for one or two keyboards." We learn, therefore, to our surprise, that crossing the hands does not necessarily indicate the use of two keyboards, a point that has a far-reaching consequence: if this technique can be applied on one keyboard, then pieces that involve it cannot be excluded from being played on the clavichord.[11] Now one of the popular traditional bases for identifying harpsichord pieces has to be dismissed, since it is no longer a determining factor.[12]

Variations 13 and 25 provide interesting parallels to the slow movement of the Italian Concerto. Both variations are planned as "arias," in which melody and accompaniment have to have individual tone colors.

All canons in the *Goldberg Variations* (with the exception of the canon at the ninth, Variation 27) are meant for one keyboard only. This causes some surprise because it stands in contradiction to all usual expectations. Would not one think that a composer would do his best to have us hear the canonic voices with greatest clarity? On the contrary, Bach hides the voice leading from us as much as he can, making the point that a canon is a piece of music which should be appreciated exclusively for its musical value, and that its "mathematical background" need not be taken as seriously as laymen usually do. That the last canon is an exception and is meant for two keyboards is most noteworthy. This canon differs from all the others by being written in just two canonic parts with no accompanying voice. The direction "two keyboards" clearly indicates the use of two different tone colors, and drastically proves once more that Bach's interest in the way his works sounded went far beyond simply letting "the lines speak for themselves."[13]

With this discussion of the *Goldberg Variations* we come to the end of all the direct information about registration given by the hand of the composer himself. The few more *forte* and *piano* signs scattered here and there do not contribute to the clarification of anything that has not yet been discussed during our survey. Scant as our new-found bits of information are, we are fortunate to have thus become acquainted with some of the basic principles of the art of registration that we could not have discovered without Bach's help. First of all, the breadth of the sections in

---

[11] Although hand-crossing is now one of the most ordinary devices of piano technique, it is noteworthy that Haydn and Mozart and even Beethoven made only sparing use of it.

[12] The Fifth Sonata in C. P. E. Bach's *Probestücke* for his *Essay*, written for clavichord, is otherwise the only piece to testify against the misconception that hand-crossing was reserved for harpsichord pieces.

[13] Compare the remark in Cornelia Auerbach's *Die deutsche Clavichordkunst des 18. Jahrhunderts*, p. 24, with these findings.

terrace dynamics and the great economy in the change of tone colors throughout a single piece are in striking contrast to the habits of most present-day harpsichordists. We also observed that short dance pieces should be played without any change in registration, since *forte* and *piano* colors usually alternate from dance to dance. Most important and helpful for the registration problems of other pieces is the fact that unless Bach wants to introduce new tone colors in a manner that will specifically create surprise, every change in registration is prepared by a cadence and often also by brief rests that make the shifting from one keyboard to the other technically very easy.

PRELUDE OF ENGLISH SUITE III IN G MINOR

If we now look around for other pieces to which the information just gained can be applied, we are lucky enough to find at least a few that show such outspoken similarities to those just discussed that their problems of interpretation can be easily solved. The concerto-grosso type was used by Bach for all preludes of the English Suites, with the exception of the first, while the French-overture type can be found most literally imitated in the Overture of the Fourth Partita and in the Toccata of the Sixth. Since a complete analysis of the registration problems in all the important keyboard works by Bach will be given later, we will restrict ourselves now to a discussion of only those pieces in which we find situations that will widen the scope of our knowledge.

No clearer example of a concerto grosso *en miniature* can be found than the Prelude to the English Suite in G minor. The cadences after each section make the distinction between grosso and concertino very easy: the grosso measures are 1–33, 67–99, 111–125, and 180–213. Yet the playing of this piece is not so simple that we need only designate the remaining measures as concertino. The first concertino section, which means *piano* in both hands, comprises bars 33 (starting after the first sixteenth) to 67 (first eighth only).[14] But from bars 99 to 111, Bach lets both hands alternate between the motives of the first grosso and the first concertino, revealing their inner relation by showing that they can be used simultaneously. The middle section of the *Allegro* of the French Overture, as well as the virtuoso-like changes between the keyboards in the first "solo" of the last movement of the Italian Concerto, provide the recipe: on the second sixteenth of bar 99, the right hand jumps to the *piano* keyboard to play the concertino motive, returns to *forte* on the

---

[14] Although most pedagogic editions recommend, during measures 33–67, a series of alternations of *forte*, *mezzoforte*, and *piano*, a connoisseur of the concerto-grosso style would certainly not consider them here.

second eighth of bar 101 for the grosso motive, etc., while the left hand is always on the alternating keyboard. In bar 110 both lower parts should be taken over to the *forte* keyboard, so that from bar 112 the general *forte* is restored.

Only one problem remains to be solved: what should we do with measures 161–180? Since measures 125–161 seem to be *piano*, and since the *forte* of the last *tutti* begins in bar 180, we are faced with the fact that playing measures 161–180 *piano* does not separate them from the preceding section, but playing them *forte* brings about the same result in regard to the final *tutti*. Since there can be no doubt about having to end the Prelude with *forte* registration, *piano* for the measures in question becomes the only possible solution, and we must examine measures 125–161 again, to see if perhaps we have been wrong there. That bar 125 marks the beginning of a *piano* section goes without saying: the correspondence with what happens in measure 33 is too obvious. Yet a closer examination of and comparison between measures 33–67 and measures 125–161 show that they are not built in exactly the same way, and that in bars 138–139 and 148–149 (Ex. 4a, b), Bach uses a manner of notation different from that in bars 44–45 and 54–55 (Ex. 3a, b).

Ex. 3a. English Suite III in G minor, Prelude, bars 44–45

Ex. 3b. The same, bars 54–55

It can easily be seen that no change of keyboards is possible in bars 44–45 and 54–55. In the corresponding bars 138–139 and 148–149, however, a change of keyboards is technically very simple. Since in all these cases *tutti* material is involved, a solution for the "terrace dilemma" of bar 161 offers itself in a very natural way. If we play the *tutti* interjections of bars 137–139, 147–149, and the cadence of 157–161 *forte*, the desired contrast in bar 161 is achieved, and we will immediately recollect that sudden interjections of *tutti* episodes in concertino sections can frequently be found in the Brandenburg Concertos and especially in Handel's

Ex. 4a. The same, bars 138–139

Ex. 4b. The same, bars 148–149

concerti grossi. It might, however, be wise to let only the right hand jump to the *forte* keyboard and keep the left hand constantly *piano*. This would not only create a differentiation in sound volume from full *tuttis*, but actually seems to be indicated by the part of the left hand in bar 157 (Ex. 5), in which the extra stem, giving g the value of an eighth note,

Ex. 5. English Suite III in G minor, Prelude, bar 157

makes jumping away not technically impossible but certainly does not favor it.[15] It cannot be denied that the same type of *tutti* material is also inherent in measures 43–45 and 53–55 of the first concertino episode,

---

[15] See p. 53 for a similar situation.

which we just recommended should be played *piano* throughout. Yet again a comparison with real concerti grossi will reveal that a first concertino section is normally not interrupted by *tutti* interjections, and the difference in notation between Examples 3 and 4 speaks strongly against such an interruption.[16]

To end our survey, it should be mentioned that the final *tutti* had better start in bar 180 in the right hand only, while the left hand may wait until bar 184 to join the *forte* keyboard.

How many registers should be used to bring out the *forte-piano* relation in this piece is a question of minor importance. If we want to use the 16′ register at all, *forte* would be the full work, *piano* the 8″ and 4″ on the other keyboard. The quick tempo would, however, make the continuous use of the 16′ register rather undesirable, since this register sounds very clumsy when used in rapid runs; therefore it seems far better to play this piece, with only 8″ plus 4″ against 8′, exactly as we treated the first and last movements of the Italian Concerto.

TOCCATA OF PARTITA VI IN E MINOR

Turning now to the Toccata of the Partita in E minor, we recognize the French-overture type, which we have already discussed. Here the 16′ register may be called to duty if we play the framing sections with the full work of the harpsichord. The middle section, however, puts problems before us that we have not yet had occasion to solve. Because it is written as a fugue, we no longer meet the strong cadences that have hitherto given us so much help in finding the *forte* and *piano* sections; indeed, we might feel rather helpless if this fugue were not written according to the principle that "developments" (sections in which the theme is led through the voices) and "episodes" or "interludes" (sections in which the theme does not appear, or where only fragments of it are used) alternate regularly.[17]

---

[16] It is embarrassing to find the same type of double stemming also in bar 125, where it seems to be absolutely senseless. We are inclined to consider it as a writing error because of the different notation in the corresponding bar 33. The lack of an autograph makes the authenticity of all notes with double stemming questionable. Inner evidence seems, however, so strongly to support our suggestions for the distribution of *forte* and *piano* that the added support by double stemming is without significance.

[17] The variety in the construction of fugues is so great that musicians have given up attempts to define a "fugue form." In order to facilitate our analysis, we will use the terms "exposition," "development," and "coda" for the three main sections that are present in every fugue. The exposition is self-evident; the coda begins with the final return of the main theme in the tonic key. To call the middle section of the fugue the development has become customary in many countries. It has also become traditional to use the word "development" for the individual presentations of the theme within the elaboration of the fugue. A "complete" development is one in which the theme appears in every voice; otherwise it is called "incomplete."

Even if we did not know, from an old tradition among organ players,[18] that developments are to be played with a fuller setting than episodes, we would understand instinctively that the difference in texture between developments and episodes is, in its acoustical demands, comparable to that between grosso and concertino. The general distribution of *forte* and *piano* is therefore relatively easy; only after closer examination will we see that some problems of greater magnitude still need to be solved.

Since no piece so far has required a richer registration than the drastic contrast of 8″ plus 4″ with 8′, let us start this fugue, too, by playing the exposition in 8″ plus 4″ and see what will happen. Very soon we discover that the structure of the first part of the fugue is much more complicated than a simple introduction of the three voices. The section that would traditionally be called the exposition ends in measure 37 on the first eighth note, and is followed by an interlude of three bars that we will play on the 8′ keyboard. In measure 40 the bass starts the theme again in the dominant key, the key in which a real fourth part would have appeared. This artistic trick, to create the impression of the entrance of an additional fourth voice in the polyphonic web, is used by Bach very frequently, and to do this entrance of the theme sufficient accoustical justice, both hands have to return to the louder keyboard after the first sixteenth or eighth of the second quarter note. That we cannot let the left hand jump alone, as might seem more natural, becomes evident two measures later. There we see that the middle voice, which also has to be played by the left hand and therefore sounds *forte*, must now be taken over by the right hand. If this hand were still on the softer keyboard, the middle voice would suddenly switch from *forte* to *piano*, which is aesthetically unreasonable.

The *forte* playing of both hands logically comes to an end at measure 43 where a new interlude begins that lasts only until measure 46, in which the theme is resumed by the alto in the key of E minor. This entrance must still be considered a part of the exposition, being a false entrance of an imaginary fifth voice, because the development of the fugue cannot start before tonic-dominant entrances have come to a stop. But where should we start playing this interlude (bars 43–46) on the softer keyboard, and how should the *forte* playing be resumed in bar 46? To our surprise we will find that a careful examination of the most minute details of Bach's writing methods gives a full answer to these questions. Let us first discuss measure 46 (Ex. 6).

---

[18] Organ players have never suffered from the disadvantage of having the tradition of their art completely interrupted. Yet the change in the principles of organ building in the second half of the nineteenth century proved as ruinous for authentic Bach interpretation as the changes in harpsichord construction.

We see immediately that the first note of the entrance of the theme in the alto is changed from its normal value of an eighth note to a sixteenth. This is obviously not done for musical reasons, because nothing prevents the alto from starting on the third eighth of this measure; the purpose is to let the right hand jump to the *forte* keyboard right on the fourth sixteenth of the second quarter. However, where would the proper place be for the left hand to return to the *forte* keyboard? Bar 46 does not give a hint, but if we go back to bar 43 we will find that Bach indicated his intentions clearly enough. When we try to decide where the change to the softer keyboard for the interlude should start, it becomes obvious that the best place for the right hand is at the very beginning of bar 43. In the

Ex. 6. Partita VI, Toccata, bar 46

left hand, however, we see that Bach has given the first note B two stems, asking that this note be held for the length of an eighth note. This means that the left hand has to stay on the *forte* keyboard for the new motive of the interlude. This interlude is written according to the principle of double counterpoint: halfway through measure 44 the parts are exchanged between the hands, and at the beginning of bar 46 the same exchange takes place again. What could be a more natural solution than to change keyboards in accordance with the change of motives? The right hand should play soft from bar 43 to $44\frac{8}{16}$, loud from $44\frac{9}{16}$ to the end of bar 45, soft at the beginning of bar 46, to resume *forte* with the entrance of the theme in the alto as Bach prescribed;[19] the left hand should stay loud until halfway through bar 44, play soft until the end of bar 45, and, since *forte* naturally starts at the beginning of bar 46, our problem is solved automatically.

It is unusually interesting to compare these measures with the version they had in an earlier autograph, the so-called *Notebook for Anna Magdalena Bach*. The comparison gives us a remarkable glance into Bach's "workshop" (Ex. 7a, b).

How infinitely more refined is the later version! How obvious it is now that the constant change of keyboards within these measures, as we

---

[19] The fractions refer to parts within the measure; thus "$44\frac{8}{16}$" indicates the eighth sixteenth note of measure 44.

outlined it, was carefully planned by Bach when he revised these bars. Most definitely the mature Bach did not take registration problems lightly but was deeply interested in co-ordinating registration with the architecture of his compositions.[20]

Ex. 7a. Partita VI, Toccata, bars 43–46. Printed version

Ex. 7b. The same. Version in the *Notebook for Anna Magdalena Bach*

Continuing the investigation of our fugue, we soon discover that new problems offer themselves. We have now come to the end of the unusually long exposition, and the first entrance of the theme in a new key (G major), which marks the beginning of the development section, appears in measure 53. The episode that starts in bar 49 takes care of the

---

[20] Bach used the same technique of double counterpoint in the middle section of the Prelude to the English Suite in G minor (discussed above, pp. 45ff.), for which a similar solution of registration problems has been offered.

necessary modulation. However, the way in which the right hand is written in bar 49 (Ex. 8) excludes the possibility of going back to the *piano* keyboard, and the fact that the left hand can play *piano* from the fourth eighth of this bar to the entrance of the theme in bar 53 does not allay our disappointment on finding that for the first time the recipe "interludes on the softer keyboard" does not work.[21] It is inevitable that we raise the question of why Bach made it technically impossible to play this interlude on the softer keyboard. Only one answer could be called a satisfactory one: if he did so, he expected a greater tone volume, a louder tonal terrace to follow. But now a dilemma arises. Having started the fugue with the dynamics 8″ plus 4″ against 8′, the next louder terrace could only be achieved by the use of the coupler; but we see at a glance that there is no place in the development section for adding the coupler, which, as we

Ex. 8. Partita VI, Toccata, bar 49

will remember, requires rests in both hands at the same time. However, bar 53, the end of the interlude, contains a rest of an eighth note's length in the left hand, just sufficient to permit drawing a new register at exactly the moment when we need it badly to mark the beginning of the development. Which single register can we use? Since no additional sound volume is available—the 16′ register would be nonsensical at this moment—it becomes obvious that we have started the fugue at too high a sound level, and a solution of striking simplicity presents itself for the entire problem: if we start the fugue with alternation of the two 8′ registers and add the 4″ register in bar 53, all difficulties in co-ordinating registration and architecture disappear. Traditionally one of the 8′ registers is somewhat softer than the other,[22] so it is still possible to maintain some distinction between the thematic entrances and the episodes of the first part of the fugue. Now the unusual position of the last interlude of the exposition, bars 49–53, which could not be played on a different level

---

[21] Up to now, this "recipe" has been only an assumption, taken from the organ players' tradition. When we analyze more fugues, it will become apparent that the same rule is meant to be applied to harpsichord fugues too.

[22] On almost all harpsichords, that 8′ which is on the same keyboard as the 4′ is the softer one. This is most logical. If this 8′ were strong, it would prevent the higher octave from coming through well, and a weak 8′ on the other keyboard would sound very feeble as a contrasting tone color. A strong 8′ goes very well with the 16′ register, which is always an auxiliary device, used only rarely for solo effects. In other words, in the combination 8″ plus 4″, it is the 4″ which gives the decisive tone color; in the combination 8′ plus 16′, the 8′ color is predominant.

from the preceding thematic entrance, appears in a new light. With ever-growing admiration we see, on closer examination, how much more important these bars are than all the previous episodes. Measures 49 and 50 extend and intensify the end of the theme. In measures 51 and 52 the first motive of the theme is used to create an impression of still greater intensity that seems to ask for a tone color brighter than that of the previous interludes. In addition, the change of registration to 8′ plus 4′ in bar 53 lends itself very well to underlining the change from minor to major. Since these bars form a *bridge* between two different tone levels, it would have been illogical to play them *softer*, since the purpose of a bridge is to connect, not to separate.

With this problem solved, the development section offers no further difficulties. The distribution of the voices between both hands and the

Ex. 9. Partita VI, Toccata, bar 57

way in which the entrances of the theme are introduced make the right registration clear immediately. The left hand plays *forte* after having drawn the 4′ register during the short rest in bar 53; the right hand follows in bar 57. It is technically simple to hold the quarter note f′ sharp on the lower keyboard, and to climb for the c′ sharp to the upper one (Ex. 9, NB). On almost all old harpsichords, the distance in height from one keyboard to the other is very small, so that manipulations like this could be easily carried out.

Because of the ever-increasing intensity of the musical lines, we may continue playing *forte* until measure 71. The wonderful interlude that starts with the last three sixteenths of this bar and that makes use of material from the opening section of the Overture is played *piano*, of course. On the last eighth note of bar 77 the right hand goes back to *forte*, followed by the left hand in bar 81, last note. A brief interruption between bars 88 and 89 allows the player time to restore the coupler and 16′ register for the concluding section.

Thus in our first experience with a fugue we learned that a thorough examination of the most minute details of the setting was necessary to find our way through the intricacies of the complicated structure of this piece. Yet it was gratifying to see that Bach's writing helped reveal his artistic intentions to a great extent. We now know that if we look for double stemming or change of note values, or for the distribution of the

5

voices between both hands at all "joints," we will get more information
about registration than we had dared to expect. A measure like bar 46 is
not an isolated case. Similar situations are found in the Toccata in C

Ex. 10. Toccata in C minor, bar 151

Ex. 11. Partita V, Gigue, bar 49

minor in bar 151, and in the Gigue of the Fifth Partita, bar 49 (Exs. 10
and 11).

We leave the other movements of Partita VI to later discussion,[23]
mentioning here only that the Corrente and Gigue are of such gigantic
dimensions that the rule "one dance, one tone color" cannot be applied,
and *forte-piano* contrasts have to be used.

THE *WELLTEMPERED KEYBOARD*

We now turn to the most crucial problem in Bach's keyboard music: the
Welltempered Keyboard. As we have already remarked, nowhere else do
the opinions of editors and artists clash more pronouncedly than in regard
to the interpretation of this collection of forty-eight preludes and fugues.
Both Spitta and Schweitzer find that neither the harpsichord nor the
clavichord is good enough to bring out the hidden beauties of these pieces.
Spitta even goes so far as to pretend that only the modern piano can be
the instrument of which Bach dreamed when conceiving them. Wanda
Landowska tries to prove that the entire *Welltempered Keyboard* is meant
to be played exclusively on the harpsichord. Arnold Dolmetsch maintains,

---

[23] See Appendix A, p. 320.

although not quite so strongly, that at least for the vast majority of it, the clavichord is the only right instrument.[24] Since all these students of Bach's language use only aesthetic reasons for defending their contradictory viewpoints, it is imperative to approach the collection from the mechanical and technical side, which has already yielded so much fruitful information.

The biggest problem with which we will have to deal in this collection is the amazing fact that Bach's fugues show an unending variety in their structure; we will find scarcely any fugue that corresponds completely in its architecture to any other. Yet there are some fugues in which development sections and episodes alternate rather regularly, and it might be wise to start our investigation of the *Welltempered Keyboard* with them, since our recently acquired experiences will be helpful here.

Fugue in C minor, W.K. I

The popular C minor Fugue of the first volume is an extraordinarily good example of this regular alternating. The exposition, to be played *forte* (8″ plus 4″), ends in measure 9 on the first note of each hand; the episode following it, to be played *piano*, of course, lasts until the entrance of the theme in measure 11. We may question only whether the left hand should return to the *forte* keyboard on the second note of this measure, or perhaps on the fifth eighth. Aside from the fact that the latter choice is

---

[24] To fill the last possible gap, the Dutchman Hans Brandts Buys, in his book *Het Welltemperierte Clavir van J. S. Bach* (Arnhem, 1944), has entered the organ in this competition of instruments, claiming the entire collection of the "Forty-eight" for it. After discussing the word *manualiter*, which is found in the so-called "Fischoff Autograph" (whose authenticity is still doubted), and after emphasizing the fact that in Christian Weber's *Welltempered Clavir*, an imitation of Bach's masterpiece, twelve fugues have a pedal part identifying them as organ pieces, Brandts Buys tries to substantiate his claim by going into some structural peculiarities of Bach's work. Yet he has to admit that no real proof can be given. According to him, the entire work sounds exceedingly good on the organ, and very good but somewhat less satisfactory on the harpsichord, because long notes cannot be held sufficiently. Many of the fugues cannot be played at all on the clavichord.

One of the chief pieces of evidence on which Brandts Buys based his conclusion that at least the first book of the "Forty-eight" is written for the organ is the fact that Bach restricts himself therein to the range of C to c‴, the traditional range of the organ, while the range of the harpsichord is larger. This argument, however, cannot be conclusive. In the brilliant C major Concerto for Two Harpsichords, the restricted range is used. In my opinion, the forty-nine arpeggios in the *Welltempered Keyboard* (most of them in the E flat minor Prelude, vol. I) sufficiently preclude the use of the organ, because a quick arpeggio is foreign to Bach's organ style. To our knowledge only one casual and unconvincing arpeggio sign has come down to us in all Bach's organ works, and this is in an entirely unimportant single Prelude in G major of which no autograph has survived (reprinted in the Bach-Gesellschaft, vol. XXXVIII, p. 85). Therefore the single sign does not prove anything. Yet, in spite of Brandts Buys' untenable approach to the instrument problem, and in spite of his exaggerated eagerness to prove the existence of motive relations between preludes and fugues, his book contains interesting tables and many fine observations.

technically easier, it seems more logical; it is not convincing to split the running sixteenths of the first part of the countersubject into soft and loud. Since this same overlapping of the end of the episodes with the entrance of the theme is repeated in measures 15 and 20, we may begin to question the aesthetic justification for believing that the countersubject of this Fugue starts with the second sixteenth of measure 3. Could it not be that the countersubject begins with the fifth eighth of this bar and that the descending scale of sixteenths is only a bridge leading to it?

This conception has become more and more convincing to me, and is strongly supported by the fact that the little ascending figure of bar 5, which comes to the forefront so unexpectedly in bars 17–19, and which obviously bears a relation to the descending scale in bar 3, is also introduced first as a bridge. Therefore, there is good reason for giving the descending sixteenth notes acoustical independence from the counter-subject, as we have done. These observations can only increase our admiration for this masterpiece, which is one of the rarest examples of Bach's unique capability for combining the most spontaneous inspiration with equally precise mathematical calculations. What listener who merely hears this Fugue being played, without looking at the score, would ever think that there is not a single note in the piece that does not have to be in its place for exactly calculated constructional reasons?

The remainder of the Fugue offers no problems. In measure 15, first the left hand returns to *forte*, then the right hand, just as in measure 11 but with inverted roles. The next interlude starts in bar 17 after the first eighth note. Bar 20 repeats the situation of measures 11 and 15: the right hand starts *forte* with the entrance of the theme, the left hand follows on the sixth eighth note. In bar 22, where the right hand returns to *piano* as in bar 9 (the corresponding bar), the left hand should be on the *piano* keyboard from the beginning of the bar. A comparison with bar 9 will explain this without words. *Forte* begins again on the second eighth note of bar 25, in which we also meet the first longer rest in this piece. Can this rest mean that one should change the registration here? No doubt about it! If we have a 16′ register at our disposal, this is the place to draw it. We can then play the powerful bass entrance of the theme in bar 26 with 8′ and 16′, just as Czerny, with his vague memory of older ways of interpretation, suggests in his edition. That Czerny starts playing octaves in the left hand immediately after the rest, however, is not justifiable, because it precedes the entrance of the theme.[25]

In bar 28 we find another rest, this time for both hands. Again we are convinced that this rest has a purpose, since, with both hands free, we

---

[25] Busoni also discusses this problem.

have exactly the conditions needed for putting the coupler into action. The eighth rest allows just enough time, and now the last bars of the Fugue can be played with the splendor of the full work of the harpsichord. On an instrument without the 16′ register, we would not be in a position to add a new color in bar 25. The left hand would simply stay on the softer keyboard until the entrance of the theme in bar 26, which would naturally be played *forte*. The application of the coupler in bar 28 would then add only one 8′ to the previous tone color, but this would be sufficient to give the end of the Fugue some extra distinction. Looking back on our experiences with this Fugue, we see that Bach gave the owner of a large harpsichord every opportunity to make good use of all the devices of his instrument, and it would be absurd to claim such a piece for the clavichord.

Fugue in G minor, W.K. I

In the Fugue in G minor, the alternation between developments and episodes is equally easy to distinguish. An analysis of this Fugue appears on Chart 2.

CHART 2

Exposition

Bars:	1–12
Voices:[a]	A S B T
Keys:[a]	T D T D

Development

Bars:	$12-18\frac{5}{8}$					$18\frac{6}{8}-20\frac{1}{4}$	$20\frac{2}{8}-24\frac{9}{16}$	$24\frac{10}{16}-28\frac{1}{8}$
Voices:	A	B	S	B	$\left(\begin{array}{c}A\\SDrM\end{array}\right)^{b}$	Episode modulating	B S A	Episode modulating
Keys:	rM	DrM	DrM	rM			SD SD T	

Coda (*Stretto*)

Bars:	$28\frac{2}{8}-34$
Voices:	S T B A T
Keys:	T T T T

[a] Abbreviations: Voices, S = Soprano, A = Alto, T = Tenor, B = Bass. Keys, T = Tonic, D = Dominant, SD = Subdominant, rM = relative major.

[b] Overlaps with beginning of episode.

Several peculiarities of the Fugue are noteworthy. Seldom does Bach separate the three main sections as clearly as he has here, by means of the distinction given to measures 12 and 28: both have a rest in the left hand sufficiently long to draw a new register if desired. The first development (bars $12-18\frac{5}{8}$) follows the exposition immediately, without any bridge. In the first development all voice entrances are in major keys; in the second development they are in minor keys. Both developments are irregularly constructed and are far from fulfilling the rules of a "school fugue." In the entire section, the tenor never gets the theme and is completely silent from bars 18–28, a wonderful proof that Bach did not "construct," but followed his creative inspirations. The first development is unexpectedly extended with the somewhat distorted entrance of the theme in the alto in bar 17, which overlaps with the bass entrance in the same bar. Yet the presence of the second half of the theme in the alto inconspicuously produces the material for the little episode in bars $18\frac{5}{8}$–$20\frac{1}{8}$. Furthermore, this same material from the second half of the theme serves as a link between the episode and the second development by appearing in inversion while the bass begins the main theme. Most noteworthy is the magnificent balance of the five thematic entrances in the coda-*stretto* with the five entrances in the first development. Also interesting is the fact that in the *stretto*, both entrances of the theme in the tonic key are in the tenor, as if Bach here wants to give to this voice some compensation for the meager role it has played so far throughout the Fugue. The two last bars of the Fugue also receive special treatment, since, in order to increase the sound volume, Bach adds a fifth voice. There can thus be no misunderstanding that the end has to be played *forte*.

How can we bring these architectural features into acoustical realization by means of registration? The only parts of the composition that need not be discussed are the *stretto* (to be played *forte*) and the episodes (*piano*). Because the second development stands between two episodes, it should naturally be played *forte*. Readers may wonder why it is necessary to mention this, since it is generally assumed that developments are to be played loudly. Yet the first development puts us in a puzzling situation. If we want to play the first development *forte*, we have to start the Fugue *piano*. But the clear-cut three-part architecture of this Fugue, so strongly underlined in bars 12 and 28, makes it evident that exposition and *stretto* have to be played at the same acoustical level, and, since Bach himself made it apparent that the *stretto* is supposed to be played *forte*, the same holds for the exposition. Yet, if we start the Fugue *forte*, we could not play the first development *forte* too, because nobody would hear its beginning. To increase the sound volume by using the coupler or 16′ is so nonsensical that we need not discuss such a possibility. If we now decide to play the first development softly, we do not know how to play the following episode (bar 18) which, of course, should also be played *piano*.

Surprisingly enough, it is possible to prove that the only correct solution is to play the first development on the soft keyboard with the 8′ register. This section is the only part of the Fugue that is written entirely in major keys. Later on we will discuss more fugues in which only one section is written in the contrasting mode, and we will always find that playing the contrasting part softly is the only possible solution. For the dilemma of the episode in bars 18–20, a simple solution, strongly supported by the structure, offers itself. This episode consists of two brief motives built on the "question and answer" principle, or better, demanding the "echo" effect. If the first half of this episode (starting on the sixth eighth of bar 18) is played *forte*, the necessary contrast with the previous development section is reached. We then play *piano* from the sixth eighth note in bar 19 to the beginning of bar 20 where we return to *forte* for the playing of the second development. That section, entirely in the minor mode, has every right to be played loudly.

Playing the first development *piano* is further justified when we want to play this Fugue on a harpsichord with one keyboard only, having for registration just two different 8' registers or 8' and 4'. In this case we have to start with both registers, release either the 4' or the louder 8' in bar 12 where the rest in the left hand makes this possible, and draw the same register again in bar 28. Although the piece will sound less rich than on a harpsichord with two keyboards, the basic architecture will come out clearly even in such a restricted situation. Now, looking back upon the entire Fugue, we need no longer wonder why Bach omitted any bridge between the exposition and first development, because the contrast between *forte* and *piano* is supplied by those sections themselves. The peculiar construction, with acoustical contrasts, of the little episode in bars 18–20 also finds its natural explanation; it makes possible the demonstration of the architecture of the Fugue by means of harpsichord registration.

Fugue in D major, W.K. I

The Fugue in D major lends itself excellently to being played with the full work of the harpsichord, owing to its pompousness and the use of the dotted rhythms of the French Overture. The Czerny edition shows some reminiscence of this way of playing, as may be seen from the advice to play the left hand with octave doublings in the last two bars. The structure of the Fugue is very simple: developments and episodes alternate regularly. Since the lower keyboard plays full work, the upper keyboard may use 8″ and 4″ as a contrasting softer tone color. The right hand plays on the softer keyboard from bar 6 after the first chord to bar 8, first chord; from bar 9, second quarter, to bar 11, first quarter; from bar 21, second quarter, to bar 22, first quarter. The left hand plays on the softer keyboard from bar 6, second quarter, to bar 7, first quarter, and from bar 17, second quarter, to bar 20, first quarter. All the rest is full work.

Prelude and Fugue in C major, W.K. I

Up to now we have deliberately omitted any discussion of registration problems in the preludes, partially because the preludes to those fugues that we have discussed lend themselves to manifold possibilities of interpretation for which our present knowledge does not supply sufficient ground on which to base conclusions, and partially because the problems that we would have met there are of no help in widening our knowledge. In the case of the famous Prelude and Fugue in C major, however, we will discuss the Prelude first. The problems offered by this piece are much greater than we might expect from a composition whose structure is so utterly simple. Schweitzer's remark, "The only thing of which we can be sure in regard to the modern way of interpreting this prelude is that there has never been a pianist who has succeeded in playing it to the satisfaction of another," is unfortunately also true of an execution on the harpsichord.[26] The Prelude consists of nothing more than single broken triads, each of them repeated immediately. By the time the coda starts, three bars before the end, we have heard the same little figure repeated sixty-four times.

It might be interesting to see some descriptions by outstanding musicologists of how this piece should be played. In his article, "Das Bach'sche Clavecymbel und seine Neukonstruktion," Oskar Fleischer, late Director of the Berlin State Collection of Early Music Instruments, singles out this very Prelude and tries to show how it could be played on the most famous of all harpsichords preserved, the "Bach Flügel."[27] "With some experience in registration one can gradually proceed from the softest *pianissimo* to the mightiest *fortissimo*. Interpreted in this manner, the first Prelude of the *Welltempered Keyboard* reveals a completely unexpected idea of its architectural construction, the principle of which seems to be this gradual increase of the volume of sound."[28]

Unfortunately, no amount of "experience in the art of registration" could enable any performer to produce the gradual increase of sound either on this or on any harpsichord with hand registration. Since this Prelude offers no rests to the player's hands, the registration on an instrument with two keyboards is restricted to the two tone colors that are prepared before the piece is begun. All that one can produce, therefore, is not a gradual crescendo, but a regular alternation in every bar between a *forte* of 8″ and 4″, and a *piano* of 8′ (Ex. 12). Even an alternation of the two 8′ registers would be sufficient to bring out an echo effect which, on

---

[26] *Bach*, p. 332.
[27] See p. 31 for a description of its disposition.
[28] Oskar Fleischer, "Das Bach'sche Clavecymbel und seine Neukonstruktion," *Zeitschrift der International Musikgesellschaft*, Jahrgang 1 (1899), p. 161.

paper at least, seems not entirely out of the question (Ex. 13). Yet the reader may be assured that no person who is at all sensitive to music would be able to stand the horror of thirty-two mechanical echos. A few measures played this way are enough to convince anybody that this type of interpretation has to be dismissed from our consideration.

Ex. 12. Prelude in C major, *W.K.* I, first half of bar 8″ plus 4″, second half 8′ only

Ex. 13. The same, alternating two 8′ registers

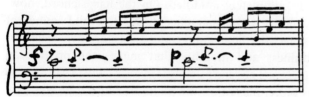

How would it be, however, if we were to entrust a "helper" with the task of producing a gradual increase of tone volume which, as players, we are unable to create by ourselves? The only registers that a helper could engage are the 4″ and the 16′. The coupler could not be used because one helper would be unable to push in the lower keyboard during the playing; two helpers would be needed, since the player has no hand free to assist. We hope that nobody could seriously believe that Bach would have reckoned with the presence of two helpers wherever this Prelude would be played. It would hardly conform to the pedagogical purpose of the entire collection. Let us therefore decide to be content with one helper and find out how great his contribution to a performance of this Prelude could be.

We would start, of course, with the softer 8″ register and after some time we would go over to the stronger 8′. Somewhere the helper could add the 4″ register, but we would then be at the end of our power to increase the volume of sound. The addition of the 16′ would change the tone color but would not contribute to a louder sound unless the coupler could be added at the same moment. This way of playing would by no means produce the impression of the progress from the softest *pianissimo* to *fortissimo* that Professor Fleischer wanted; we can dismiss it without having to decide where these registers should be added because we would never find two people who would agree on the right places for these manipulations.

The only way of playing that remains to be discussed and is technically possible is to perform the entire piece in one registration from beginning to end. This has been recommended by musicologists who consider indifference to sound media an outstanding characteristic of the *entire* baroque era. Karl Nef gives a vivid description of this form of interpretation for the Prelude: "When played, the lower tones of the harpsichord on the left side of the keyboard sound for a longer time than the same notes would on a piano if the pedal were not used. This beautiful sound of sustained low notes is a frequently used special effect of old keyboard music. Let us take the most famous example, the C major Prelude from the first volume of the *Welltempered Keyboard*. On the piano one cannot play it without pedal because of the resulting dull tone; with the pedal it sounds completely muddled. On the harpsichord, however, the two sustained notes sound magnificent, like the mild sounds of bells, while the agile sixteenths float lightly and transparently. It is this contrast between restfulness and mobility that makes the prelude an incomparable masterpiece. The harpsichord player will realize this immediately, while this piece, played on the piano, remains a puzzle even to the Bach connoisseur."[29]

It is, alas, not so easy to produce on the harpsichord the sound effect Nef so vividly describes. Tones that are located so close to each other as the notes of the Prelude indicate inevitably have the same tone color and are therefore either all mild bells or all transparent. Only if one always plays the first two notes of each figure on the lower keyboard in 8′ and 16′ registration and plays the remaining notes on the upper keyboard in 8″ color, does one come rather close to Nef's sound picture. Yet the result obtained is far from being satisfactory. The left hand now gets a prominence which the texture does not imply, and we hear two voices competing which were obviously not planned to be exposed in such a fashion. Nor can this protect us against the dryness and machinelike monotony produced by the sixty-four repetitions of the same figure in the same tone color. Even the most ardent enthusiast of the harpsichord must admit that hearing this piece in such a way is much more torture than pleasure.

Thus, for the first time during our inquiry we find a piece that seems absolutely incapable of performance on the harpsichord. We could try to minimize this fact and call it merely accidental, if this were not an offense

---

[29] Karl Nef, "Clavecymbel und Clavichord," *Jahrbuch der Musikbibliothek Peters,* Jahrgang 10 (1903), p. 15.

to the genius of Bach. Furthermore, it is strange that this should happen in the very first piece of a collection in which so many of the pieces are masterfully designed to produce a colorful performance on a harpsichord of the larger type. How can we dare accuse Bach of such a negligence when this Prelude is, in all other respects, a masterpiece that fulfills exactly the task assigned to it: to be the portal for the entire *Welltempered Keyboard*! Therefore, would it not be only natural to ascribe this piece, which is apparently written in a style different from that of all those previously discussed, to the clavichord?

A clavichord piece needs no rests anywhere for drawing registers; in this respect the Prelude is perfectly suited for a performance on this instrument. Weigh the possibility of playing the piece on the clavichord, thereby giving it everything it wants and needs—a performance of utter refinement and delicacy, even making Professor Fleischer's proposed gradual crescendo possible to some degree—against the alternative of hearing the sixty-four monotonous repetitions of the same figure in the same tone color on the harpsichord. It would certainly seem strange that any sensitive musician could ever seriously consider the harpsichord the right instrument for this piece.[30] Yet let us admit that it is impossible to

---

[30] Nobody regrets more than this writer that the discussion of harpsichord and clavichord problems has persistently been a polemic matter instead of a united search for truth. For this reason we are abstaining from discussing registration and playing methods on phonograph records of the harpsichord, in spite of the fact that they undeniably represent a kind of pedagogic edition of Bach's keyboard works. Only once, for this Prelude in C major, do we feel compelled to make some startling observations about one well-known recorded performance by a very prominent player. During the first bars (5, 7, 11, and so on), one will already hear obvious crescendos and decrescendos, which could be produced on a harpsichord only by gradual application of registration pedals. On p. 38 we criticized this practice (which of course could never be used on historical instruments) as being one of the most abused tricks possible on modern pedal instruments, since, at the moment of its application, the harpsichord is transformed into a clavichord. That the player on this record felt it necessary to apply gradations of tone volume in the Prelude in C major is a flagrant although certainly involuntary admission that the unchangeable tone of the harpsichord does not satisfactorily fit this piece and that the clavichord is the right instrument for it.

Moreover, it seems highly questionable that (in a clavichord performance, of course) a crescendo, starting in the second half of bar 11, should turn into a diminuendo at the end of bar 12. We would prefer to play the end of bar 11 diminuendo, start a crescendo in bar 12, lead to a climax in the first half of bar 13, and then return to diminuendo. The addition of a 16' register to every first G which we hear in bars 24ff. is hardly necessary but is at least technically possible on a historical instrument if just this note is played on the 8', 16' keyboard (prepared in advance) and all the others on the second keyboard with 8". The end of the Prelude again raises a challenge. Despite our respect for improvisations possibly made by eighteenth-century players, we are not enthusiastic about the contra-C added at the very end. How heavily has Czerny been blamed for doing the same at the end of the Prelude in B flat major, *W.K.* I! Equally unsatisfactory is the omission of any c" sound in the last improvised C major arpeggio. This leaves the leading note b of the penultimate bar acoustically unresolved. It is true that Bach often resolves a leading note into the tonic, a major seventh below, but I cannot recollect a single case where he resolves this note into the third of the tonic triad. Although in earlier versions of this piece e' is indeed the highest note, it is there the result of the correct and traditional resolution of a dominant seventh: the highest note in the preceding bar is f'.

prove the good cause of the clavichord "scientifically" by this Prelude alone, in spite of the considerable amount of circumstantial evidence we have supplied. We will have to see whether we get more substantial proof from an analysis of the Fugue belonging to it.

This Fugue deserves even more admiration than the Prelude. It combines unbelievable craftsmanship with delightful elegance, and one cannot help feeling that for the opening fugue Bach deliberately wrote a "showpiece." There are no episodes, but in constant series of *stretti* the theme is cited twenty-three times[31] within twenty-seven measures. The

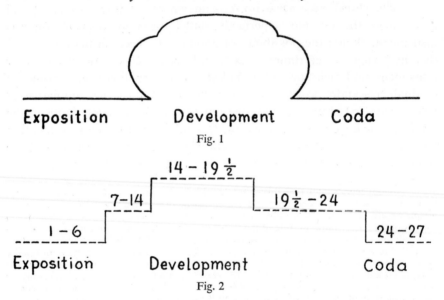

Fig. 1

Fig. 2

organization is most beautifully balanced. The exposition (measures 1–6) is followed by a development built in three sections, as follows: two *stretti* of two voices, each of which is followed by an entrance of the theme; one *stretto* of three voices followed by one *stretto* of four voices; then again, two *stretti* of two voices, with an increase in distance between the

---

[31] Hans Brandts Buys' count of twenty-four is wrong. This dismisses the fantastic conclusion that the twenty-four entrances are a symbol for the twenty-four preludes and fugues. The figure "twenty-four" can only be attained by counting the false entrance of the theme in bar 15 (soprano). Then, however, the false entrances of the bass in bar 20 and of the soprano in bars 24–25 must also be added, making the total number twenty-six. When Bach uses mathematical symbols (on pp. 254ff. we will discuss them extensively), they are never on as low a level as Wilhelm Wercker's *Studien über die Symmetrie im Bau der Fugen und die Motivische Zusammengehörigkeit der Präludien und Fugen des "Wohltemperierten Klaviers" von Johann Sebastian Bach* (Leipzig, 1922), tries to make us believe. It is a pity that Brandts Buys often applies Wercker's methods, although he does not consider himself a blind adherent of Wercker. Wercker's assumption that the theme of Bach's Fugue in C major is a reincarnation of the famous old "L'homme armé" melody has been unanimously repudiated by all authorities. Yet Brandts Buys not only makes Wercker's theory his own, but calls every line of four descending seconds in the *Welltempered Keyboard* a "l'homme armé line."

entrances of the second *stretto*. A coda containing one *stretto* of two voices, followed by a "free fantasy," brings the Fugue to an end. The wonderful symmetry of this Fugue caused Busoni to make an "architectural drawing" (Fig. 1). In the "language of terrace dynamics," this could perhaps be changed to the diagram shown in Figure 2.

The task of the harpsichord player is herewith clearly set: three terraces have to be planned, and for quick understanding of the technical

Ex. 14. Fugue in C major, *W.K.* I, bar 7

Ex. 15. The same, bar 14

Ex. 16. The same, bar 19

Ex. 17. The same, bar 24

implications we present here the four decisive measures 7, 14, 19, and 24 (Exs. 14–17) in which the changes of registration have to be made.

If we were to try the Fugue first on a small harpsichord (two keyboards, one with soft 8″ and 4″, the other with loud 8′), the three terraces would be soft 8″ for the exposition, loud 8′ starting in the right hand in bar 7, and then in the left hand in bar 10. In bar 14 we could quickly draw the 4″ register and play the climax of the piece, the *stretti* of three and four voices, with the 8″ and 4″ color. So far everything would be perfectly satisfactory. Now, however, our troubles begin. The climax comes to an end in bar 19. Here we would have to leave the 8″ and 4″ keyboard and return to the 8′ color, but where and how should we do this? Far from making the usual clear cut between sections, Bach "chains" the end of the climax to the beginning of the next section by having the two overlap. With "finger-breaking acrobatics" we could perhaps master the situation by letting the left hand jump to the softer keyboard on the second sixteenth, and by making the right hand play the alto notes e, f sharp, and g with a gliding thumb on the soft keyboard, keeping the soprano notes on the other keyboard. It is, however, somewhat doubtful whether this can be done well enough without endangering the player; in fact, in other places where Bach seems to ask for simultaneous playing on two keyboards, the technical situation is generally simpler.

Even if we manage to overcome this difficulty, a new dilemma awaits us in bar 24. Here we should return to the soft 8″, but only a helper could take away the 4″ register; furthermore, the overlapping of the voices would force the right hand to wait for the fifth eighth note before being able to join the left hand, which would jump to the soft keyboard after the first note of this bar. Acoustically, however, this abrupt change in the right hand suits only the alto part, but the soprano line is so clearly an unbroken one that an interruption after the fifth eighth would destroy its coherence. A similar acoustical problem in bar 19 forces us to abandon the idea of trying the acrobatic stunt. For the tonal balance of this bar it is necessary for the left hand, which gives the foundation for the I_6–II_6–V–I cadence, to be played as loudly as the upper voices; therefore it makes no sense to descend from the highest terrace to the next lower one in this bar.

The inevitable result of this examination is the realization that registration and form of this Fugue cannot be brought into co-ordination. In bar 19 we have to stay on the louder keyboard; moreover in bar 24 nothing is gained by permitting the left hand to return to the 8′ keyboard, because the pedal point of this hand is as important as the voices in the right hand. The picture of the terrace dynamics would therefore look like Figure 3 in our harpsichord interpretation, and it stands in obvious contrast to the architecture of the Fugue.

Nothing would be gained by trying the Fugue on the largest type of harpsichord with coupler and 16' register. We would start with 8' (loud), have the 8" and 4" ready from the beginning for use in measures 7 and 10 for right and left hands respectively, add coupler and 16' in bar 14, which causes a small but not too obvious interruption—and from then on we are faced with the same problems as in the first version. Similarly, it would be impossible for us to accept the unsuitable compromise suggested by

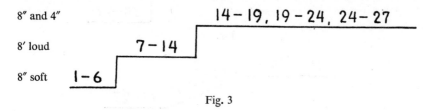

8" and 4"   14 − 19, 19 − 24, 24 − 27

8' loud   7 − 14

8" soft   1 − 6

Fig. 3

Brandts Buys, namely, to change registration only once, going from soft to loud in bar 14. This would give the Fugue the misleading sound picture shown in Figure 4.

Since the three fugues that we have analyzed before have shown us how superbly Bach made use of the harpsichord to explain inner architecture by the means of acoustics, it would be very strange if in the case of this Fugue the composer should now have completely neglected to take similar care. We had better admit that this piece is also not meant to be executed on the harpsichord, and we must inevitably arrive at the same solution which proved to be the only one possible for the Prelude: to play the Fugue on the clavichord. It goes without saying that a clavichord interpretation does not reproduce the terrace dynamics we had

14 − 27

7 − 14

Fig. 4

symbolized in Figure 2, and if we should try to achieve this effect we would be ignoring the spirit of the clavichord. A thorough examination of the Fugue reveals, however, that our drawing was correct only in regard to the outer architecture, but inaccurate in regard to detail in three places.

In bar 19 Bach did not make a clean break between the terraces, but caused the beginning of the new section to overlap with the end of the preceding one. In other words, he rounded the corner so that the picture in Figure 5 should be changed to the one in Figure 6. In bar 24 the same situation exists. The right hand cannot make an abrupt break, so that once more we have to smooth a corner, playing what we might call the *diagonal* between the terraces (Fig. 7). This figure can have only one acoustical meaning: a diminuendo, which is exactly what the clavichord, and only the clavichord, can do.

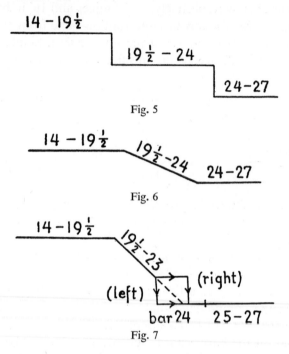

Fig. 5

Fig. 6

Fig. 7

If we now re-examine the first part of the Fugue, we will discover another inaccuracy. Although it is true that the development begins in bar 7, and the climax of it with bar 14 (Fig. 8), only the right hand is ready

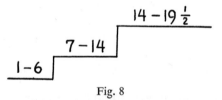

Fig. 8

to change keyboards at bar 7; the left hand has to wait until bar $10\frac{1}{2}$ before it can join the right hand. Our drawing must therefore be changed accordingly (Fig. 9).

Although, as we have shown before, this terrace plan can be realized on the harpsichord, a comparison of the diagrams of bars 1–14 and 19–27 shows their complete correspondence. Therefore bars 7–14 do not contradict a dynamic interpretation on the *diagonal*, this time a crescendo. It is noteworthy to see with what skill Bach systematically builds up the sound sonorities in bars 7–12. Every thematic entrance intensifies the crescendo, and we see that Bach has done everything possible to help the clavichord sound to advantage. The diagram of the complete Fugue should now be drawn as in Figure 10, or, to correspond better with our detailed figures, as in Figure 11.

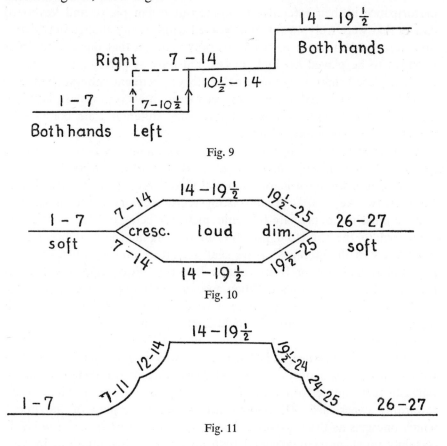

Fig. 9

Fig. 10

Fig. 11

I hope we have succeeded in proving that this Prelude and Fugue are meant to be played on the clavichord. Only those who are satisfied to hear both the Prelude and the Fugue in one registration from beginning to end, pretending that "the lines speak for themselves," are undefeated in their insistence that these pieces as well as the entire collection of the "Forty-eight" should be played on the harpsichord. In opposition to this "anti-acoustical" (or even "antimusical") solution, let us again repeat our reasoning: it seems absurd to assume that Bach would have opened a collection of forty-eight preludes and fugues written specifically for the harpsichord just with two pieces that are perfect in every respect except that they show this instrument at its poorest; furthermore, that the same Bach would have done so who has proved many times over, both in other fugues of the *Welltempered Keyboard* and in larger works, such as the

Italian Concerto, that he had a perfect knowledge of how to write well for this instrument.

One of the chief arguments used by the defenders of the one-color performance is their reference to numerous organ pieces and keyboard dances that were truly meant to be played without any change in registration. In regard to dance pieces let us only mention that these were never intended to be played as single pieces, but only as parts of suites where the next piece brings a new tone color; this is frequent enough change to avoid acoustical boredom. The organ pieces, however, when played in one registration, contain not one but three different tone colors—the colors of the two manuals and the pedal—which are interesting enough to be listened to for a considerable time. We might say that such pieces give us a "vertical" enjoyment to substitute for a "horizontal" one.

No doubt the harpsichord too will give "vertical" enjoyment if one plays on two keyboards in contrasting register colors at the same time, and we must not depreciate this enjoyment for being only a twofold one compared to the threefold possible on the organ. Many dance pieces, quite a few of the preludes (as we shall see later), and, notably, the two-part Fugue in E minor from volume I of the "Forty-eight" will profit from this kind of treatment. When special conditions, however, like the need to avoid terrace dynamics or a writing method that compels both hands to play on the same keyboard, enforce upon the player a one-registration performance for an entire fugue of complicated structure and high artistic significance, it is hard to see why one should feel satisfied with such shabby acoustic results when another instrument is available that can turn the performance of the same piece into an infinitely more rewarding experience. The enjoyment of the "interplay of the lines" which one gets as the only reward in the one-registration performance is certainly much more intellectual than aural; the differentiations in tone volume provided by hearing sometimes four voices at a time, sometimes only three or two, can hardly give much pleasure to the ear compared with the wealth of refined shading possibilities that a clavichord can offer in addition to the same degree of enjoyment of the lines. For this reason alone, we are at a loss to understand the truly hostile attitude of so many excellent musicians, notably professional harpsichord players, toward any attempt to give back to the clavichord its due share in the Bach repertoire.

However, nothing strengthens our repudiation of one-color registration for this Prelude and Fugue more than the fact that it is possible to write in an interesting way for a harpsichord with one keyboard only, hence with a single color. As we have already mentioned, this technique, developed by the virginalists, lived on into Bach's time in the art of improvising accompaniments. We would certainly underrate Bach's genius if we did not believe that he was capable of finding an acoustically satisfactory method of writing in one tone color when all who served as accompanists were able to solve this problem. The single fact that Bach did not adopt this technique for his writing suffices to prove that he was not even considering the harpsichord as a medium when he wrote a keyboard composition which is not "multicolored."[32] The assumption that Bach could ever have been content to write for the harpsichord without using any variety of registration becomes entirely impossible when we see that our experiences with the C major Prelude and Fugue are not isolated instances; there are many similar pieces in the same collection.

Fugue in G sharp minor, W.K. I

In contrast to the long examination necessary for determining the right way to perform the C major Fugue, the problems of the Fugue in G sharp minor can be solved in a few moments. Here developments alternate with episodes, yet nowhere will we find any clearly separated sections. Each development is connected with the next episode by over-lapping voices, and a glance at measures 13, 21, 28, and 34 is sufficient to see that if we play the exposition on the soft keyboard (which might seem logical) and go to the loud one in bar 11, we have to stay on it to the end. The continual overlapping of voices prevents us from returning to the soft tone color. Playing this Fugue, too, on the clavichord remains the only possible solution.[33]

Fugue in D minor, W.K. I

To come to a decision about the appropriate instrument for the Fugue in D minor is somewhat harder. This Fugue has much in common, structurally, with the C major Fugue, the most important feature being a strong cut in bar 21, comparable to that in bar 14 of the other piece. Because of this break the D minor Fugue has sometimes been called an example of binary form. Yet, in spite of the obvious recapitulations in the

---

[32] In connection with this problem it may be noticed that Prince Leopold had bought in March 1719 an "unusually large and expensive harpsichord from Berlin, made after specifications by J. S. Bach" (see Friedrich Smend, *Bach in Cöthen*, Berlin, 1952, p. 17). Bach research has established a link between the acquisition of this instrument and the wealth of keyboard music Bach wrote in his Cöthen years (see Heinrich Besseler, *Zur Chronologie der Konzerte Joh. Seb. Bachs*, Max Schneider Festschrift, Leipzig, 1955, p. 119).

[33] Everything that has been said about this Fugue holds also for the Fugues in F sharp minor and A flat major of volume I. We invite the eager student to investigate both these pieces in order to get more experience in the method of architectural analysis. For the Fugue in F sharp minor the decisive measures are 11, 15, 18, 20, 25, 29, 32, 37; for the A flat major Fugue we want to mention only bars 10, 13, 19, 21, in which change of keyboards is manually impossible.

second part (see the correspondence between measures 30–34 and 9–12, and between 39–42 and 17–20), the constant massing of ever-new combinations of thematic material seems to contradict this formal scheme, which, in my personal opinion, covers only the "paper facts." The form of the Fugue may be analyzed as follows. The exposition contains one additional entrance of the theme in the soprano, and ends in bar 12 with the magnificent yet entirely inconspicuous combination of the second half of the theme in the bass with the first half of it inverted in the alto. The development is constructed in three sections: *stretti* of two voices in bars 13–20, *stretti* of three voices in bars 21–30, and finally, *stretti* in which simultaneous entrances of the theme occur in two voices. In the last two measures, the only ones that can be called "coda," since the measures before are a recapitulation of part of the first development section, alto and tenor split to form a six-part setting. This makes it possible to cite the original and inverted forms of the first measure twice, at the same time.

What can the harpsichordist do to bring acoustical clarity into this complicated organization? Measure 13, which marks the beginning of the development, is written in "overlapping style" so that no change of keyboards can take place there. Because no rest suitable for drawing additional registers is to be found in the entire Fugue, we cannot have more than two tone colors at our disposal. The only places at which Bach's writing method allows any change of keyboard are in bar 21, in which the left hand, and bar 22, in which the right hand could move over to the other keyboard, and in bars 27 and 28, where a similar switch could be carried out. Brandts Buys actually suggests that changes be made at these bars so that measures 21–27 are played either softer or louder than the rest of the Fugue. This, however, creates an acoustical three-part form which receives no justification from the formal organization of the piece. Since a harpsichord player would actually need four terraces to bring out the contrapuntal structure of this piece and since Bach clearly indicates at the decisive place, bar 13, that he does not want an application of terrace dynamics, the only remaining solution, once more, is to play the Fugue on the clavichord.

This Fugue confronts us, for the first time in our investigations, with a problem that is most puzzling to laymen as well as to professional players: how should one treat the theme when it reappears continually throughout a fugue? Should one always play it very prominently as the vast majority of pianists do, or should one mix it discreetly with the countersubjects and contrapuntal lines of the other voices, which are certainly not unimportant? A general answer covering every possible situation can, of course, not be given. In each case the decision will depend on the artistic importance given to the "additional material." Yet one basic answer comes from the instruments themselves. Only the modern piano and the clavichord are capable of "bringing out" the theme at any time under all possible conditions. On harpsichord and organ, however, a theme can be played prominently only if it can be singled out on a separate keyboard, something that does not happen very often, except in fugues in two parts. The longer we think about the consequences of these basic acoustical facts, the clearer it becomes that they form a new and most important tool that can help us in the selection of the right instrument.

Before making general statements, for which we should prefer to have discussed more material, let us see what the application of this principle adds to a better understanding of the D minor Fugue. In this Fugue the entrances of the theme play the most prominent role, and Bach constantly uses them to create surprise. We can never guess beforehand in which voice or in what form (original or inverted) the theme will appear next. Within forty-four measures we find only six in which the theme does not appear directly: bars 10 and 11, to which bars 31 and 32 correspond, and bars 20 and 42, both of cadential nature and, again, corresponding ones. The mechanism of the harpsichord does not allow a singling out of these entrances, while it is the special feature of clavichord technique that every line, every single note, can be played in a prominent way, whenever we want to do so, by regulating the touch. Therefore, the thematic structure of the Fugue also makes it evident that the clavichord is the only appropriate instrument for its interpretation.

Fugue in F minor, W.K. I

Although it was the frequency of thematic entrances that supported the selection of the clavichord as the right instrument for the D minor Fugue, it is the rarity of such entrances that will make us come to the same decision for the Fugue in F minor of the same volume. A detailed analysis of this Fugue will be especially illuminating, because it is seldom that we come across one in which developments and episodes alternate with such regularity; consequently, on first glance we would have the right to assume that this piece is ideally suited for the harpsichord. The theme is three measures long, and the entire Fugue is built on the alternation between three measures in which the theme appears and three measures of episode. Even in the exposition the entrance of the fourth voice is delayed by the insertion of an episode (bars 10–12) and, strangely enough, all episodes are built following one rhythmical scheme. Only once is this pattern extended: at measures 22–27 the episode is six measures long.

Let us now find out how this rigid scheme lends itself to that type of treatment on the harpsichord which is the only one possible in such cases: thematic entrances in 8″ and 4″ registration, episodes in 8′. The result of such a survey, which makes it necessary to examine every third measure for possibilities of changing keyboards, is most illuminating.

Measure 10   Beginning of episode I: possible.
         13   Theme enters in soprano: impossible.
         16   Beginning of episode II: not convincing but possible.
         19   Theme in tenor: impossible in the right hand, seemingly possible in left hand; however, proved to be inaccurate by the necessity of playing parts of the countersubject in the left hand in bar 20.
         22   Beginning of episode III: possible.
         25[34]   No necessity for change because episode III extends over six bars, or more correctly, five and a half.
         27   Theme in bass: possible on sixth eighth but very awkward.
         30   Beginning of episode IV: possible.
         34   Theme in alto: impossible or most awkward on second eighth.
         37   Beginning of episode V: impossible.
         40   Theme in tenor: impossible.
         43   Beginning of episode VI: possible.
         47   Theme in soprano: possible.
         50   Beginning of episode VII: impossible.
         53   Theme in bass: impossible.

No further discussion is necessary after this revealing investigation. Evidently this Fugue can be played only on the clavichord. Let us add that it is a godsend for this piece that the harpsichord has to be excluded. The regular and monotonous alternation of sound volume at every third bar would produce almost as devastating an effect as the alternation, already discussed, of the same sonorities in every bar of the C major Prelude. Busoni is fully aware of this peril when he writes in his edition: "From the beginning of the second development a certain rigidity in the form and monotony in the harmonic and contrapuntal evolution are perceptible, which gradually ruin the effect of the magnificent and promising first part. For this, in our opinion, the unbroken tripartite rhythm (12/4) is chiefly to blame. And then comes the monotonous succession of the alternate entrances of the theme and the episodes; one

---

[34] The abbreviation of one-half measure in this episode is responsible for the break in the three-measure pattern; on the other hand, episodes IV and VI are lengthened by the addition of two quarter notes each, in measures 30 and 43.

follows the other with pedantically strict regularity. The episodes themselves elaborate unchangingly a motive of not exactly remarkable charm." Indeed, only the "singing out" of the wonderful melodic line of the theme that can be achieved on the clavichord saves the interpretation of this Fugue from utter dryness.[35]

Fugue in E minor, W.K. I

In order to avoid becoming "anti-harpsichord-minded," it might be wise to return to some fugues in which Bach utilized the assets of the harpsichord to good advantage. Although it would be wrong to ascribe every piece written in two parts to a harpsichord with two keyboards, it is obvious how well this type of harpsichord is suited to a plastic reproduction of such pieces. It would be interesting to find out whether experiences applicable to other pieces can be gained from the Fugue in E minor, the only one of the "Forty-eight" written in two voices. This brilliant Fugue shows the use of an obbligato countersubject and also of regular alternation between developments and episodes. Nothing could be more natural than playing the theme in 8″ and 4″ color, the obbligato countersubject in 8′, and the episodes in 8′ for both hands. Only for those places in double counterpoint (bars 15–18 and 34–37), which are within the two corresponding large episodes, might there be good justification of alternating each hand between 8″ and 4″ and 8′ from bar to bar, just as we did in the middle part of the Prelude to the English Suite in G minor. For the famous unison of both voices in measures 19 and 38, 8″ plus 4″ in both hands is the only right conclusion. The registration, therefore, is shown on Chart 3.

It is a delight to listen to such a lively display of tone colors which, at the same time, makes every architectural detail clearly audible.

---

[35] Brandts Buys feels exactly the same way when he writes in his chapter on registration: "Fortunately, on organ and harpsichord it is almost impossible to commit the sin of always playing the theme in an overaccentuated way, the illness of almost every pianist. . . . Yet, there is in the *Welltempered Keyboard* one fugue wherein, in spite of the emphasis that must be given to three countersubjects, and in spite of all the technical difficulties involved, I dare to commit this sin; it not only sounds very well, but seems to give a more profound content to this fugue. It is the Fugue in F minor, from the first volume. There I play all nonthematic material with a soft 8′ on the upper keyboard, the theme always on the lower keyboard with 16′ and coupler. In this way the restfulness and the calming effect, which is the characteristic feature of this fugue, is strengthened by the severity of the chromatic theme. Furthermore, the long quarter notes of the theme get enough power to stand out against the sixteenths of the countersubjects" (*Het Welltemperierte Clavir*, p. 142). If only the theme could always be singled out and played on the lower keyboard! With the exception of the alto entrance in bar 4, there is, in the entire Fugue, not a single entrance of the theme where other voices do not have to be played with the same hand; therefore, Brandts Buys' description remains wishful thinking—describing most accurately, although involuntarily, an interpretation that can be achieved only on the clavichord.

CHART 3

Right hand: f^a 1–3⅓ p 3⅔————10 f 11–13⅓ p 13⅔–15 f 16

Left hand: f 3————5⅓ p 5⅔————12 f 13————15 p 16

Right hand: p 17 f 18–20⅓ p 20⅔–21 f 22————24⅓ p 24⅔————31

Left hand: f 17 p 18 f 19————————22⅓ p 22⅔————29 f 30—

Right hand: f 32————34 p 35 f 36 p 37 f 38–42

Left hand: 32⅓ p 32⅔–34 f 35 p 36 f 37————42

---

[a] $f = forte$ (8″ and 4″), $p = piano$ (8′).

Fugue in B flat major, W.K. I

Equipped with this experience, we are well prepared for meeting the challenge of the B flat major Fugue in the same volume, which is a very complicated one. The theme is accompanied by two countersubjects, each of them of unusually plastic shape. All the episodes are built from thematic material, and the notes are so cleverly distributed among the fingers of both hands that it is very easy to discover which parts of the Fugue are meant to be played on one keyboard, and where possibilities for separating the hands on the two keyboards arise. The exposition is enlarged by a false fourth entrance in the dominant, which may be due to Bach's desire to confirm the obbligato character of both countersubjects by immediately presenting a second combination of all three subjects. The development section brings two complete statements of the theme, in G minor and C minor, followed by a somewhat distorted entrance of the theme in the alto that takes care of a modulation to E flat major.

It is rather doubtful whether the only remaining entrance of the theme before the final return to B flat major, namely, the entrance in E flat major in bar 37, should be considered a continuation of the development or—perhaps better—the beginning of the coda. It cannot be denied that this entrance is so closely linked with the final entrance of the theme in B flat major (bar 41) that it is almost impossible to consider them as separate units. To build a coda with the tonal relation subdominant-tonic, which in itself is nothing more than a counterbalance to the tonic-dominant relation of the exposition, is a practice often used by Bach and other writers of fugues. The last doubt about the formal disposition of the entrance in E flat major disappears when we discover that if we consider it part of the coda, the development remains entirely in minor keys. This formal principle is one that was very frequently applied and is most beautifully represented in the *Welltempered Keyboard* by the Fugues in G major, volume I, and E minor, volume II. The inner organization of the B flat major Fugue may therefore be described as in Chart 4.

CHART 4

	Exposition	Extension	Episode	Development	Episode	Coda
	$1\text{–}17\frac{1}{16}$	$17\frac{2}{16}\text{–}19\frac{1}{16}$	$19\frac{2}{16}\text{–}22$	$22\text{–}30\frac{1}{16}$	$30\frac{2}{16}\text{–}37\frac{1}{16}$	$37\frac{2}{16}\text{–}48$
Entrances:	S A B S			A B	(A)	S A
Tonalities:	T D T D		modulating	rm[a] SDrm	modulating	SD T

[a] rm = relative minor.

In regard to registration, one could hardly call it unintentional that the entire exposition, including the additional fourth entrance (bar 13), the section of the development in C minor (bars 26–30), and the subdominant entrance which we consider part of the coda, is written in such a way that the theme can always be singled out to be played on a separate keyboard; this would, of course, be the loud one. On the other hand, at the entrance in G minor (bar 23), at the distorted entrance in C minor modulating to E flat major (bar 35), and at the last entrance in B flat major only one keyboard can be used. This immediately clarifies the registration for all thematic entrances (Chart 5).

CHART 5

Bars:	1–4	5–8	9–12	13–19	22–26	26–30	35–36	37–41	41–48
Thematic entrances:	S *f*	A *f*	B *f*	S *f*	A *p*	B *f*	A *p*	S *f*	A *f*
Countersubjects:		*p*	*p*	*f*	*p*	*p*	*p*	*p*	*f*

The remaining episodes (bars 19–22 and 30–35) are written in double counterpoint, which makes it reasonable to play them on two keyboards. The right hand plays *piano* from the second sixteenth in bar 19 to the first sixteenth in bar 22, *forte* from the second eighth, bar 30, to the first sixteenth of bar 33, then *piano* again until the entrance of the soprano in bar 37; the left hand is always on the other keyboard. Altogether, this Fugue is another marvelous document of brilliant writing for the harpsichord.

Preliminary Conclusions

At this point we might be allowed to break off further investigations of registration problems temporarily. For the moment, I hope to have succeeded in proving that when Bach wants to write brilliantly and effectively for the harpsichord, he certainly knows how to do so; furthermore, that the quantity of pieces in which the sound effects of the harpsichord cannot be used is much too great for the solution of playing them in one tone color from beginning to end, instead of giving them the well-shaded and refined performance that can be achieved on the clavichord. Let us not forget that on the harpsichord, regardless of what mastery of the art of touch we may have acquired, exposition, development, episodes, and coda all sound alike if we cannot distinguish between them by the art of registration. The favorite excuse of the defenders of "unregistered" performances, "Let the lines speak for themselves," may perhaps be valid for those fortunate few whose musicianship is so accomplished that they are capable of enjoying a piece of music in full merely by reading the score. (Maybe Bach was thinking of such an ideal audience of "sightseers" when he wrote the *Art of the Fugue*.) If, however, we play music for our own or other people's enjoyment, we have to reckon with the human ear and must make every performance as lively and plastic as possible. A little dance piece may and very often must be played in *one* registration only; but the next dance—dance pieces never stand alone—will be played in another tone color. What Bach has to tell us in a fugue is much too important to be treated in this manner, especially when there is the possibility of giving the piece a most vivid performance on a clavichord. Finally, we hope that nobody would dare construct an artificial *forte-piano* or *piano-forte* relation analogous to the relation between two consecutive dance pieces, in an attempt to save for the harpsichord the preludes and fugues that seem to have been written for clavichord.

Before we close this chapter we want to draw the attention of the readers to the fact that our most recent experiences enable us to give a more specific answer to the important question raised before: how should the subject of a fugue be treated during a performance? Should it always be played *ben marcato*, or are countersubjects and other contrapuntal lines of equal weight? A summary of the types of fugues written by Bach will help us arrive at the correct answer.

Although the variety of formal principles that Bach applies in his fugues is overwhelmingly rich, we now begin to see that three categories of fugues can be rather clearly distinguished: (1) those in which developments and episodes alternate rather regularly; (2) those in which the theme is cited only sporadically in one or another voice; (3) those that are filled with overlapping entrances and the application of all the contrapuntal "artificialities" possible (augmentation, inversion, and so on). Fugues of the first type (those in G minor, A minor, and D major, *W.K.* I) seem to be destined by nature for the harpsichord.[36] In them a thematic entrance *cannot* be given individual prominence, since *forte* and *piano* contrasts are reserved for developments and episodes in their entirety. A fugue of the second type, in which the rarity of thematic entrances makes this event a highly important one, should be played on the harpsichord only if the theme itself can *always* be played on a single keyboard, a necessity with this type of construction. (Because this proved to be an impossibility, the Fugue in F minor, *W.K.* I, must be played on the clavichord.) The fugues of type 3 (Fugues in C major and D minor, *W.K.* I) almost always have to be reserved for the clavichord, because the terrace dynamics of the harpsichord are generally too inflexible to do justice to their highly complicated structures. On the clavichord, touch can give prominence to every individual thematic entrance.

This classification into three fundamental building types will prove to be invaluable when we have to deal with fugues which at first glance seem to allow execution on both instruments. Up to now, all the fugues that we have assigned to the clavichord have been constructed in such a way that a proper execution of them on the harpsichord was technically impossible. Yet there are also fugues that we would like to play on the clavichord, for aesthetic reasons, even though their basic architectural plan can be fulfilled literally by the technical possibilities of a harpsichord. Our examination of fugue types would be incomplete if we did not face the special problems of such pieces.

Fugue in F sharp major, W.K. I

Rarely could we find a better example than this Fugue in F sharp major to prove that the artificialities of contrapuntal treatment are by no means an indispensable requirement for a good fugue. The only "fugal" events after the exposition are five simple statements of the theme: in the tonic (soprano, bar 11), dominant (alto, bar 15), relative minor (bass, bar 20), subdominant (alto, bar 28), and, at the end, one last entrance in the tonic (soprano, bar 31). These statements are connected by episodes that mostly use fragments of the theme, such as the first four notes, the interval of a fourth, or the descending interval of the second, c sharp to b, from the second bar. The countersubject (soprano, bars 3–4) seems at

---

[36] No wonder that the vast majority of organ fugues are constructed according to this principle, which is, of course, the one best suited to displaying the various tone colors of an organ with several keyboards.

first to be obbligato, but is used only partially or is even completely missing later on. From bar 7, however, a little figure of four sixteenths, two ascending, two descending, becomes obbligato and is used almost unin-terruptedly throughout the entire fugue. This little figure, and similar ones, were often used by Bach, Handel, and other composers of this period to suggest the idea of water. Therefore, if we want to help poetically inclined laymen enjoy the composition more than conscience would normally allow in the case of a fugue, we might even give this piece the nickname "Little Brook" Fugue, or "Little Barcarolle."

If we now go into architectural details, we see that this Fugue is related both to type 2 (rarity of thematic entrances) and to type 1 (regular alternation of developments and episodes). To our dismay, we will soon discover that this relatively short Fugue, which is such a miracle of beauty and simplicity, will cause us much more trouble than we would normally expect from a piece of such formal clarity. For our first orientation we might try to separate developments and episodes, because, if this can be done successfully, the distribution of the piece on the two keyboards of the harpsichord is immediately clarified. The first bar to be investigated is bar 7, in which the "official" part of the exposition comes to an end. However, it is important to realize that the contents of bars 7–11 are an extension of the exposition and not the first episode, a point that we will prove with the following discussion.

In bar 7 there appears inconspicuously and for the first time the above-mentioned motive of four sixteenths, which will play such an important role throughout the rest of the Fugue. How should this motive be articulated? The Busoni edition warns in a special remark "not to yield to the temptation to phrase trochaically" (♪), since he believes that the proper phrasing is iambic (♪).

But Hermann Keller, in his book *Die musikalische Artikulation, insbesondre bei Joh. Seb. Bach*, suggests ♪.[37] Schmidt-Lindner, in the Schott edition, suggests ♪.

---

[37] (Stuttgart, 1926), p. 126.

These three totally different versions give us a foretaste of the difficulties into which we will run when we come to a discussion of the general
problems of articulation. If applied to the entire Fugue, each version
would give it a completely different character. I personally am convinced
that in this particular case Keller found the right version, as can be proved
by the great quantity of similar "wave figures" that Bach marked with
this type of articulation in other compositions.[38] This articulation clearly
gives a negative answer to the question of changing keyboards in bar 7.
Such a change could take place only after the first sixteenth of this bar,
since the leading tone in the alto must first be resolved. Made after the
first sixteenth, however, a change of keyboards would tear the motive of
four sixteenths into pieces. Therefore it cannot be done, and we have to
stay on the same keyboard until bar $11\frac{1}{2}$.

On which keyboard should we start this Fugue; on the loud one,
using 8″ plus 4″, or on the soft, using only 8? The traditional prescription
would call for the loud. However, there now arises a dilemma in that we
have to shift to the soft keyboard in bar $11\frac{1}{2}$, where the development
section normally requiring *forte* tone begins. Unorthodox as this may be,
we could perhaps comfort ourselves with the fact that Bach also ignores
the rules of a "school fugue" here by starting the development section in
the tonic. Yet new trouble waits for us in bar 13. The citation of the theme
ends, and an episode begins on the fifth eighth note of this bar. The alto,
however, is tied over and keeps the right hand on the soft keyboard,
preventing any shift that would clarify the beginning of the episode
acoustically. Yet it is good that such a shift cannot be made; to which
keyboard could we have gone at this moment other than to the loud one,
which is not generally desirable for playing episodes? So we stay soft and
can finally play *forte* from the entrance of the theme in the alto, bar 15.
The left hand can share the *forte* playing at the second sixteenth of this bar.

The *forte* can be kept up until the first notes of bar 17, where the
new episode begins and brings us back to *piano*, unfortunately only by
cutting into the four-note motive in the alto. In bar 20 both hands could
resume the *forte* after the first note, in order to mark the entrance of the
theme in the bass. The next episode starts in bar 23 and can be played
softly only by cutting into the four-note motive again. *Forte* can be
resumed in bar 28, for the right hand on the second eighth note, while
the left hand must wait until the last quarter. The last episode appears in
bar 30, and for the entrance of the theme in bar 31 one can switch to the

---

[38] See the last chorus of the first part of the *St. Matthew Passion*. Busoni's version cannot
be executed conveniently, because of the speed of the Fugue. Bach reserves the iambic organization of four notes for slower speeds, usually for the description of steps or footsteps. See the
famous duet, "Wir eilen mit schwachen Schritten" from Cantata 78, in which the motive is
written out in eighth notes.

loud keyboard with the right hand, followed by the left hand on the tenth sixteenth note.

I heartily wish that I could now take the reader to a harpsichord in order to demonstrate what we have just described in such dry terms. Without an ear test we cannot really know whether the theoretical distribution of this Fugue on two keyboards will sound convincing. After trying it one must admit that although the distribution just outlined is technically—or better said—manually possible, we have little reason to be proud of it. The impossibility of changing keyboards in bars 7 and 13, the necessity of playing a development section *piano* (bar 11),[39] and the cutting into the four-note motive are all disadvantages that weigh heavily against adopting our solution. Furthermore, the frequency of the changes from *forte* to *piano* gives our interpretation an abruptness and restlessness that are very much in contradiction with the heavenly serenity of the piece.

We will therefore have to start again in order to see whether this Fugue, which seems to resent the separation of developments and episodes according to type 1, can be more effectively registered when we try to bring out the sporadic appearances of the theme characteristic of type 2. We start the theme on the loud keyboard, but let the right hand play softly from the second note of bar 3 to the middle of bar 11. The left hand plays the alto and bass entrances on the loud keyboard, returning to the soft on the second eighth of bar 7. From then on the only places to be played *forte* by the right hand are these: from the tenth sixteenth of bar 11 to the first note of bar 17; from bar 28 after the first eighth note to the first note of bar 30; finally, from the sixth eighth note of bar 31 to the end. The left hand plays *forte* from the entrance of the theme at bar 20 to the first sixteenth of bar 23, or perhaps better, only to the first eighth note of bar 22; it then joins the right hand in playing *forte* from the last quarter of bar 28 to the first note of bar 30, and may or may not support the *forte* of the right hand at the end of the Fugue, from the sixth eighth note of bar 33, or preferably from the sixth eighth of bar 34, to the end. The end can also be played soft by both hands, with the right hand returning to the soft keyboard on the tenth sixteenth of bar 33.

Acoustically this solution is a little more satisfactory; yet the weak spots in its distribution of *forte* and *piano* are also evident. Let us just mention the troubles this version shares with the first: the impossibility of returning to *piano* in the middle of bar 13 and the division of the four-note motive in bars 17 and 23. Much more weighty is the fact that our desire to single out the thematic entrances cannot be achieved without

---

[39] Another unsatisfactory consequence of this procedure is that the *comes* appearance of the theme in bar 15 is played in a different tone color than the *dux* in bar 11, to which it is an answer.

also letting other voices share the limelight involuntarily, particularly the alto in bars 11–13, 28–30, and from bar 31 on. Actually, the bass entrance in bars 20–21 is the only place after the exposition where our basic idea can be fulfilled. Therefore, the situation in regard to this Fugue is exactly the same as with the F minor Fugue, where the harpsichord was also incapable of singling out the few but important entrances of the theme. Again the clavichord is the only instrument that can do justice to this Fugue in F sharp major, whose intimacy alone should have been sufficient to suggest this instrument immediately. The only reason, however, for this lengthy twofold exploration is that in this Fugue a distribution of the material upon two keyboards is *manually* possible, while in the F minor Fugue the technical impossibility of this procedure could be proved at the outset

Fugue in F major, W.K. I

It is necessary that we analyze one more fugue in order to discuss a representative type 3 (abundance of contrapuntal "artificialities"), in which we find the same situation: namely, that a harpsichord solution is manually possible, but the clavichord is the only proper instrument. We will select the Fugue in F major, which shows in its architecture a surprising similarity to the Fugue in C major, *W.K.* I; however, its passepied-like character and restriction to three voices make the F major Fugue a much less serious affair. Both pieces have in common the increase and following decrease in the quantity and proximity of *stretti*, as well as the marked break in the middle where the relative minor key is reached (bar 46 in the Fugue in F major). But in the F major Fugue there are two episodes, a feature that is entirely lacking in the C major one. Chart 6 describes the architectural construction of this Fugue. The construction can be represented in terraces, as in Figure 12.

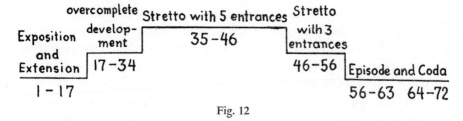

Fig. 12

From this diagram we see the striking similarity between the F major Fugue and the C major Fugue, and this time Bach's writing allows us to prepare the harpsichord for the three terraces: soft 8″, loud 8′, 8″ plus 4″. In bar 21 the left hand has the rest necessary for drawing the 4″ register, and if we are afraid to do this so quickly, we can even play the first notes

CHART 6

Exposition	Extension in the form of an episode	Development	Episode	Coda
	13–17	17–55		
1–13		(1) Overcomplete development: (5 entrances) 56–63		64–72
		S bar 17 A bar 21 B bar 25		Two entrances in *stretto* S bar 64 varied A bar 65 distorted
		A bar 27 (in *stretto*)		
		(2) *Stretto* with 5 entrances: B bar 34 S bar 36 A bar 38 B bar 40 S bar 42		
		(3) *Stretto* with 3 entrances: B bar 46 A bar 48 S bar 50		

of the alto entrance in bar 22 with the right hand to allow more time. The 8″ and 4″ registration becomes effective, for the left hand at the last eighth in bar 34, for the right hand in bar 36, also at the last eighth. In bar 53 we again find the rest necessary for taking away the 4″ register so that the end of the Fugue can be played with 8″ soft. We will remember that in the C major Fugue the absence of any rest that could be used for removing the 4″ stop was one of the decisive factors in proving that the Fugue could not be handled properly on a harpsichord. Here, however, the possibility of having three terraces is clearly available, and we could play this Fugue as shown in Figure 13.

We can hardly deny that this diagram looks rather attractive, and we might even deserve some praise for the cunning way in which we almost succeeded in hiding from the eye and the ear the fact that our interpretation has some weak spots. Looking back at our first draft (p. 83), we see that we have made some changes. Moreover, our first draft itself contains one obviously very debatable spot: it is not easy to justify playing the only real episode and the coda in the same tone color. Yet the way in which Bach connects episode and coda in bar 64 makes any change of keyboards at this moment impossble, in addition to the fact that neither a louder nor a softer terrace would solve the problem. Playing the coda louder would destroy the architectural picture of the Fugue completely, since we would then end louder than we began; a softer terrace in the coda could only be created with the participation of coupler and 16′ register, which is technically impossible.

Looking at the episode, we might think it a good idea to let the left hand play on the louder of the two 8′ keyboards from $50\frac{2}{8}$ to $63\frac{2}{8}$, as this would give us a chance to make the beginning of the coda, in bar 64, audible; indeed, there is a certain justification for this procedure, since

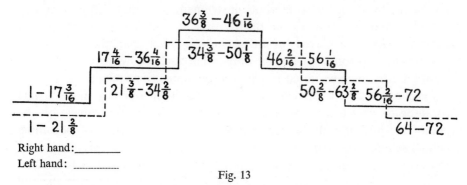

Right hand: _____
Left hand: _____

Fig. 13

everything that this hand does during those measures has some importance. The part of the left hand in bars 56–59 is remarkable for the threefold repetition of the inversion of the first bar of the theme, while from 60–63 the same hand plays the third bar of the theme three times (slightly varied the third time). Unfortunately, a glance at the right-hand part tells us that this hand does exactly the same thing at the same time, only in the opposite order. Therefore, the only logical way to play this episode would be to apply the principle of double counterpoint to the registration, as we have already done so often. Again, however, Bach's writing method in bar 64 forbids this because there would be no way of returning to 8″ registration with the right hand if that hand were to go to the louder keyboard and the left hand to the softer one in bar 60.

But this is not the only place where our interpretation does not stand above criticism. In bar 17 one can move to the second sound terrace only with the help of a bold "gliding procedure," the necessity of which is certainly not indicated in the picture of the notes. Also, in bar 13, where the real exposition ends and an "extension in the form of an episode" follows, Bach clearly does not want any change of keyboards.[40]

---

[40] Here Bach's writing method is exactly the same as in bar 7 of the F sharp major Fugue.

7

If we weigh all these incongruities together, it seems evident that Bach could not have planned this Fugue for a harpsichord interpretation, but that this piece, too, must be reserved for the clavichord.

SUMMARY

The examination of these last fugues was indispensable in order to show that there are cases in Bach's keyboard music where only a very perceptive investigation will reveal that the harpsichord is not the correct instrument for a composition for which it may seem well suited technically. We will go even one step further, and will admit not only that there are quite a few pieces by Bach for which both instruments can make equal claims,[41] but also that occasionally in Bach's time it may have happened that compositions were played on an instrument other than that of his predilection. A person who owned only a harpsichord with one keyboard would hardly have hesitated to play on it compositions meant for a larger harpsichord or for a clavichord as well, just as in our day music lovers continue to play transcriptions of orchestral and chamber music on the piano (in spite of radio and phonograph) for the purpose of becoming better acquainted with the music. Yet a pianist who plays one of Beethoven's symphonies for his own pleasure in a two-hand or four-hand setting is fully aware that he does not get from his instrument the full meaning of such a piece, and we may safely assume that in former days also, the owner of a small harpsichord was well aware of the restrictions in tone volume and color forced upon him by his instrument.

Nevertheless, such a situation could not have occurred frequently enough to be of any importance in formulating the principles of performance of keyboard music in the baroque period. To cultivate music as a "little hobby," as is nowadays customary in the circle of our "music lovers," who generally do not realize on how low a level their enjoyment of music stands, was entirely unknown in those almost "golden days" of music. Either one lived with music as a real connoisseur, even without being a professional, or one had nothing to do with it. From many sources, especially from the Bach family, we know that a large harpsichord, a clavichord, and a pedal (sounding keyboard for the feet) were considered standard equipment for a real musician, and were often augmented by the home organ.[42]

This instrument, a little church organ, usually without pedal and sometimes so small that it could be carried around (*Portativ*), was rather

---

[41] The details for the pieces in question will be given in Appendix A.

[42] See Spitta, *Johann Sebastian Bach*, vol. II, p. 968. C. P. E. Bach writes in his *Essay*, "Every keyboardist should own a good harpsichord and a good clavichord" (p. 37).

popular in the baroque period. We have no document proving that the
Bach family owned one, but it is well known that such an organ was used
in the school of St. Thomas. Some influence of this instrument upon
certain preludes and fugues by Bach is undeniable, even though we have
no more definite proof at our disposal than considerations of style and
the prevalence of long, sustained notes. The Prelude in E flat major,
Prelude and Fugue in B flat minor, *W.K.* I, and the Fugues in E flat
major and E major, *W.K.* II, perhaps also the Prelude and Fugue in C
sharp minor, *W.K.* I,[43] and the Prelude and Fugue in B flat minor, *W.K.*
II, which seems to be too powerful for any harpsichord—all these pieces
are so remarkably different from the normal keyboard style in the "Forty-
Eight" that designation of them for the home organ seems to be the most
satisfactory solution for the problems they offer. In this respect it is interesting to recall the casual way in which Czerny refers to playing the
collection on the organ, in the preface to his edition of the *Welltempered
Keyboard* (see p. 16 above). Yet not many more preludes and fugues
from our collection than those just mentioned could be assigned to the
organ with justification.

Actually, themes of fugues for the large church organ are built in a
very different manner from harpsichord and clavichord themes. This
difference has become nearly unanimously acknowledged by Bach research.[44] The vast majority of the themes of Bach's organ fugues make
use of figures like Example 18, all of which are built in such a way that

Ex. 18

they are easily playable on the pedal keyboard. Because Bach does not
have to reckon with such playability in his *manualiter* pieces, similar
figures are not found in his works for clavichord and harpsichord. The
very few fugues that use them sporadically—the Fugues in C minor and
E minor, *W.K.* I, and those in C major and G major, *W.K.* II—prove
beyond question that they stem from a different chamber of Bach's heart.

---

[43] It would not be difficult to design a pedal part for this Fugue; for example, the bass
entrance in bar 37 and the bass line at the end.

[44] See among others, Schweitzer, *Bach*, p. 293. A comparison of the themes of the "long"
Fugue in A minor for Harpsichord in 3/4 time, and that of the "great" A minor Organ Fugue
in 6/8 time, shows the difference most clearly. The themes are almost identical in their musical
contents. Yet the theme of the harpsichord Fugue could never be played effectively on an
organ pedal, while the theme of the organ Fugue is not at all difficult for the feet in spite of its
brilliance.

It would certainly have been very strange for Bach to have been indifferent to the enormous contrast between performances of the same piece on a harpsichord and a clavichord, especially when he differentiated so clearly between organ and klavier pieces. Because he could expect every serious keyboard player to own a harpsichord and a clavichord, it was therefore not unusual that Bach made collections of pieces for various keyboard instruments and felt perfectly certain that those people into whose hands they were given would know how to deal with them. I hope that our examination of the technical aspects of Bach's keyboard music has proved that in reality there is a very refined differentiation between harpsichord and clavichord pieces. The old legend, that in all these pieces Bach's only artistic goal was to make us enjoy the playing of the lines, must therefore be dismissed.

The overwhelming richness and variety of Bach's keyboard music, and the many different types of formal principles he applied, especially in his fugues, make it impossible to formulate infallible rules for ascribing every piece to its proper instrument. Only general procedures can be stated here, which will help steer the individual examination of every piece in the right direction. We must:

1. Examine the general architectural plan to determine the presence or absence of terrace dynamics.

2. Inspect rests occurring at the "seams" of a piece, to find out whether they might be meant for making changes in the registration possible. A rest or a fermata in both hands at the same time almost always indicates the use of the coupler.

3. Carefully examine all cadences, to find out whether a change of keyboards is expected. All episodes have to be examined to see if they are connected with, or separated from, the adjacent parts.

4. Examine thematic entrances to determine whether they can and should be singled out from the other voices by being played on a separate keyboard.

If it is impossible to make the architecture and registration of a piece correspond on the harpsichord, the piece should be reserved for the clavichord.

CHAPTER 3

Dynamic Problems

GENERAL REMARKS

Of all the problems offered by Bach's keyboard works, that of choosing the proper instrument is probably the most far-reaching. Nothing is more important to the inner spirit of a performance than the aura, the atmosphere created by the instrument. Our examination of the various types of Bach's keyboard works has shown that almost every piece displays in its structure, as if written with invisible ink, the stamp of its instrumental destination; indeed, this is done with such a degree of clarity that a musician of the period would have had no difficulty in understanding the message. Might it be possible that a similar situation exists in regard to the problems of dynamics, tempo, ornamentation, and articulation; that for the solutions of these problems, too, we need only to make the "invisible ink" readable?

In the case of dynamics, the answer can be given immediately in the affirmative. Although only a small number of *forte* and *piano* signs in Bach's own hand have come down to us, and although most of them, as we know from the previous chapter, are nothing other than indications for registration, the instruments themselves reveal Bach's intentions with infallible clarity. We need therefore not wonder that he found it unnecessary to provide us with more detailed information.

For pieces written for the harpsichord, problems of dynamics are practically nonexistent once we have chosen the proper registration. The number of sound levels will correspond to the number of terraces to be used. As we have said before, short pieces, especially dance movements, do not need more than one tone color from the beginning to the end; in other cases the normal number of terraces is two: single tone and tone with octave doubling. Here and there, for works of large proportions, a third terrace, full work, may be used. Rests in both hands or a fermata generally indicate the start of the third terrace, since the full work cannot be applied without having both hands free for coupling the keyboards.

Because nearly all movements of major size are built either in concerto-grosso form or as fugues with regular alternation of development and episodes,[1] it is nearly impossible to make mistakes in regard to *piano* and *forte* distribution in those pieces. For toccata-like pieces the liberty in interpretation that is so characteristic of this genre eliminates the possibility of any serious error and spared us the necessity of analyzing them in the previous chapter. Runs in which both hands join to play a single line, such as those at the beginning of the Chromatic Phantasy, the D minor and C minor Toccatas, and the cadenzas in the D minor Harpsichord Concerto, are to be played at least in octaves if not with the full work. Comparisons with similar situations in organ toccatas leave no doubt about this problem.

Even fewer suggestions need to be given for clavichord pieces. The instrument itself does not allow the range of dynamics to go beyond the limits of *ppp* and *mf*, and the design of the lines is sufficient to show us how to keep the interpretation flexible and alive. The warning against overuse of the *Bebung* (p. 10) should be taken most seriously. However, nothing is more decisive for the understanding of the dynamics of a clavichord piece than our basic approach to the music. Together with the sonatas and suites for unaccompanied violin and cello, the clavichord pieces represent the only part of the composer's creative output where the veil covering Bach the man is lifted a little. These pieces are real "confessions," "pages from a diary," and show us the depths of soulfulness and tenderness that are the counterpart of Bach the giant. If we approach them in the same manner in which we would read a lyric poem to ourselves, or in which we would sing for our own pleasure, without any intention of impressing an audience, then we will find the right style. Bach has been called a baroque, even a gothic master. In the light of our study of the clavichord pieces we may add—with more justification—Bach the romantic.

THE EXECUTION OF BACH'S KEYBOARD WORKS ON THE PIANO

The discussion of the problems of dynamics and registration has brought us so close to those questions which puzzle every conscientious piano

---

[1] For fugues of the largest dimensions (e.g., Chromatic Phantasy, last movement of the Concerto in C major for Two Harpsichords, etc.), Bach uses this type of construction exclusively.

player that, although we have not yet dealt with tempo, ornamentation, and articulation, we might turn immediately to the most crucial of all problems: what should we do when we take Bach's keyboard works out of their native soil and transplant them from harpsichord and clavichord to the only keyboard instrument available in our time, the piano?

The mere description of the mechanisms of the harpsichord and clavichord gave us sufficient cause to question the justification of playing compositions written for these sound media on the piano, especially when they are transferred exactly, with no adjustments. Now that we have seen the ingenuity displayed by Bach in dealing with the mechanical possibilities and limitations of the harpsichord and clavichord, it is imperative that we compare the piano with both these instruments in a most serious examination.

Even to those readers who have never heard any of Bach's works performed on the original instruments (in regard to the clavichord, which is still virtually unknown, this means almost 99 per cent of the music lovers), it must have become increasingly evident that we are dealing with a problem of primary importance. It is only too apparent that our modern piano has very little in common with the old instruments. Furthermore, its superiority over its predecessors is much more questionable than we have been led to believe, especially by those who have constantly assured us that Bach would have been sublimely happy could he ever have heard his compositions played on this miraculous instrument.

Actually, the situation is not really too bad for compositions written for the clavichord, because here at least the written notes correspond to the notes that we are expected to hear. Yet even the art of touch of the greatest piano virtuoso cannot compete with the much more refined shadings possible on the tiny clavichord, not to mention the unique and inimitable effect of the *Bebung*, the vibrato of a single tone. Whoever has become familiar with the tone production of a clavichord will perhaps agree that the relation between this instrument and the piano is something like that between a butterfly and a bat. When it comes to the relation between a harpsichord and a piano, however, we have to admit in all frankness that there is none. No bridge leads from the inflexible plucked tone of the harpsichord to the shadings of tone possible on the piano. Yet what a poor substitute are these shadings for the variety of tone colors and octave combinations produced by the registers of the harpsichord!

The most satisfactory solution for this problem, one that would spare us many of these troubles, would, of course, be the revival of harpsichord and clavichord. Indeed, the renaissance of both these instruments is no longer a utopian dream, but has become one of the most outstanding events in the musical life of our time. The revival of the harpsichord, started so courageously by its "first lady," Wanda Landowska, has now been accepted by the entire musical world, and a conductor who still uses a piano for continuo purposes has to reckon with severe criticism for lacking a "sense of style." Even the clavichord has begun to awake from its long slumber in museums. Not only professional instrument makers but many hobbyists as well have become fascinated by the beauty of its tone, which is produced by the simplest of mechanical devices. Furthermore, the low price for which a clavichord can be manufactured is an added stimulus for its ever-increasing revival. Whoever becomes the lucky owner of one or the other, or even of both instruments, would probably never want to play Bach on the piano again—not out of snobbishness, but because of the holy conviction that only on the old instruments can Bach's keyboard music display its full splendor. Nevertheless, a solution has to be found for those innumerable music lovers who can own only a piano, and who still, and most justifiably, do not want to give up playing Bach on the only keyboard instrument available to them.

Clavichord Works on the Piano

For works written for clavichord the solution is fairly simple: one must forget the enormous dynamic range of the piano and play, with utter discretion, within the limits of *ppp* and *mf*, just as one would talk to oneself. No display of hyper-romanticism is tolerable; yet one should apply all the tenderness that can be found in the finest lyric poetry. Using a spinet piano, with its smaller tone volume, instead of a big grand would prove most advantageous. It is a tragedy that from the first modest beginnings the developments in piano building have always tended toward production of greater tone volume, generally at the expense of the soft tone, which has become less and less flexible. Is it not grotesque that we casually put into the small living room of a modern apartment an instrument which could easily be transferred to a concert hall without weakening its sonority? Nothing is more horrible than having to listen, in such a drawing room, to the exhibition of young talent playing in "concert style."[2]

The arrival of the spinet piano is only the first step made by our present-day piano factories in the direction of giving us a piano for home use. One need only play some square pianos from the period 1790–1840 to become amazed at the richness of nuance in the soft tones that such

---

[2] I feel unable to suppress the observation of how closely the *ff* possibilities of a modern piano in a small room are related to the horsepower of a modern car waiting to be released, with such deadly results, on our highways.

small instruments can provide. A piano like the "piano console" by J. H. Pape (built in Paris in 1839), now in the Berlin State Collection, exceeds every modern piano in tonal beauty. Not before 1850, approximately, did the grand piano begin to achieve the enormous tone volume with which we now reckon and which was exploited for the first time in Liszt's brilliant piano works. The grand piano owned by Chopin, which was exhibited years ago in the Pleyel factory in Paris, testifies vividly to what he called "*fortissimo*"—so much less than the thunderstorm produced by present-day virtuosi—and is a good reminder that this greatest master of the piano tone hated the concert hall and preferred to play to a small but responsive audience in the salons of Parisian aristocracy. Only if we approach the works of Bach written for the clavichord with a similar conception—that we have to play them for ourselves and not for a crowd, just as Bach's favorite subtitle, "For the enjoyment of the soul of connoisseurs and true amateurs,"[3] suggests—will we be able to grasp the wonderful discretion with which Bach remains the master of his feelings.

Harpsichord Works on the Piano

In the case of Bach's compositions for harpsichord, the transfer to the piano offers far greater difficulties. The glaring fact that gradations of crescendo and decrescendo were technically impossible on the organ and harpsichord is irrevocable. Equally irrevocable is the fact that these instruments, as well as the clavichord, had no device equivalent to the piano pedal. Are the purists right when they go so far as to forbid any use of the pedal and to exclude all shadings of piano tone from a conscientious Bach interpretation? Does this not mean that we have to deprive the piano of everything that makes listening to it a pleasure for our ears?

No doubt, these questions put a severe load of responsibility upon the artistic conscience of every player. In regard to pedaling, utter discretion is imperative. Never should the damper pedal be used for creating "veils of harmony." He who can apply the singular art of beautifying individual tones with the help of indescribably small pedal applications, however, has acquired a "license" for use of the piano pedal from which he should not hesitate to profit.

In regard to the application of crescendos and decrescendos, one has to bear in mind that no player of a clavichord or of a stringed or wind instrument, and naturally no singer, would ever have entertained the absurd idea of not using them to underline the ups and downs of the

---

[3] "Denen Kennern und Liebhabern zur Gemütsergötzung." I purposely translate *Liebhaber* as "true amateur," as a reminder that the dilettante of that period was far superior in his knowledge of musical matters to the music lover of our time (see p. 19).

musical texture. Although Bach never wrote the words "crescendo" and
"decrescendo,"[4] the oboe d'amore solo in the aria "Phoebus, deine
Melodie" from the cantata "Phoebus and Pan," which he wrote out in a
remarkable way (Ex. 19),[5] proves that the use of the crescendo was not

Ex. 19. "Phoebus and Pan," aria "Phoebus, deine Melodie," oboe d'amore

foreign to him. Also, the emphasis on "cantabile playing" in the preface
to the Inventions indicates very clearly his attitude in regard to shadings.
Of course, long crescendos through several measures, which we might
instinctively be seduced into applying to a pedal point (Ex. 20), are

Ex. 20. Italian Concerto, Movement 1, bars 124–128

absolutely "un-Bachian." As is generally known, they were used for the
first time by the Mannheim orchestra. When playing harpsichord compositions on the piano, small crescendos and decrescendos should by no
means be avoided, because without them the tone of the modern piano
would sound unbearably dull. On the other hand, one must be very
careful to establish well-separated sound levels for the different terraces;
"echo effects," in particular, have to be faithfully rendered.

---

[4] These words did not come into general use before Jomelli introduced them in Mannheim
about 1757–1760. For the earlier "secret" history of the application of crescendo and diminuendo, see *Origins of Musical Time and Expression* by Rosamond Harding (London, 1938). A
crescendo mark, reported by Riemann in his edition of the Trio for Two Violins and Continuo
in G major by G. Pergolesi (but not mentioned in Harding's book), could not be checked by
this writer for its authenticity. Johann Kuhnau used the term *più piano* in addition to *forte*
and *piano* in the sonata "Jacobs Heirat" (probably a clavichord piece, at least by preference).

[5] Bach's use of *piano* and *forte* is identical with a way of notation used by Christoph
Bernhard in his *Kompositionsschule*, written in 1648 (republished under the title *Die Kompositionslehre Heinrich Schützens in der Fassung seines Schülers Christoph Bernhard* by Josef
Müller-Blattau, Leipzig, 1926). For singing long notes, the author recommends: "For whole
and half notes one uses *piano* at the beginning and end, and *forte* in the middle. One must
watch that one does not go suddenly from *piano* to *forte* and vice versa, but that one lets the
voice gradually increase and decrease; otherwise, what should be a masterly achievement
[*Kunststück*] will sound miserable." This is, of course, the same technique which, in the
eighteenth century, became generally known as *messa di voce*.

The most crucial aspect of the transfer of a harpsichord composition to the piano arises when we start taking registration into consideration. No mental adjustment can help us hide the fact that these problems are identical with those that come up when we try to transfer an organ piece to the piano. By now everybody acknowledges that in the case of organ music playing the mere notes would be nonsensical, and that bars like Example 21 from the Prelude in E flat major for organ should be played on the piano in an arrangement like Example 22. This gives at least an

Ex. 21. Prelude in E flat major. For Organ

Ex. 22. The same. Piano arrangement

approximate account of how such a piece sounds on the organ. How strange that when the Italian Concerto, written specifically for "a harpsichord with two keyboards," is played on the piano, everybody is content to play and to hear just the mere written notes; how few realize that bars like Examples 23 and 24 should sound like Examples 25 and 26, and that only bars like Example 27 should really sound as written.

These few examples are sufficient proof that playing just the written notes of the Italian Concerto on the piano is not only a misinterpretation but actually a gross caricature of the inner meaning of this glorious piece, in which the juxtaposition of different sound masses is a *sine qua non* for making it sound like a concerto grosso, as its title asks. Whether we like it or not, the only way to be at all fair to a major composition for harpsichord when playing it on the piano is to use an arrangement, a transcription—be it for two pianos or for four hands on one—in which the sound volumes are distributed exactly the same way that they would be on the harpsichord.[6]

Ex. 23. Italian Concerto, Movement 1, bars 1–2   Ex. 25

Ex. 24. The same, bar 31   Ex. 26

Ex. 27. The same, bars 129–130

No special "instructive editions" are needed for making such arrangements. For playing on two pianos the only prerequisites are two copies of the piece in question, a minor item, and—what is, alas, a major investment—a thorough knowledge of the problems of formal analysis. Should the acquisition of the latter not belong to the equipment of any person seriously interested in music? It is one of the saddest aspects of our present-day musical education that the acquisition of technique and touch now occupy the minds of young piano students nearly exclusively,

---

[6] Busoni and Petri, in their famous Bach edition (Breitkopf and Härtel), were the first ones to realize that nothing is achieved in Bach interpretation by the playing of the literal notes. They added octaves and even "mixture" sounds in the parts of both hands. Petri's setting of the French Overture is a nearly perfect transcription of this monumental piece. Yet, when editing the Italian Concerto, the realization that ten fingers are not enough to produce all the sounds necessary made Petri give up writing a transcription. He retreated to a literal copying of the original notes, adding in brackets the words "*Tutti*" and "*Solo*" to give at least an idea of the problems involved.

while all theoretical branches of musical knowledge are considered a *quantité négligeable*. This unforgivable attitude is supported by many teachers, who eternally complain that assignments in theory prevent the student from having enough time for practicing; indeed, the matter comes up regularly for discussion at faculty meetings in nearly every conservatory. Our analytical discussions of Bach's fugues should certainly have convinced readers that knowledge of the problems of musical structure is an indispensable prerequisite for a performer. We know that every good musician of Bach's period was thoroughly equipped to deal with such problems.[7] Nothing would be more beneficial for raising the standard of our students' musical conceptions than an intensive study of the structural problems offered by Bach's keyboard music.

The procedure for arranging a piece for two pianos is simple. After having decided which parts of a harpsichord composition are meant to be doubled in octaves, one is ready to play on two pianos from the original copies. For the *piano* sections either one player may play or both players may play only one hand each, to give them the pleasure of continuous occupation; of course everything has to be played where written. For *forte* sections one player plays both hands as written, the other plays one octave higher to produce the 4' doublings. The register combination 8' and 16' is, of course, imitated if one player plays both hands one octave lower. The lute stop, which in Bach's works seems to be applicable very rarely, can, at least to a certain degree, be imitated by applying a very fine and thin staccato touch, supported by una corda pedal but without damper pedal. Even the register combination 4' and 16' coupled, perhaps the most charming of the color effects possible on a harpsichord, can be reproduced if one player plays the original part of the right hand simultaneously one octave higher and one octave lower than written while the second player does the same with the left-hand part. The effect of the full work of the harpsichord, however (8', 8", 4", 16' coupled), cannot be achieved with any kind of transcription for two players: a third player on a third piano would be needed for this purpose. But we had better stop now; this fact is mentioned merely to remind the reader of how many notes a harpsichord is able to produce simultaneously with only ten fingers playing.

In cases where two pianos are not available, a four-hand setting for one piano will give a good idea of the real meaning of a harpsichord

---

[7] That even laymen were familiar with such problems can be seen from the very interesting "vocation" given to Bach by the Konsistorium of the Liebfrauenkirche in Halle, when he considered becoming the successor to Wilhelm Zachow, Handel's teacher (December 14, 1713). In this document the good people of Halle prescribed to Bach in detail which registers of the organ he should use for accompanying the congregational singing. See Hans T. David and Arthur Mendel, *The Bach Reader*, p. 65.

piece. The *piano* sections are played with only one hand on a part. For *forte* sections the *Primo* player plays Bach's original right-hand notes with the left, doubling them an octave higher with his right hand; the *Secondo* player does the same in the opposite direction, his right hand playing the original notes of Bach's part for the left hand, and his left hand doubling them an octave lower.[8] Again, any normal printed edition can be used for this type of four-hand playing by marking *col 8va* above and below the places that need doubling. Such an application of doublings would correspond to a harpsichord registration of 8″ and 4″ on one keyboard contrasted with 8′ and 16′.

When we play Bach's major harpsichord compositions in such home-made arrangements, we should do so in the same frame of mind in which we play transcriptions of symphonies or chamber music works by the great classic masters: we know that in this way we get a foretaste of the real meaning of the composition, which will prepare us well for the moment when we are privileged to hear or to play the same composition on the authentic instrument. And if we play this composition again by ourselves on the piano, just as it is written and as everybody has played it thoughtlessly hitherto, no harm will be done; after our experience in four-hand playing we will be fully aware that one person can produce only the *skeleton* of the piece in question.

There is only one serious and seemingly cruel consequence that we cannot avoid facing: Bach's major harpsichord compositions will have to disappear from the concert programs of our piano virtuosi. Actually, we should not shed too many tears at this loss. The ever-increasing quantity of harpsichord recitals will provide more and more opportunities to hear these works in an authentic manner. Even the famous arrangements of Bach's organ compositions made by Liszt, Tausig, and Busoni,[9] which for decades were most effective "program-openers" of our greatest virtuosi, are now played much less often, and for good reason: the chances of hearing these compositions in their original form, even on authentic copies of baroque organs, have increased tremendously.[10] As a matter of fact, the contributions of professional pianists toward making the keyboard works of Bach better known have, with a few laudable exceptions, been very small. How often do we ever hear the magnificent preludes and

---

[8] In my book *Der Vortrag alter Klaviermusik*, I have added as a supplement arrangements of the first movement of the Italian Concerto and of the Fugue in G minor (*W.K.* I) for piano, four hands.

[9] For these compositions, too, we prefer the homemade four-hand arrangements for piano to any well-intended transcriptions.

[10] For the same reason, no pianist nowadays plays Liszt's fantastically well-made arrangements of Beethoven's symphonies, which for years were the arranger's favorite numbers on his own concert program; however, in their time they fulfilled a mission that can never be overestimated.

fugues from the second volume of the *Welltempered Keyboard* in a public performance? Who ever cares to play the Third or Fourth Partita in a concert program? The artificial "homage to Bach" in the opening number of a standard concert program (90 per cent of the time the Chromatic Phantasy) has certainly never contributed to a "Bach cult." We should not regret seeing this falsified show-number disappear from the concert programs, and a pianist who feels any responsibility for his profession should restrain himself from playing something not meant for his instrument. If he still feels that he must perform such a work, he should at least inform his public with a little notice: "Originally written for harpsichord."

However, there does exist one group of pianists who may have an excuse to profit by the situation: the duo-pianists, who have become so very popular during recent years. Bach's harpsichord pieces could provide them with a well-justified enrichment for their all-too-small repertoire, which hitherto has consisted primarily of arrangements whose quality could be very seriously questioned. If Bach's major harpsichord compositions need a place in the concert halls at all—and this is to be doubted, since the spirit in which they were written has very little in common with public performance—their legitimate place is here, in the recitals of the duo-pianists. But it is not my intention to help these performers with the publication of ready-made arrangements, in order that they may get their material the easy way. An intensive study of the inner architecture of Bach's most formidable harpsichord pieces cannot and should not be spared to them. For the imitation of the various register colors on two pianos, our previous remarks give all information necessary. Nothing could be more beneficial than for every musician to study the methods with which a creative artist handles his tools. If the problems offered by Bach's keyboard works could convince the young music students of our time of the necessity of giving most serious study to the analysis of the hidden laws of musical architecture, these works could become the cornerstone for the most decisive development in their inner growth: the transformation from an amateur into a connoisseur.

CHAPTER 4

Tempo

Our initial surprise that Bach dared to write down nothing more than the naked notes for most of his keyboard music has begun to subside. We have seen that the structure of each piece reveals the proper instrument for performance; we have seen that the instruments and the form of the pieces give us the necessary information about dynamics. Will we be equally fortunate in regard to the problems of tempo?

Again, the sources of direct information are very few. Here is the list of tempo marks in Bach's keyboard music, not entirely complete, but with no work of any importance omitted.

1. Tempo marks found in autographs or printed editions published by Bach himself

Welltempered Keyboard, vol. I:	Prelude 2, bar 33, *adagio*; bar 35, *allegro*
	Prelude 10, bar 23, *presto*
	Prelude 24, *andante*
	Fugue 24, *largo*
Welltempered Keyboard, vol. II:	Prelude 3, second part, *allegro*
	Prelude 16, *largo*
	Prelude 24, *allegro*
Partita II:	Sinfonia, *grave, adagio*; bar 8, *andante*
Partita V:	*Tempo di menuetto*
Partita VI:	*Tempo di gavotta*
Italian Concerto:	Second movement, *andante*
	Third movement, *presto*
Goldberg Variations:	Variation 15, *andante*
	Variation 22, *alla breve*

2. Tempo marks found in contemporary copies of generally recognized quality

Toccata in F sharp minor:	*Presto e staccato*
Toccata in C minor:	*Adagio* (three times); at the end, *presto*
Toccata in D minor:	Fuga, *presto, adagio*
Toccata in D major:	*Allegro, presto*
Toccata in G major:	*Adagio, allegro e presto*
English Suite IV:	Prelude, *vitement*
English Suite VI:	Prelude, last bar, *adagio*; then *allegro*
Chromatic Phantasy:	*Andantino* in the *recitativo*
Capriccio on the Departure of His Brother:	*Arioso adagio, adagiosissimo* [*sic!*], *adagio poco*
Adagio in G major (transcribed from Sonata in C major for Violin Solo):	*Adagio*
Sonata in D minor (after Sonata in A minor for Violin Solo):	*Adagio, allegro, andante, allegro*
Concerto in A major for Harpsichord:	Third movement, *presto*
Concerto in F major for Harpsichord:	Third movement, *allegro*
Concerto in C major for Two Harpsichords:	Second movement, *adagio ovvero largo*
Sixteen concertos after Vivaldi, etc.:	All of these concertos have tempo indications except eight first movements, which have none. All indications are traditional. In the tenth Concerto, the last movement is marked *prestissimo*.

This is a small list indeed, and would have been almost negligible had we restricted ourselves to reporting only those tempo marks authenticated by an autograph. In the works for organ, tempo indications are so rare that it does not seem worthwhile to list them at all; in regard to works other than keyboard music the situation is not significantly better. The *St. Matthew Passion* contains five tempo marks in the entire score! The Mass in B minor has only twelve tempo marks, among which *vivace ed allegro* for the setting of "Et expecto" (in the Credo) may be mentioned. In the cantatas (church and secular) we find approximately 150 tempo marks for about 1,520 single numbers. In the field of chamber music,

8

however, most movements of the Brandenburg Concertos[1] and *almost all* sonatas for one or several instruments are marked.

Before making any evaluation of this tabulation, we must comment about the use of the Italian tempo indications. In Bach's time most of the Italian terms still did not have the meanings that we attribute to them nowadays. The emphasis was more on the mood or the so-called "affect"[2] of the piece, rather than on direct tempo information. Thus *allegro* and *grave* meant "gay" and "serious" respectively, giving the performer a clue to an appropriate tempo. Because of this vagueness and the variability of these moods, the harvest of information that we can draw from the relatively large number of marks on the vocal and instrumental works is not as great as the figures might imply.

If we now look over the list of authentic tempo marks, we find very few that are of particular interest. *Prestissimo* and *adagiosissimo*, the extreme speed indications, are each used only once.[3] The *allegro e presto* in the G major Toccata, the *grave, adagio* in the Second Partita and the *vivace ed allegro* from the "Et expecto" of the B minor Mass each combine two words which in present-day usage indicate different gradations of speed. The explanation for this seemingly twofold tempo indication is, however, very simple. The purpose of the double terminology is to give additional information about the affect involved. *Tempo di minuetto* and *tempo di gavotta*, used as tempo indications in the partitas, confirm the fact that dance movements had their own typical speed, known by tradition.

It is perhaps not too surprising that the chamber music, including the Brandenburg Concertos, provides the greatest quantity of tempo indications, since these works depended least on Bach's personal participation in performances. The cantatas and the Passions were hardly ever directed by anyone other than the composer himself. On the other hand, the "connoisseurs" who played the chamber music certainly did not have to be reminded constantly that the organization of a *sonata da chiesa* was slow, fast, slow, fast, and that a concerto almost always consisted of three movements in the order of fast, slow, fast. We must therefore admit that we are at a loss to find a convincing explanation for Bach's frequent generosity in giving tempo information where the need did not really

---

[1] Only the first movements of the first, second, third, and sixth concertos are unmarked.

[2] We will treat this subject in more detail in Chapter 7, Articulation.

[3] Extreme speeds, especially in piano music, were developed only recently, as a result of the deplorable ambition of modern virtuosi to be called "speed kings." But certain pieces in the orchestral repertoire also suffer nowadays from being played at entirely unjustifiable speeds, for instance, the Overture to the *Marriage of Figaro*, the "Champagne Aria" from *Don Giovanni*, the *Scherzo* from *A Midsummer Night's Dream*, and the 6/8 variation in Brahms's *Variations on a Theme by Haydn*.

exist, and of his reticence in regard to the vast majority of his compositions. If he could act this way, however, it is obvious that in his time there must have existed enough of a tradition about tempo problems so that it was not too difficult to find the right speed for a piece. A brief excursion into the history of tempo marks will show us that enough documents have survived to clarify this matter to an appreciable degree.

HISTORICAL REVIEW

Italian tempo marks began to appear around 1600, and Adriano Banchieri (1567–1634) is credited with the first use of them in his *L'organo suonarino* (1605).[4] It is interesting to see that Frescobaldi's *Canzoni da sonar* were published in 1628 without tempo marks but that in 1634 a second edition used them. However, their use was not generally adopted before the second half of the eighteenth century. This does not mean that in earlier periods anarchy dominated the field of tempo. For several centuries there had existed a system of notation that clarified the absolute value of the single note, and that made specifications of tempi by the use of descriptive words unnecessary. This *integer valor notarum*, which gave a certain kind of note an average duration, was often brought into relation with the human pulse.[5] In 1618 Michael Praetorius tried to reckon out how many measures at moderate speed could be played in a quarter of an hour, and came to a figure that corresponded almost exactly to the beat of the human pulse.[6] Christoph Simpson, in his *The Principles of Practicle Music*, compared four quarter notes to a "leisurely counting of one, two, three, four,"[7] a description that was used nearly verbatim by Henry Purcell in the Preface to *A Choice of Lessons for the Harpsichord or Spinet* (London, 1696). In 1702 St. Lambert said about C time: "Grave and slowly; its four quarters should move like the steps of a man walking quite slowly."[8] Even as late as 1767 Jean Jacques Rousseau stated in his *Dictionnaire de Musique* in the article "Tempo": "The time signatures

---

[4] Banchieri seems to have been preceded only by the Spaniard Luis Milan, the master of the lute, who used the words *a priesa* for "quick" and *a espacio* for "slow" in his *El Maistro* (1535; modern edition by Leo Schrade, *Publikationen älterer Musik*, vol. II, 1927). See also W. Apel, *The Notation of Polyphonic Music* (Cambridge, Mass., 1942), p. 190.

[5] It is beyond the scope of this book to give an extensive report on the extremely interesting history of the relation between note values and tempi. Readers who want more detailed information are referred to Apel's *The Notation of Polyphonic Music*, chapter IV, section I, "Proportional Time Signatures and Tempo," and also to Ralph Kirkpatrick's paper, "Eighteenth Century Metronomic Indications," *Papers of the American Musicological Society* (1938), p. 30.

[6] *Syntagma Musicum* (1615–1629), III, 87–88.

[7] (London, [1665]), pp. 21–23.

[8] M. de St. Lambert, *Les principes du clavecin* (Paris, 1697), chapter VIII.

also fixed the relative value of the notes" (*Ces signes fixaient aussi la valure relative des notes*).[9]

The longest elaboration of tempo problems is found in Johann Joachim Quantz's *Versuch einer Anweisung die Flöte traversière zu spielen*, written in 1752, two years after the death of Bach. The prolixity of Quantz's writing makes it inadvisible to give a literal translation of his chapters dealing with tempo, which—along with the entire book—should be carefully studied by everybody interested in eighteenth-century music. We will restrict ourselves to a condensed report of those paragraphs that are of special importance to us.[10]

In paragraph 45 Quantz promises to give a method that will help a performer to find (*erraten*) the right speed for every piece, and he regrets that composers do not have a device to indicate the desired tempo. He knows about the invention of Loulie's Chronometre (1698),[11] the most important forerunner of Maelzel's metronome (paragraph 46), but recommends for measuring time the pulse of a healthy person (paragraph 47), coming to the conclusion, like Praetorius, that an average speed has eighty beats per minute. In paragraph 55 he jokingly discusses the objection, which can easily be raised, that the temperaments of various people may cause some marked aberrations; but he reckons that five pulses, more or less, add or subtract, within forty measures, only one sixteenth of a pulse per bar, an amount which is too small to be significant. He then defines four basic speeds for the performance of "concertos, trios, and solos" (paragraph 49):

1. *Allegro assai*, which also includes *allegro di molto* and *presto*;
2. *Allegretto*, which includes *allegro ma non tanto, non troppo, non presto*, and *moderato*;
3. *Adagio cantabile*, which includes *arioso, larghetto, soave, dolce, poco andante, affetuoso, pomposo, maestoso, alla siciliana*, and *adagio spirituoso*;
4. *Adagio assai*, which includes *adagio pesante, lento, largo assai, mesto*, and *grave*.

He adds that all the terms in one group are really differentiations in character rather than in speed.

Quantz continues, saying that *allegro assai* is the fastest tempo, *allegretto* is twice as slow (*noch einmal so langsam*), and the remaining ones are similarly slower. In *alla breve* time one has to play the eighth notes as one played the sixteenth in C time. The decisive conclusion comes in paragraph 51:

---

[9] (Ed. 1824), p. 274.
[10] Book XVII, part 7, paragraphs 45–60. An English translation of most of these paragraphs can be found in Rosamond Harding's *Origin of Musical Time and Expression*, pp. 2–6.
[11] Described by Harding, pp. 9ff.

Because it would be impossible for a violinist or a woodwind player to play more than eight notes in the time of one pulse beat, the following rule can be given:

For common C time

Allegro assai	one pulse beat for half a bar
Allegretto	one pulse beat for each quarter
Adagio cantabile	one pulse beat for each eighth
Adagio assai	two pulse beats for each eighth

For ₵ time

Allegro assai	one pulse beat for each bar
Allegretto	one pulse beat for each half bar
Adagio cantabile	one pulse beat for each quarter
Adagio assai	two pulse beats for each quarter

Less detailed and less clear rules are given for 3/4 time in paragraph 5, among which the following are the most interesting: "In 3/4 time, if the piece is obviously *allegro* and sixteenth notes are used, the tempo cannot be fixed by the pulse directly. However, if one takes two bars together, the pulse indicates the first and third quarter notes of the first bar, and the second quarter note of the second bar." In other words there are only three pulse beats for six quarter notes. Quantz suggests modifications of his basic rules according to the note values used by the composer (paragraph 51): "If, for example, an *adagio cantabile* in 3/4 time consists only of quarter notes, the quarter note should get one pulse beat. On the other hand, an *alla siciliana* (12/8) would be too slow if each eighth note gets one beat. However, if one divides two pulse beats into three parts, one gets one beat for the first, and the next for the third eighth. Then one must stop watching the beat of the pulse, or the third eighth will become too long." This method will serve, Quantz assures us (paragraph 54), to find the right speed for every composition, just as the composer wanted it. Finally, in paragraph 60 he remarks that composers would do well to write their works in so unmistakable a mood that everybody could easily find the right speed.

These remarks by Quantz sound so clear and definitive that at first glance we might be tempted to rejoice; it seems that we now have a tool which gives, at least for compositions that carry an Italian tempo indication, almost the same degree of accuracy as would have been possible had Maelzel's metronome existed. Unfortunately, our expectations will be considerably disappointed when we transform Quantz's recommendations into accurate figures. Fulfilling literally his prescriptions of the proper relation between pulse and note values, we get the tempi as shown in Chart 7.

CHART 7

For common C time		For ¢ time	
Allegro assai	♩ = 80 M.M.	*Allegro assai*	♩ = 160
Allegretto	♩ = 80	*Allegretto*	♩ = 80
Adagio cantabile	♩ = 40	*Adagio cantabile*	♩ = 80
Adagio assai	♪ = 40	*Adagio assai*	♪ = 80

These diagrams reveal immediately the impracticality of Quantz's scheme.[12] *Allegro assai* at ♩ = 160 is obviously much too fast for a tempo *alla breve*, in which eighth notes still occur. The last movement of the Italian Concerto, which as a *Presto* in ¢ is an example of the greatest speed ever prescribed by Bach, would become a miserable race, technically impossible on the harpsichord and in very poor taste on the piano where a virtuoso might perhaps be able to maintain such a speed. The last movement of the Fourth Brandenburg Concerto, also marked *presto* ¢, is equally impossible at this speed. In regard to common C time, the same holds for *allegro assai* at ♩ = 80. Quantz himself confirms (paragraph 50) that at this speed (*allegro assai*) a composer still uses runs of sixteenths throughout the bar, which is again a technical impossibility if a half note equals 80. On the slow side scarcely a piece exists that could stand the inertia of a tempo in which ♪ = 40. Even Variation 25 of the *Goldberg Variations* is timed by Kirkpatrick at ♪ = 46, while Bischoff thinks that ♪ = 84 and Czerny that ♪ = 88 might be right. For the *Adagiosissimo* of the Departure Capriccio, ♪ = 40 would be completely ridiculous. (Bischoff gives it ♩ = 60.) Even the organ prelude "O Mensch, bewein Dein Sünde gross" would become a caricature if played in this tempo, in spite of the fact that it is probably the slowest piece Bach ever wrote.

One cannot help thinking that Quantz elaborated his scheme for the

---

[12] In his recent publication, *Rhythm and Tempo* (New York, 1953), p. 34, Curt Sachs severely criticizes Quantz for misleading the reader completely with these tempo differentiations, since "his alleged tempi are simply the assignments of different note symbols to one and the same beat—in fact, *proportiones* in the sense of the Renaissance. They do not become actual tempi without those imponderables that every good performer knows: the same metronomic tempo can be given a driving or a hesitant character." We cannot help feeling that Dr. Sachs, the illustrious Senior of musicology in our time, has taken issue too strongly with the statements of Quantz, which, in our opinion, are merely the formulations in plain language of a practical musician and not the carefully worded elaborations of a learned theorist. Of course Quantz's "alleged" tempo marks represent only one and the same beat expressed in various note values. However, there can also be no doubt that Quantz intended the Italian tempo marks to represent moods and affects only, rather than actual tempi (see Quantz, Schering ed., p. 266). In our opinion, the only thing that matters in these paragraphs of Quantz is that he puts the emphasis upon the existence of relations between the inner beats inherent in various presentations of "human affects."

beauty of its appearance, without being too concerned about its practicality in performance; in fact in the same chapter one finds some casual remarks that weaken his categorical statements. In paragraph 51 Quantz states that there is a speed between *allegro assai* and *allegretto* which should be used for pieces that cannot stand excessive velocity because of quick runs (*Passagien*). This speed is indicated by the terms *poco allegro*, *vivace*, or *most often* by *allegro* alone, which is Bach's most common tempo mark. The addition of the *allegro* tempo is an important break in the regularity of Quantz's scheme and makes it highly probable that similar compromise speeds might have existed between the other extreme tempo prescriptions.

Most important is a side remark attached to paragraph 50, in which Quantz says that the generation before his own was accustomed to play almost twice as slowly, so that what was called *allegro assai* was played in those bygone days as one would now play *allegretto*. This remark would have to be kept clearly in mind in connection with Johann Sebastian Bach if we want to acknowledge the validity of the idea that our composer belongs spiritually to the generation before Quantz.[13] Indeed, many musicologists are inclined to deny completely the accuracy of relating Quantz's writings to Bach's artistic views. However, even if we were to reduce Quantz's speed designations to almost half, his scheme would still be impractical; it would now be technically possible to play Bach's fastest pieces, but the slowest ones would reach a degree of inertia beyond discussion.

The speeds which Quantz assigns to some French dances also make it evident that his tempi do not represent Bach's period. To believe that Bach could have wanted "entrées, loures, and courantes" to be played pompously (*prächtig*), at the speed of one pulse beat for a quarter note, is as impossible as the record speed of one measure to a pulse for bourrées and rigaudons.[14] So we have to dismiss almost completely any literal application of Quantz's elaborations, and can consider them only as a kind of guide, pointing to the direction from which a general treatment of tempo problems may emerge.

We shall not include detailed reports about tempo fixing by a few French writers of the eighteenth century, because they restrict themselves primarily to the discussion of dance speeds. Aside from the fact that they all differ considerably among themselves and also with Quantz, so that no binding conclusions can be drawn from their writings, we have to

---

[13] In reality Bach was only twelve years older than Quantz. For a full translation of this paragraph see p. 122.

[14] Quantz, paragraph 58.

remember that under Bach's hands each dance gets a stylization that excludes the possibility of making practical use of any of these figures.[15]

That certain aspects of C. P. E. Bach's famous *Essay* no longer represent the spirit of his father's time is rather well known and, in general, correct. Nevertheless, the single paragraph in which he deals with problems of speed is irreproachable in its validity: "The pace of a composition, which is usually indicated by several well-known Italian expressions, is based on its general content as well as on the fastest notes and passages contained in it. Due consideration of these factors will prevent an allegro from being rushed and an adagio from being dragged."[16]

Also interesting to read is a remark by Bach's pupil Kirnberger in the preface to his *Recueil d'airs de danses caracteristiques* (Berlin, 1771). "How is it possible for the performer to give the piece he executes the appropriate expression which the composer imagined if he cannot designate, *with the help of the various types of notes* that occur with the piece exactly which movement and which character are appropriate to each kind of tempo? In order to acquire the necessary properties of good interpretation nothing better can be done by the performers than to practice all kinds of characteristic dances. Each piece of this dance music has its proper rhythm, its caesuras of the same length."[17]

Finally, let us quote from Leopold Mozart's *Versuch einer gründlichen Violinschule*:

This [the explanation of the note values] is only the normal mathematical distribution of a measure, which we call tempo and tactus. Now comes the main thing: the manner of movement. One must not only be able to beat time correctly and evenly, one must also be able to find out from a piece whether it asks for a slow or a somewhat faster motion. One puts before a piece descriptive words, such as *allegro* (gay), *adagio* (slow), etc. But slow and fast also have further gradations. And even if the composer tries to explain the type of motion with additional words, it is impossible to define exactly that mood which he wants to be expressed in the interpretation of his piece. *Therefore one has to find this out from the piece itself, and here one will infallibly recognize a true connoisseur. Every piece of music contains at least one phrase from which it is possible to determine with certainty the type of movement most appropriate to the piece.* Indeed, it should be remembered that if one is only attentive to a piece one is often simply forced into its natural motion. But it is important to know

---

[15] One must use caution in taking information about the speed of dance pieces from books describing dances and dance steps. In Mattheson's book *Das beschützte Orchester* (Hamburg, 1717), vol. II, p. 138, we find this important remark: "An allemande for dancing and one for playing are as different as heaven and earth." Mattheson goes on to say that this is true of all dances except, perhaps, the sarabande.

[16] C. P. E. Bach, *Essay*, p. 151.

[17] Quoted by Yella Pessl, "French Patterns and Their Readings in Bach's Secular Music," *PAMS* (1941), p. 8 (italics mine).

that for this type of knowledge extensive experience and the ability to judge well are prerequisites. Who would contradict me if I count this among the highest achievements of the art of music?[18]

It seems rather obvious that these eighteenth-century documents all reveal—between the lines—the existence of a tradition, still in the possession of the musicians' guild, that brought time signatures and note values, and consequently the affect, into a relation with absolute speed. This relation was doubtless an aftermath of the old methods of notation that were still alive in the sixteenth century and were abandoned only gradually during the seventeenth century.[19] Frederick Dorian, in his *The History of Music in Performance*, goes so far as to state that "Indications for determining the correct time are likewise furnished by the score script itself. Time signatures and notation automatically provide the necessary information for the tempo. That is to say, signs such as 2/2, 3/4, not only indicate the rhythmic disposition of the notes, but simultaneously are definite tempo connotations."[20]

DISTRIBUTION OF TIME SIGNATURES

Although Dorian's blunt statement undoubtedly oversimplifies the problem, at least it shows the direction from which we can start an un-biased investigation. Therefore, let us make a table (Chart 8) that shows how the various time signatures are distributed in Bach's keyboard works. The list is complete, with the exception of a few of those single pieces that form only an appendix to his works. No piece of any distinction is omitted, but dance movements are excluded in order not to overcrowd the list with material that has no relation to our problem. It is well known that all dances have their traditional time signatures that vary only in the case of the gigue, which can appear in 3/8, 6/8, 9/8, 12/8, 12/16, C, or 2/1. The different time signatures for courantes and correntes are symbolized by their names: 3/2 for courantes, 3/8 or 3/4 for correntes. However, those pieces from Bach's suites that do not belong to the common dances, such as "Air," "Scherzo," "Burleska," are included on our list.

We also have omitted the concertos for one or more harpsichords and strings, since almost all of them are transcriptions from violin concertos. The "legality" of giving each of the thirty *Goldberg Variations* a separate

---

[18] (Augsburg, 1756; new ed., Vienna, 1922), section I, part 2, paragraph 7 (italics mine).

[19] See W. Apel, *The Notation of Polyphonic Music*, p. 195. The author gives as the latest example some bars in triple metre, following bars in normal C time from G. See also Muffat's *Apparatus musico-organisticus* (1690), vol. II. Another example from approximately the same date can be found in the last variation of Johann Christian Bach's Sarabande with Variations, republished by Riemann (Steingräber, 1892).

[20] (New York, 1942), p. 143.

CHART 8

The Distribution of Time Signatures in Bach's Keyboard Works
(252 Compositions)

Left portion

Composition[a]	Time Signatures[b]					
	C	3/4	₵	3/8	2/4	Other
Inventions:						
1 C major	x					
2 C minor	x					
3 D major				x		
4 D minor				x		
5 E flat major	x					
6 E major				x		
7 E minor	x					
8 F major		x				
9 F minor		x				
10 G major						9/8
11 G minor	x					
12 A major						12/8
13 A minor	x					
14 B flat major	x					
15 B minor	x					
Sinfonias:						
1 C major	x					12/8
2 C minor	x					
3 D major	x	x				
4 D minor	x					
5 E flat major		x				9/8
6 E major		x				
7 E minor	x					
8 F major	x	x				
9 F minor				x		
10 G major		x				
11 G minor				x		
12 A major	x					
13 A minor						9/16
14 B flat major	x					
15 B minor			x			
French Suites:						
II (Air)	x					
IV (Air)						

Right portion

Composition[a]	Time Signatures[b]					
	C	3/4	₵	3/8	2/4	Other
The *Welltempered Keyboard* volumes I and II:[c,d]						
15 G major	P¹ F¹ P²	P²				P¹–24/16
16 G minor	F¹ F²	F²		F²		F¹–6/8
17 A flat major	F¹ P²	P¹ P²				P¹–6/8 / F²–6/8
18 G sharp minor						F¹–9/8
19 A major	P¹ F²					
20 A minor	F¹ P² F²		F¹ P²			P²–12/8
21 B flat major	P¹	F¹ F²				P¹–9/8
22 B flat minor	P¹		F²			P²–12/16
23 B major	P¹ F¹ P²		P²	F²		F²–3/2
24 B minor	P¹ F¹					
Italian Concerto	3	b	c		a	a²–6/8
French Overture		14	a¹	3½	h	1–9/8 / 1–12/8
Goldberg Variations[e]	3		3½		2	1–12/16 / 2–6/8
C minor Phantasy	x					
Chromatic Phantasy and Fugue	x					
A minor Phantasy and Fugue	F		P			
A minor Phantasy (early)	x	x				
A minor Fugue (with short Prelude)	P					
A minor Prelude and Fugue (later Triple Concerto)	P	F				F–12/16
Aria variata in A minor	x					
Toccatas: E minor	b, c, d					a–3/2
F sharp minor	a, c					b–3/2
C minor	a, b, c					d–6/8
D minor	d					

English Suites:	I						12/8
(preludes	II		x				
only)	III				x		
	IV	x					
	V						6/8
	VI						9/8
Partitas:[c]	I	a					
	II	a^1	a		e	f	
	III		e		a	f	
	IV	a				d	a–9/8
	V		a				
	VI	a^2		a^1, d			
The *Welltempered Keyboard* volumes I and II:[d]							
	1 C major	$P^1 F^1 P^2$				F^2	
	2 C minor	$P^1 F^1$ $P^2 F^2$					
	3 C sharp major	$F^1 P^2$ (½) F^2			$P^1 P^2$ (½)		
	4 C sharp minor			F^1			P^1–6/4 P^2–9/8 F^2–12/16 [P^2–12/8]
	5 D major	$P^1 F^1$		$P^2 F^2$			
	6 D minor	$P^1 F^2$	$F^1 P^2$				
	7 E flat major	$P^1 F^1$		F^2			P^2–9/8
	8 D sharp minor	$F^1 P^2 F^2$					P^1–3/2
	9 E major	F^1	P^2	F^2			P^1–12/8
	10 E minor	P^1	F^1	F^2	P^2		
	11 F major				F^1		P^1–12/8 P^2–3/2 F^2–6/16
	12 F minor	$P^1 F^1$				$P^2 F^2$	
	13 F sharp major	F^1	P^2	F^2			P^1–12/16
	14 F sharp minor	$P^1 F^2$	P^2				F^1–6/4

	D major	a, b, c					d–6/16
	G minor	c, e					a–24/16
							b–3/2
							d–3/2
	G major	a, b					c–6/8
Duets:	E minor				x		
	F major					x	
	G major						12/8
	A minor			x			
Departure Capriccio		a, b, d, e, f	c				
12 Small Preludes:[f]							
	1 C major	x					
	2 C major	x					
	3 C minor		x				
	4 D major	x					
	5 D minor		x				
	6 D minor	x					
	7 E minor		x				
	8 F major	x					
	9 F major	x					
	10 G minor		x				
	11 G minor		x				
	12 A minor						9/8
6 Small Preludes:[f]							
	1 C major	x					
	2 C minor		x				
	3 D minor				x		
	4 D major					x	
	5 E major	x					
	6 E minor				x		
Totals		106½	46	21½	20	12	46[g]

[a] Parts of compositions are considered in the total as well as entire ones. When the whole composition is included under one time signature, it is represented by "x."
[b] The time signatures are given in order of the five most frequent. Compositions under "Other" are listed by the specific time signature.
[c] Movements are indicated by letters in alphabetical order: "a" equals first movement, "b" equals second movement, etc. Superscripts indicate parts of movements.
[d] For the *Welltempered Keyboard* both volumes are combined. "P" equals Prelude, "F" equals Fugue; superscript "1" indicates volume I, superscript "2" indicates volume II. "P" and "F" are also used in other prelude-fugue compositions.
[e] The numerals indicate the number of variations in each time signature; the theme is, of course, included in the figure for 3/4 time.
[f] The numbers follow the Steingräber edition.
[g] Broken down: 9/8—10; 6/8—9; 12/8—8; 3/2—7; 12/16—5; 6/4—2; 6/16—2; 24/16—2; 9/16—1.

place and number may be debatable. In defense it may be said that every variation is an outspoken "character piece" in which the time signature selected by Bach bears a close relation to its spiritual content. Furthermore, each variation is longer than almost any of the "short" preludes, which in our opinion have almost less right to be represented on this list.

The final figures in Chart 8 show to what a surprising extent the pieces in C time are in the majority. They comprise about 42 per cent of the entire output, a figure that would have been even higher had we omitted the thirteen variations in 3/4 time in the *Goldberg Variations*; the variations bring the pieces written in 3/4 time to second place, with 18 per cent. Next on the list are those in ₵ time with 8.5 per cent, and in 3/8 time with 8 per cent.

To make this basic material more meaningful, we have separated it into a series of tables, putting together those compositions that have the same time signature and express the same affect—hence those that might be played at similar speeds (see Appendix B). For each work we have used the minimum number of notes necessary for easy identification. This time, however, we have added examples of dance pieces and harpsichord concertos wherever they might be helpful for comparison; sometimes we have included the first bars of pieces other than keyboard music in order to show the similarity of the tempo problems throughout the entire works of Bach. We also found it illuminating to indicate, for most of the pieces, metronomizations from some current standard editions; these reveal strikingly the vastness of the disagreement about speed among the Bach authorities.

Whoever is familiar enough with Bach's keyboard works so that a few representative notes can recall to him the wealth of beauty and wisdom contained in each composition cannot pass his eyes over these tables without some feeling of awe and humility. Indeed, we feel a little embarrassed to have to expose these works to such cold-blooded examination.

Before we go into a systematic inquiry about the problems of speed, let us make just a few random observations about the tempo tables in Appendix B. Starting perhaps with the tables of works in 3/8 time (Va–c), we notice that quite a few pieces are built with almost identical rhythmical organization. There is no difference in patterns between the Fugue in F major, *W.K.* I (Va, 4), the Fugue in B minor, *W.K.* II (Va, 8), the chorus "Sind Blitze, sind Donner" (Va, 24) from the *St. Matthew Passion*, the Passepied of the Fifth English Suite (Vc, 1), or the French Overture (Vc, 3). Another group of nearly identical pieces is represented by the Prelude in E minor, *W.K.* II (Va, 6), the Invention in D minor (Va, 2), the Fantasia from the Third Partita (Va, 11), the Organ Toccata in F major (Va, 21) and the "Little" Prelude in D minor (Va, 16; No. 3 of the six "Little" Preludes). In this time signature thirty-second notes are nearly absent, with the exception of two pieces in E minor, the Corrente of the Sixth Partita (Vc, 8) and Duet I (Vb, 4).

That similar rhythmical organization is often paralleled by identical keys is a fact of which we should take notice.[21] It is also interesting that the figures played by the violin in the middle section of the last movement of the Violin Concerto in E major (Va, 20) are the same ones that predominate in the E major Invention (Vb, 1; NB). Moreover, there is a rhythmic relation between the last movements of the Harpsichord Concerto in F minor (Va, 18), and the Violin Concerto in E major in spite of the gulf between them in key and mood.

If we look for a moment at the metronome marks that have been given to a few of these pieces, we can make some startling observations. The Passepied of the Fifth English Suite is marked by Bischoff at ♩. = 76; the Passepied of the Fifth Partita, however, is marked ♩. = 60; and the Passepied of the French Overture ♩. = 63. What might have caused Bischoff to make such fine differentiations for identical types of dance pieces? The Fugue in B minor, *W.K.* II, is marked by Bischoff at ♩. = 54, but by Czerny ♩. = 76, a rather large difference of opinion. The Fugue in F major, *W.K.* I, however, which uses exactly the same rhythmical scheme as the B minor Fugue, shows both editors in closer agreement: Czerny indicates ♩. = 66, Bischoff ♩. = 60. Since both these fugues are obviously passepieds, according to these metronome marks the range of speed for passepieds is from ♩. = 54 to ♩. = 76. How would it be if we were to try all these pieces at a unified speed in the middle of both extremes, perhaps at ♩. = 65? The experiment might be worthwhile, but for the moment let us put it into the back of our minds as an avenue of approach to be used later on. However, before leaving the 3/8 table we should notice that the two pieces in this group which do make use of thirty-seconds are marked by Bischoff at greatly divergent speeds: ♪ = 96 for the Duet in E minor and ♪ = 132 for the Corrente in E minor from the Sixth Partita.

Turning now to Table VIa, which contains works in 6/8 time, we find a series of compositions so completely like those of the 3/8 table as far as rhythmical organization is concerned that by hearing alone we would probably not realize that they are not in 3/8 time; for example, the Fugue in G major, *W.K.* I (VIa, 1), and the Prelude from the Fifth English Suite (VIa, 3). The same is true for the 12/8 group, of which the

---

[21] To avoid anticipating here the remarks that should be reserved for Chapter 8, Symbolism, in which tonality problems will be treated, we will simply add "NB" when we find such similarities during the ensuing discussions.

Prelude in F major, *W.K.* I (VIIIa, 2) and the Invention in A major (VIIIa, 1) are shaped almost identically with the 3/8 pieces. We also see that the pieces in 12/16 time bear a decided relation to those in 12/8 time: the sixteenth note simply substitutes for the eighth. However, in 6/8 and 12/8 time we find several pieces in which sixteenths are either entirely or nearly completely absent, such as the Fugue in G sharp minor, *W.K.* II (VIb, 1) the Gigue from the Fourth French Suite (VIc, 4), the Prelude in E major, *W.K.* I (VIIIb, 2), and the Prelude from the First English Suite in A major (VIIIb, 5), which is very closely related to the Prelude in A (NB), *W.K.* II (VIIIb, 4). Again we ask in vain why Bischoff wants ♩. = 69 for the Prelude from the Suite and ♩. = 92 for the Prelude from the *Welltempered Keyboard.*

Looking at the 4/4 tables we quickly discover the inherent relation between all those first movements that are in concerto-grosso form: those of the Brandenburg Concertos 1, 2, 3, 5, and 6 (Id, 19–23), the Harpsichord Concerto in D minor (Id, 10), the concertos for two and three harpsichords (Id, 13–15), the Violin Concerto in E major (Id, 24), the Concerto for Two Violins in D minor (Id, 25), and the Prelude of the Fourth English Suite (Id, 3). To this list we can add from the 2/4 table the first movement of the Violin Concerto in A minor (IIIa, 9) and that of the Italian Concerto (IIIa, 3). A brief look at the 3/4 table shows us, if we just listen to the pieces that are really "little concerti grossi"—the Prelude of the A minor English Suite (IVa, 6), the Fugue of the Chromatic Phantasy in D minor (IVa, 10; NB), the last movement of the Harpsichord Concerto in D minor (IVa, 24), and that of the Concerto for Two Violins in D minor (IVa, 25)—that through all these pieces there swings one rhythmical pendulum, identical with that of the concertos just mentioned on the 4/4 table. Does it not seem that all these pieces cry for a somewhat unified speed?

Other strange observations can be made from the 4/4 tables. Landshoff calls the first Sinfonia *andante* at ♩ = 80 and the Sinfonia in D major *allegretto* at ♩ = 76. Czerny states that the speed ♩ = 80 is *andante con moto* when applied to the Fugue in G minor, *W.K.* I; *lento moderato* for the Prelude in E flat major, *W.K.* I; *allegretto moderato* for the Fugue in C minor, *W.K.* I. But for the Prelude in B flat major, *W.K.* I, he calls the speed ♩ = 84 *vivace*! Bischoff states that ♩ = 104 is *lento* for the Fugue in B flat minor, *W.K.* I, but *allegro* for the Fugue in E flat major, *W.K.* I. The speed of ♩ = 108 he calls *allegro* for the Prelude in F sharp minor, *W.K.* I, but *allegretto* for the Prelude in A flat major, *W.K.* I; ♩ = 100 is *molto moderato* for the Fugue in C sharp minor, *W.K.* I, but *allegro* for the Fugue in C sharp major, *W.K.* I.

Further rather remarkable differences of opinion are found in regard to the proper speed for the following pieces: for the Invention in C major Keller suggests ♩ = 63, but Czerny ♩ = 120; the Invention in B flat major is marked ♪ = 88 by Keller but ♩ = 88 by Czerny; the Prelude in B flat minor, *W.K.* I, is marked ♪ = 92 by Bischoff and Czerny, ♪ = 56 by Keller. In the *Goldberg Variations* Kirkpatrick suggests ♪ = 46 for Variation 25, where Bischoff wants ♪ = 84. The figures for Variation 8 are ♩ = 86 by Kirkpatrick and ♩ = 120 by Bischoff and Czerny. In addition to the conflict between editors, let us notice the highly divergent speeds at which the same editor often marks similar pieces. To those of the *Goldberg Variations* that display virtuosity, Kirkpatrick gives the following assignments: ♩ = 94 in Variation 1; ♪ = 156 in Variation 5; ♩ = 86 in Variation 8, 80 in Variation 14, 108 in Variation 17, 86 in Variation 20, 102 in Variation 23, and 80 in Variation 28. For the six allemandes in the English Suites, which are surprisingly uniform in character, Bischoff makes the following distinctions: Suite I, ♩ = 76; II, ♩ = 92; III, ♩ = 88; IV, ♩ = 76; V, ♩ = 80; VI, ♩ = 72. Apparently Bischoff believes that no allemande should be played at the same speed as any of its sister pieces.

Where can we find a good starting place for seeking out the system followed by the musicians of the eighteenth century? It does not make sense to begin with those pieces that carry tempo information from Bach's own hand: they are not numerous enough to allow us to draw any convincing conclusions, and furthermore, what type of conclusions could be drawn from words as vague as the Italian tempo marks? How simple our task would be if it were necessary only to distribute Bach's compositions among the four basic speeds of Quantz; unfortunately, as we already proved, Quantz's speeds are impracticable in their literal execution. However, it is hard to think that Quantz would have formulated such an elaborate scheme if it were not related at all to the contemporary tradition, and we would certainly be somewhat better off with four or five basic speeds for Bach's works than with the dozens of varieties suggested by present-day editions.[22]

PIECES IN 4/4 TIME (Table I)

That a speed as basic as the "pace of the human pulse," which is identical with "the pace of a man walking slowly," has to be found is obvious. Since the vast majority of Bach's keyboard compositions are in 4/4 time, we may try to find our basic pace on this table; indeed, at first glance we see several pieces which, because of their note values and affects, seem to

---

[22] The fifth speed is the "common *allegro*" that Quantz placed so casually between *allegretto* and *allegro assai*, without letting it participate in the "multiplying system."

want a "moderate" speed. After a most careful and repeated examination, we assigned forty-five pieces out of 103.5[23] written in 4/4 time to the speed "*moderato*," which may be represented by the metronome mark of $\downarrow$ = 80 (see Table Ia).

At this point of our first metronomization, it must be understood that we are not asking for a religious adherence to exactly the same speed for all these pieces. Small modifications in one or the other direction are absolutely justifiable, according to the temperament of the performer and even the instrument on which he is playing: harpsichord, clavichord, or piano. Since the tone of the piano lacks any kind of "individual character" that can be compared to the "halo" which surrounds every tone on the clavichord and, to a certain degree, on the harpsichord, a somewhat greater speed for playing on the piano might seem desirable. We frankly admit preferring $\downarrow$ = 84 as a "moderate" speed on the piano.

It will prove highly instructive to play and replay for oneself substantial parts of the pieces found on Table Ia, in order to regain that approach to a piece of music which was the traditional and natural one in Bach's period: the grasping of the affect whose proper representation was the goal of the composer. In Chapter 7, Articulation, we will deal at greater length with the subtleties of the doctrine of affections (*Affektenlehre*). For our present purposes it will be sufficient to be familiar with the "basic condition" of the human soul that was generally expressed by moderate speed; this is most accurately represented by the word "moderate." The more often we play through these selections, the greater will become our admiration for the overwhelming richness of Bach's palette, especially if we try to build for ourselves a kind of "inner crescendo" from the perhaps least interesting piece, Prelude 14, *W.K.* I (Ia, 18)—which acquired this stigma by nearly general acclaim—through Numbers 23, 20, and 6, to the heights, or should we say depths of Numbers 30, 24, and 16. Let us bring to the attention of those who play these selections that two of them, Numbers 24 and 16, are the only ones in which note values of sixteenths are almost completely absent.

Some of the compositions on this table make use of a rhythmical and expressive device that deserves special mention, since we will find the same device later on in the ¢ and 2/4 tables: it is the so-called "sigh motive," a repeated note followed by a falling second, either major or (mostly) minor, ♪ ♫. This plastic motive, which expresses a true

---

moderato affect (we sigh only when we feel "moderately badly"; utter hopelessness and sighing do not go well together), is best known to the music lover from the popular F minor Prelude, *W.K.* II, in 2/4 time. On Table Ia we find it in the Invention in C minor, the Prelude in A major, *W.K.* I, the Prelude in G sharp minor, *W.K.* II, the Phantasy in C minor, and the last movement of the Concerto in C major for Two Harpsichords, called *Allegro* (Nos. 2, 20, 30, 33, 39). How important this motive is as a means for determination of tempo will become apparent later.

Eleven selections on this table contradict in essential attitudes the spirit of moderation: Numbers 12, 13, 19, 21, 22, 27, 28, 32, 33, 37, and 39. All of these might be called "sparkling" or "filled with energy," culminating in the real "fury" of Number 32, the Fugue in A minor, *W.K.* II. It may at first seem baffling to the reader to find these pieces on this table, where they apparently do not belong in regard to affect; but, as we will remember from the quotations from C. P. E. Bach, Kirnberger, and Leopold Mozart, the note values are also a decisive factor in finding the right speed.

A closer examination of our "dissenting" examples shows that we can divide them into two categories. Numbers 12, 13, 19, 21, and 39 are all built on the rhythm ♪♪♩ with the accent on the eighth note, the rhythm of the anapaest. This rhythm, which is generally considered to have more energy than its reverse form, the dactyl, was used by the ancient Greeks as the favorite rhythm for marching and battle songs. Whenever Bach uses the anapaest pattern in abundance, for instance, in the first movement of the Third Brandenburg Concerto, the result is always that of "brisk energy."[24] In our examples this rhythm is not used quite as abundantly, but still often enough to create the effect of "subdued energy" at *moderate* speed. For the remaining Numbers 22, 27, 28, 32, 33, and 37, another common denominator can be detected: they all make use of note values faster than sixteenths, either triplets of sixteenths or thirty-seconds. The culmination of this group, as we already stated, comes in the furious explosion of the A minor Fugue, which is nearly unique in Bach's work.

At first the two types of compositions at moderate speed, types which we could classify as "passive" *moderato* and "active" *moderato*, might seem arbitrarily chosen. For the conclusions supporting the choice, I must ask the reader to wait until we have studied all the pieces in C time.

---

[24] Other pieces are the Fugue of the Chromatic Phantasy, the second movement of the Violin-Harpsichord Sonata in A major, which is in *alla breve* time, the "Et expecto" from the B minor Mass, and so on. The sporadic appearance of anapaest figures in pieces like Numbers 1a, 3, 6, and 9 has, of course, nothing to do with the problem.

9

I must also warn most strongly against any resentment toward tempo designations that stems merely from the habit of having hitherto played one or the other piece at a totally different speed. The fundamental differences of opinions about tempo among the most widely acknowledged Bach editors prove only too well that any real foundation for establishing tempi does not yet exist. Our heritage of tempo conceptions, which we owe to the highly individualistic keyboard literature of the nineteenth century, has made us almost incapable of dealing rationally with the completely different tempo problems of the earlier periods. In spite of the relatively short time that separates us from Bach's period, Bach research belongs to the domain of musical archeology. If one has not "lived with Bach" for many years, one is simply not ready to throw overboard as many well-established traditions as one must when embarking on such a study.

There is even more evidence for grouping the pieces on Table Ib under a similar tempo than there was for those on Table Ia. Here we have brought together those compositions in 4/4 time that seem to require less speed than *allegretto-moderato*, namely, those which Quantz assigned to *adagio cantabile*. The unity of affect among these pieces is so complete that it cannot be overlooked. They maintain a kind of inner tranquillity, an absence of emotion or "longing"; it is an equanimity of mind that is almost the private property of Bach, not found in the work of any earlier or later composer. What our rather clumsy words mean is better understood when we play the themes of these fugues in Table Ib, one immediately after the other: Numbers 12, 13, 14, 16, 18, and 19 (to which we may add the Fugato of the D major Toccata, No. 24). All these pieces, which could be described by the popular definition of a fugue as "a serious discussion of a serious matter among serious people," appear to the layman to be perhaps the most drastic examples of "absolute music." These are pieces that cannot be approached with any display of personal emotion, pieces that can never become his friends in the way that he might "just adore" this or that composition by Beethoven or Chopin. Therefore he leaves them mostly to the professional, believing that only he can understand what there is to be appreciated; whereas the more advanced Bach lover will probably find in these seemingly indifferent pieces the glow of an inner warmth less obvious but more consistent than that found in pieces of much more popular appeal. Through them he will learn to understand the language of Bach's supreme epic, the *Art of the Fugue*.

If we now look more carefully at the pieces of Table Ib, we find only one work of totally divergent character, the Fugue in D major, *W.K.* I, Number 6. However, this piece need not cause us any trouble since it represents the French-overture type. We will discuss it in connection with other overtures by Bach, which offer a special problem. In the "meditative" fugues we find very few note values other than eighth notes and sixteenths, but Numbers 2, 8, 11, 17, 20, and 22 use thirty-seconds in somewhat larger quantities. We could, for that reason, almost call them a group within a group, in which an inner link between Numbers 2, 11, and 21 cannot be overlooked: their keys are B flat major, G minor, and B flat major. Number 7, the Prelude in D minor, *W.K.* I, is the only one that uses triplets of sixteenths. In Number 10 we find, to our surprise, the anapaest rhythm discussed in connection with Table Ia. Fortunately it shows its new meaning—dragging burdensomely along—so clearly that interpreting it any other way is not possible. Finally, let us mention that one authentic tempo mark, *andante* (No. 22), and two *adagio* marks from rather reliable copies (Nos. 25 and 26), remind us of the small difference in meaning between these two Italian words, to express which only a minimal modification in speed is necessary; in fact the prevalence of eighth notes in the two *adagio* pieces takes care of this adjustment automatically.

What speed should be used for all these pieces? That Quantz's recipe "twice as slow" (♩ = 40) is complete nonsense can be proved in a minute by a practical experiment with a metronome. However, since Quantz talks about another tempo group, *adagio assai*, which should move twice again as slowly, therefore at ♪ = 40, and since there are a few pieces by Bach that are obviously slower than those of Table Ib (we have put them together in Table Ic), the solution for our tempo problem is not difficult to find.

An experiment with a metronome shows that the very slowest pieces, those on Table Ic, can just stand a tempo close to ♩ = 40, but that this speed is the limit in slowness for Bach's music.[25] Logically, the right speed

---

[25] In spite of the many startling disagreements among editors about the tempi of individual pieces, they all, to our knowledge, seem to avoid going beyond this extreme with three notable exceptions: Kirkpatrick suggests ♪ = 46 for the famous Variation 25 of the *Goldberg Variations*, and ♪ = 54 for Variation 15; Keller prescribes ♪ = 56 for the Prelude in B flat minor, *W.K.* I. These three indications strongly contradict those of other editors. For Variation 25 we find that Bischoff suggests ♪ = 84, Czerny, ♪ = 88; for Variation 15 Bischoff and Czerny agree on ♪ = 108; and for the Prelude they agree on ♪ = 92. Although Variation 25 is of unique beauty, even in Bach, we feel unable to share the opinion of the noted editor of the *Goldberg Variations*, whose excellent edition (Schirmer) is a landmark in scholarship, that this piece deserves a unique tempo. Of course we cannot claim that Bach would have written a special tempo mark for it had he wanted to distinguish it from the other variations, but it is noteworthy that he did prescribe *andante* for Variation 15 where a misunderstanding might easily have occurred. This hints that he might have added *largo* or *adagio* for Variation 25 if he had so desired. However, the general texture of this variation is so closely related to that of Variation 13, marked by Kirkpatrick at ♩ = 40, that we see no reason for assigning to Variation 25 a speed so enormously different. Since Variation 15 is called *andante* and not *adagio*, the tempo designation of ♪ = 54 seems to be beyond the province of the indication. On p. 130 we will have more to say about the problem of Variation 25.

for pieces that are just too slow for the $\downarrow$ = 80 speed, but on the other hand clearly distinguishable from a still slower group ($\downarrow$ = 40), should be the speed $\downarrow$ = 60. A metronome test proves immediately that there is no piece on Table Ib that sounds mistreated when played at this speed.

Nothing special needs to be said about the pieces on Table Ic, which are the truly slow compositions in C time. The only remarkable feature is their small quantity. The fact that five of them are distinguished by specifications of *adagio, largo,* or *grave,* while only two carry no tempo marks, makes the conclusion almost inevitable that in Bach's time very slow speeds were rare and needed a special warning.

Do not think for a moment that we have lost track of the fact that all our assignments to speed groups have been made by arbitrary proceedings. However, let us postpone counterchecking our method until we have finished the investigation of pieces in C time. For the pieces in 4/4 time *faster* than moderato, Quantz is even less of a help than before. Although he recognizes two speeds slower than the basic speed of the human pulse, he reports only one doubling of tempo, *allegro assai,* in which $\downarrow$ = 160. For pieces in which sixteenths predominate,[26] this is mechanically impossible on the harpsichord. However, Quantz did allude to an intermediate speed, the common *allegro,* which stands between *allegretto* and *allegro assai.* We need only remember the experiment we made with his recommendations for slow speeds, look over the relatively few "fast" pieces, on Tables Id and Ie, and we will quickly find the answer to our problem.

It is not difficult to discover those pieces that ask for the greatest speed. Either they carry the *presto* mark (Id, 8; Ie, 3) or, if unmarked, they have to be virtuoso pieces, such as the *perpetuum mobile* D major Prelude, *W.K.* I (Ie, 2). Experiments with the metronome show us that the limit of speed, determined by the fastest notes of a piece—as recommended by C. P. E. Bach—is definitely around $\downarrow$ = 120 for the harpsichord. This corresponds exactly with our findings in regard to slow pieces, where we discovered that the slowest tolerable tempo for Bach is half as slow as that recommended by Quantz. Herewith we can conclude that the fastest tempo, *allegro assai,* should be around $\downarrow$ = 120, and consequently that the probable speed for pieces of common *allegro* character would then be about $\downarrow$ = 100. It must be understood, of course, that all these speeds are approximate evaluations allowing for flexibility in both directions.

If we now examine in detail Tables Id and Ie, our first observation —and for many readers a rather surprising one—is that the number of

---

[26] *Allegro* pieces by Bach that use only quarter and eighth notes are always written in ₵ time; for example, the final movement of the Italian Concerto, marked *presto.*

fast pieces is very small: there are only five truly fast ones and not more than eighteen pieces belonging to the common *allegro* group. The limit of speed, which, for the harpsichord at least, we set at ♩ = 120–126, is nearly always respected by Bischoff and Keller; each goes beyond it only once, Bischoff in the D major Prelude, *W.K.* I, with ♩ = 132, and Keller in the *Presto* of the E minor Prelude, *W.K.* I, with ♩ = 126. That Czerny, the master of finger dexterity and velocity, often gives the highest speed suggestions, should cause us neither to wonder nor to be concerned. We might almost praise his moderation when we see that he reaches Quantz's top speed only once, in the *Presto* of the E minor Prelude, for which he suggests ♩ = 80. Otherwise he goes as far as ♩ = 144 only once, for the Prelude in C minor, *W.K.* I, and once to ♩ = 132, for the Prelude in D major, *W.K.* I. Although, as we have said before, there is no reason to take Czerny as a Bach authority, in fairness we should mention that there are more than a few cases in which his metronome mark is not the fastest given by other editors.

Among the pieces that give the *allegro* table its special flavor, the most outstanding are no doubt the first movements of various concertos. For this reason we also included there the first bars of five Brandenburg Concertos, the E major Violin Concerto, and the Concerto in D minor for Two Violins, as well as the beginnings of the Italian Concerto and the Violin Concerto in A minor (Id, 19–27). Although both last pieces are written in 2/4 time, their "inner swing" is obviously the same as that of the 4/4 *allegro* movements. This confirms that there are clear links leading from one time signature to another, an observation already hinted at in our first casual survey. Of the compositions on Table Id that are not concerto movements, the Prelude of the Fourth English Suite (No. 3, which received the strange tempo indication *vitement* from someone other than Bach) and the Toccata in G major (No. 6, called "Concerto" in an old copy) are actually concerto-grosso movements in form and therefore belong to the concerto group. Nearly all the other compositions, especially the toccatas, are written in *concertante* style. Hardly anywhere else on these tables will we find as large a group of pieces with such a homogeneous character, and the urge for a uniform treatment of all these pieces in regard to tempo seems so obvious that it simply cannot be overlooked.

We now have a difficult problem to bring to the foreground. Our modern conception that the ₵ sign indicates the doubling of the basic speed, although acknowledged by Quantz, proves to have only limited validity in regard to the works of Bach; he used C and ₵ interchangeably, as has been known for quite some time. We see from Table Id that all the first movements of the Brandenburg Concertos and some movements of other concertos are written in ₵, but still others, such as the first movements of the two concertos for two harpsichords, are not. The first movement of the D minor Harpsichord Concerto has come to us in an older version in C time, but that which we consider to be the final version is written in ₵.[27] The famous Double Concerto in D minor for Two Violins has the time signature ₵ in the violin version and C in the two-harpsichord version, with autographs for verification in both cases. That in all these pieces the "inner beat" is 4/4 and not 2/2 is too evident to need proof; no conductor could hold the players together by beating *alla breve*. Therefore these pieces have been included on the 4/4 table.

It does not lower our admiration for the two preludes that begin the short Table Ie if we call them "studies in velocity." In addition, the Fugue of the G minor Toccata, which uses triplets of eighth notes only, instead of the customary sixteenths of the other toccatas, deserves a place on this table. With somewhat less conviction we included the *Presto* from the D minor Toccata, although only out of respect for the *presto* mark found in contemporary copies. It can be played at a speed around $\downarrow = 120$, even though in some measures the left hand has quite an assignment. However, to do the same with the *Presto e staccato* of the F sharp minor Toccata is impossible for musical reasons: the texture is too complicated to be heard at that speed. *Nolens volens* we had to give it a place on Table Id, 8, although we are not happy about placing two movements marked *presto* on different tables.

Before we discuss the entire output of true ₵ pieces, we should try to make a résumé of our experiences with the compositions in 4/4 time, and especially try to discover possible sources of error in our individual assignments to the various speeds. A few conclusions seem to us beyond the realm of "trial by jury," particularly the placement of limits for slow and fast speeds around $\downarrow = 40$ and $\downarrow = 120$, in contrast to Quantz's suggestions of $\flat = 40$ and $\downarrow = 160$. We do not want to argue whether a speed slower than $\downarrow = 40$ might still be tolerable, since this is a matter of taste; however, there can be no doubt about the impossibility of $\downarrow = 160$ because the mechanism of the harpsichord gives sufficient proof. He who might think that $\downarrow = \pm 120$ is too slow a limit for high speed should be warned by a paragraph from Quantz, already mentioned on page 107, which we now translate in full:

In bygone days everything was played twice as slowly as in our time: what was called *allegro assai, presto, furioso*, etc., was written the same way but was played not faster than one writes and plays an *allegretto* nowadays. The many fast notes in the instrumental pieces of former German composers thus looked much more formidable than they really sounded. The French composers of

---

[27] No autograph exists for this composition.

our time have generally kept this type of medium speed for vivacious pieces even now.[28]

If we want to maintain that Quantz's general opinions cover a period spiritually different from Bach's, an opinion which we share only with great reservation since there is no authoritative answer to the problem, this paragraph is of greatest importance. It reveals, too, how loosely Quantz used terms like "twice as slowly," which cannot have had a literal meaning, for who would play a piece such as Bach's Prelude in D major, *W.K.* I, at ♩ = 80! Furthermore, this would not stand up against Forkel's description of Bach's playing, that in general he took the tempi for his pieces "very vivaciously" (*sehr lebhaft*).[29]

If we have succeeded in finding five distinguishable speeds between ♩ = 40 and ♩ = 120, which makes the result of our examination stand very close to Quantz's fundamental statements, the figures 40, 60, 80, 100, and 120 offer themselves very naturally as a condensation—or better, compression—of Quantz's system. I hope it has been made sufficiently clear that we do not want to insist that every piece can invariably be attributed to only one inflexible speed. Especially between the speeds of ♩ = 60 and ♩ = 80, "in-between" or even "exchange" possibilities might easily be found, depending on the temperament of the individual. We can foresee that here and there many people would prefer speeds faster than those indicated in this book. Let us emphasize, however, that one must take into serious consideration the person who is playing: a virtuoso, a student, or an amateur. Especially in regard to Bach's Inventions, one cannot stress strongly enough that they were written for people whom Bach called "beginners." This should explain the relatively slow speeds to which we have assigned them. A modern piano virtuoso can certainly play Schumann's "Wild Horseman" at a terrific speed without any feeling of a truly wild ride, while a child who has just reached "grade two" in piano playing will be able to imagine the allusion of Schumann's title even at *allegretto* speed. In the final analysis let us point out that our chief goal has been and is to free Bach's keyboard compositions from being played at innumerable individual speeds, and to bring the Bach player to meditate most seriously about the *true affect* expressed in each piece he plays, as well as in its numerous sister pieces. The more he knows about the other pieces expressing similar attitudes, the better his performance will become, just as our conception of the world around us achieves a clearer shape when the unity between microcosmos and macrocosmos begins to have some meaning for us.

In addition to the true affect, which was always the most significant

---

[28] Quantz, *Versuch*, XVII, 7, paragraph 50.
[29] *Über Johann Sebastian Bach's Leben, Kunst und Kunstwerke*, p. 35.

factor in assigning a composition to a particular speed group, the note values involved also played an important role in our decisions. The necessity of considering this factor became apparent when we assigned pieces like the D sharp minor Fugue, *W.K.* I, and the Prelude in B minor of the same volume to the speed ♩ = ±80. It arose again when we decided to place the *Adagios* of the Toccatas in G major and C minor on the *andante* table, Ib, to which they do not seem to belong.[30] The case of the Prelude in B minor, *W.K.* I, is especially puzzling, since it is the only piece on the *allegretto* table that carries the prescription *andante*. However, it is possible to find a rational explanation for these instinctive adjustments.

All four pieces just mentioned share the feature of moving in eighth notes rather than sixteenths. Transferring them to a faster group than the one to which they seem to belong, at least according to the Italian tempo marks given to three of them, is supported by the remark from Quantz, cited on page 105, that if an *adagio cantabile* consists only of quarter notes, the quarter note gets one pulse (instead of the eighth). This really means that any piece in this category that consists only of quarter notes should be transferred to the *allegretto* group. We treated the B minor Prelude in a similar way quite instinctively, finding that because of the lack of sixteenths, it sounded terribly clumsy at ♩ = 60. But why Bach distinguished this Prelude with a tempo mark and did not do the same with the Fugue in D sharp minor, *W.K.* I, we are unable to answer. It is interesting to notice that in the so-called "Autograph D," described by Spitta[31] and also by Bischoff, the B minor Prelude has *no* tempo indication while the Fugue is marked *largo*.

Now we might find an additional explanation for the unusually high percentage of tempo marks—five out of seven—on the pieces of Table Ic. Perhaps the reason for it is that, with the exception of the Sinfonia in F minor, all of them look to the unsuspecting eye as if they were normal *moderato* pieces.[32] Again we have to ask why Bach did not care to give tempo marks to the Sinfonia in F minor and to the Prelude in B flat minor, *W.K.* I. Are the three different rhythmical levels in the famous Sinfonia (quarter notes for theme I, eighth notes for theme II, sixteenth and thirty-second notes for theme III) clear enough to make a wrong speed impossible?[33] Is the true affect of the Prelude obvious enough to fulfill the same purpose? We have even asked ourselves whether possibly

---

[30] See p. 119.

[31] *Bach*, vol. II, p. 837.

[32] The (authentic) slurs in the B minor Fugue could easily lead to the misunderstanding that this Fugue belongs to the group of pieces using the sigh motive, discussed on p. 116.

[33] How much less conspicuous are the three rhythmical levels of Bach's only other composition with a similar construction, the Prelude in A major, *W.K.* I; its levels are differentiated by quarter notes, eighth and sixteenth notes, and syncopations.

it is wrong to place both these pieces on the table of slowest speed. All editors have given the Sinfonia tempo marks closer to ♩ = 50 than to ♩ = 40. When we play the B flat minor Prelude unpretentiously and intimately on the clavichord,[34] it sounds more convincing to us even at a speed close to ♩ = 60[35] than it does at the fantastically slow speed suggested by Keller, ♪ = 56, which can be played only with a "false" pathos certainly foreign to the Bach period. Yet what is really true in regard to both these pieces can probably only be judged by a musician who has grown up in the spiritual mentality of the eighteenth century.

Our lengthy discussion of all the problems encountered in studying Bach's compositions in 4/4 time will considerably shorten our investigations in other time signatures. For further examinations we may apply the same tools that proved to be so helpful for the classification thus far: the exploration of the true affect and the conclusions to be drawn from the note values.

PIECES IN ₵ TIME (Table II)

We have already mentioned Bach's habit of using the ₵ sign in such a way that it does not always designate true *alla breve* motion. On Table IIa we have put down those pieces in which *two beats a measure* are the moving unit. That the inner relation of Numbers 1–13 (perhaps with the exception of 4 and 5) is as strong as the exterior similarity of note values becomes immediately apparent. In addition, two links between the *alla breve* and 4/4 tables show us that *moderato*, the speed of the human pulse, is common to both signatures. (In *alla breve*, of course, the indication is ♩ = 80.) First, the second theme of the famous Fugue in C sharp minor, *W.K.* I (IIa, 1), which has three obbligato subjects, corresponds literally with the third theme of the only other fugue with three subjects, the Fugue in F sharp minor, *W.K.* II (Ia, 29). Furthermore, the Fugue in F sharp major, *W.K.* II (IIa, 5), makes ample use of the sigh motive found so frequently on Table Ia, which is logically written here in double values.

Three pieces carry tempo indications, of which the *alla breve* for the last movement of the Triple Concerto (IIa, 12) has no particular significance. The unauthentic *allegro* on the last movement of the Concerto in C major for Three Harpsichords (No. 13) could tempt us to transfer this piece to a higher speed if the runs of sixteenth notes in the harpsichord

---

[34] The selection of the clavichord is justified by the fact that this Prelude is clearly written "after" a Prelude in F major from Kaspar Ferdinand Fischer's *Musikalisches Blumenbüschlein*, which is reserved by the author for clavichord (see p. 21).

[35] In this respect it is of great importance to note that we will find the same melodic line, but with doubled note values, in the Prelude in B flat minor (NB!), *W.K.* II, which we have assigned to the speed group of ♩ = 60 on Table IIb.

parts did not make this technically impossible. Somewhat puzzling, however, is Number 7, the Prelude in B minor, *W.K.* II. This piece has come to us, through "Altnikols copy I," in a version in 4/4 time without any tempo indication, and written in values twice as fast—obviously an authentic earlier version.[36] In this form, the patterns used resemble very much the Invention in B flat major (Ib, 2), which might incline us to assign the piece to $\downarrow = 60$ for the $\mathbb{C}$ version. On the other hand, the fairly frequent appearance of the well-known sigh motive would bring this Prelude, for reasons of stylistic coincidence, into the speed group $\downarrow = 80$. Because of the many sixteenth notes and because of the weight of Bach's authentic *allegro* prescription, we think that the faster of the two tempi, $\downarrow = 80$, is preferable. This way the piece corresponds in speed with the last movement of the Concerto in C major for Three Harpsichords (IIa, 13), which also uses sixteenths and has *allegro* marked in contemporary copies. Furthermore, a comparison with the Prelude in B minor, *W.K.* I (Ia, 24), called *andante* by Bach and timed by us, for very special reasons, at $\downarrow = 80$, makes the juxtaposition of *allegro* at $\downarrow = 80$ and *andante* at $\downarrow = 80$ very convincing.

The two compositions that we assign to a slower pace on Table IIb need only a brief discussion. That the right speed for the Fugue in B flat minor, *W.K.* I, is not $\downarrow = 40$ but $\downarrow = 60$ is made evident by the absence of eighth notes; for the Prelude in the same key from the second volume, one might still feel at first glance that the slower speed would be justifiable. Remember that we felt equally doubtful about the right speed for the Prelude in B flat minor, *W.K.* I (Ic, 2), which has the main melodic line in common with the Prelude of *W.K.* II. It is hard to believe that this coincidence is accidental, because in the B minor Fugue, *W.K.* II, Bach obviously cites some bars of the B minor Fugue of *W.K.* I, which must have a symbolic meaning.[37]

What speed to give to the *Presto* movement of the Italian Concerto (IIc, 1), which is the only really fast piece in the *alla breve* group as far as compositions for keyboard instruments are concerned, may perhaps best be decided by comparing it with the four compositions placed beneath it on the table for this purpose. It is most closely related to the final movement of the Fourth Brandenburg Concerto (IIc, 2), which is also marked *presto*. For reasons of clarity and because of the frequent appearance of the anapaest rhythm, $\downarrow = 100$ seems an appropriate

---

[36] We hardly need mention the numerous cases in which Bach changed the basic metre of a composition. Especially notable cases are the Gigue of the Sixth Partita, which was transferred to 2/1 from $\mathbb{C}$ as it appears in the *Notebook for Anna Magdalena Bach*, and the frequent examples in the *Art of the Fugue*.

[37] Compare bars 19 and 20 of the Fugue in B minor, *W.K.* I, with bars 86–90 of the Fugue in B minor, *W.K.* II. For more details on these coincidences see p. 240.

choice. If we feel able to display finger dexterity, $\half = 120$ could be tolerated, since the "bravura" spirit is certainly not foreign to this great composition.

On Table IId we place the first measures of two compositions by Bach, both of which seem to have received a time signature contrary to the common meaning of C and ₵. It is impossible to feel the Fugue in D major, *W.K.* II (IId, 1), as an *alla breve* piece. Having no sixteenth notes, it belongs to the same group as the Fugue in D sharp minor, *W.K.* I, and the Prelude in B minor (Ia, 16 and 24), which would give it the speed of $\quarter = 80$. The metronomizations of Bischoff and Czerny show that they also felt the necessity of making the quarter note the basic beat. In the case of Duet IV (IId, 2), written out in C time, the inner beat is clearly *alla breve*, and the speed $\half = 80$ may be taken from the Invention in A minor (Ia, 5) with which this piece shares not only the key but also the melodic material.

We have also made another appendix to the ₵ tables, Table IIe, which includes the first measures of those pieces by Bach that are either real French overtures, or are at least closely related to them by the deliberate application of rhythmical figures like ♩. ♪. Some of these overtures are written out as *alla breve* pieces, others have the C sign, and a clear differentiation between the types assigned to either time signature is impossible; to the eye, the Overture to the Fourth Partita, in ₵ time, and the Overture from the *Goldberg Variations* (Variation 16), in C time, look exactly alike.[38] A unified speed around $\half = 60$ for the three real overtures (Nos. 1–3) seems to be appropriate, while the Sinfonia of the Second Partita, with its warning *grave, adagio,* apparently needs a slower speed, perhaps $\half = \pm 40$. (Notice that the dotted rhythm is represented here by a dotted sixteenth and a thirty-second note.) However, in the Toccata of the Sixth Partita, which shows such a close relation to the overtures, it almost looks as if the Introduction and Postludium should be played at the speed of $\half = 80$, because the middle part uses the same melodic material. It is the sigh motive that makes us assign this part to that speed. On the other hand, to differentiate the "framing" sections by using the speed of $\half = 60$ might also be defensible.[39]

PIECES IN 2/4 TIME (Table III)

Table III, the 2/4 table, is twice linked with the 4/4 table. Since the first movement of the Italian Concerto (IIIa, 3) does not differ from any of

---

[38] It should be mentioned that all orchestral overtures by Bach are written in C time.
[39] See pp. 320ff.

the concerto-grosso movements in C time (see Table Id), it establishes for this table also an *allegro* group at ♩ = 100. One may also observe the inner relation between the theme of the Capriccio of the Second Partita (IIIa, 4) and a well-known motive from the Concerto in D minor for Two Violins in C time (IIIa, 10). The same material is recognizable even in the final movement of the Violin-Harpsichord Sonata in C minor (IIIa, 11). The "Echo" from the French Overture in B minor (IIIa, 6) also has a cousin, if not a brother, in the Badinerie of the famous Suite for Flute in the same key (IIIa, 12).

Three pieces that use the sigh motive establish the *moderato* group at ♩ = 80 for the 2/4 table, too (IIIb, 1–3). We also assigned the first movement of the Harpsichord Concerto in F minor (IIIb, 4) to this group instead of giving it the concerto-grosso speed of ♩ = 100. This piece and the first movement of the Triple Concerto in A minor (along with the Prelude in A minor for Harpsichord, Ia, 37, which is the spiritual father of this concerto) are the only concerto-grosso movements in which triplets of sixteenths are used in abundance; therefore, the reduction of the speed to ♩ = 80 is fully justified.

Only one piece in 2/4, the fifteenth variation of the *Goldberg Variations* (IIIc, 1) needs a still slower speed, and it is nice to see that Bach found it worthwhile to give this piece the indication *andante*. Again, we know of no other explanation for Bach's procedure than that he wanted to avoid having the eyes take this variation as a normal *moderato* piece, the same reason which we used to explain the *largo* on the Fugue in B minor, *W.K.* I (Ic, 3). Assigning it to the speed ♩ = 40 and not to ♩ = 60 (because of the indication *andante*) will be justified later when we will use the same speed in pieces in 3/4 time.[40]

DANCE PIECES IN C AND ¢ TIME (Table IIf)

Before we leave the tables of "even time," we must examine the dance pieces that belong to this group. They are neither numerous—only allemandes, gavottes, bourrées, three gigues, and one anglaise are involved —nor do they offer any puzzling problems. It would be nonsensical to have the theme of every individual dance on our tables (this is also true of dance tables in other time signatures) so we have written out only the minimum number necessary for demonstration purposes.

That allemandes belong to the *moderato* group needs no special proof because they are supposed to contrast with the following fast dance, the courante. The unity of character among the allemandes of the French and

---

[40] See p. 130.

English Suites is so obvious that we have already questioned Bischoff's overrefined differentiations in speed. Beginning with the Third Partita Bach stylized his allemandes more and more: the rhythms become increasingly complicated, thirty-seconds and triplets of sixteenth notes are used, and, in probably the most beautiful of all, the Allemande of the Fourth Partita, the character is changed so completely that the piece is a veritable *arioso*, comparable to the second movement of the Italian Concerto. For allemandes of this type the average speed must doubtless be reduced to *andante*, ♩ = 60.

The speeds that Quantz suggests for gavottes and especially bourrées so strongly contradict the character of Bach's pieces that they are beyond consideration: for gavottes, 𝅗𝅥 = 120–132; for bourrées, 𝅗𝅥 = 160.[41] We are probably on the right track when we distribute the speeds as follows: 𝅗𝅥 = 80 for gavottes and anglaises, and 𝅗𝅥 = 100 for bourrées. It is interesting that the Gigue from the First French Suite (IIf, 13), which represents a rare type cultivated by the French lutenist Gaultier, is written out in C time, but the older version of the Gigue of the Sixth Partita (IIf, 14a) is written in ¢ in the *Notebook for Anna Magdalena Bach*. We give them the tempi of ♩ = 80 and 𝅗𝅥 = 80, respectively. However, what to do with the Gigue of the First Partita (IIf, 15) cannot be stated with authority by anyone. There will always remain the problem of whether or not this piece, which is so much more than a gigue, should be played brilliantly on the harpsichord or tenderly on the clavichord. I am inclined to assign it to the clavichord[42] and to play it at the speed of ♩ = ±140, which is as unique in our scheme as the piece itself.

PIECES IN 3/4 TIME (Table IV)

Our routine for distributing Bach's keyboard pieces among various speeds according to affects and note values has now become well enough organized so that we will have no difficulty in recognizing the most characteristic features on the 3/4 tables. We can even say that without them we would be at a loss in dealing with our next examples, because the prescriptions that Quantz gives for pieces in 3/4 time are especially confusing and often impossible in practice. His rule[43] for bringing the pulse into relation with triple-metre *allegro* pieces in which sixteenths are prevalent means, in the language of the metronome, that ♩ = 160, or ♩. = 53⅓. This speed is so excessive, if one has to play sixteenth notes, that it is beyond

---

[41] It is a joy to see that for the most natural human activity, marching, he does find a speed corresponding to the pulse and indicates a tempo of 𝅗𝅥 = 80.

[42] See discussion in Appendix A, p. 312.

[43] Cited on p. 105.

discussion.[44] Nobody could ever play the so-called "Long" Fugue in A minor (IVe, 2) at that tempo. Two more categories of pieces in 3/4 time that Quantz describes cannot be found in Bach's works, namely, "*presto* pieces using eighth notes only," and "*adagio cantabile* pieces in which only quarter notes are used."

However, another of Quantz's remarks, that "*adagio cantabile* pieces in which the bass moves in eighth notes" have to be played at the speed of one pulse beat to the eighth note, has unexpected consequences: it helps us see a controversial problem in a new light. In footnote 25, above, we voiced concern about Kirkpatrick's metronomization of Variation 25 of the *Goldberg Variations* at $\flat = 46$, the slowest speed suggested anywhere for Bach's keyboard works. We mentioned then that the texture of this variation reminds us very much of Variation 13, which Kirkpatrick thinks should be taken at almost double the speed, with $\downarrow = 40$. Thus a large gap is created between these closely related variations. Quantz's remark gives us the authority to put the two variations together, on Table IVd ($\downarrow = 40$), along with a very famous piece that even bears a tempo mark from Bach's own hand: the *Andante* of the Italian Concerto.[45] By comparing these three pieces, it becomes evident that not only is the texture of the right hand the same in each case, but that the movement of the left hand is also identical: the bass moves in eighth notes, just as Quantz mentioned. Indeed, without his remark we would hardly have thought of adding the bass moving in eighth notes to the list of characteristic note values that help indicate the speed of a piece. (I hope I will not be accused of sophistry if here and there I take Quantz as an ally and then reject his opinions when I do not agree with him.) However, one cannot help feeling that a thorough comparison of the inner structure of these pieces indicates the probability that Bach's *andante* for the slow movement of the Italian Concerto stands "in secret ink" as the tempo indication for the two variations also.

In order to get tangible results for the other problems on the 3/4 tables, we have to rely on our method of comparison of note values and affects. The first surprise is that in triple metre the fast pieces form the majority, even when we discard the seven individual numbers contributed by the *Goldberg Variations*. Since several of the pieces on the *allegro* table, IVa, are of the concerto-grosso type (Nos. 6, 8, 9, and 24), it is not difficult

---

[44] Even in piano pieces of outspokenly virtuoso-like character, speeds around $\downarrow = 160$ are rare. We find them, for example, assigned to two of Chopin's Etudes, Op. 10, No. 12 and Op. 25, No. 12, in the Peters Edition (Scholtz).

[45] The indication *adagio* is actually found on the second movement of the E major Violin Concerto in the arrangement for harpsichord and strings, made by Bach himself. (The autograph of the Violin Concerto is lost.) The pattern of this movement corresponds with the three pieces on this table.

to assign the speed of $\downarrow = 100$ to this group. All the fugues (Nos. 2, 7, and 10) except Number 5 are constructed with regular alternation of developments and episodes, a construction closely related to the formal principles of the concerto grosso. In general, the pieces on Table IVa share the spirit of vivacity, with the exception of Numbers 5 and 12–16, in which there are no sixteenth notes. No wonder, therefore, that these pieces sound "twice as slow" and breathe tranquillity in spite of the seemingly fast beat.

The true *moderato* spirit is common to Numbers 1–5 and 7 on Table IVb; its most beautiful manifestation appears in the "Cradle Song" in E major, *W.K.* II (IVb, 4).[46] The only contrasting pieces on this table either use an unusual rhythmical pattern, such as the G minor Fugue, *W.K.* II (No. 6), which almost reminds us of the chorus "Lasset uns den nicht zerteilen" from the *St. John Passion* (No. 10), or they add thirty-seconds (No. 8) or triplets of sixteenths (No. 9).

The list of pieces slower than *moderato*, Table IVc, is smaller. At first glance this group might not seem so far removed from the *moderato* pieces, but closer comparison reveals the extent to which the pathos and declamation have increased. It is this which must have caused Bach to distinguish the Invention in F minor with so many slurs for articulation. Numbers 6 and 7 link this table, which we assign to $\downarrow = 60$, with the dance piece in 3/4 time; both examples represent the sarabande type although they have not been called so explicitly.

On the slowest table, IVd, we find only the three pieces already discussed at length: the slow movement of the Italian Concerto, and Variations 13 and 25 of the *Goldberg Variations*. The two truly fast pieces of Table IVe manifest their showy character so clearly in the display of finger dexterity that no comment is necessary. Since $\downarrow = 40$ and $\downarrow = 120$ are the most natural speeds for these two extremes, all the pieces in 3/4 time are divided among five speed groups between 40 and 120 for the quarter note, corresponding to our findings for 4/4 time.

The dance pieces in 3/4 time (IVf) are more numerous than those in 4/4 and 2/4 time. This is caused not so much by different dance types as by quantity, since two of the standard dances of the suite, the corrente and sarabande, are in 3/4 metre. In addition, among the "voluntary" dances that are traditionally placed between the sarabande and the gigue, the menuet, also in 3/4 time, enjoyed great popularity with Bach. These dances in triple metre will give us a little more trouble, because within the individual groups themselves there seems to be a greater variety of types than we encountered in the dances in 4/4 time.

---

[46] In many places the left hand of this piece corresponds with the bass part of the aria "Schlafe, mein Liebster" from the *Christmas Oratorio* (see Chapter 8, pp. 250–251).

The very slowest and fastest dances offer no problem. Sarabandes could hardly be played slower than ♩ = 60. Even the most stylized of all sarabandes, that of the Sixth Partita (IVf, 3), can be executed at this speed and is thereby brought into closest relation with the beginning of the Toccata of the same Partita with which it is thematically so obviously linked.[47] The fastest dances on the 3/4 list are the correntes that use sixteenth notes, and, for mechanical reasons, these cannot be played much faster than ♩ = 120. This might also be the right speed for the Corrente of the Fourth French Suite (IVf, 6) and that of the First Partita (IVf, 7), which use triplets of eighth notes, a pattern relatively rare in correntes.[48] The Corrente of the C minor French Suite (IVf, 8), which uses eighth notes exclusively, would, however, be very clumsy at this speed; it has to be raised one level to ♩ = 140 or even more; only the feeling for three beats to a bar must still be maintained.

Among the menuets we also meet with several types that preclude one common tempo: pieces in which quarter and eighth notes alternate (Sixth French Suite, IVf, 14); pieces with eighth notes only (First Partita, IVf, 18); pieces with triplets of eighth notes (Fifth Partita, IVf, 19); with quarter notes almost exclusively (First Partita, Second Menuet, IVf, 20); and finally even pieces with occasional sixteenths, like the beautiful third piece of the Three Menuets from the *Notebook for William Friedemann Bach* (IVf, 12), a real *arioso* representing the most stylized of all menuets.[49]

The slowest must be the menuet applying sixteenths, with a speed of approximately ♩ = 100 (IVf, 12). For the fastest menuet, that from the First Partita (IVf, 18), which uses eighth notes only, the answer is not so easily given. If we play this Menuet, and then immediately after it the Corrente of the Second French Suite (IVf, 8), both of which look very much alike on paper, we get the following impression, which might be decisive for determining the proper speed: the inner beat of the Corrente remains "one-two-three," so that we still count the quarter notes in spite of their great speed; but in the case of the Menuet we feel a compelling desire to count only "one-one-one," a single pulse beat for the whole bar, thus using a counting method that we have not had to apply up to now.

---

[47] This increases the possibility that ♩ = 60 might be the best speed for the Introduction and Postludium of the Toccata, a question which we could not answer on p. 127. Compare, however, Appendix A, p. 320.

[48] Other examples in the same category are the Corrente of the D minor Suite for Violin Solo, and to a certain extent the Corrente of the Suite for Unaccompanied Cello in E flat major.

[49] It is not yet common knowledge that nearly all dance pieces from the *Notebook for Anna Magdalena Bach*, which are so immensely popular with elementary piano teachers all over the world, have come to be regarded by Bach authorities as apocryphal works (see Hermann Keller, *Die Klavierwerke Bachs*, p. 93).

Had we followed Quantz's recommendations, we would already have played bourrées at the speed of one pulse beat for the bar with $\circ = 80$, which, without hesitating, we have the right to call completely non-sensical. Strangely enough, however, the recommendation that Quantz makes for *all* menuets works rather convincingly in this particular case. Briefly, he says that for menuets *one* pulsation has to be taken for *two* quarters,[50] a speed that we have already calculated to correspond to $\downarrow = 160$ or $\downarrow. = 53\frac{1}{3}$. This speed is, as we will remember, the same one that Quantz suggests for "*allegro* pieces with runs of sixteenths." While it was proved completely impossible to play pieces containing sixteenths at this galloping speed, in the Menuet from the First Partita, in which only eighth notes are involved, we encounter no technical difficulties.

Since $\downarrow. = 53\frac{1}{3}$ is an ugly figure, and since all of our metronome assignments give only approximate average figures, would it be considered far-fetched to identify this value with $\downarrow. = 60$?[51] Might we thereby be able to apply our old landmarks of 60, 80, and so on, in a new situation, this time to complete bars? This is, of course, mere speculation. Yet, theoretically, it is clear that the more we deal with time signatures of smaller units, like 3/8 and 6/8, the more often will the whole bar become the counting unit. It will be very interesting to see whether Bach's compositions in 3/8 time, which are rather numerous, will give us opportunities to answer this question.

Having finished the survey of Bach's compositions in 3/4 time, we may stop again for a brief review and a comparison of these findings with the previous ones in duple time. In triple metre it was again very logical to find five outspokenly different speed groups, and links between pieces of similar organization in duple and triple time signatures offered themselves very naturally. Only in one respect are the pieces in 3/4 time markedly different from those in duple time: while of the latter pieces the vast majority belongs in the *moderato* group, in 3/4 time the greatest number of pieces is in the *allegro* group. Again we must admit that one could question our arbitrary policy of using Quantz as a witness whenever we like what he says, and rejecting him when his writings do not meet with our personal approval. Yet we hope that at least one line of direction in our method of treating Quantz now begins to emerge: it is always about the extreme speeds that we disagree with him, but in the center field of moderate speeds nothing of importance has to be refuted.

---

[50] XVII, 7, paragraph 58.

[51] It is interesting that Bischoff, by far the most conscientious of all Bach's editors of the nineteenth century, gives this Menuet as well as that of the Third French Suite (IVf, 17) the metronomization of $\downarrow. = 60$, while for all other menuets he uses the quarter note as the unit of counting. We agree with him and ask the same also for the Menuet from the Fifth Partita (IVf, 19), in which only a very few quarter notes interrupt the regular flow of the eighth notes.

PIECES IN 3/8 TIME (Table V)

Where will Bach's center of interest appear when we turn from pieces in 3/4 time to those in 3/8 time? The answer to this question is given on Tables Va and b in an almost dramatic way. Out of all these pieces, only four form a group of their own insofar as their "inner beat" is unquestionably the eighth note (Vb). All the other examples show a unity of patterns found nowhere else up to now. Their most outstanding features are that they all share the whole bar as the counting unit and that they are almost without exception disguised dance pieces, some leaning toward the passepied type (Va, 4, 5, 8, and 14), others having elements of the corrente. In our first casual survey we noticed the remarkable similarity between the Fugue in F major, *W.K.* I (Va, 4) and the Fugue in B minor, *W.K.* II (Va, 8), and also the similarity among Numbers 1, 2, 6, 11, and 16; to the last group we can even add the "concerto grosso" represented by the Prelude of the English Suite in G minor (Va, 9), especially because of its concertino section (beginning in bar 33). Most illuminating is the comparison of these pieces with their spiritual brothers in orchestral and vocal music, among which we find some of Bach's most glorious compositions.

For the specification of the speed to which all these pieces should be assigned, the most convincing clues come from a comparison of the Corrente of the Fifth Partita (Ex. 28; Vc, 7) and the Fugue in G major,

Ex. 28. Partita V, Corrente

Ex. 29. Fugue in G major, *W.K.* II

Ex. 30. Partita I, Menuet

W.K. II (Ex. 29; Va, 7) with the Menuet of the First Partita (Ex. 30; IVf, 18).

Since the main patterns of these pieces are the same, differing only in that the note values in the Corrente and Fugue are just twice as fast as those in the Menuet, it is not difficult to feel the similarity of the inner beat in all three. We may therefore assign to the compositions in 3/8 time on Table Va a speed corresponding to $\downarrow$. = 60 in 3/4 time, namely, $\downarrow$. = 60.

We can, however, apply still another method for the specification of the right speed for this group of pieces. We saw on Table Id that the first movements of all the Brandenburg Concertos, with the exception of the Fourth, correspond completely in patterns and speed. When we assigned them uniformly to the tempo of $\downarrow$ = 100 we did so because they belong to the common *allegro* group and not to *allegro assai*; this was made evident by the prevalence of runs of thirty-seconds, which prohibit a higher speed. Does the Fourth Brandenburg Concerto in 3/8 time stand entirely apart from the others? Instinctively we feel no difference. This piece also moves in sixteenth notes, and the same runs of thirty-seconds also appear in the sections for the solo violin. What would happen if we were to play the sixteenths in this piece at the same speed as in all the others, a procedure that was successful in 3/4 time when we set the speed for all pieces of concerto-grosso type at $\downarrow$ = 100? To find the metronome mark in 3/8 time that corresponds to $\downarrow$ = 100, we must go through the following calculations: four sixteenths = 100, two sixteenths = 200, six sixteenths = $\dfrac{200}{3}$ = 66.6. We get $\downarrow$. = 66 as our corresponding speed, which is close enough to $\downarrow$. = 60, the figure previously decided!

The speed of $\downarrow$. = 66 gives us an additional satisfaction. When we tried to reckon the speed for the fastest menuet in 3/4 time, we arrived at the figure of $\downarrow$. = $53\frac{1}{3}$, which we increased to $\downarrow$. = 60—a procedure clearly as unscientific as possible. Now mathematical calculations give us the value of $\downarrow$. = 66, which is approximately as much faster than 60 as 53 was slower. We could hardly find a better justification for taking 60 as the *average* value, and for reminding ourselves that no metronome mark should be considered an exact value, but is open to a variety of gradations.

Because we will see later that the average speed of $\downarrow$. = 60 is the right one for all pieces of *allegro* character on the 6/8, 9/8, and 12/8 tables as well as on those for 6/16, 12/16, and 24/16 (here, of course, $\downarrow$. = 120), we cannot help coming to a conclusion of unusually far-reaching importance: it seems as if the *sixteenth note* has a kind of absolute value through all pieces of *allegro* character in all possible bar times. This conclusion receives very convincing support from the basic technical principles for stringed and wind instruments. All players of *average* technical skill seem to agree in regard to a basic *allegro* speed at which detached sixteenth notes can be bowed comfortably on a stringed instrument and produced by simple tonguing on a wind instrument. In correspondence with the first primitive seventeenth-century attempts to determine speeds, in which word descriptions such as "man slowly walking" or "leisurely counting one, two, three, four," were used, we can now add a new popular device for finding *allegro* tempo: just say "ta-ta-ta-ta" at a comfortable speed. This, together with the second foothold for finding fundamental speed, which we get from the law that *moderato* corresponds to the beat of the human pulse, helps explain why speed prescriptions were unnecessary in a period where rules so close to human nature were the governing factors.

We return now to Table V in order to examine the remaining pieces. For those four in which the "inner speed" is determined by the beat of an eighth note, we have to lower the tempo to the next slower category, ♩. = 40 or, much more logically, ♪ = 120. In the case of Duet I (Vb, 4), the speed might even be lowered to ♪ = 100, because this piece seems almost to represent an *andante* type. We would perhaps hesitate to include the Sinfonia in G minor (Vb, 2) in this group, were it not that the ornamented version of it brings to our attention the melancholy elements which one might easily overlook.

Piano players will probably complain bitterly that we have not created a truly fast speed group for the popular Prelude in C sharp major, *W.K.* I (Va, 3). However, this piece is misunderstood by most piano students, who see in it a rare opportunity for the display of finger dexterity. On the surface the Prelude seems to invite such treatment because its main figure looks like a study in "side movement," a special type of arm technique; only a closer examination reveals that the figure of the right hand has to be understood as simply another case of "arpeggio ornamentation of background harmonies," such as Bach used in the C major Prelude, *W.K.* I, as well as in the C sharp major Prelude, *W.K.* II.[52] This becomes especially apparent in the second part of the piece where the staccato playing begins, as one can see by a comparison of Examples 31,

Ex. 31. Prelude in C sharp major, *W.K.* I, bars 87–88

---

[52] Other pieces of the same type are the well-known "Little" Prelude in C minor and the Prelude in C minor, *W. K.* I. A more modern example is the Etude, Op. 25, No. 12, by Chopin.

32, and 33. With this approach one will discover that the left-hand part of our Prelude is more important than the light figures of the right hand, and the predominance of the *tranquillo* spirit over the *agitato* elements will become more and more evident.

Ex. 32. Prelude in C major, *W.K.* I

Ex. 33. Prelude in C sharp major, *W.K.* II

One might also claim that we underrated the basic speed of the Corrente of the Fifth Partita (Vc, 7), in which the right hand is closely related to the C sharp major Prelude just discussed. However, one only has to glance at the second part of this Corrente to find out that here also the "singing elements" come to the foreground. The melodic line (Ex. 34)

Ex. 34. Partita V, Corrente, bars 33ff.

becomes indistinguishable from the patterns of the passepieds (Table Ic) or from Numbers 4 and 8 on Table Va. No further comments regarding the examples on Tables Va–c are necessary. That the Corrente of the Sixth Partita, the only one using thirty-seconds in abundance, has to be brought down to the next lower speed unit, $\quad \downarrow \cdot = 40$, really goes without saying.

PIECES IN 6/8, 9/8, AND 12/8 TIME (Tables VI, VII, VIII)

Numbers 1–7 on Table VIa, pieces in 6/8 time, are obviously nothing more than a continuation of the patterns in 3/8 time from Table Va.

Justified in this way, we assign them also to the group of ♩. = 60. There are only two pieces in 6/8 time for which this speed does not apply: Numbers 1 and 2 on Table VIb, in which the eighth note is the basic unit of motion. When we go on to the gigues in 6/8 (VIc), we are amazed at the richness of possibilities that Bach has in store for us. We need four speed groups for them, with the slowest at ♩. = 60, in order to do justice to the complicated texture of the Gigue from the Fifth Partita (VIc, 1), which one may compare to the Prelude of the Fifth English Suite (VIa, 3), and the fastest at ♩. = 120 for the tarantella-like runs of the Gigue in the Second English Suite (VIc, 5).

The first group of Table VII, pieces in 9/8 time, contains those that continue the patterns of normal 3/8 time (VIIa, 1–4); therefore, we will again assign the tempo of ♩. = 60. The Prelude in C sharp minor, *W.K.* II (VIIb), represents the *arioso* or *andante* type (♩. = 40), while Numbers 1 and 2 on Table VIIc, in which there are no sixteenths, have to be transferred to the next higher speed of ♩. = 80, just as we did before when the type of note values changed. It is significant that of those pieces on Tables VI and VII which we assigned to the speed of the pulse, ♩. = 80, the wonderful Double Fugue in G sharp minor, *W.K.* II (VIb, 1), the Sinfonia in E major, and the Prelude in E flat major, *W.K.* II (VIIc, 1 and 2), are unanimously outspoken examples of true *moderato* character. Variation 24 of the *Goldberg Variations* (VIIc, 3) looks different. For very special reasons we want to postpone its discussion until we have discussed the Prelude in D major in 12/8 time.[53] The Invention in G major (VIId) is the only example of *allegro assai* in 9/8 time, and is an early brother to the gigantic Gigue that Bach wrote in 9/16 time for the Fourth Partita.

As was to be expected, Table VIII, containing the pieces in 12/8 time, continues the rolling sixteenths of 3/8 and 6/8 time; this makes the speed of ♩. = 60 inevitable. Those pieces in which sixteenths are rare or nearly absent (VIIIb, 1–4) are once again models of *tranquillo-moderato* spirit and are set at ♩. = 80. The two gigues in 12/8, in which sixteenths are completely missing, must, of course, proceed at the same speed as the corresponding gigues on the 6/8 table: ♩. = 120 (VIIIc, 1 and 2).

We could not put down examples of *alla siciliana* pieces (which, owing to their prescribed 12/8 time, would also belong to this table), because for unknown reasons Bach never wrote a piece in this popular fashion for keyboard solo. We find them only once in his organ works (Trio Sonata I, second movement), here and there as middle movements in chamber music,[54] and in some of the harpsichord concertos; they are

---

[53] See pp. 139–140.

[54] See, among others, the second movement of the Flute Sonata in E flat major, this time in 6/8.

always in the stylized form of *ariosos*, generally using sixteenths and even thirty-seconds, sometimes marked *larghetto*, sometimes *adagio*. Because of the richness of the ornamental detail, their speed seems to be ♩. = 40, but for the "naked" form, which employs only the patterns ♩ ♪ and

♫ ♩ ♩, the metronomization ♩. = 60 is better.[55]

One piece on our 12/8 table asks for detailed discussion, namely, the Prelude in D major, *W.K.* II (VIIIb, 3), which carries the unique tempo indication ₵, 12/8. That the ₵ has no connection with an *alla breve* rhythm is very obvious. Furthermore, in regard to the rhythmical patterns and note values involved, this magnificant piece, one of the most triumphant Bach ever wrote, is without any real companion. Of all the keyboard pieces, only the Sinfonia in C minor (VIIIb, 1) and the twenty-fourth variation of the *Goldberg Variations*, in 9/8 time (VIIc, 3), show related features; these are chord figures, similar rhythmical subdivisions

between eighths and sixteenths, ♩ ♫♫ (which in this case have

nothing to do with the passepied), and the motive of the "falling octave,"

Bach's favorite symbol for majesty. That the rhythm ♩. ♩ in the D major

Prelude is identical with the rhythm ♩ ♪ (with 3) in both the other pieces is

generally accepted, since this manner of notation represents a widely used tradition of Bach's time.[56] But it is less clear whether the eighth notes in

the second bar should be played evenly or as if "dotted" $\left(\text{♩} \atop 3 \text{♪} \right)$. The

latter is probably correct, but full authority cannot be given to it.

The inner meaning of the Prelude becomes very clear when we compare it to its three "big brothers" in the organ and vocal music of Bach: the equally triumphant Organ Prelude in C major which is in 9/8 time, the opening chorus of Cantata 65, "Sie werden alle aus Saba kommen," and finally, nothing less than the "Sanctus" from the B minor Mass. The fact that this last is written in C time is proof of our statement that the ₵ of the Prelude under discussion has no real meaning. "Praise the Lord" is the message of all these pieces, which express the noblest

---

[55] Sicilianas without ornamentation, written so frequently by Scarlatti and Vivaldi, are found only among Bach's vocal works. Two examples are the "Shepherd Music" from the *Christmas Oratorio* and the tenor aria "Ich will leiden" from Cantata 87. The Organ Pastorale in F major (first movement) is also a "naked" siciliana, but its authenticity is open to question.
[56] See p. 197 for further discussion of this problem.

elevation of the soul and which are united by the majestic motive of the falling octave. Because, in spite of the many sixteenths present, the "triplets" of eighth notes are the decisive factor for determining the inner beat of the Prelude, neither an *andante* nor an *allegro* tempo will do. The only natural one is *moderato*, ♩. = 80. Fortunately, this speed has never been contested by the various editors, whose speed suggestions—as we see on our table—are rather close to our own figure.

When we turn from these pieces to Variation 24 of the *Goldberg Variations* (VIIc, 3), we again read the message "Praise the Lord" between the lines. This determines not only its speed, at ♩. = 80, but also the fact that this variation needs for its registration the full work of the harpsichord rather than the "pastoral style" (using only a single 8′ register) in which it is most often heard. Played with the full work, the contrast with the following variation—the "crown of thorns" as poetic souls have called the twenty-fifth—is noticeably enhanced, and Variation 24 fares much better in its illustrious neighborhood.

PIECES IN 6/16, 12/16, AND 24/16 TIME (Table IX)

The unity of all examples on Tables IXa, c, and d, which represent 6/16, 12/16, and 24/16 metres, is a complete one for the eye as well as for the ear: the basic unit of all these pieces is the dotted quarter, and they move at the tempo of ♩. = 60. The Prelude in G major, *W.K.* I (IXd; Ex. 35a),

Ex. 35a. Prelude in G major, *W.K.* I

Ex. 35b. Prelude in D minor, *W.K.* I

has the rare 24/16 time signature only in the right hand; for the left hand Bach prescribes C time, which is, of course, the true counting time for this piece. One sees immediately its similarity to the Prelude in D minor from the same volume (Ex. 35b), and it is therefore natural to assign the speed of $\jmath. = 60$ to the G major Prelude, corresponding to the speed of $\jmath = 60$ for the D minor Prelude. This closing of rings of similar speeds between different time signatures proves from another angle that we were right when we established groups of pieces with the basic tempo of $\jmath. = 60$ or $\jmath. = 60$ for a whole bar.

The only "foreign" element on Table IX comes from the two pieces in 9/16 time, which belong, of course, to a different rhythmical group (continuing the spirit of 9/8 time). No wonder that the Sinfonia in B minor (IXb, 1) is a spiritual cousin to the E major Sinfonia (VIIc, 1), even in spite of the former's glittering figures of thirty-seconds, which, when played well, need not interrupt the inner tranquillity of this beautiful "Little Barcarolle." Its natural speed is *moderato* at $\jmath. = 80$. The formidable Gigue of the Fourth Partita (IXb, 2) is a spiritual brother to the tumultuous gigues in the English Suites (written in 6/8 or 12/8 time) and has to join them by being played at $\jmath. = 120$.

PIECES IN 6/4 AND 3/2 TIME (Table X)

Although there are very few pieces on our last table, which contains those in 3/2 and 6/4 time, they are all very important ones. This adds to our responsibility when we try to assign proper speeds, a task that is particularly difficult this time because hardly any material from other tables gives us direct supporting evidence. In regard to the two pieces in 6/4 time, the Prelude in C sharp minor, *W.K.* I (Xc, 1), and the Fugue in F sharp minor of the same volume (Xc, 2), editors differ widely in their solutions for basic problems. Keller feels that $\jmath.$ is the inner beat for the Prelude, but not for the Fugue. Czerny and Bischoff take the quarter unit as the inner beat for both pieces, but emphatically disagree with Keller concerning the speed for the C sharp minor Prelude. Keller, on the other hand, nearly agrees with them about the speed for the Fugue. We personally feel so strongly that $\jmath.$ is the inner beat for both pieces that we have some difficulty in understanding how anybody could come to different conclusions, especially in view of the absence of sixteenths in both pieces. Only in the F sharp minor Fugue can a link to other pieces be found: the "chain of sighs," we might almost say of "teardrops," in the counter-subject corresponds rather closely to similar patterns in Variation 15 of the *Goldberg Variations*. (The famous "rain of tears" from the chorus "O Mensch, bewein dein Sünde gross," at the end of the first part of the *St. Matthew Passion*, cannot be used for comparison, since there the lines of sixteenths are only an accompaniment for the vocal parts which determine speed and mood.) On Table IIIc, 1, we assigned Variation 15 to ♩ = 40, a speed which had an interesting justification on Table IVd, 1, where the same speed could be assigned to another piece with the authentic tempo mark *andante*, the second movement of the Italian Concerto. If we want to translate the speed ♩ = 40 from a piece in 2/4 time into 6/4 time with two inner beats, ♩ = 40 becomes ♩. = 40, a speed which fits both pieces here extremely well. It is somewhat faster than the speeds suggested by Bischoff and Czerny, but it prevents the danger of "false pathos," which can hardly be avoided at slower paces.

The problems offered by the three pieces in 3/2 time are even more difficult. For the famous Prelude in E flat minor, *W.K.* I, which Busoni beautifully describes as "Bach's prophetic forecast that in the fulness of time a Chopin would arise," 𝅗𝅥 = 60 is obviously as much too fast as 𝅗𝅥 = 40 is too slow. We therefore give it the speed assignment of 𝅗𝅥 = 50, a figure not previously used in our schemes. We do not want to make artificial excuses by saying that this Prelude, unique in Bach's works, also deserves a unique speed. If we had such low intentions as trying to save the honor of full coherence for our system of speed distribution, we could better say that the figure of 40, the lowest on the metronome, always has more symbolic than actual meaning for us. We constantly feel tempted to speed up to approximately 48 those pieces that are assigned to the slowest level. This frees the Prelude from the stigma of not fitting into our general scheme.

We must be more concerned about the two remaining pieces in 3/2 time, the Prelude in F major, *W.K.* II, and the "Cathedral" Fugue[57] in B flat minor of the same volume (Xa, 2 and 3). In neither case can we possibly agree with the speeds suggested in printed editions. For the Fugue in B flat minor Czerny goes beyond all others, suggesting the sluggish speed of 𝅗𝅥 = 104, which can only be rejected with horror when tried. The minimum flow for this piece cannot be attained at any speed less than 𝅗𝅥 = 80. In regard to the Prelude in F major, *W.K.* II, it seems impossible to us to co-ordinate the authentic slurs over four notes with speeds like 𝅗𝅥 = 60, suggested by Bischoff and Keller, or even Czerny's 𝅗𝅥 = 50. The only pieces that offer the eye some substance for comparison are the Double of the Sarabande from the Sixth English Suite (Xb, 4b), and some courantes, in which slurs over four eighth notes can frequently be found. The Double of the Sarabande, however, gives misleading visual information that is not confirmed by the ear; it is obvious that our Prelude has nothing in common with sarabande style. Much more enticing is the idea of calling it a kind of courante, which would bring it up to the speed of

---

[57] This name was suggested by Busoni in his edition.

$\downarrow$ = 80. Yet we have to confess that even this speed is not satisfying. The speed of $\downarrow$ = 100 seems to us to be necessary in order to get this piece moving, especially when it is played on the clavichord, on which the tied notes fade out before the voice moves again unless we play the piece as fast as suggested. We cannot help feeling that this Prelude could easily have been written out in note values twice as fast, using 3/4 time with running sixteenth notes; but since we are unable to provide any circumstantial evidence for our theory, we have to abandon this discussion after having given only our "minority report."[58]

The last group of pieces to be discussed is made up of the dances in 3/2 and 6/4 time and requires only a few words. Sarabandes in 3/2 time are in no way different from those in 3/4 time, and both types share M.M. $\downarrow$ = 60 as the speed of the unit of beat. While the majority of Handel's sarabandes are written in 3/2, Bach uses this notation only in the Sixth English Suite, perhaps in order to get better readability for the Double (Xb, 4b); indeed, this might also be an explanation for his use of 3/2 time in the F major Prelude just discussed. For the courantes, with their famous traditional changes between 3/2 and 6/4 time, 3/2 is generally the basic one. Only in the Courante of the Third French Suite (Xd, 1) does Bach acknowledge that the situation is reversed, by giving 6/4 as the official time signature. For reasons of clarity no speed greater than $\downarrow$ = 160 ($\downarrow$ = 80) seems possible for these dances. The old-fashioned, ceremonious French loure is represented once,[59] in the Fifth French Suite. Since it is close to the sarabande, a similar speed, $\downarrow$ = 120, seems reasonable.

CONCLUSIONS

We are now at the end of our attempts to find the proper tempi for Bach's keyboard works.[60] Not for a moment do we hesitate to admit that in order to reach our conclusions we had to rely upon "inner evidence" and "reading between the lines" more than in any previous chapter, and that

---

[58] In Chapter 8, Symbolism, we will raise a conjecture which might indeed contribute to justification of this speed (p. 249).

[59] The only other loure by Bach is that from the Suite in E major for Solo Violin.

[60] The reader has probably noticed that this writer does not refer anywhere to Fritz Rothschild's book, *The Lost Tradition in Music* (New York, 1953). Mr. Rothschild's theory that metre and note values alone present exact information about the proper tempo of every composition, following a tradition that was lost after Bach's death, has already been refuted by enough Bach scholars to spare us from repeating the arguments that weigh heavily against it. The mere fact that quite a few times Bach notated the same composition in different metres (see p. 126) proves that he did not consider time signature and note values *alone* to be the source of information about tempo. See, among others, the review by Arthur Mendel in *Music Quarterly*, vol. XXIX, no. 4 (October 1953), p. 617.

the results achieved are undoubtedly open to debate. However, we have accomplished the one thing that was our chief goal throughout this investigation: we have shown that there does not exist in Bach's works an unending variety of tempi, but that there are a limited number of tempo groups and that each piece, according to its affect and its rhythmical organization, belongs in one or another of these groups.[61]

In contrast to Quantz, we decided on *five* groups of speed, roughly described by the words *adagio, andante, moderato, allegro,* and *presto.* This is, of course, no new discovery; it is as much a platitude as it is a truism; but the symmetric organization, with *moderato* as the pivot for oscillations to both sides, represents a principle that Bach uses more than any other composer for the formal construction of single pieces as well as of cycles of pieces. How often does Bach say the most important thing in the middle of a piece, building "ascending" and "descending" sections to serve as balancing counterparts.[62]

Although our basic metronome marks for these five speeds—M.M. 40, 60, 80, 100, and 120—may, at first glance, seem to have been selected for the "beauty of their appearance" (as we accused Quantz), they have not been arbitrarily chosen. The pivot of 80, corresponding to the heartbeat, needs no justification. That the upper limit of speed could not have been far above ♩ = 120 because of the mechanism of the harpsichord can be proved by every *historic* instrument (modern harpsichords cannot be considered authentic in this respect). On the other hand, human instincts seem to agree that the limit of slowness cannot be much below ♩ = 40. Therefore, only the speeds of ♩ = 60 and ♩ = 100 remain debatable subjects. Whether the speed of ♩ = 60, the length of a second, is also built into the reactions of human nature in a way analogous to the heartbeat is perhaps a problem for psychologists; however, in regard to the speed of ♩ = 100 as that of a natural, average *allegro,* it seems that there is an agreement among almost all musicians.

That the unity of these inner beats crosses the lines of the various time signatures, that ♩ or ♩ = 80 can be found in C, 2/4, and ¢ as well as in 3/4 time, that the unit ♩ = ±60 can also be deduced by applying Quantz's system (based on 4/4 time with ♩ = 80), that the average values of ♩. = ±60 can be deduced from 4/4 time at ♩ = 100 by equating

---

[61] As a counterexperiment one may try to tabulate Beethoven's thirty-two piano sonatas in a similar way. The impossiblity of such an undertaking will quickly become apparent, and will show more effectively than words the differences in the mental attitudes of the periods toward problems of tempo.

[62] See the Fugue in C major, *W.K.* I (pp. 64ff.), or the use of the "Royal Theme" in the middle of the second movement of the Trio Sonata from the *Musical Offering*, splendidly analyzed by Hans David in his monograph on this work, *J. S. Bach's Musical Offering* (New York, 1945).

sixteenth notes, and that ♩. = 60 in the time signature of 24/16 is identical with ♩ = 60—these are startling observations; yet they all stem from the period in which time signatures served as absolute time indications (see pp. 103ff.).

As we have said before, all these tempo suggestions should be understood as approximations. Although the beat of the human heart seems to remain steady, the "inner pulse of mankind" has undoubtedly become faster since Bach's time, and we ourselves would be the first to admit that metronome figures like ♩ = 48, 66, 84, 108, and 126 probably represent to our time the same reactions that the metronome marks previously set meant to the baroque period. At any rate, when Bach's keyboard works are played on the piano, such a "seasoning" of tempi becomes almost a necessity.

Whether we assigned every piece, without error, to the correct and only group to which it belongs is a matter that should not be of too great concern to anybody. Interpretative genius can do miracles in suggesting speed while playing relatively slowly, and vice versa. The decisive thing is always to find the "true affect" of a piece from the "various types of notes." Whoever has acquired this knowledge, through "extensive experience and the ability to judge well," will be the first to agree that dictatorial metronome marks are never an ultimate goal. Nobody has expressed this better than Beethoven, who, after a period of enthusiastically endorsing the invention of his friend Maelzel, made this famous statement to Schindler: "*No* metronome anymore: he who has the right feeling will not need it, and he who does not have this feeling will derive no help from it and will still run away with the entire orchestra."

CHAPTER 5

Ornamentation

HISTORICAL REVIEW

The correct execution of the ornaments in Bach's keyboard works has always appeared to be a most unpleasant problem, both to musicians and to laymen. It is usually approached with the doubt that any serious efforts bestowed upon its solution may not really be worthwhile. The chief reason for this almost unanimous reaction is the widespread belief, allegedly supported by the "authorities," that the baroque composers prescribed their ornaments only as a device to help prevent the evanescent tone of the harpsichord from fading out too soon. Since this condition no longer exists on the modern piano, most editors advise omitting the majority of these ornaments, thus considering them only a kind of temporary gown not essential for understanding the true spirit of the music. Even the editors of the Bach-Gesellschaft did not consider it necessary to report on the presence or absence of the same ornament in the various manuscripts, declaring that most of them were added "by unauthorized hands" (*von unberufener Hand*). This prejudice goes so far that the more ornaments a manuscript contains, the more its authenticity is questioned by those editors.

It is to the great merit of Ludwig Landshoff, editor of the magnificent *Urtext* edition of the Inventions and Sinfonias, for which I had the privilege of making a modest contribution by adding the fingering, to have proved for the first time in an irreproachable manner that the multitudes of ornaments found in the Fourth, Seventh, Ninth, and Eleventh Sinfonias represent precisely the way in which Bach wanted these pieces to be played.[1] Landshoff's *Revisionsbericht* is one of the most

---

[1] J. S. Bach, *Inventions and Sinfonias*, ed. L. Landshoff (Peters, 1933).

146

important publications of the entire Bach literature, but unfortunately it has not yet been translated into English.[2] Aside from showing that the so-called "second autograph" of the Inventions is unauthentic, its most important contribution was to place the role of the ornaments in the right perspective.

Owing to our better understanding of the art of the baroque period, for which we are especially indebted to the research of Heinrich Wölfflin,[3] we now view this great period not as an era of decadence—as previous generations were wont—but as one of natural reaction against the Renaissance. The flamboyant passion in the curves of the architectural lines of the baroque, so strongly contrasting to the restraint of the Renaissance, is identical with the role of melodic ornaments in baroque music. "To suppress these ornaments," says Landshoff rightly, "would be the same as to remove the protruding ornaments from a piece of sculpture or the rich stucco ornaments from the walls of baroque palaces, or to replace the spiral columns of the baroque with classic ones: it would destroy the entire meaning of these pieces of art."[4]

Friedrich Ehrhard Niedt of Jena, author of the *Musikalische Handleitung*, which Bach used in his teaching, writes that embellishments are actually the life of the music.[5] C. P. E. Bach also testifies for the importance of the ornaments: "No one disputes the need for embellishments. This is evident from the great numbers of them everywhere to be found. They are, in fact, indispensable. Consider their many uses: They connect and enliven tones and impart stress and accent; they make music pleasing and awaken our close attention. Expression is heightened by them; let a piece be sad, joyful, or otherwise, and they will lend a fitting assistance. . . . Without them the best melody is empty and ineffective, the clearest content clouded."[6]

It is true that one has to be cautious in taking C. P. E. Bach as a crown witness for his father, to whose musical taste he was actually opposed in many respects. In this particular case, however, his opinion obviously agrees with his father's, as Landshoff was able to prove.[7] In contrast to general belief, C. P. E. Bach used fewer ornaments than his father, and warns against their abuse when he writes that too many spices "may ruin the best dish."[8] That from external evidence he seems to have

---

[2] Ludwig Landshoff, *Revisionsbericht zur Urtextausgabe von Joh. Seb. Bach's Inventionen und Sinfonien* (Leipzig, 1933).

[3] Heinrich Wölfflin, *Kunstgeschichtliche Grundbegriffe* (Munich, 1915).

[4] *Revisionsbericht*, p. 26.

[5] *Musikalisches A B C* (Hamburg, [1708]), p. 32. For Bach's use of Niedt, see Spitta, *Musikgeschichtliche Aufsätze* (Berlin, 1892, 1894), p. 121.

[6] C. P. E. Bach, *Essay*, p. 79.

[7] *Revisionsbericht*, p. 27.

[8] *Essay*, p. 81.

used more results from his careful indication of every embellishment; during the lifetime of his father, however, it was the practice to distinguish between *essential* ornaments, which had to be written down by composers, and *arbitrary* ones, which were to be added by every intelligent interpreter.[9]

Actually, Bach is not very consistent in following this method. On the one hand he omits quite a few essential ornaments, such as trills at cadences, which must then be added by interpreters. He also very often puts down an ornament only at the first appearance of a phrase (for example, in the Sinfonia in F major), leaving it to the interpreter to add it again wherever the phrase reappears. On the other hand, he writes out a good many of the *arbitrary* ornaments in full note values, apparently not trusting the interpretative capabilities of his fellow musicians. For this procedure he got the famous rebuff from his personal enemy, Johann Adolf Scheibe: "All embellishments, all little ornaments, and almost everything that *belongs to the method of playing* are written out by him in real notes."[10]

This attack was directed more against Bach the man than against Bach the composer. Essential in it is the hurt pride of the professionals, who felt that their ability in providing skeleton melodic lines with the necessary embellishments was an integral part of their artistry.[11] Especially in Italy the art of improvising good embellishments was considered the private property of singers. We find these rather amusing lines in Pierfrancesco Tosi's *Opinioni de' cantori antichi e moderni o sieno osservazioni sopra il canto figurato* (Bologna, 1723), translated into German in 1757 by Bach's pupil Agricola:

When the pupil is sufficiently familiar with appoggiaturas . . . he can only laugh at those composers who write them out either because they want to be considered up-to-date, or because they want to make people believe that they can sing better than singers. Why do they not also write out the *arbitrary* embellishments that are much harder and much more indispensable than the appoggiaturas? If they write them out, however, in order not to lose the glorious title of a "virtuoso *à la mode*," they should as least admit that this requires only a little effort and study. Poor Italy! Is it really true that today's singers no longer know where these appoggiaturas have to be added if the composer does not put his finger upon the place? In my time one was intelligent enough to find

---

[9] Brandts Buys gives a good list of them (*Het Welltemperierte Clavier van J. S. Bach*, p. 130).

[10] *Der Critische Musikus*, Part I, ed. by Johann Adolf Scheibe (Hamburg, 1738), pp. 46–47. Italics mine.

[11] Handel had much more respect for this tradition than Bach, and most of his arias at slow speed, as well as the slow movements of his instrumental music, need many additional embellishments. The Aria with variations in his D minor Suite is one of the rare cases where he wrote out the full ornamental line.

them. Oh, what an insult this is to you, you singers of the newest fashion, if you accept lessons from the composers that should be given to children only.[12]

This complaint stems from the same attitude that caused Scheibe's outbreak, and brings to the fore the undeniable fact that we should learn how to find those places in Bach's works where ornaments should be added instead of trying to discard those that have come down to us.

When we begin to study the problems presented by the ornaments in Bach's keyboard works, we find a situation fraught with diversity of opinion. Not only do all printed editions disagree in their advice about execution, but the same is true of the books and tables of ornaments from Bach's period to the present time.[13] These facts alone make it clear that great flexibility in handling ornaments not only was tolerated but was customary in baroque music. Although it will never be possible to establish fixed rules which cover every case that may arise, we still have the task of clarifying the problems involved, as far as this can be done with the material at our disposal, and of eliminating many absolutely wrong interpretations of ornaments that are offered in traditional editions.

If we were now to give our readers a general description of the contemporary sources on ornaments, and were to add a report on the comments made by modern writers—to which we would then have to add our comments on these comments—we would achieve nothing beyond that feeling of absolute frustration and hopelessness which overcomes everybody doing research in the field of ornamentation. We will therefore try another approach in the hope that it may be easier to come to general conclusions and to escape from the labyrinth of inconsistencies and contradictions if we explore specific situations first: our method will be to study the problems of the various ornaments where they occur in the music itself. The most appropriate starting point is, of course, the table

---

[12] These lines from Tosi are cited and translated from Landshoff, *Revisionsbericht*, p. 29.

[13] There exist more than two hundred books and tables written between 1600 and 1800 that deal with ornaments. I refer readers who are interested in firsthand information to the tables by Jean Henri D'Anglebert (1689), Boehm (1690), K. F. Fischer (1696), Dieupart (1710), Couperin (1713), and Gottlieb Muffat (1735–1739?). See the Bibliography for complete references; see also the books already mentioned by Quantz, C. P. E. Bach, and Leopold Mozart, which, however, represent only in part the situation as it was in Bach's time. The most important modern publications are: Edward Dannreuther, *Musical Ornamentation* (London, 1893–1895); Arnold Dolmetsch, *The Interpretation of the Music of the Seventeenth and Eighteenth Centuries* (London, 1915, 1946); Putnam Aldrich, "The Principal Agrements of the Seventeenth and Eighteenth Centuries: A Study in Ornamentation" (doctoral dissertation, Harvard University, 1942, not yet completely printed). This monumental study contains by far the most complete compilation of the source material that has yet been made, combined with a thorough discussion of it. Schweitzer also deals with the problems of ornamentation in his Bach biography, and gives a list of some additional but less important literature on this subject (*Johann Seb. Bach*, pp. 319–326). Of recent date is Walter Emery's *Bach's Ornaments* (London, 1953), an excellent, condensed guide through this labyrinth of problems. One of its special merits is that the very learned author nowhere tries to enforce solutions where lack of information makes this impossible.

of ornaments that Bach wrote out in the *Notebook for William Friedemann Bach* (1720), his eldest son. Although it is often reproduced, we print it again, in Plate VII.

What has happened to this table when it has been reproduced on various occasions is representative of the entire situation in ornament problems. In the Preface to the third volume of the Bach-Gesellschaft, the last ornament, called *"Idem"* by Bach, is erroneously given the sign

ᘓᘓ (*doppelt cadence*) instead of ᘓᘓ ; the same mistake is also

found in Schweitzer's book.[14] In Moser's biography a trill sign, *tr*, is given at this place,[15] and the penultimate ornament, *accent and trillo*, which in

Schweitzer's book is misprinted ᘓᘓ, has the misprint ᘓᘓ in

Moser's!

In itself, this table is interesting enough as a document. The solutions given by Bach are in every case identical with those of contemporary French composers, while the names are a strange mixture of German, French, and Italian! Unfortunately, for practical purposes the table is not as helpful as we would like it to be; it covers only average problems, revealing nothing about the subtleties of the art of embellishment for which C. P. E. Bach needs sixty pages. However, it seems obvious that the elder Bach did not want to go into more detail because his table was written for a boy of nine who would have been more confused than enlightened by anything more than the basic information.

THE TRILL

When we examine the way in which Bach uses the trill, we notice immediately that he alternates between ᘓᘓ, ᘓᘓ, and *tr*, on long or short notes, without any particular system; in fact, ᘓᘓ and ᘓᘓ are often written in the form of a little wave line, ᘓᘓ, which makes it very difficult to count the number of oscillations. In the Invention in C minor Bach uses the sign *tr* at the end of bar 2, but in bar 24, an identical place, he uses ᘓᘓ.

In regard to the correct execution of trills, all sources of French origin from the second half of the seventeenth century and the beginning of the eighteenth agree that the trill has to begin on the upper auxiliary. Since the vast majority of German sources also support this treatment, we shall consider this rule a basic one. In essence it means that the trill is

nothing more than a quick repetition of appoggiaturas: ᘓᘓ ᘓᘓ. It is

---

[14] *Bach*, p. 320.
[15] *Johann Sebastian Bach*, p. 235.

totally inexcusable that even now one can buy editions which do not observe this practice, and that one can still hear artists of the highest repute who start every trill on the main note. The only problem concerning the trill is whether or not there are exceptions to this rule of starting with the upper auxiliary note.

Dannreuther states six cases in which the trill begins on the *main* note:

a. When the shake starts *ex abrupto.* Fugue XIII. [*W.K.* II], part ii.—

b. When the shake starts after a note staccato—or after a rest. Fugue VI. [*W.K.* I], part i., bar 2—

c. When the repetition of a note is thematic. Prel. XIII. [*W.K.* I], part i., F sharp maj., bars 7, 12, 13, and 19.

d. When the melody skips, and the shake thus forms part of some characteristic interval; as, for instance, the interval of the seventh in the theme of Fugue XV. [*W.K.* I], part i., bars 25 and 26—

e. When the movement of the bass would be weakened if the shake were begun with the accessory. . . . Fugue IV. [*W.K.* II], part ii., bar 32—

f. Franz Kroll's hint to teachers[16] may be quoted here: "Whenever an appoggiatura from above would be out of place, then the shake had better not begin with the accessory."[17]

Dannreuther points out that cases *b* and *e* also come under the rule "melodic outlines must not be blurred."

Schweitzer, clearly influenced by Dannreuther, says, "The trill normally begins on the upper auxiliary. It may begin on the main note only in exceptional cases. For somewhat longer trills it is strongly recommended that one wait for a moment on the main note and then start the trill on the upper auxiliary, especially if a movement or a theme begins with a trill (see Fugue XIII, *W.K.* II) or if the upper neighbor note has just been played."[18]

Unfortunately, Dannreuther's rules were taken from the clear blue sky; they have never been found in any verbal formulation in contemporary sources, with the exception of the phrase "melodic outlines must not be blurred," repeatedly used by C. P. E. Bach,[19] from whom Dannreuther apparently took it. "It may be wise to warn the reader here against the frequent incorrectness and inaccuracy of Dannreuther's discussion . . . in spite of the general excellence of the book."[20] Yet, there are puzzling

---

[16] Franz Kroll edited the *Welltempered Keyboard* for the Bach-Gesellschaft.

[17] *Musical Ornamentation*, pp. 165–166.

[18] *Bach*, p. 320.

[19] *Essay;* see also p. 152 below.

[20] Ralph Kirkpatrick, Preface to the G. Schirmer edition of the *Goldberg Variations* (New York, 1938), p. 11. Aldrich says, "The greatest shortcoming of this writer [Dannreuther] is in his treatment of the ornamentation of J. S. Bach; here Dannreuther seems to throw all his laboriously collected source material to the four winds and to offer his personal interpretation" ("The Principal Agrements," p. 11).

places in Bach's keyboard works which make it rather hard for us to insist that to begin a trill with the upper auxiliary is a rigid rule tolerating no exceptions. Unbiased discussion will allow such places to speak for themselves and will show that some of Dannreuther's "rules," which he presents in such a misleading way, may perhaps not be entirely unjustified.

There does exist one inviolable rule, nowhere contradicted, to which ornaments as well as all other aspects of music are subject: the rule of *clean voice leading*, avoiding forbidden fifths and octaves. C. P. E. Bach cites this rule twice in regard to ornaments. In the section on appoggiaturas he writes, "Hence, as with all embellishments, the introduction of an appoggiatura must not corrupt the purity of voice leading."[21] And again, in the discussion of the trill, "Because, as already mentioned, ornaments must not corrupt the purity of voice leading, it is better to employ either the normal or the descending trill in Figure 112, for the ascending trill [ᴍᴋ] creates forbidden fifths" (Ex. 36).[22]

Ex. 36. Figure 112, from C. P. E. Bach, *Essay*

Evidence that this rule for purity of voice leading pertains also to the works of J. S. Bach can be found in bar 16 of the Invention in F minor (Ex. 37a). If the turn is begun on the main note (Ex. 37b), parallel fifths occur. In the *Notebook for William Friedemann Bach*, we find the same turn written out in large notes (Ex. 37c), and in Forkel's edition of the Invention (published by Hoffmann and Kuhnel) we find the version given

Ex. 37. Invention in F minor, bar 16

in Example 37d. Although only the version from the *Notebook* is authentic, both Examples 37c and 37d show the desire to avoid parallel fifths. Bach

---

[21] *Essay*, p. 95.
[22] *Essay*, p. 110.

occasionally sinned against this rule[23] (the haste with which he had to compose one cantata after another easily explains many such slips), but there is no case in his works in which he wrote such parallels for the purpose of a "challenge." In the light of this fact, let us discuss the 24 cases appearing on the Trill Table (see Appendix B).

With one glance at these examples we can see that in every case the playing of the upper auxiliary at the beginning of the ornament leads not only to ugly hidden fifths or octaves, but frequently even to intolerable parallels. The quantity of these cases, which in all probability is only a small part of many more that have escaped my vigilance, is too large for them to be dismissed as slips of Bach's pen. Some of them are real "horrors," like the unison parallels in bar 13 of the Invention in C minor (No. 2) and the open fifths in bar 13 of the Prelude in F minor, *W.K.* II (No. 6).[24] In fact, quite a few present parallels between the outer voices, where they are considered a major crime; in this position they are so obvious to the ear that even a beginner in composition cannot remain unaware of them. Now we are thus faced with the predicament of having to find out what Bach might have played in these situations. Because the majority of the cases in question concern trills on relatively short notes, it might be appropriate to study these cases first.

The sign used by Bach for a short trill is nearly always the ominous . How easy would our situation be if the simple rule, with which the majority of our generation grew up, were correct: that represents a mordent, to be played as , and that represents an "inverted mordent," equal to .[25] As a matter of fact, this rule was

---

[23] See the famous correction made in bar 11 of the first movement of the Fifth Brandenburg Concerto, where Bach discovered that the viola part contained parallel octaves with the solo violin and overlooked the fact that his correction caused a series of much worse parallel fifths with the harpsichord part (*Revisionsbericht*, Bach-Gesellschaft, vol. XIX). Brahms made a list of the parallels he discovered in Bach's works, recently published by Heinrich Schenker under the title *Brahms Oktaven, Quinten u.a.* (Universal Edition, Vienna, 1953). We give one example, bar 21 of the aria "Ich halt es mit dem lieben Gott," from Cantata 52 (Ex. 38).

Ex. 38. Cantata 52, aria "Ich halt es mit dem lieben Gott," bar 21 (three oboes)

[24] The marvelous unisons between both voices in the two-part Fugue in E minor, *W.K.* I, have, of course, nothing to do with our problem.

[25] See, among others, Czerny's edition.

considered authoritative by at least 98 per cent of the teachers all over the world. Alas, in this drastic form it is entirely fictitious. The official term "inverted mordent" does not appear in any treatise written before Bach's death, and during his life the trill on short notes followed basically the same rule as the trill on longer ones. It, too, started on the upper auxiliary, and the only change was a reduction in the number of oscillations, the minimum length of the trill being four notes. C. P. E. Bach writes that "In very rapid tempos the effect of a trill can be achieved through the use of the appoggiatura."[26] However, in none of the cases that we have shown would an execution of four notes or the replacement of the trill by an appoggiatura be a remedy for the parallels; the only

solution possible would be the use of three notes: . The question

arises, therefore, as to whether this method of execution is really as foreign to Bach's idiom as most Bach authorities of our day pretend.

If we want proof, we have to see whether Bach ever wrote out this kind of short trill in full note values, as he did with so many other ornaments, including the mordent. Several examples can be found, including not only bar 17 of the A minor Fugue, *W.K.* I, which Dannreuther discovered (Ex. 39), but also bar 16 of the First Harpsichord Concerto after Vivaldi (Ex. 40), and four very interesting measures (bars 11–14)

Ex. 39. Fugue in A minor, *W.K.* I, bar 17

Ex. 40. First Harpsichord Concerto after Vivaldi, last movement, bar 16

from Variation 15 of the *Goldberg Variations* (Ex. 41). The two "inverted mordents" (let us use this term until we come to a discussion of nomenclature) in bar 11 of the Variation were written voluntarily, but the ornament in bar 14 *had* to be written as a consequence of inverting the

---

[26] *Essay*, p. 105.

canonic line; it is therefore a true "inverted mordent," being the inversion of the mordent in bar 13.[27]

Ex. 41. *Goldberg Variations*, Variation 15, bars 11–14

If we are hunting for a slower version of these three notes, we have an example from the Sonata for Violin and Harpsichord in G major (Ex. 42) and one from the Violin Concerto in E major (Ex. 43). We hardly

Ex. 42. Sonata VI for Violin and Harpsichord in G major, bars 38–39

Ex. 43. Violin Concerto in E major, last movement, Violin I, bars 121–124

---

[27] In bars 3 and 4 of this variation a similar situation exists: the middle voice has an "inverted mordent" in bar 3, which is answered in bar 4 in the inverted canonic soprano by a real mordent, also written out in full.

The appearance of an inverted mordent as a result of the inversion of a normal mordent is, in itself, an interesting problem. Bach does not always allow an inverted mordent to arise in this situation: in the Gigue of the Sixth French Suite (bars 2 and 26) the issue is avoided by the addition of an appoggiatura; in the Gigue of the Second French Suite a true inversion is destroyed by answering the mordent of bar 2 with a trill (∿∿) in the corresponding bar, 34. But another example of a genuine normal inversion relation is found in bars 1 and 2, 17 and 18, of Variation 12 of the *Goldberg Variations*.

need emphasize that cases like Example 44a have nothing to do with our problem; their true meaning is shown in Example 44b.

Ex. 44a

Ex. 44b

Of the following cases, the first (Ex. 45) is probably a genuine example of the ornament in question; Example 46 could also be explained as an *accent with trillo* (in accordance with Bach's table), which is written out in full in bar 4 of Variation 25 of the *Goldberg Variations* (Ex. 47).[28]

Ex. 45

Ex. 46. Toccata in C minor, bar 19

Ex. 47. *Goldberg Variations*, Variation 25, bar 4

---

[28] In Variation 12 of this set we find the same ornament in bar 4, but this time in the abbreviated notation (Ex. 48).

Ex. 48. *Goldberg Variations*, Variation 12, bar 4

It is evident that the figure in Example 47 is the "little brother" of the formula *accent with mordent* on Bach's table (Ex. 49): it is found so frequently in his works that no examples need be given.

Ex. 49

Before we investigate the pertinent material from eighteenth-century treatises, let us try to find some solutions for those cases of longer trills where it seems undesirable to begin on the upper auxiliary. For this problem we were able to find only five situations in which Bach wrote out his intentions explicitly. Unfortunately we do not feel that we have the right to draw conclusions from the first three (Exs. 50, 51, and 52), since

Ex. 50. Toccata in E minor, fourth and fifth bars before the end of the fugue

Ex. 51. Concerto VIII after Vivaldi, Movement 1, bar 35

Ex. 52. Organ Prelude (B.G., vol. XXXVIII, p. 22), bar 7

one might also consider them "melodic oscillations" that took the form of a trill by chance.

The remaining cases are of a different nature. In the Fugue in F sharp major, *W.K.* II, Bach twice wrote the solution for the trill in bar 1 (Ex.

53a). The second of the two illustrations (Ex. 53c) is the more important one. Looking at the first case (Ex. 53b) one might think that Bach simply

Ex. 53. Fugue in F sharp major, *W.K.* II

a. Bar 1   b. Bar 20   c. Bar 70

wanted to "smooth" the line in a particular situation. However, by the second appearance of this solution it becomes evident that a system rather than a local situation determined the notes. Obviously he wanted to demonstrate that "the melodic line should not be blurred" and that the leading tone should get its due emphasis. A similar treatment of the leading tone also occurs in the Allemande of the Violin Sonata in E minor (Ex. 54). No autograph is preserved.

Ex. 54. Violin Sonata in E minor, Allemande, bars 10–11

The Fugue in D minor, *W.K.* I, gives us further information about the correct execution of the trill. The interval of the descending third in the second bar of the theme (after the staccato sign) is such an important part of the melodic line that it should not be obscured by starting the trill with the upper auxiliary. It is a godsend that bar 12 (Trill Table, No. 12), in which there are the most ugly potential parallel fifths, proves that Bach could not have intended this trill to start on the upper auxiliary. This case also shows that a note does not have to be a leading tone in order to be treated in this way.

It is of greatest importance that the examples in both fugues agree as to their manner of execution. They teach us that for such trills the first note to be played is the main note, which receives a value twice as long as that used in the trill. However, the oscillations that follow obey the traditional rule and begin on the note above. It is impossible to deny that Dannreuther's rules a, b, and d, although nowhere mentioned in contemporary sources, do have their historic foundation in these cases.[29]

---

[29] That Bach's solution was more than a personal preference, but was founded on tradition, can be proved by innumerable trills written out in full in the works of Frescobaldi, with

The problem of when to apply this execution of a trill in order to avoid blurring a line is one that demands for its solution a high degree of artistic responsibility. While Dannreuther was no doubt correct in giving the inversion of the theme of the Fugue in G major, *W.K.* I, as one case (Ex. 57), Schweitzer's inference that one should apply this method

Ex. 57. Fugue in G major, *W.K.* I

of execution to all situations where the "upper neighbor has just been played"[30] seems to widen the gate too far. At any rate, every individual situation should be examined very carefully before one applies the exceptional solution. For example, for the trill in the theme of the Fugue in F sharp major, *W.K.* I, one is more inclined to recommend the traditional solution given above, rather than the trill with a stop on the main note.

An additional piece of evidence which shows that Bach likes a clear harmonic explanation of the first note of a piece can be found in the opening bar of Variation 13 of the *Goldberg Variations* (Ex. 58). Here, contradictory to all contemporary rules, Bach writes out a turn beginning on the main note,[31] and the same pattern is repeated throughout the

---

which Bach was familiar. Example 55 shows the end of Toccata IX by Frescobaldi, *Il secondo libre di toccati* (Rome, 1637), p. 26; reprinted in Archibald Davison and Willi Apel, *Historical*

Ex. 55. Girolamo Frescobaldi, Toccata IX, three last bars

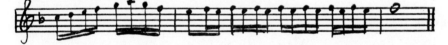

Anthology of Music (Cambridge, Mass., 1946, 1950), II, 19. See also bar 10 of the same composition and bars 13–15 in the Praeludium by Tunder (*ibid.*, II, 61). Tunder was in all probability Frescobaldi's pupil around 1640.

Frescobaldi's trill corresponds completely with Giulio Caccini's explanation of the *gruppo* or *double relish* in the Foreword to his *Le nuove musiche*, written in 1602 (Ex. 56). See Oliver Strunk, *Source Readings in Music History* (New York, 1950), p. 384.

Ex. 56

[30] *Bach,* p. 320.
[31] A few more examples of turns starting on the main note can be found in the second movement of the Italian Concerto.

variation. It would not be too far-fetched to conclude that the way in which Bach handles the turn here suggests the possibility of treating the trill in a similar manner.

Ex. 58. *Goldberg Variations*, Variation 13, bar 1

Another case in which the trill has to start with the main note is frequently found at the ends of phrases where the melodic line descends from the third above the tonic, through the second, to the tonic itself, as, for example, in the Sarabande of the Fifth French Suite (Ex. 59). Yet,

Ex. 59. French Suite V, Sarabande, two last bars

when we say that this trill starts with the main note, we describe the situation only as it offers itself to the eye. Closer examination reveals that from the aural point of view the trill really begins on the note b′, and could almost have been written by Bach as in Example 60. This is analogous to Rousseau's execution of the *cadence pleine* (Ex. 61).[32] The case therefore reduces itself to Bach's *accent with trill*, this time only partially written out.

Ex. 60. The same

Ex. 61. Rousseau, *cadence pleine*

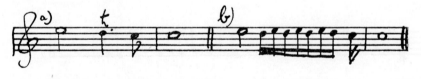

---

[32] J. J. Rousseau, *Methode . . . pour apprendre à chanter* (1788), p. 58. See Aldrich, who rightly places this case under the heading "Fallacy of the trill from the main note" (pp. 428–430).

These examples represent all the evidence regarding Bach's attitude toward trills that we were able to assemble from his music. Obviously, neither for the short nor for the long trill can a start on the main note be entirely ruled out. If we now turn to the contemporary sources for further information about the long trill, we can cull several pertinent facts.

Although from the second half of the seventeenth century there was a unanimous preference in France for the trill from above, in Italy there was a predilection for starting on the main note throughout that century. In the majority of cases the Italian composers wrote the trill out in full note values, as we have shown in the keyboard works of Frescobaldi; needless to say, many trills starting with the upper auxiliary can also be found. Frescobaldi's German pupil, Kaspar Kerll, continued the traditions of starting the trill on the main note and of writing it out in full.[33] Both composers' works belonged to the standard repertoire of the Bach family. Even as late as 1703, Franz Xaver Murschhauser, a pupil of Kerll, gave the explanation of the trill sign shown in Example 64;[34] and Adam

Ex. 64. Franz Xaver Murschhauser, explanation of trill

Reinken, with whom Bach came into personal contact when playing for him in Hamburg in 1720, explained the trill thus in the Preface to the *Hortus Musicus* (1687): "*A Tremul qui superne tonum contingit*,"[35] which

---

[33] Here are two examples chosen from many possibilities in his works (*Denkmäler Deutscher Tonkunst*, II, 2, 28, 8 (Ex. 62, 63).

Ex. 62. Frescobaldi, Canzona II

Ex. 63. Frescobaldi, Toccata II, bar 5

---

[34] *Denkmäler Deutscher Tonkunst in Bayern*, XVIII, 313.
[35] Reprinted in *Publicaties van de Vereeniging voor Noord-Nederlandsch Muziekgeschiedenis*, vol. XIV (1886).

has been understood by quite a few people to have the meaning as shown in Example 65. Alas, Reinken did not give an explanation in notes, and

Ex. 65

this case remains therefore undecided. It is well known that Bach arranged two trio sonatas from this work for the keyboard.

Let us summarize this discussion with the following statement by Putnam Aldrich:

> The chief point of conflict between the French and German styles of trill is the question whether the ornament should begin on the main note or on the auxiliary. The French *tremblement*, as we have seen, *always* starts on the note above the written note, whereas the Italian *tremolo* (or *trillo*, as it was later called) is less definitely crystallized in form and often begins with the main note.
>
> There is little doubt that all the composers mentioned above [Boehm, Fischer, J. S. Bach, G. Muffat] accepted the French interpretation of the trill. Oddly enough, most of these composers were apparently unaware of the existence of any conflict. This is evidenced by the fact that they often used the Italian name or the Italian sign, or both, when they were obviously referring to the French ornament. . . . J. S. Bach's terminology, in the table he prepared for Wilhelm Friedemann, is a curious mixture of Italian, French and German nomenclature, in spite of the fact that his realisations of the ornaments are all purely French. . . . Owing to the fact that *some* musicians (we do not know the proportion) must have continued to follow the Italian tradition until *at least* [italics mine] the first decade of the eighteenth century, it is impossible to determine the exact date of the establishment of the French *tremblement* in Germany. It is clear, however, that the period during which the use of the trill was based primarily upon the French models coincides approximately with the lifetime of J. S. Bach (1685–1750). After this time, the trill takes on a more German character.[36]

This statement clarifies the historical position and use of the trill extremely well.[37] There is no doubt that in the majority of cases Bach

---

[36] Aldrich, pp. 313–314, 316.

[37] Everyone working in the field of ornamentation is indebted to Putnam Aldrich for the painstaking care with which he prepared his excellent treatise. We have only one reservation in regard to his treatment of the trill: in our opinion the source material for the trill starting on the main note was not given sufficient representation. Aldrich's chapter "Superior Oscillations Starting with the Main Note" has no individual section of Italian sources, as all the other chapters have, and the material that shows the use of the Italian trill is mentioned only sporadically on pp. 299–300 under the heading, Superior Oscillations Beginning with the Auxiliary. The section on German sources for the trill beginning on the main note mentions

follows the French taste. The only addition that we want to make is to call attention to the fact that, in the light of the earlier Italian influence, those few cases in which we find it necessary to start the trill on the main note are less unusual and unexpected than they seemed at first; the survival of some Italian influence in middle Germany is undeniable, and we know that Bach was familiar with music that contains ornaments in the Italian style.

The confusion in the contemporary documents reaches its climax in regard to the *short trill*, ♪. Names like "short trill," "half trill," "*Pralltriller*," and "*Schneller*" are used interchangeably and arbitrarily, although one can see that some theorists are eager to make specific distinctions between them. C. P. E. Bach reserves the name "*Pralltriller*" for only one situation: a short trill on the second note of a descending second. The first note may be written at its real value or as an appoggiatura, as shown in his examples (Exs. 66, 67).[38] He calls the *Pralltriller* the

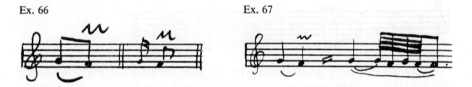

Ex. 66   Ex. 67

most attractive ornament, one that adds life and brilliance, but says at the same time that it is the most difficult embellishment, since "It must literally crackle . . . the upper tone must be snapped . . . with such exceeding speed that the individual tones will be heard only with difficulty."[39] We can get an idea of what C. P. E. Bach thinks of the mechanical qualities of the pianoforte in contrast to those of the harpsichord and clavichord, if we note that for him this ornament is insuperably difficult to produce lightly on the piano. "I doubt that the most intensive practice can lead to complete control of the volume of the short trill at the pianoforte."[40]

When we look at the realization of the *Pralltriller* as described by C. P. E. Bach, which "must not sound as frightening as it looks fully written out,"[41] we observe that the notes actually played are identical with those of the "inverted mordent." However, the delay caused by the tying

only Hummel and the period after him, but the cases of Murschhauser and Reinken remain entirely undiscussed, appearing only in the tables of the Appendix. Considering the great emphasis put on the influence of French taste throughout Aldrich's book, the statement just cited appears surprisingly generous to the Italian tradition.

[38] *Essay*, pp. 110–111.
[39] *Essay*, pp. 110–111.
[40] *Essay*, p. 112.
[41] *Essay*, p. 111.

of the first note is an integral part of the entire ornament, which is therefore nothing more than a special case of an oscillation starting on the
upper auxiliary. Considering how small the time value of this delay is, we
need not wonder that players found it more practical to disregard the tie
and to start the trill immediately, thereby playing an "inverted mordent."
Marpurg describes this as follows: "If in the execution of the tied simple
trill, the first note is passed over and the trill is begun, contrary to the
rule, directly with the main note, and the oscillation is shortened and
limited to three notes, then there results an incomplete trill which, however, is nevertheless more useful in certain cases than the ordinary
complete trill. . . . Mr. Bach [C. P. E.] calls this trill a *Pralltriller* on
account of the speed with which its three notes (and no more) must be
performed."[42] In the edition of 1756 Marpurg gives an illustration as
shown in Example 68.

Ex. 68. Marpurg, explanation of *Pralltriller*

   We do not fully understand why Aldrich severely criticizes Marpurg
for this "practical solution," as in the quotation following, and why he
holds Marpurg's statement "responsible for a good deal of the confusion
that has arisen between the *Pralltriller* and the three-notes *Schneller*."[43]
According to Aldrich,

it is hard to believe that Marpurg would have deliberately misrepresented C.
P. E.'s teaching. But, since he had certainly both read the *Versuch* and heard its
celebrated author perform, it seems equally incredible that he can have misunderstood the passage we have just cited above [C. P. E. Bach's description
of the *Pralltriller*; author's note]. The only plausible explanation of this direct
contradiction is that, in Marpurg's opinion, the speed of the ornament is so
great that it is quite impossible to perceive whether the tie in the realization is
actually performed as a tie or not, and that, consequently there was no use in
encumbering the student's mind with it.[44]

We are fully convinced that nothing other than practical considerations
prompted Marpurg's statement. His words "contrary to the rule" show
clearly enough that he wanted his suggestion to be considered an exception,
and we are glad that Aldrich finally concedes that "the tie was often
disregarded in actual performance."[45]

---

[42] Friedrich Wilhelm Marpurg, *Die Kunst das Clavier zu spielen* (1750, 1756), I, IX, vi,
8; cited by Aldrich, p. 371.
[43] The *Schneller* will be discussed later.
[44] Aldrich, pp. 371, 373.
[45] Aldrich, p. 371.

C. P. E. Bach writes out a figure, nearly identical with Marpurg's, as an example of a "short trill," but he does not give a solution for it (Ex. 69).

Ex. 69. C. P. E. Bach, explanation of short trill

Löhlein also describes the same figure. However, since most Bach authorities are very hesitant about acknowledging the authenticity of any information coming from what they call "the generation after Bach," Ludwig Landshoff's evidence of similar treatment of the short trill, gathered from Bach's own musical environment, is of greatest importance. Johann Ludwig Krebs, one of Bach's favorite pupils, who studied with him around 1735, wrote out in the "Hanschriftlicher Sammelband" a

table of ornaments that contains the following explanation:

should be played  .[46] This corresponds completely

with the solutions by Marpurg and Löhlein.

We are happy that we can add one more piece of evidence from the hand of an even more distinguished pupil of Bach, Johann Philipp Kirnberger. In bar 26 of the C sharp minor Fugue, *W.K.* II, we find the situation given in Example 70; however, in Kirnberger's copy this measure is written out in full notes (Ex. 71). Although the case is not a literal

Ex. 70. Fugue in C sharp minor, *W.K.* II,   Ex. 71. The same. Kirnberger's copy
　　　bar 26

Pralltriller according to C. P. E. Bach's definition, it is in itself a very important example of the execution of a *short trill*, and is obviously a

---

[46] Johann Ludwig Krebs, "Handschriftlicher Sammelband," MS. 803, Staatsbibliothek, Berlin.

12

practical solution for avoiding the awkwardness of playing it as in Example 72. Let us mention that Kirnberger was Bach's pupil from

Ex. 72

1736 to 1741, just those years during which the second volume of the *Welltempered Keyboard* was assembled.

The documentary value of this testimony from two of Bach's most talented disciples cannot be overestimated; it gives direct proof that in a descending line the "inverted mordent" becomes a permissible tool when the speed of a piece makes the execution of a four-note trill impractical.

Only one case, the sigh motive with a short trill (Ex. 73), seems to withstand any documentary explanation. Strangely enough, whenever it

Ex. 73

appears, it nearly always leads to forbidden fifths if it is played with four notes. No solution other than the three-note "inverted mordent" seems to offer itself. In C. P. E. Bach's *Essay*, the "inverted mordent" is never mentioned as an independent ornament. However, he describes an ornament called "*Schneller*," which, he claims, is not mentioned by other writers. This ornament, he says, must invariably be written in small notes:

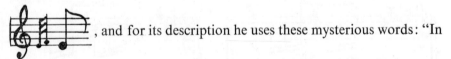 , and for its description he uses these mysterious words: "In

its employment as well as its shape it is the opposite of the mordent, but *its tones are identical with those of the short trill.*"[47]

It is not easy to ascertain what C. P. E. Bach means by these words. Does he imply that there exists a short trill consisting of three notes, or does he only want to identify the notes of the *Schneller* with those of the

---

[47] *Essay*, p. 142. Italics mine.

short trill that actually sound?[48] It is not possible to decide this. No trill of three notes is ever mentioned in the paragraphs on the "short or half trill," and the *Pralltriller* situation is clearly a restricted one, with the 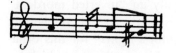 sign on the second note of a falling second. We are searching for a solution of the opposite situation, a sign on the *first* note of a falling second.

To our great astonishment, we find among the examples that C. P. E. Bach gives for the *Schneller* the figure in Example 74, to which he adds

Ex. 74. C. P. E. Bach, *Schneller*

that this is frequently used "*at caesurae* [*sic!*]."[49] We naturally identify this solution with the sigh motive which we have already claimed can only be played this way. Unfortunately the case is still more complicated. In the section on the *turn*, we again find the sigh motive, shown in Example 75, which is almost identical with J. S. Bach's Prelude in F minor, *W.K.* II.

Ex. 75. C. P. E. Bach, turn and sigh

In the explanation of this example C. P. E. Bach writes that the turn "may replace the trill in those cases where the latter is difficult to perform owing to the presence of another voice in the same hand. The substitution may be made only on a relatively short note, for others cannot be completely filled in by the turn."[50] His solution this time is therefore the figure in Example 76. But even this is not the end of the story of the sigh

Ex. 76

---

[48] That the latter supposition might be the explanation becomes more probable when we find C. P. E. Bach describing the *mordent* in these words: "It should be observed that the mordent is the opposite of the short trill" (*Essay*, p. 131).

[49] *Essay*, p. 143. Italics mine.

[50] *Essay*, p. 115.

motive, for we find it cited a third time in the section on appoggiaturas
(Ex. 77).[51] Yet, because only the three-note solution is able to avoid the

Ex. 77

undesirable parallels that frequently arise when ornamentation is applied
to Bach's sigh motive, playing what is actually an "inverted mordent"
remains the only way out of this impasse; this is true in spite of the fact
that C. P. E. Bach could almost claim "inventor's rights" for this ornament, and required that it always be written out in small notes, which his
father never did.

C. P. E. Bach offers three different solutions for the sigh motive.
Should we conclude from this that in J. S. Bach's works we should also
give it different solutions, depending on whether undesirable fifths arise
or not? Should we really play three notes in the Prelude in F minor,
W.K. II, and a four-note trill or the turn solution in the Partita in E minor
where there is no problem of parallels? To us, the plasticity and expressive
power—let us again call it the affect—of the sigh motive is so great that
we feel it to be an unchangeable value and cannot bring ourselves to play
it in three different ways. It is very surprising that the peculiar problems
of this deeply human motive—no other figure is mentioned in C. P. E.
Bach's *Essay* three times—are never mentioned in any other treatise. It is
still more surprising that such a great connoisseur of Bach's language as
Ludwig Landshoff takes the existence of the "inverted mordent" for
granted, calls it simply *"Pralltriller,"* and applies it even where no
descending second is involved (the decisive factor for C. P. E.), although
no contemporary document stands behind this type of treatment.

Looking further back into the history of the trill, we find "inverted
mordents" used as tremolos in Diruta's *Il Transilvano* in 1593 (Ex. 78).[52]

Ex. 78. Diruta, *Il Transilvano*, "inverted mordent"

---

[51] *Essay*, p. 91.
[52] G. Diruta, *Il Transilvano* (Venice, 1593); quoted by Dannreuther, p. 8.

Mersenne and the lutenists also used it.[53] Then, for almost 150 years it seems to have remained unmentioned. Since Bach actually wrote out the "inverted mordent" on more than one occasion, and since there is no other way in which to make so many applications of  in Bach's works sound right other than by playing an "inverted mordent," we must acknowledge that this shortest of trills had gone "underground" for that period but that it emerged again during Bach's lifetime. It is decidedly not foreign to his idiom, as many writers have tried to make us believe.

One special interpretation of the trill that has found its way into many modern editions still needs to be mentioned: the habit of stopping

a trill like  on the main note at the beat of the dot be-

fore proceeding with the notes of the afterbeat. This practice has been sharply condemned by Aldrich, who claims that "this interpretation seems to miss the point entirely, for in it the closing notes neither stand for a mordent nor do they provide a smooth transition between the trill and the following note."[54] There cannot be any doubt that, in general, this way of execution is unjustifiable; yet four times Bach writes out a trill that seems to have serious implications in this direction (Exs. 79, 80, and 81).

Ex. 79. French Overture, 2nd *Grave*, bar 2

Ex. 80. Prelude in E minor, *W.K.* I, bar 10 (same in bar 12)

---

[53] In Mersenne's *Harmonie universelle* (1636) and Gaultier's *Pièces de Luth* (1660), the sign ""′″ stands for "*tremblement*," as follows:

[54] Aldrich, p. 336. The mordent mentioned by Aldrich is, of course, an inverted one, an ornament that he does not recognize.

The first two examples do not correspond completely with our problem because Bach interrupts the trill with a rest instead of with a

Ex. 81. Concerto for 3 Harpsichords in D minor, Movement 2, two last bars

prolonged note, and this rest covers only half the value of the dot. Furthermore, in these cases the final note is ascending, so that the three last notes together give the impression of a slide. However, the example from the Concerto for Three Harpsichords fits the case exactly, and proves that stopping on the main note is not totally foreign to Bach's idiom.

TURN AND SLIDE

The execution of the turn in Bach's keyboard works gives no trouble. The rule that it consists of only four notes,[55] beginning on the upper auxiliary, is always applicable except for the few cases previously mentioned where Bach writes out a turn of five notes in full values.[56] Turns of *four* notes are written out in the Fugue in G major, *W.K.* I, the Gigue from the French Overture, and the Fugue in E minor, *W.K.* II, as well as

in other pieces. The special case of ♪ ⌒ ♪ has apparently never changed;

it was generally executed in Bach's time just as it is treated now.[57]

In regard to the slide, which is also often written out in full, nothing more has to be said than that it should always be played on, and never before, the beat—a fact which is generally understood for the turn also.

THE MORDENT

The mordent, too, offers almost no problems, in contrast to the serious trouble that its "illegal brother," the "inverted mordent," gave us. That the auxiliary note of the mordent is always its diatonic neighbor is so

---

[55] That nearly all turns in Haydn's and Mozart's works, and in Beethoven's earlier works, should also be played with four notes is still not generally known.

[56] An example of such a turn can be seen in Example 58.

[57] The only exception to this rule of which I have become aware has been discussed on p. 152.

well known that we need hardly mention it. In a few cases it is hard to know whether to play more than one oscillation, a procedure usually indicated by the sign ∿, because the same sign is sometimes used for the *trill with termination* and is therefore equal to ∿. Yet this problem does not arise in any major work. More often than any other ornament, the mordent is written out in full notes; indeed, sometimes we are unable to explain why Bach did not use the symbol instead.[58] Then again, whether

every appearance of a figure like 𝄢 should be called a mordent is

hard to decide. Only with greatest hesitancy would we include the theme of the popular C minor Fugue, *W.K.* I (Ex. 82a), among such cases, as Aldrich does (Ex. 82b).[59] Nevertheless, Bach's elaboration (Ex. 83) of the measure from the second movement of Marcello's Oboe Concerto (Ex. 84)

Ex. 82a. Fugue in C minor, *W.K.* I

Ex. 82b. The same. Aldrich

Ex. 83. Marcello, Oboe Concerto, Movement 2. Bach's elaboration

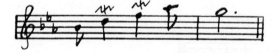

Ex. 84. The same. Marcello's original

---

[58] For example, the Italian Concerto, second movement, bars 35, 36.
[59] Aldrich, Table 22.

speaks in Aldrich's favor.[60] On the other hand, the Prelude in A flat major, *W.K.* I (Ex. 90a), looks, and must be felt equally "un-Bachian" when written with *agréments* (Ex. 90b).

Ex. 90a. Prelude in A flat major, *W.K.* I   Ex. 90b. The same, with *agréments*

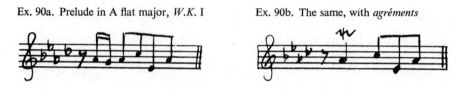

---

[60] If we concede this, however, we must make the same concession in the following cases (Exs. 85, 86, 87), which involve the "inverted mordent" in a flagrant way.

Ex. 85. *Magnificat*, aria "Et exultavit," bar 12, violin part

Ex. 86. Cantata 63, No. 7, bar 2 (B.G., vol. XVI, p. 53)

Ex. 87. Cantata 125, No. 3 (B.G., vol. XXVI), bar 1

The bass part of the chorale "Freuet euch und jubiliert," meant to be interpolated into performances of the *Magnificat*, is particularly striking (Ex. 88).

Ex. 88. "Freuet euch und jubiliert," bass part

Finally, to give an example from the work of another composer, see bars 24–25 of the aria "Without the swains assidious care," from Handel's oratorio *Susanna* (Ex. 89).

Ex. 89. Handel, *Susanna*, aria "Without the swains assidious care," bars 24–25

THE APPOGGIATURA

The chief problem encountered in dealing with the appoggiatura resembles that presented by the trill: very frequently a literal application of the rules found in the textbooks proves impossible, in spite of the fact that these rules are in general clearer and less open to arbitrary solution than those pertaining to the trill. It would have been easy to avoid any difficulty with appoggiaturas, had it been agreed to write them out in their real note values; instead, they were played with all possible variations of duration, and the symbol used in no way designated the actual length of the note. Once more we will follow the practice of not discussing the rules in general, but of exposing individual rules to their practical consequences when applied to Bach's works.

As confirmed by Bach's own table, the normal length of the appoggiatura is half the value of the main note. However, Nos. 1–4 on the Appoggiatura Table (see Appendix B) all lead to bad parallels when executed this way.

That the rule of clean voice leading must be strictly observed in regard to appoggiaturas is explicitly underlined by C. P. E. Bach: "As with all embellishments, the introduction of an appoggiatura must not corrupt the purity of voice leading."[61] His own illustrations of treatments that had "better not be put into practice" are shown in Example 91.[62]

Ex. 91. From C. P. E. Bach

For an appoggiatura before a dotted note, the "official" rule of the textbooks is that two-thirds of the value of the dotted note goes to the

Ex. 92

appoggiatura and one-third goes to the note itself (Ex. 92). Yet this execution, too, is sometimes excluded by the threat of parallels (see

---

[61] *Essay*, p. 95.
[62] *Essay*, p. 95.

Appoggiatura Table, Nos. 5–11). C. P. E. Bach gives such an example (Ex. 93) and states, "If the appoggiatura is held beyond its written length,

Ex. 93. From C. P. E. Bach

it will create open fifths."[63] It is interesting to see how sensitive he is to harsh voice leading. He repudiates the use of quarter-note appoggiaturas in the cases in Example 94, because "the fifths struck against the bass will

Ex. 94. From C. P. E. Bach

Ex. 95. From C. P. E. Bach

sound ugly."[64] About Example 95, he says that the appoggiatura "must not be prolonged or the seventh will sound too harsh."[65]

Would his father have felt the same way? That Johann Sebastian sometimes consciously enjoyed "rough" voice leading cannot be denied. One can see it in the magnificent excerpt from the Prelude in C sharp minor, *W.K.* II (Ex. 96). There is, however, a considerable difference

Ex. 96. Prelude in C sharp minor, *W.K.* II, bars 9–10

---

[63] *Essay*, p. 95.
[64] *Essay*, p. 95.
[65] *Essay*, p. 95.

between these "bold rough" sounds and "obviously ugly" sounds, which the elder Bach would have wanted to avoid. An example of the latter occurs in the Toccata of the Partita in E minor, where the sigh motive is involved. Although in most pieces in which this motive is used, bad parallels appear when we try to start the  on the upper auxiliary, no direct parallels occur (as already mentioned on p. 168) in this Toccata.[66] However, if we take a broader view, the empty octaves in bars 69 and 70 (Ex. 99; see bars 40 and 41 as well) sound so hollow that we almost feel

Ex. 99. Partita in E minor, Toccata, bars 69–70

---

[66] This is true, however, only of the final version. In the version found in the *Notebook for Anna Magdalena Bach*, we see that bars 63–64 were originally written as in Example 97, which Bach later changed to the bars shown in Example 98.

Ex. 97. Partita in E minor, Toccata, bars 63–64 as in *Notebook for Anna Magdalena Bach*

Ex. 98. The same. Final version

If we take the addition of a  on the main note of the sigh motive for granted (nowhere in the first version was the  sign written out), we see immediately that the "four-note solution" produces another case of parallel fifths. Might this have been the reason Bach altered the lines for the final version?

them as parallel octaves; we therefore issue a strong warning that for this piece also, the "inverted-mordent" solution of the sigh motive is obligatory. A comparison of these "octaves" with the ugly-sounding fifths of C. P. E. Bach's example shows the striking similarity between them.[67]

The flexibility in the treatment of appoggiaturas went so far that even at the end of a piece the rule that two-thirds of the value of a dotted note goes to an appoggiatura before it did not invariably hold; this is beautifully proved by the last bars of both sections of the second movement of the Flute Sonata in B minor (Ex. 101). The eighth note written

Ex. 101. Flute Sonata in B minor, Movement 2, last bars of first and second parts

out in the harpsichord part at the end of the first section leaves no doubt that the appoggiatura at the end of the second section must be treated the same way.

---

[67] Yet—and here again we are made aware of the tragic dilemma to which the student of the secrets of Bach's art is so often exposed—Bach himself contradicts the theory that he would rather have avoided writing such parallels at large distances, as we see from the bars of the "Augmentation Canon" of the *Art of the Fugue* in Example 100. The unusual care that

Ex. 100. *Art of the Fugue*, "Augmentation Canon"

was applied in the elaboration of this canon, made known to us by the numerous alterations to which Bach subjected it, excludes the possibility that these parallels were caused by carelessness or oversight, and adds to the "riddle of the sigh motive." Fortunately, these bars do not disturb the validity of our repudiation of the parallels in the examples quoted on p. 152. Note that this is, as far as I know, the only case where Bach uses an appoggiatura before the sigh, corresponding to C. P. E. Bach's notation cited on p. 167, instead of the ⌇⌇ above the first note.

Other interesting cases in which Bach indicates the proper length of the appoggiaturas involved can be found in Numbers 11a and b on the Appoggiatura Table. His placing of the figures of the thorough bass (at NB) shows that the appoggiaturas are not to be given their usual value, but the length of an eighth instead. This was obviously done to avoid parallels. How minute the examination of individual situations must sometimes be in order to find an implied solution becomes evident when we study the examples from the *Largo* of the Harpsichord-Violin Sonata in G major (Nos. 12a, b, and c). Bar 2 shows that the value of a quarter for the appoggiatura is impossible on account of the resulting parallel octaves; bar 17 excludes the value of a sixteenth because of parallel fifths. The only length for the grace note that fits all three bars is that of an eighth, notwithstanding the parallel fourths in bar 6, which were certainly pleasing to Bach. He used them, for example, in the Prelude in C sharp minor, *W.K.* II (see Ex. 96, above), and in bar 13 of the Fugue in D sharp

Ex. 102. Fugue in D sharp minor, *W.K.* II, bar 13

minor, *W.K.* II (Ex. 102). From all these examples it becomes obvious that no general rule for the duration of an appoggiatura can be given.[68]

Not very well known among Bach players are the following special cases, cited by Quantz (Ex. 103)[69] and C. P. E. Bach (Ex. 104).[70] How far

Ex. 103. From Quantz

Ex. 104. From C. P. E. Bach

---

[68] A rather ingenious "practical recipe" for appoggiaturas has been offered by Hans Joachim Moser. He suggests that the length of the appoggiatura, which is not always half the value of the main note, is, however, always identical with half the value of the *counting unit*, the inner pulse of a piece ("Zu Frage der Ausführung der Ornamente bei Seb. Bach," *Bach-Jahrbuch*, 1916, p. 8; *Johann Sebastian Bach*, Berlin, 1935, p. 234). We have not been able to check his rule through the entire keyboard literature, but his examples are very convincing.

[69] *Versuch*, Table VI, Figures 15 and 16.

[70] *Essay*, pp. 90f.

their range of application extends is still unclarified. The example in 6/8 time sounds rather convincing when applied to bars 1, 2, 17, 28, 29, 30, 31, and 32 in the Gigue of the French Overture, and to bar 16 in Variation 7 of the *Goldberg Variations*. The same rule applied to bar 8 of this Variation (Appoggiatura Table, No. 13) would, however, "blur the melodic line," as Kirkpatrick points out in his edition. It would be equally impossible to apply it to Numbers 14 and 15, and to the two examples from Bach's chamber music, Numbers 16 and 17. In 4/4 or 2/4 time, I know of no case where the rule could be applied.

About the rule shown in Example 105[71] (an appoggiatura to a note followed by a rest is played in such a way that the appoggiatura takes the

Ex. 105. From C. P. E. Bach

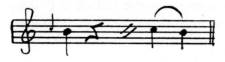

place of the main note; the latter note is deferred to the rest), very little is known. The only place where it might be possible to use it is in bar 2 of the Prelude in E flat major, *W.K.* II (Ex. 106). Yet neither a quarter nor

Ex. 106. Prelude in E flat major, *W.K.* II, bars 1–2

an eighth note could be ruled out convincingly for the length of the appoggiatura.

When all these cases are considered, it seems beyond doubt that no textbook rule exists which was not abandoned by Bach here and there, for reasons not always easy to determine; even in regard to what we call "pure voice leading," Bach apparently had opinions of his own that were not shared by everybody. We will therefore have to be content with avoiding flagrant violations of good taste in our execution of ornaments, and we must admit that for a few very puzzling pieces, like the Aria of the *Goldberg Variations*, the Sarabande of the Fifth Partita, and the ornamented version of the Sinfonia in E flat major, universal agreement will probably never be reached. Nevertheless, it would be absolutely wrong to think that these are problems of minor importance.

In the first of these highly problematic pieces, the theme of the

---

[71] *Essay*, p. 91.

Goldberg Variations, the question of the proper length for the appoggiaturas appears in virtually every second bar. With all due respect for Kirkpatrick's thoughtful remarks in his masterful edition, we have to disagree with him about his solution for bar 18. Here he gives the appoggiatura the length of a quarter note, while in all corresponding places (bars 2, 4, 6, 20, 25, and 26) he assigns the length of an eighth. He even stresses that he does this in bar 26 for reasons of consistency. Actually, the situation in bar 18 seems exactly the same as that in the other bars. We doubt, too, that it is necessary to give the appoggiaturas in bars 21 and 22 the length of a sixteenth in order "to avoid parallel sevenths"; these sevenths were probably a source of special enjoyment for the bold ear of the master, who did not hesitate to write them in the C sharp minor Prelude, *W.K.* II, as well (see p. 174).

Another unsolved mystery is the proper length of the short appoggiaturas in Variation 13 of the *Goldberg Variations*, where the traditional solution leads, in bar 17, to very ugly parallel octaves, and in bars 25 and 26 to equally bad parallel fifths. In this case Busoni is the only editor who was aware of the problem, at least in bar 17; yet he overlooked it in bars 25 and 26. His solution of interpreting the appoggiatura as a *Nachschlag* (connecting it with the note before) is probably the best way out of the impasse, and at the same time removes the ugly sound of the empty octave in bar 2. Yet Kirkpatrick's citation of C. P. E. Bach's remark: " 'When the appoggiatura sounds the octave of the bars, it cannot be long, because the harmony would be too empty' (*Essay*, II, 2, 14)" is no cure for the parallels in bars 17, 25, and 26.

The Sarabande of the Fifth Partita offers, at first glance, some notation puzzles. Why did Bach write the "upbeat note" of the melody mostly at its real value of a sixteenth but in bars 4, 20, and 22 as an eighth? And why did Bach write an appoggiatura on the first beat of the same bars (4, 20, 22) but real notes in bars 8 and 34? Closer examination, however, shows that no inconsistency from Bach's side is involved. In bar 8, it is the bass part which forces Bach to give the "upbeat g" the correct value. It would have looked very odd if he would have written here an appoggiatura before a dotted quarter and then an eighth note, meant to be played at the same time as the sixteenth of the left hand (the traditional rule that governs this type of playing is explained in detail on p. 193). In bar 34, the rest which Bach wanted in the highest part forced him to write correct values for all voices. In bars 4, 20, and 22 no such complications were involved. Bach could therefore feel certain that the traditional "upbeat rule" would be respected by every player.

In the famous "ornamented version" of the Sinfonia in E flat major, which is almost never played, it is doubtful whether the soprano line of bar 23 is a decisive indication that all appoggiaturas in this piece should follow the "rule of the tied note" (see p. 178), as Landshoff suggests. In bar 20 this version leads to ugly parallel fifths, which Landshoff tries to avoid by changing the short appoggiaturas of bars 19 and 20 into *Nachschläge*. This is a very artificial device. Giving all appoggiaturas the length of an eighth note, which also removes the parallels, seems to be the most reasonable solution.

Our reason for advocating this interpretation has far-reaching consequences, inasmuch as the appoggiaturas very often represent a "sigh," almost identical with the sigh motive. We do not want to call every appoggiatura before a note a second lower a sigh, but we can at least state that whenever the affect of the piece in question makes a sigh reasonable, the length of the appoggiatura should not be more than one-half the value of the main note when the latter is a quarter, one-third when the metre uses a dotted quarter. The famous duet "So ist mein Jesus nun gefangen," from the *St. Matthew Passion*, is completely distorted when it is sung as in Example 107, instead of as in Example 108; the former way,

Ex. 107. *St. Matthew Passion*, "So ist mein Jesus nun gefangen"

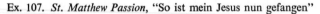

Ex. 108. The same

unfortunately, is still recommended occasionally. It can hardly be doubted that the affect here calls for the sigh. Furthermore, Bach gave us additional proof in the C minor Fantasy for Organ, bar 59, where he wrote out in full notes the bars in Example 109, which are clearly related to the melodic

Ex. 109. Fantasy for Organ in C minor, bar 59

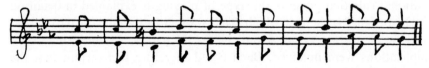

line of the duet. In Rameau's *Pièces de Concert* we find the measures in Example 110, from the slow movement of the Third Concerto, "La

Timide," Second Rondeau, which indicate that the sigh motive belongs
to the "international vocabulary of music."

Ex. 110. Rameau, Third Concerto, "La Timide," Second Rondeau, bars 13–14

Although these examples should be sufficient to prove that the
eighth-note solution is correct when the sigh affect is involved, the extraordinary fame and beauty of the duet from the *Passion* and the prominence
of some people who advocate the "long" appoggiatura cause us to go into
more detail in this special case. The fact that we know of no argument
that could support the "long" solution on musical grounds may be called
a matter of personal opinion; however, several points favor the "short"
version:

    1. The "long" solution gives the impression of ¢ instead of C time.[72]

    2. The harmonic skeleton that underlies the melodic line at the
beginning is clearly that illustrated in Example 111; but the "long"
appoggiaturas create a false impression, shown in Example 112, in which

Ex. 111

Ex. 112

the tonic (NB) is emphasized instead of the dominant. A similar situation
arises in bars 9 and 10 (Ex. 113), where the "long" execution puts undue

Ex. 113. *St. Matthew Passion*, "So ist mein Jesus nun gefangen," bars 9–10

---

[72] Moser's formula that appoggiaturas should get half the value of the counting unit
(see footnote 68, above), which in this case is the quarter note, is based in part on this example.

emphasis on the $\frac{6}{4}$ chords and creates the impression shown in Example 114, in place of the cadential formula I–V (Ex. 115).

Ex. 114   Ex. 115

3. The cries of the chorus, "Lasst ihn, haltet, bindet nicht," in bars 43–45, smother the resolution of the appoggiaturas if the dissonances are made "long."

4. The "long" solution requires that the flute parts in bars 43–45 be played as in Example 116. The parallel fifths occuring here are the final

Ex. 116. *St. Matthew Passion*, "So ist mein Jesus nun gefangen," bars 43–45

proof that the "*short*" solution is the only right one. Again we see to what extent details have to be examined in order to find solutions that were probably natural and traditional in Bach's period.

Nothing more needs to be added at the present to our discussion of ornament problems.[73] The rather rare cases of acciaccatura and arpeggio will be dealt with, wherever they occur, in Appendix A. In regard to the arpeggio, we need only mention here that it too, like all other embellishments, must be played *on* and not *before* the beat (as is customary nowadays). We do not expect that readers, asking desperately for guidance, especially in regard to onerous problems connected with the long trill, the short trill, and the appoggiatura, will be completely satisfied with the information given by us. Yet we felt obliged to show the *actual* situation in the field of ornamentation, with all its unsolved questions, instead of imposing textbook laws that, as we proved, were often broken by Bach. It may be pardonable and understandable that many writers and editors, in their endeavor to help the cause of Bach performance, have offered their tentative proposals as authentic solutions. But we have to raise a warning voice to make it clear how far we are, even now, from an authoritative interpretation of the ornaments in the keyboard works of Bach.

---

[73] A Bach student eager to get more "systematic" information on ornaments is urged to consult Walter Emery's excellent book, *Bach's Ornaments*, which will give him plenty of additional material for thought.

CHAPTER 6

Conventional Alterations
of Rhythms

NOTES INÉGALES

In contrast to present-day custom, which considers it the duty of a composer to write out the rhythmical values of a piece in such a way that the interpreter is never left in doubt about their treatment, there existed in earlier periods quite a few situations in which the notation of a rhythm did not correspond to the way in which the rhythm was meant to be executed. The most formidable of these, to which François Couperin refers in his famous statement in *L'Art de toucher le clavecin*: "We do not play as we write,"[1] is the case of the *notes inégales*, a problem whose mere existence is still nearly unknown to today's interpreters. The solution of this problem, in accordance with the rules found in numerous treatises written between 1600 and 1800, is so important to the correct interpretation of early French music that its neglect is indefensible. All sources agree that the application of the rules of "inequality" was restricted to French music. However, because Arnold Dolmetsch,[2] and more recently others, have advanced the theory that these rules should be applied to the interpretation of Bach's works, we will give a condensed report on the chief aspects of the problem.

The basic rule of "inequality" is that in passages of predominantly conjunct motion, pairs of notes of *equal* length that are one degree shorter in value than the lower figure of the time signature (for example, quarter notes in 3/2 time, eighths in 3/4, sixteenths in 3/8 or 6/8 time, and so on)

---

[1] (1716; complete edition, Paris, 1933), vol. I, p. 41.
[2] *The Interpretation of the Music of the Seventeenth and Eighteenth Centuries*, pp. 53f.

are supposed to be played *unequally*, the first being prolonged at the cost of the second. The length of such a prolongation varies, according to the character of the piece, from a slight hold to an actual dotting or even double dotting: from ♩♩ to ♩ ♪ to ♩.. ♫ . This type of playing was sometimes specifically prescribed by words like "*louré*" (for slight hold), "*piqué*," or "*pointé*" (for outspoken dotting), while words such as "*notes égales*," "*détaché*," "*décidé*," or "*marqué*" were written when no rhythmic alteration was desired. A complicated system of rules governed the application of "unequal playing," but how common it was can easily be deduced from the fact that composers used to indicate the places where "inequality" should *not* be applied more often than they explicitly asked for it.[3] What justifies the pretension of Arnold Dolmetsch and later writers that this French mannerism should be applied to the works of J. S. Bach? Is there any source material of German origin that would validate this procedure? The enormous prestige enjoyed by French music everywhere in Europe at this time leaves no doubt that any composers and writers of more than provincial stature were acquainted with the French practice. Georg Muffat, who studied for six years in Paris, described "inequality" as "used by the Lullists" in the Preface to his *Florilegium Musicum* (1698).[4] Johann Gottfried Walther also mentions "inequality" in the notes on "*lourer*" and "*quantitas notarum*" in his *Musikalisches Lexicon*.[5] More important than these two statements, of which Muffat's underlines the restriction of *inégalité* to French music, is a paragraph in Johann David Heinichen's *Der Generalbass in der Composition*, in which he says that "as is well known [*bekanntermassen*], the first and third notes in groups of equal value are always inherently long."[6]

---

[3] Readers interested in obtaining more detailed information about this problem may consult the article by E. Borrel, "Les notes inégales dans l'ancienne musique française," *Revue de Musicologie*, vol. XV, no. 40 (November 1931), p. 278; and Wilfrid Mellers' book, *François Couperin and the French Classic Tradition* (London, [1949]), pp. 295ff.

[4] *Florilegium Musicum, Denkmäler Oesterreich. Tonkunst*, II, 24.

[5] (Leipzig, 1732; facsimile reprint: Kassel, 1953).

[6] (Dresden, 1728), p. 27. Unfortunately, Heinichen's paragraph is open to various interpretations. He says only that in groups of four notes the individual notes are *called* long and short according to their inner (harmonic) value, and it is indeed possible that he refers only to a problem of nomenclature rather than to one of performance. This interpretation is supported by Kellner's statement: "Notes of equal value have not only *quantitatem extrinsicam* but also *intrinsicam*. Externally they can be *treated* equally slow or fast, but in regard to their inner value, one is long, the other short" ("*Es haben die Noten von gleichem valore nicht allein quantitatem extrinsicam, sondern auch intrinsicam, vermöge welcher sie zwar äusserlich eine wie die andre gleich langsam oder gleich geschwinde tractirt werden können, innerlich aber ist die eine lang, die andre kurz. Zum Exempel, es wären in einem Takte 8 Achtelteile, da wären nach der innersten Geltung die erste lang, die zweite kurs U.S.W., da sie doch nach ihrer äusserlichen Geltung eine wie die andre gleich lang oder gleich kurz ausgehalten werden möchten*"; Daniel

Finally there is a long paragraph in Quantz's *Versuch* that contains the essence of the French rules of "inequality";[7] it omits the reservation of the rule for French music and adds two rules that are never mentioned by French writers.

That the technique of inequality was unknown to Bach is highly improbable. When he visited the court of Celle he had ample opportunity to become acquainted with all kinds of French music, and his works do contain many obvious traces of French influence. Yet there does not exist a single bar in Bach's entire work that gives external evidence that inequality should be applied. Since equal playing was often explicitly indicated in French music, as we have seen, at least a few direction marks for it should appear here and there in Bach's music if inequality was meant to be applied as frequently as Dolmetsch wants it to be. Some modern interpreters go so far as to play not only nearly all the sarabandes of the suite collections but also the Prelude of the First Partita and the Aria of the Sixth almost wholly in unequal values. We know that Bach trusted so little in the correct execution of ornaments that he wrote a great number of them out in full. Would he not, at some time, have written out in full the rhythmical values of the *notes inégales* if he desired that type of execution? Might this not be expected in pieces in which he wrote out ornaments in abundance, such as the second movement of the Italian Concerto, Variation 13 of the *Goldberg Variations*, or the Prelude in F sharp minor, *W.K.* II?

To my knowledge, there are in Bach's keyboard works only two places where, for a moment, one might suspect the traces of the French technique. The first is in the harpsichord version of the Violin Concerto in E major. In transcribing measures 23 and 24 of the second movement, Bach changed the even rhythm of the violin version (Ex. 117) into a dotted line (Ex. 118). However, the slur over all four notes reveals that he

Ex. 117. Violin Concerto in E major, bar 23

Kellner, *Treulicher Unterricht im Generalbass*, Hamburg, 1732, p. 11). In the light of our present knowledge, it is impossible to draw binding conclusions about the role of inequality in Germany.

[7] *Versuch*, XI, paragraph 12. In discussing the examples of appoggiaturas, Quantz also says explicitly that the right way to play these ornaments "derives from the French manner of playing" (VIII, paragraph 6). Quantz's paragraph, which is the only clearly written testimony on this subject, cannot be taken too seriously. Quantz lived in Paris for seven months and shows obvious leanings toward French taste in both his writing and his music.

simply intended a "lombardian" variation of the original line[8] and did not mean to write out in notes the French *coulé*, which always refers to only two consecutive notes.

Ex. 118. The same. Harpsichord transcription

The second case that might seem to indicate the use of the French technique, one that even offers a sample of the revoking of unequal playing by the use of dots above the notes, occurs in the French overture of the *Goldberg Variations*, a piece in which Bach deliberately imitates French style (Ex. 119).

Ex. 119. *Goldberg Variations*, French overture, bars 8–9

Yet these dots really prove nothing, because similar marks are found in other pieces where there can be not the least suspicion that equal playing had to be requested; in reality they merely ask for a *martellato* execution. See, for example, bar 93 of the last movement of the Concerto in A major for Harpsichord.

In my opinion, the richness and flexibility of Bach's articulation, which has no equal in French music, is so great that it makes the artificial application of unequal playing unnecessary and unwanted. Moreover, a comparison of the innumerable slurs found in Bach's chamber and vocal music with those that Couperin wrote down for the application of the French technique makes us realize that Bach's use of the slur has a totally different meaning.

DOTTED NOTES

While the problem of the *notes inégales* had better be discarded, or at least put aside until more convincing evidence can be produced than has

---

[8] Bar 7 of the theme of the *Goldberg Variations* contains another example of the relatively rare application of the "lombardian" effect in Bach's works.

hitherto been at our disposal, another feature of French music has to be considered very seriously, namely, the problem of *dotted notes*. There is no doubt that the well-known rule[9] of giving a short note following a dotted one a shorter duration than that indicated by its mathematical value had been unanimously adopted by German composers. It was applied not only to a single note, so that ♩. ♪ was meant to be played like ♩.. ♬, but also to groups of short notes, such as those that can be found in nearly every French overture; ♩. ♬ was therefore to be played like ♩. ♬.[10] It is interesting to notice that a brief rest could be taken before playing the short note (or notes): ♩. ♪ could be played like ♩. ♪.[11]

Of greatest importance and very little known is the custom, reported by Quantz, that the Frenchmen (*Die Welschen*) also used the rule of abbreviation for an eighth note following a quarter "in bourrées, entrées, rigaudons, gavottes, and rondos in 4/4 or 2 time, and in loures, sarabandes, courantes, and chaconnes in 3/4 time."[12] When the rhythm ♩. ♪ coincided with the rhythm ♩. ♪♪♪ in another voice, the eighth note was also played as a thirty-second: . It is to the merit of Joseph Ponte that he pointed out that the original print of the Sarabande of the Fifth Partita reveals this clearly and indisputably in the way in which Bach had the music set (Ex. 120).[13] (The situation is the same in the print of bars 9, 10, 13, 23, and 25, also.) Yet, when we try to apply this rule more widely to Bach's works, we should not be surprised if we find trouble again.

---

[9] See Quantz, *Versuch*, V, paragraphs 20ff.

[10] The version ♩. ♬, found in many pedagogic editions, is not "short" enough.

[11] Quantz, *Versuch*, XVII, 7, paragraph 58.

[12] Quantz, XVII, 7, paragraph 58.

[13] Joseph Ponte, "Problems in the Performance of J. S. Bach's Clavierübung, part I" (unpublished honor thesis, Harvard University, 1952), p. 11.

In the "real" overtures, such as the French Overture, the Overture to the Fourth Partita, the Sinfonia of the Second Partita, and Variation 16

Ex. 120. Partita V, Sarabande, bar 11

of the *Goldberg Variations*, no difficulties arise. However, the range of influence of this "French rhythm" extends still further, and in many cases the problem of where to draw the line for the application of the "abbreviation" is a very delicate one. The Gigue of the First French Suite (Ex. 121a) is so saturated with dotted rhythms that there can be no doubt about its correct execution (Ex. 121b).[14] When we look at the earlier

Ex. 121a. French Suite I, Gigue

Ex. 121b. The same

version of the Gigue of the Sixth Partita, written in the second *Notebook for Anna Magdalena Bach* (Ex. 122), we instantly realize that this piece

Ex. 122. Partita VI, Gigue. Earlier version

---

[14] Bar 5 of this Gigue even gives direct proof that this conclusion is correct. The collision 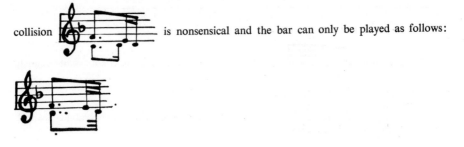 is nonsensical and the bar can only be played as follows:

seems to ask for the same treatment. We should therefore not hesitate to try the final version, which Bach wrote in double values (Ex. 123), in the same style.

Ex. 123. The same. Final version

At first, this incomparable piece seems to sound still bolder and more sparkling than it would when played as written. Yet, with this change, there are new problems to solve. The first one, whether we should continue to play in the "overdotted way" (as we may be allowed to call the procedure of playing ♩... 𝄾 instead of ♩. ♪) when Bach's writing changes from ♩. ♪ to ♩ ♫, need not disturb us. Both are the same rhythms and can be treated alike. What, however, should we do when figures like ♫♩ or ♩♫ begin to appear? Following the rules cited on page 187, we have the right to play ♫♩. or ♩. ♫ respectively.[15] Alas, when figures like ♫♫ show up (from bar 18 on), we lose our courage at the thought of playing ♩. ♫♫♩., and when we arrive at bar 20 we are certainly at our wit's end. Here we are confronted with the situation pictured in Example 124, and would therefore have to

Ex. 124. Partita VI, Gigue, bar 20

---

[15] These figures are also found in the Gigue of the First French Suite, which has the same rhythmic configurations and belongs to the same tempo group as the E minor Gigue. However, they appear there only in bar 21, where they pass almost unnoticed and fit well into the general picture when played:

play the bar as in Example 125. Immediately we hear that on the second quarter (at NB) the glorious dotted rhythm comes to a complete standstill,

Ex. 125. The same

which is as disturbing as it is illogical. In addition, the twofold role of the note e′ in the alto, which serves not only as the end of a phrase but also as the beginning of the following theme, is no longer clear; for the latter purpose its value would have to be that of a thirty-second instead of a dotted eighth. On these grounds alone one could come to the conclusion that any thoughts of applying "French dressing" to this Gigue have to be abandoned.

A comparison of this bar with the corresponding one in the first version of the Gigue produces further interesting evidence (Ex. 126a). It shows that this figure in the alto of the final version (Ex. 126b) had not

Ex. 126a. Partita VI, Gigue, bar 20. Earlier version

Ex. 126b. The same Final version, alto figure

originally been part of Bach's plan, but was added later as a kind of "bridge," a procedure often used by the mature Bach when he made alterations on his "early" works. We can only admire the exquisite knowledge and taste which Bach exhibits in using the rhythmical pattern

♩ ♫ ♫ ♪ for this purpose. Although we have now shown that the "bridge rhythm" should not be dotted, whether the pattern ♩. ♪ should also *not* be played in the "overdotted" way ♩... ♬, still remains undecided. In the first version this can be done with ease at the critical place, bar 20. We might almost regret that in the second version Bach smoothed out the magnificent harmonic clash of e′–c′–B, which occurs in the first version of this bar, by inverting the interval of the third between e′ and c′ and thus making it a sixth.

In the second part of this piece another problem arises that adds to the previous complications. From the third bar on, groups of four consecutive eighth notes appear in nearly every measure (only six out of twenty-four do not contain them), and we have to decide whether we should play them as written or as *notes inégales*! Technically, "unequal" performance would be much easier, because it would spare us the constant vigilance over which rhythms to play "overdotted" and which to play as written. But, since most of these groups of eighth notes are in *disjunct* motion, one cannot apply the French treatment in good conscience. On the other hand, if inequality is taken away from the groups of eighth notes, as well as from all the groups with the 🎵 or 🎵 rhythm, the playing of ♩...𝄾 in "overdotted" style becomes so awkward that even fingers accustomed to these rhythms inevitably protest against such obstacles. It is an undeniable fact that such rhythmical complications are not found in French literature.

Since the substitution of ♩...𝄾 for ♩. ♪ cannot be disproved for general application with the evidence available in this Gigue, we will have to look for other pieces in which similar problems arise. It is quite obvious that in the Prelude in F sharp major, *W.K.* II, the overdotted playing creates no difficulties at all, and it is rather hard to deny that the Prelude gains considerably in "sparkle" by being treated this way.

If we now apply this method to the Prelude in A flat major, *W.K.* II, playing all notes following dotted ones at "top speed," as shown in Example 127, bar 7, serious doubts arise as to whether we are not changing

Ex. 127. Prelude in A flat major, *W.K.* II, bar 7

Ex. 128. Prelude in E flat minor, *W.K.* I

the heavenly dignity and tranquillity of this deeply religious piece into very earthly and courtly pomp. The character of the Prelude in E flat minor, *W.K.* I, is also changed completely when it is played in the French style (Ex. 128), as is recommended by Dolmetsch.[16]

Even in the Fugue in D major, *W.K.* I, which is filled with all the elements of French-overture style, only the beginning sounds convincing

if we play  for ⌐⌐, as Dolmetsch again suggests.[17] We cannot

help feeling very strongly that in bar 9, singled out by Dolmetsch to illustrate his execution (Ex. 129), our ear would accept the $\frac{6}{4}$ harmony

Ex. 129. Fugue in D major, *W.K.* I, bar 9. Dolmetsch execution

(NB) much more willingly if it were played with the emphasis of the value of a sixteenth, as it is written, rather than in the shortened version, which makes the chord sound accidental. Bar 17 sounds equally bad, if not worse, when played the same way (Ex. 130). It is noteworthy that Dolmetsch, who was the first to advocate the introduction of unequal playing

Ex. 130. The same, bar 17

into Bach interpretation, and who advises that the Sarabande of the French Suite in D minor (Ex. 131) be played in 9/8 time with *notes*

Ex. 131. French Suite in D minor, Sarabande

---

[16] *Music of the Seventeenth and Eighteenth Centuries*, p. 64.
[17] *Music of the Seventeenth and Eighteenth Centuries*, p. 65.

inégales (Ex. 132),[18] does not dare recommend unequal playing of the sixteenths, following the French rule, in the D major Fugue (Ex. 133).

Ex. 132. The same. Dolmetsch execution

Ex. 133. Fugue in D major, *W.K.* I, bar 9

Actually, unequal playing could certainly be performed much more easily than his own version.

All these cases do not yet throw much light on our basic problem of whether overdotted playing can rightfully be added to Bach's idiom; however, interesting and pertinent ideas can be gained by considering a neighboring situation, a peculiar tradition with which most piano players are familiar.

In a piece in which dotted rhythm is used regularly, whenever a phrase begins in the middle of a beat, its first note and the rest preceding that note are written in equal rhythmical values; however, in actual playing, the first note is made as short as the other short notes following

dotted ones in that piece. Thus, the phrase   has

to be played like this:

In Bach's keyboard works, the best-known piece in which this rule has to be taken into consideration is the Sinfonia of the Second Partita. Here nothing seems to speak against such an execution (Ex. 134), which sounds convincing and natural. Only in bar 6 does a complication arise.

---

[18] *Music of the Seventeenth and Eighteenth Centuries,* p. 86.

If we apply the rules of dotting to this bar, which Bach notated in dotted sixteenths (Ex. 135), a problem is created in the second beat. Should we

Ex. 134. Partita II, Sinfonia

Ex. 135. The same, bar 6

dot the second g of the upper voice of the left hand, as in Example 136, or not, as in Example 137? The dotted version is much easier to play than

Ex. 136   Ex. 137

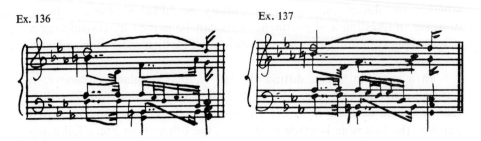

the other, which is rather awkward; yet it also takes the liberty of dotting notes that do not actually belong to those categories which allow alteration. On the other hand, one glance at Bach's version, and our instincts demand that the three notes, a' flat, d, and B, be played at the same time. Again, a convincing decision cannot be reached with the information available, although we are very much inclined to think that Bach did not expect anyone to be puzzled and wrote down what seemed to be the simplest way of notation. If every sixteenth were played "overdotted," this eighth sixteenth should be played the same way, following the custom of the period; Bach might have felt sure—to use Brahms's classic remark —that "every donkey could see it." We refer our readers, however, to page 196, where we will show that the entire problem can perhaps be seen in another light.

At this point, an excursion into French-overture situations in the cantatas produces some additional material on the case of double dotting. Dotted rhythms appear in the duet "Die Armut, so Gott auf sich nimmt" of Cantata 91, "Gelobet seist Du, Jesu Christ."[19] In an older version of the cantata, reprinted in the Appendix to the volume of the Bach-Gesellschaft, the dotted rhythm is always written out as ♪ 𝅘𝅥 𝅘𝅥𝅮𝅘𝅥𝅮𝅘𝅥𝅮 . However, in the final version, of which we have the autograph, the same rhythm appears as ♪. 𝅘𝅥 𝅘𝅥𝅮 , and twenty-seven times Bach went to the trouble of writing out this more elaborate figure.[20] Did he do so to avoid misinterpretation?

The bars (Ex. 139) from the first violin part of Cantata 108, "Es ist Euch gut, dass ich hingehe,"[21] are rather puzzling. It is hard to come to

Ex. 139. Cantata 108, "Es ist Euch gut, dass ich hingehe," first violin, bars 7–8

any conclusion other than that the differentiation between sixteenths and thirty-seconds was planned and meant to be executed. The strangest case, however, is found in the "Trauerode" (Ex. 140).[22]

The strength of this example, together with the previous ones, seems great enough to lead us to conclude that the mature Bach (all these pieces were written after 1727 when Bach was in Leipzig) notated the *real* values of the notes, just as so many times he wrote out melodic ornaments in

---

[19] Bach-Gesellschaft, vol. XXII.

[20] The real reasons for all the "approximate" types of notation were, of course, the time-saving factor and the advantage of having a less cluttered score. Double dots were not yet in use, although the first appearance of which we are aware can be found in the Bach-Gesellschaft. In volume XLV we find bar 18 of the Courante from the Suite in E minor printed as in Example 138, presumably after a copy by Krebs. Alas, no autograph is extant for verification.

Ex. 138. Suite in E minor, Courante, bar 18

[21] Bach-Gesellschaft, vol. XXIII, p. 205.
[22] Bach-Gesellschaft, vol. XIII.

full. If we are willing to accept this theory, we need not only *not* be afraid to play the Preludes in F sharp major and A flat major, *W.K.* II (which were certainly not composed before the Leipzig period) just as written, but we may also be allowed to take back our inference on page 194, that in the Sinfonia of the Second Partita (published in 1727, the year of the "Trauerode") all dotted situations might be played the "French way." Therefore, the problematic bar 6 can also be played as written by Bach.

Ex. 140. "Trauerode"

Nothing supports this theory more effectively than the structure of Fugue VI of the *Art of the Fugue,* the Fugue "*à la française.*" To play in this Fugue both a sixteenth following a dotted eighth and an eighth following a dotted quarter as short as possible, as Gustav Leonhardt[23] recommends, completely ruins the masterly architectural-mathematical plan which links Fugues V–VII so obviously and convincingly. We also strongly repudiate Leonhardt's second recommendation to apply the rules of "inequality" to all runs of sixteenths in this Fugue. At the speed prevailing, the overdotted playing of these sixteenths does not add anything to the stateliness and dignity of the French overture but produces the impression of whipped, galloping horses—an impression strangely confirmed by the fact that this rhythm is identical with the "flagellation rhythm."[24] This rhythm is, however, always written out by Bach in full note values. Moreover, it seems so far to have escaped general attention that the use of sixteenths in groups of four notes is a novelty, introduced by Bach into the texture of French overtures. The "real" French overture does not make use of the groups and restricts "overdotting" to quarters and eighths. Although in French literature inequality is frequently applied

---

[23] Gustav M. Leonhardt, *The Art of Fugue: Bach's Last Harpsichord Work* (The Hague, 1952).

[24] See the *St. Matthew Passion,* Recitativo, "Erbarm es Gott," and also p. 252 below, where we identify the Prelude and Fugue in G minor, *W.K.* II, as a "flagellation scene." Similar situations will frequently be found in Handel's works, for example, in the Prelude of the F minor Suite.

to groups of sixteenths in an overture, such groups represent a foreign element and belong under the rubric of fast notes, which in all French treatises are recommended to be played as *notes égales*. The same considerations hold, of course, for the Fugue in D major, *W.K.* I, and it is nice to see how a sound instinct warned Dolmetsch against application of the French system for this piece, as mentioned previously.

Another problem that cannot be solved authoritatively arises when a dotted rhythm collides with a triplet in another voice, a situation that affects the interpretation of the Correntes of the Fourth French Suite and the First Partita, the Gavotte of the Sixth Partita, and in *W.K.* II, the Prelude in D major and the Fugue in E minor, just to mention a few. Regarding this subject, Quantz and C. P. E. Bach completely disagree. Quantz writes, "The short note after the dot should not be played at the same time as the third note of the triplet, but after it. Otherwise one would get the impression of 12/8 time."[25] On the other hand, C. P. E. writes, "With the advent of an increased use of triplets in common or 4/4 time, as well as in 2/4 and 3/4, many pieces have appeared which might be more conveniently written in 12/8, 9/8, or 6/8. The performance of other lengths against the notes is shown in Figure 177 [Ex. 141]."[26]

Ex. 141. Figure 177 from C. P. E. Bach

Although the advice given in our conventional editions unanimously advocates C. P. E.'s version, it seems as if J. S. Bach took the middle road once more. It would be hard to deny that for the two Correntes just mentioned (Partita I, French Suite IV), Quantz's overdotted version seems to be the more convincing one. For the Fugue in E minor, *W.K.* II, however, there cannot be any doubt that C. P. E. Bach's version is the only possible one. The same can also be said, with some justification, of the Prelude in D major, *W.K.* II, with its puzzling ¢–12/8 problems. The *Tempo di gavotta* of the Sixth Partita seems to invite Quantz's interpretation. It would certainly be helpful in solving the puzzle of the opening

figure, 𝅘𝅥𝅮𝅘𝅥𝅮𝅘𝅥 , which, when interpreted the "French way," 𝅘𝅥𝅮𝅘𝅥,

---

[25] *Versuch*, V, paragraph 22.
[26] *Essay*, p. 160.

makes good sense, especially in the rhythmic collision of bar 6 (Ex. 142).
The problem of bar 22 (Ex. 143) would also be solved the same way, by
applying the rule for series of short notes (Ex. 144). Nevertheless, all these

Ex. 142. Partita VI, *Tempo*
  di gavotta, bar 6

Ex. 143. The same, bar 22

Ex. 144. The same

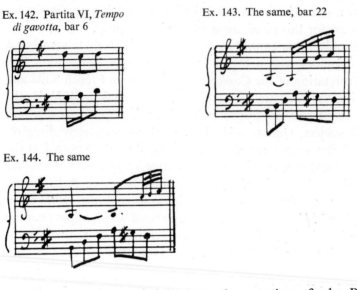

considerations do not help answer the question of why Bach suddenly
changed his notation in two places, writing triplets in bars 12 and 20

Ex. 145. Partita VI, *Tempo di gavotta*

Ex. 146. The same

(Exs. 145 and 146). This unexplainable procedure makes all our worries
almost superfluous.

The Allemande of the Fifth Partita is of special interest, insofar as

here Bach made a careful differentiation between ♩. ♪ and ♪♪♪

written against triplets of sixteenths in the other hand (see bars 4, 10, 20).

Did he want two notes in one hand against three notes in the other to be played with mathematical accuracy? This question should in general be answered almost certainly in the negative. Too many documents prove that this manner of playing, which seems so formidable to piano players of modest talent, was still circumnavigated in the eighteenth century by unequal playing of the group of two notes, a custom that we could almost consider a germ of influence from the technique of *notes inégales*, were this not a basically different situation.

This treatment of "two against three" is confirmed by evidence found in the Triple Concerto in A minor. Bars 128–129 (Ex. 147), reproduced

Ex. 147. Triple Concerto in A minor, Movement 1, bars 128–129

in the Bach-Gesellschaft[27] after "an authentic copy from Bach's pupil Müthel," certainly seem to indicate that the "easiest version" is meant, which should then probably be played at ✳ as well as at NB. It is noteworthy that the questionable notes of the harpsichord player are doubled in other instruments, where the figure is executed in the ordinary way, with even sixteenths. Does this mean, perhaps, that Müthel wrote down what he planned to play, thinking that the situation was not worth any special care since it is practically inaudible?

Other cases, however, seem to prove that sometimes Bach deliberately planned the collision of two rhythms, as, for example, in the Sonata in G minor for Viola da gamba and Harpsichord obbligato. The rhythms

Ex. 148. Sonata in G minor for Viola da gamba and Harpsichord obbligato, last movement, bars 3–5

---

[27] Vol. XVII, p. 245.

appear first in separate instruments (bars 3–5) before the harpsichordist is exposed to playing them simultaneously in bars 17–18 (Exs. 148, 149).[28]

Ex. 149. The same, bars 17–18, harpsichord part

The many collisions between triplets in sixteenths and regular sixteenths which take place in the first movement of the Fifth Brandenburg Concerto (bars 10, 12, 27, 42, and so on, harpsichord part) never involve the problem of another instrument's playing the same part at the same time. Yet, it seems almost impossible to think of any other way of execution than the literal one. On the strength of these examples it may certainly be said that here also, as in so many other cases, Bach is ahead of his time, and that the literal combination of the two antagonistic rhythms cannot be called "un-Bachian."

---

[28] Other places where the combination of rhythms seems obligatory are the middle section of the last movement of the Sonata in E major for Harpsichord obbligato and Violin; bar 42 of the first movement of the Harpsichord-Flute Sonata in B minor; bar 15 of the Prelude in F sharp minor, *W.K.* II.

Articulation

HISTORICAL REVIEW

The problems of articulation will quickly reveal themselves as being by far the most puzzling of all the problems related to the interpretation of Bach's music. This may come as a rude awakening to many Bach lovers, because very little attention has been bestowed by performers and editors upon this fact. In contrast to our study of ornaments, in which we had to sort through an embarrassing amount of information, our present subject suffers from a severe dearth of source material. Very few articulation marks are found in Bach's keyboard works, very rarely does a contemporary source mention these problems at all, and musicology has barely started to lay the groundwork for an investigation of this hitherto entirely unexplored field.

The latter circumstance sounds almost incredible in light of the fact that the dictum, "Let the lines speak for themselves," has been used so often for minimizing the importance of the instrument problem. The meaning of this assertion is that a good pronounciation and declamation of the musical lines were more essential to the performance of music of Bach's period than the actual sounds emanating from a harpsichord or clavichord.[1] Logically, it should follow either that the baroque traditions of articulation were known and understood, or, if not, that serious efforts were being dedicated to solving this problem. Yet, in addition to a few pages in Schweitzer's Bach biography,[2] and the remarks of some editors

---

[1] In addition to the statement of Cornelia Auerbach (see p. 18 above), I cite as one example from among many others the following sentence from Schweitzer's *Bach*: "Truly, the chief role in Bach's works belongs not to dynamic shadings but primarily to phrasing and articulation" (p. 338).

[2] Pages 338–352.

of distinction and responsibility, such as Landshoff and Kirkpatrick, there now exists only one book that deals with this subject at all: Hermann Keller's *Die musikalische Artikulation, insbesondre bei Bach*, which has not yet been translated into English. Since Schweitzer and Keller come to totally different conclusions in nearly every case in which they try to analyze the articulation problems of the same composition,[3] there is unfortunately no exaggeration when we state that the entire field of articulation is still *terra incognita*.

Even the real meanings of the terms "articulation" and "phrasing" are so often misunderstood and confused that it might not be superfluous to define them. "Articulation" means the plastic pronounciation of melodic lines, in accordance with their true meaning, through the application of varieties of touch from *legatissimo* to *staccatissimo*; "phrasing" means the "clear rendering in musical performance of the phrases of the melody."[4]

Although source material is extremely rare, concerning both authentic articulation marks in the works of Bach and remarks about legato, staccato, and touch in contemporary treatises, we must start by collecting the material at our disposal. In regard to articulation marks, we would not be wrong in saying that approximately 95 per cent of all the keyboard works by Bach carry no indications at all. Of the Inventions, only those

---

[3] Some illustrations are shown in Example 150.

Ex. 150a. Fugue in C major, *W.K.* I   Ex. 150b. Fugue in F minor, *W.K.* I

Ex. 150c. Fugue in B flat major, *W.K.* I

[4] Willi Apel, "Phrasing," *Harvard Dictionary of Music* (Cambridge, Mass., 1947), p. 573.

in D major and F minor are well provided with slurs. Rather interesting is a lonely slur for a falling second in bar 8 of the Invention in C minor: it looks like an outburst of emotion during writing. A few important suggestions for the Invention in B minor have come to us from Gerber's copy, which, we now know as a result of Landshoff's investigation, must be given serious consideration. The three little slurs at the end of the Invention in A major have no significance. In the Sinfonias we find two slurs ensuring a sigh interpretation in bars 22 and 23 of the E flat major piece, and one informative slur in the first bar of the F minor one. The ornamental version of the G minor Sinfonia is distinguished by slurs that appear unexpectedly in bars 22–28.

In the first volume of the *Welltempered Keyboard* we find the following indications: two sigh slurs in the Prelude in C sharp minor, one *tenuto* sign and one slur over four notes in the Fugue in D minor; two slurs in the Prelude in E flat minor; three slurs, connecting two notes, in the *Andante* section of the Prelude in E minor; one slur in the last bar of the Fugue in E minor; two slurs in the Prelude in G sharp minor; and six slurs in the theme of the Fugue in B minor, telling us that the descending seconds are sighs. In bar 30 of the same Fugue, two slurs appear to indicate individual articulation for the alto part.

In the second volume we can as quickly cover those slurs that are worth mentioning. The complete list is:

Prelude in C sharp minor	3 slurs to connect ornamental notes
Prelude in D major	8 slurs, each connecting two notes
Prelude in D minor	3 slurs for "mordent figures"
Prelude in D sharp minor	2 appoggiatura slurs
Fugue in D sharp minor	1 slur connecting two notes
Prelude in E minor	1 slur to connect an ornamental note
Prelude in F major	Several slurs over groups of four notes
Prelude in F minor	2 slurs for sighs
Prelude in F sharp major	1 slur for an appoggiatura
Prelude in F sharp minor	1 slur for an appoggiatura
Prelude in A flat major	2 *tenuto* slurs, 1 for an appoggiatura
Prelude in G sharp minor	Several slurs for sighs
Fugue in B flat major	4 slurs, each connecting two notes
Fugue in B flat minor	1 slur for an appoggiatura
Prelude in B major	2 slurs, each connecting two notes
Prelude in B minor	A few *tenuto* slurs, a few for sighs, 2 slurs, each over four notes

For other Bach keyboard works the list is hardly any greater. The suite collections are not of much help, even though they contain somewhat more slur material, because of unsolved problems in the available sources; no autograph of the English Suites has survived. Some important authentic slurs are to be found in the Italian Concerto and in the *Goldberg Variations* (theme, and Variations 2, 5, 7, 13, 15, 16, 20, 25, and 30), but this brings us to the end of the basic and direct information from the hand of Bach as far as works for keyboard alone are concerned. Hardly any general conclusion can be drawn from this evidence. Although the slur is often used, specifically to prevent the sigh motive from being misinterpreted, many of Bach's indications are casual and inexplainable in nature.

A few slurs, however, like the ones in the Inventions in D major and F minor, are of decisive importance for the understanding of these pieces, and it is disheartening that we have to admit the impossibility of ever having found them ourselves. Since both these pieces are in no way products of complicated declamation but use quite normal material of Bach's language, they illustrate how almost hopeless it is ever to expect a full clarification of the articulation problem.

The mystery that surrounds the placing of so little information in the keyboard pieces becomes much greater when we look at Bach's works for stringed and wind instruments. There he was incredibly liberal in revealing the meaning of the musical design by means of slurs and staccato marks. Why did he put down thousands of slurs in works for other instruments, when in his keyboard music he was so reluctant to do the same? Will these slurs in the string and wind parts help us fill the gaps in our knowledge pertaining to the keyboard works?

The articulation problem is further aggravated by the tragic fact that the slur sign now carries two completely separate meanings. A slur was originally the symbol for legato playing when used in keyboard music. In string and wind parts, it indicated that the notes which it linked should be played without changing the bow or without taking breath in between. Gradually, however, the slur also became the symbol for phrasing, used to show the length of a musical idea; in this sense its ending is equivalent to the punctuation marks of our written language—the dash, semicolon, comma, period, and so on.[5] How much musical art has suffered from the

---

[5] Couperin applied the comma sporadically in his keyboard works, and Mattheson analyzed a minuet in his *Kern melodischer Wissenschaft* (Hamburg, 1737), with the help of some commas, semicolons, and periods. In 1926 Professor Jacob Fischer of Vienna published a valuable essay on this subject, followed by the edition of a series of pieces from Bach to Mendelssohn that he had provided with such signs as , ; . ! ?, a sign for "and" (&), and even the very important signs ⌒ and ⊃ for distinction between heavy and light accents. Although one might say that here and there, in dealing with the most minute details of the musical lines, Fischer overdid the application of his method, nevertheless his system represents

unbearable burden placed on the slur is beyond saying. If both meanings are applied simultaneously, but with the use of separate slurs, everything is fine, as Example 151 from Brahms's "Romance," Op. 118, No. 5, shows.

Ex. 151. Brahms, "Romance," Op. 118, No. 5

But whether a single slur is meant to indicate legato playing or phrasing, will, alas, in too many cases never be clarified.

We do not even know exactly when the slur took over the function of indicating phrasing. That Bach was not unaware of the possibility of expressing phrasing with the help of the slur can be proved by the example from the first movement of the Violin-Harpsichord Sonata in E major (Ex. 152, bar 4; see also bar 28).

Ex. 152. Violin-Harpsichord Sonata in E major, Movement 1, bar 4

The same treatment also occurs in bar 36 of the aria "Jesu, beuge doch mein Herze" from Cantata 47.[6] A few double slurs can also be found in the Violin-Harpsichord Sonata in C minor: one is in the pen-ultimate bar of the first movement, another in the third movement, fourth bar before the end. Yet these few examples seem to be the only cases in Bach's works, as far as I have been able to discover, in which two slurs appear together.

Luckily, in the keyboard works of Bach it seems that a slur was never used to symbolize anything but legato playing. In regard to wind and string parts, however, we witness a fight of long standing between editors and players about the true meaning of Bach's slurs: do they indi-cate only legato playing or were they also put in for purposes of phrasing? Joseph Joachim, generally revered as one of the most conscientious players

a tremendous step forward in bridging the deplorable abyss between a composer's inner conception of a musical composition and its actual picture on paper. Conscientious teachers should show at least one example of Fischer's editions to their pupils to acquaint them with his method of thinking.

[6] Cited in Moser, *Johann Sebastian Bach*, p. 103.

of all times, was the first to print the original version of the solo violin sonatas and suites, together with his own edition. In many cases he did not hesitate to deviate from Bach's slur prescriptions for no other reasons than "intuition" or "easier playability." One cannot help feeling that many of today's players also seem outspokenly unwilling to subjugate themselves to the playing conditions of Bach's time. They dismiss rather quickly the real problems of the faithful rendering of his articulation marks, emphasizing in their comments the striking changes in playing techniques and in instrument construction that have taken place since his time. Therefore, any real evaluation of the true meaning of Bach's slur material for these instruments will be impossible until experiments, similar to those that we are now carrying out with harpsichord and clavichord, are also undertaken with historical stringed and wind instruments.

A comparison of Bach's attitude toward indicating slurs in works for orchestra with that of Handel and Vivaldi shows that these composers were somewhat less generous in giving away information than the composer from Leipzig. Although we would not dare to draw binding conclusions from this fact, it is in itself interesting. Can it, to a certain degree at least, be explained by local circumstances? Did not those composers usually have more professional musicians at their disposal than Bach, who was so dependent on high-school boys, students, and amateurs for the execution of his cantatas? Was it perhaps Bach's knowledge of his players' lack of general experience, plus wise anticipation of saving precious time during the short rehearsal hours available for the ever-changing Sunday cantata, that led him to be more explicit in this music? In regard to keyboard music, on the other hand, Bach and Handel agree in their practice: slurs are nearly completely absent in Handel's works also. We could, of course, demonstrate that the keyboard compositions were written almost exclusively for the personal use of the composer himself, along with a limited circle of pupils and "connoisseurs." If pupils played the works of their teacher, oral information was the chief means of instruction for the true manner of execution. In addition, since the musical culture of the keyboard player was in general higher than that of his fellow fiddling or blowing musicians—be it only because of his up-bringing, in which he was preparing himself to become a future *maestro al cembalo*—it might be possible that he also got the necessary information about the basic rules of articulation during his apprentice years. Unfortunately, all these speculations do not solve the enigma of the scarcity of slurs in Bach's keyboard music.

The problem becomes even more puzzling when we discover that one great composer of this period, François Couperin le Grand, took a different attitude toward slurs. Not only does almost every harpsichord piece by Couperin carry a tempo mark, but the quantity of slur material that he supplied is absolutely unique in the field of baroque keyboard music. He also created an interesting problem for us in that he did not add a single slur to the picture of the naked notes in his organ works. It is true that quite a few of the slurs, especially those in his chamber music where we also find them in ample quantities, are meant only to differentiate between *notes égales* and *inégales* (discussed on p. 183). Yet what remains after deducting these special slurs is still much more material than Bach ever wrote out, and it is further enlarged by a source from which we would never have expected to get information about articulation: the so-called "tempo marks." The words which Couperin used for this purpose are so unusual that we have to give a list of the most important ones.

Couperin's "Tempo Marks"

Real tempo marks	Marks describing affects	Marks describing articulation
sans lenteur	gracieusement	légèrement
(très) vivement	majesteusement	marqué
un peu vivement	tendrement	d'une légereté tendre
vif	(fort) gaiement	d'une légereté modéré
animé	nonchalammant	légèrement et flate
d'une vivacité	affectueusement	coulé
modéré	languissement	très lié
sans vitesse	naïvement	luthé et lié
modérément	impérieusement	luthé-mesuré
très vite	relevé	coulemment
pesamment	fièrement	d'une légereté gracieuse
gravement sans	agréablement	et lié
lenteur	noblement	uniment
sur le mouvement	galament	également
des berceuses	gaillardement	louré
	douloureusement	pointé
dans le goût de	dans le goût Burlesque	dans le goût de la Harpe
Cornemuse	delicatement	marqué et d'une grande
	voluptueusement	précision
	grotesquement	
	badinage tendre	
	gravement firme	
	amoureusement	
	audacieusement	

Closer examination reveals that only fourteen of these directions for interpretation are related to the customary Italian tempo marks, whereas twenty-four describe human affects and eighteen have to do with articulation. Once more the affects, which played such an important role when we examined the problems of tempo, come to the foreground. It is, therefore, only logical to turn now to the books of Bach's time in order to find out how much information we can get about articulation, particularly about the influence of the affects upon it.

LINKS BETWEEN AFFECT AND ARTICULATION

Scarce as they are, some sources are highly instructive. C. P. E. Bach writes in the chapter of his *Essay* devoted to performance:

In general the briskness of allegros is expressed by *detached notes* and the tenderness of adagios by *broad, slurred notes.* The performer must keep in mind that these characteristic features of allegros and adagios are to be given consideration *even when a composition is not so marked*, as well as when the performer has not yet gained an *adequate understanding of the affect of a work.* I use the expression, "in general," advisedly, for I am well aware that all kinds of execution may appear in any tempo.[7]

He goes on:

In order to arrive at an understanding of the true content and affect of a piece, and, in the absence of indications, to decide on the correct manner of performance, be it slurred, detached or what not, and further, to learn the precautions that must be heeded in introducing ornaments, it is advisable that every opportunity be seized to listen to soloists and ensembles . . .

Above all, lose no opportunity to hear artistic singing. In so doing, the keyboardist will learn to think in terms of song. Indeed, it is a good practice to sing instrumental melodies in order to reach an understanding of their correct performance.[8]

Quantz gives the same advice in his chapter entitled "On Good Interpretation":

Each instrumentalist should try to interpret the *"cantabile"* just as a good singer would. The singer, on the other hand, should try to achieve in vivid music the "fire" of good instrumentalists, as far as the voice is able to do this.[9]

Most revealing is paragraph 16 of the same chapter:

The degree of passion of a piece can be recognized with the help of the occurring intervals, according to whether they are close or remote ones, and

---

[7] *Essay*, p. 149. All italics are mine.
[8] *Essay*, pp. 150, 151-152.
[9] *Versuch*, XI, paragraph 19.

whether the notes are to be slurred or played staccato. *Slurred* and *close* intervals express the caressing, the sorrowful and the tender; *staccato notes* and
distant jumping intervals, also figures where a dot is given to the second note[10]
express the gay and the bold [italics mine]. Dotted and sustained notes express
the serious and the pathetic; mixing notes of the length of a half or a whole bar
with fast ones represents the splendid and the *"grandezza."* Finally, the prevailing affect is indicated by the marks at the beginning of a piece, such as
*allegro, allegro andante, andantino, arioso, cantabile, spirituoso, affectuoso, grave,
adagio, adagio assai, lento, mesto*, etc. All these words, when they are thought-
fully selected, ask for a special type of execution. It need not be emphasized that
each piece may contain a great variety of mixtures of the above-mentioned
types of pathetic, caressing, gay, splendid, or joking ideas. Therefore, in each
measure one must be able to express a different affect—now sad, now gay, now
serious; this is a very important tool for performance. He who has learned this
art will never miss getting the applause of his audience and his interpretation
will always be a moving one [*rührend*]. However, one should not think that such
refined differentiations can be learned in a short time. You can hardly expect
anything of this type from young people, who are usually too lighthearted and
impatient for this.

All these passages make it evident that the connection between
articulation and affect is at least as great as that between affect and
tempo. No wonder that the writers of the eighteenth century elaborate on
all the varieties of the shadings and gradations of human affects. Marpurg,
in his *Kritische Briefe über die Tonkunst* (Berlin, 1759–1763), gives a list
of twenty-seven affects or groups of affects that music can express, which
is interesting enough to be reprinted here.

Marpurg's Affects[11]

1. Sadness
2. Gladness
3. Contentment
4. Repentance
5. Hope
6. Confidence, fright, anxiety, uneasiness, despair, terror
7. Longing
8. Uncertainty, inconstancy
9. Despondency
10. Love
11. Hate
12. Envy, ill will
13. Sympathy, mercy
14. Jealousy
15. Anger
16. Love of honor
17. Bashfulness
18. Courage, manliness, deter-mination, intrepidity, perse-verance, timidity, cowardice
19. Impudence, audacity, pride, arrogance
20. Modesty, humility

[10] This obviously describes the "lombardian" rhythm.
[11] *Kritische Briefe*, vol. II, p. 273.

21. Friendliness, goodness, affection, favor, kindness, affability, generosity, conciliatory spirit, gentleness, friendship, harmony, gratefulness

22. Vengeance, vindictiveness, curse, malediction, fury, rage, discord, irreconcilability

23. Insensibility, indifference, ingratitude

24. Innocence

25. Laughter, joyfulness, weeping

26. Impatience, commotion

27. Malicious joy, scoffing

A comparison of this list with Couperin's "tempo indications" shows that nearly all of Couperin's twenty-four words describing affects correspond to an affect on Marpurg's table. Here are a few of the less obvious and common examples:

Couperin	Marpurg
fièrement	pride
audacieusement	intrepidity
nonchalamment	indifference
agréablement	contentment
noblement	manliness
gravement firme	determination

It would not make sense to condemn Marpurg's list because of the oddities it contains. No doubt, affects like "ill will, bashfulness, vindictiveness, ingratitude," and many more, can hardly be described by musical means with infallible success. Yet it is only our present rationalistic way of thinking that causes us to be so extremely critical of the extravagances of "descriptive music." That a most vivid imagination and profound sensitivity must belong to the basic equipment of any person dealing with music goes without saying. There is no fundamental difference between Mendelssohn's famous statement that music is clearer in what it says than words could ever be,[12] or Schumann's "pedagogical" attempt to find a poetic title for a piece already written,[13] and Marpurg's very enlightening declaration that "even the viola players would play a piece in a different manner if they were provided with a title for it instead of being given only information like 'allegro,' 'adagio,' or 'presto,' without

---

[12] In his "Character Pieces," Op. 7, Mendelssohn uses affects as titles: "Gently and with expression," "With deep emotion," "Strongly and fiery," "Fast and with flexibility," "Seriously and with increasing animation," "Longing," "Light and airy."

[13] In a well-known letter to Simonis de Sire, Schumann wrote, "The titles of all my compositions occur to me after I have finished them." Equally famous is this quotation from a letter to Moscheles: "The Carnaval was written for a special occasion; its titles were added later."

knowing whether they should express a gay or irate velocity, a proud or a sad, slow speed."[14]

Marpurg's list is truly a remarkable document, insofar as it describes to us the realms in which the artistic imagination of players and connoisseurs dwelt in this period. That Johann Sebastian Bach not only painted in notes whatever could (or sometimes could not) be painted—teardrops, Adam's fall, bread-breaking, the horses of Phoebus, drunkards, and so on, often to the great consternation of his puritanical biographer Philipp Spitta—but also gave, in every vocal work, a picture of the general mood expressed in the words, leaves no doubt that he was not opposed to the theory of affects.[15] Not only did he adhere to its basic doctrine "one piece, one mood," but he used the "colloquial terms" of its musical language: "rhythmic, melodic, and motivic formulas developed for the expression of various affects."[16] That he did this with so much more skill and profundity than any other composer is what makes him such a genius;[17] yet, we have good reason to believe that he achieved it without giving much conscious thought to the aesthetic problems of the *Affektenlehre*. No authentic word referring to his awareness of the existence of this doctrine has come to us, and the fact that C. P. E. Bach talks so rarely about it in his *Essay* indirectly proves the same. Maybe Bach would not have gone so far as to state, as Georg Neidhardt did, that "the ultimate goal of music is to illustrate all affects by means of tones and their rhythms."[18] Had he ever uttered anything about the ultimate goal of the musical language, so hotly debated among the theorists of the time, he might have used words similar to those found in the noble statement by Andreas Werckmeister in his treatise, *Der edlen Musickunst Würde, Gebrauch und Missbrauch* (1691): "Music is the tool of the Lord, and the Holy Spirit

---

[14] Marpurg, *Historisch-kritische Beiträge* (Berlin, 1754–1762), vol. III, p. 535.

[15] May we be allowed to make the almost sacrilegious statement that precedents for each of the titles of Mendelssohn's "Character Pieces" (mentioned above) easily can be found in Bach's works; for example: "Gently and with expression" for the Preludes in F major, A major, E flat major, *W.K.* II, and the Prelude of the First English Suite; "With heavy emotion" for the Prelude in C minor, *W.K.* I, the Prelude and Fugue in D minor, *W.K.* II, and the Fugue in A minor, *W.K.* II; "Strongly and fiery" for the Prelude of the Second English Suite; "Fast and with flexibility" for the "Great" Fugue in A minor; "Seriously and with increasing animation" for the five-part Fugue in C sharp minor, *W.K.* I; "Longing" for the Sinfonia in E minor (Mendelssohn's piece in the same key shows a clear relation to the Bach model); "Light and airy" for the Fugue in F major, *W.K.* II.

[16] Walter Serauky, *Die musikalische Nachahmungsaesthetik 1700–1850* (Münster, 1929), p. 58.

[17] No more beautiful expression of this fact can be found than what Zelter wrote to Goethe, answering his question as to which composers used tone painting: "With Bach and Handel every casual superficiality becomes an ocean of sentiment" (translated freely; in German "*ein Abgrund von Empfindung*"). *Letters between Goethe and Zelter* (Leipzig, Reclam Edition, 1902), III, 90.

[18] Johann Georg Neidhardt, *Vorrede zu Die beste und leichteste Temperatur des Monochordi*, [1706].

by which he arouses some blest, agreeable emotions in the soul of man."

Those simple words are very close to Bach's description of the dignity of the thorough bass, which has to serve "in the honor of the Lord and for the enjoyment of the soul."[19] Bach would also have agreed with Kuhnau, who said in his famous novel, *Der musikalische Quacksalber*: "Music tries to move the hearts and to lead them toward the road to heaven."[20] In his treatise, *Texte zur Leipziger Kirchenmusik*, the same composer gives a description of the creative process which is a document of such profound sincerity and insight that we cannot help being deeply moved when reading it:

> Sometimes (when setting to music the words of the Bible) the original language can be of great help in stirring the creative imagination. If the first words, "*Wohl dem*" [Blessed is he who; author's interpolation], do not arouse any musical idea in my mind, I then read the Hebrew words "*Aschóre hāîsch.*" In a certain sense this can mean "*O, beatudines huius viri,*" "*O, der Glueckselig-keit dieses Mannes,*" or in French, "*O, que lui heureux est le personnage.*"
>
> What orator, what tongue, is able to express with adequate words the feelings of bliss that such a man can truly call his own. Although I know that the word "*aschóre*" is not always used with such emphasis, this meditation inspires me to compose the words "*Wohl dem*" with the force of many voices, or in several choirs, or, if I do not have these resources at my disposal, in rich passages, using coloraturas and similar devices in one or a few parts. One could also bestow upon the German "*dem*" a special distinction by repeating it or setting it in an unexpected *tonos*, thus drawing the attention of the audience to it.[21]

One could hardly imagine a description that comes closer to the heart of the psychological background of this mysterious process, the preparation, by self-intoxication, for the creative act. The most startling thing about these lines, however, is that Kuhnau seems to describe exactly the way in which Johann Sebastian Bach condensed the essence of the hymns into his miraculous chorale preludes, which Max Reger so aptly called "symphonic poems *en miniature*."[22]

That many of the melodic and rhythmic formulas used by Bach for the expression of affects were not his private property, but were used by all his contemporaries in somewhat similar ways is now common knowledge, owing to the work of Schweitzer and Pirro.[23] Arnold Schering has

---

[19] Spitta, *Johann Sebastian Bach*, vol. II, p. 216.
[20] (1700; new edition ed. Curt Benndorf, 1900).
[21] (1710), p. 174.
[22] See also Erwin Bodky, *Das Charakterstück* (Berlin, 1932), p. 4.
[23] A comparison of those bars in Kuhnau's "Biblical" Sonata, "The Combat between David and Goliath," in which he describes the death of Goliath, and Bach's setting of the words "Et sepultus est" in the B minor Mass, is especially revealing. See p. 244 for these examples.

given perhaps the best summary of the general aspects of this problem: "Each age has its peculiar . . . individually shaped rhythms and motives of joy, special formulas for sorrow, elegy, pride, unrest, etc. Furthermore, each age also possesses typical motivic formulas for the imitation of noises, movements, and events in lifeless nature ('tone-painting formulas'). With the help of these figures symbolizing the affects, which are familiar to him from repeated hearings, the listener is able to understand the meaning of the music as it is heard, and can adjust his imagination to grasp its progress."[24]

However, Schering goes on to point out, most correctly, that in the Preface to his *Der Generalbass in der Komposition*, Johann Heinichen stresses the fact that "this method can do no more than give some help to the stimulation of the artistic imagination, as is the purpose of the *loci topici* in the art of speech." Because it comes from an authority who lived in the heyday of the *Affektenlehre*, this clarification of the quite restricted position that the vocabulary of the affects had in the shaping of a composition as an entity is especially interesting. It is also of help in giving Schweitzer's "affect-motive tables" their proper place among the tools that help us understand Bach's artistic goals.

Herewith ends our survey of the remarks from books of Bach's time that might be of help in disentangling the problems of articulation. It is, of course, true that none of these comments gives us sufficient information to put even one slur upon a Bach theme with complete authority. Yet there is also no reason to minimize the importance of the general information gained. We learned that once the "true content and affect" of a piece is understood, definite conclusions not only about tempo but also about articulation, "be it slurred, detached, or what not," can be drawn by the interpreter. "Brisk *allegros*" are meant to be played with emphasis on detached notes; "tender *adagios*" with emphasis on broad, slurred notes. Close intervals suggest legato; distant jumping intervals are generally detached or played staccato. It is also of major interest that C. P. E. Bach twice emphasizes that the absence of articulation marks does not excuse the performer from having to know how to deal with this matter. Such a comment seems to point to the existence of an oral tradition in this field also, which has contributed toward making articulation so difficult a problem for us late-comers.

AUTHENTIC SLUR MATERIAL

Before we start to apply these fundamental principles to Bach's themes, we have to see how much help we can get from the wealth of slur material

---

[24] Arnold Schering, Review of Hugo Goldschmidt's *Die Musikaesthetik des 18. Jahrhunderts, ZMW*, I, 5 (February 1919), p. 305.

found in the vocal and orchestral works. A complete and systematic survey of this material has never been undertaken. Remarks such as that made by Schweitzer: "Whoever studies the dots and slurs in the orchestral parts of the *Brandenburg Concertos* and of certain cantatas will know how to deal with the phrasing problems of Bach's keyboard works,"[25] and Keller's statement that "Bach gave us, in the many thoroughly prepared parts of his cantatas, his chamber music, and other works, enough clues to the way in which his keyboard and organ works should be articulated," seem to indicate that such a study would easily solve the entire problem.[26] Yet Schweitzer and Keller, as already reported, disagree nearly completely about every theme that they have both provided with suggestions for articulation. But Keller, who made the first well-founded and serious attempt to examine the articulation problems in his book, *Die Musikalische Artikulation,* had to admit that the marks which he proposed for the fugue themes of the "Forty-eight" and the greater organ works *most certainly* do not exclude other equally well-justified solutions.

Startled by the incredible discrepancies found in the numerous Bach editions, I decided many years ago to make a thorough study of all the slur material that has come down to us from Bach's hand, hoping that the answers to the problems of articulation could be found therein. This enterprise seemed even more justified, since the concept of the unbroken unity of Bach's language in his keyboard, orchestral, and vocal works had been so widely acknowledged that it actually formed a pillar of any Bach research. "It is the magnificent unity of Bach's language that makes it lawful to apply the articulation marks from works in which he wrote them out, to unmarked works," wrote Keller.[27] With sadness it must be said that the result of this investigation, which has cost countless hours of hard labor, was bitterly disappointing. In contrast to all expectations, and to the assertions of Schweitzer and Keller cited above, it became apparent that the cases of concurrence are infinitely less frequent than anticipated, and that the relatively few examples given by Schweitzer and Keller cannot be measurably enriched by more thorough investigation.

---

[25] *Bach,* p. 339.

[26] Herman Keller, *Die Klavierwerke Bachs* (Leipzig, 1950), p. 31. Ernst Kurth, who edited the sonatas and suites for unaccompanied violin and cello, omitting all slurs, since "probably all were added by foreign hands" (!), says in the Preface to his edition, "To everyone who understands the meaning of the lines [*den Linienstil*] in Bach's works, his phrasing is no problem at all [*versteht sich von selbst*]" (*Drei Masken Verlag,* München, 1921, pp. 12f.). That Kurth mixes up phrasing and articulation, and in reality means articulation alone, becomes evident as one reads further in his Preface.

In the *Bach-Gedenkschrift* Walter Reinhard states, "The articulation can always be defined by the musical meaning of the line. Whoever studies the complete edition of Bach's works thoroughly will find so many original articulation signs that it will not be too difficult [!] to apply them to the other works in which they are missing, in accordance with the principles demonstrated by the Master" (*Bach-Gedenkschrift, 1950,* p. 90).

[27] *Die Musikalische Artikulation,* p. 80.

Yet, even though the main goal was not achieved, it cannot be said that this search was entirely without results. The longer it lasted, the more evident it became that the general assumption about the over-all unity of Bach's language had to be modified. It is true only insofar as the smallest as well as the largest composition of this inimitable master clearly carries the personal stamp, "made by Bach." In regard to technique, however, it gradually became clear that Bach applied an individual type of melodic organization to every branch of music. We have already discussed the fact that there is a major difference in basic structure between themes meant for the organ and those meant for the harpsichord or clavichord. In the overwhelming majority of cases, the themes of instrumental and vocal music also have a language of their own, dance rhythms and dance-like melodic patterns excepted. Only one nearly literal derivation of an organ theme from instrumental music can be found, the well-known A major Fugue, which owes its theme to the orchestral introduction of Cantata 52. The very few cases of close relation in the field of *Klaviermusik* will be reported shortly.

The new element that appears in the vocal music of Bach can probably best be described as being "word-bound." This means that certain motives owe their shape, and therefore their articulation, to the desire for a clear pronunciation and sometimes even a pictorial explanation of the words to which they are set. Bach consistently built his melodies in such a way that the clearest possible rendering of the words could be achieved. However, when he gave vocal motives to accompanying instruments, he did not hesitate to indicate different articulation wherever he felt that it would be better suited to instrumental execution. This is doubtless a strong point in favor of Keller's opinion that there is more than one justifiable way in which to articulate many of Bach's motives. On the other hand, if this were true in all cases, then any decision about articulation made with the help of an analogy involving Bach's vocal works would have only limited authenticity. It is therefore hard to understand how Schweitzer and Keller could so boldly say that a thorough study of the articulation marks in the vocal and instrumental music would solve the problems of articulation in the keyboard music.

We cannot reproduce here all the authentic slur material that has come to us in Bach's vocal and instrumental works. It is so large a collection that it would form a separate book—one which would be helpful only to the very few people who are so thoroughly familiar with every keyboard piece that they could pick out the related situations and draw their own conclusions. We must restrict ourselves to listing on our Articulation Tables (see Appendix B) only those slurs that are more than casual and that throw some light on the problems of the keyboard repertoire. Unless otherwise marked, all the examples are from scores that are generally considered to be autographic.

Tables Ia–c contain material that is "word-bound." These phrases might have been articulated in a different way, had the words not dictated a special treatment. The information obtained from these tables is certainly embarrassing, although not completely unexpected. We see that when the motives are of this type, Bach's instrumental articulation sometimes agrees in full, sometimes only partially or not at all, with the vocal articulation. Here and there we actually see strokes of genius in the application of the means of articulation; for example, in the selection from Cantata 114 on Table Ib, 1a, the two staccato marks help emphasize the words "*nun nicht*," which would otherwise not get as much attention as Bach's deep religious feeling wants to put upon them.

Table II contains the musical material that shows direct relation to keyboard works—not in single little figures, but in real thematic dependance. That fewer than two dozen unmistakable examples of mutual reference can be found is an amazing testimonial to the wealth of Bach's creative imagination. However, our immediate profit, in terms of being able to put authoritative slurs in the keyboard works, is correspondingly small. In addition, we find once more that Bach's information is not always definitive. Number 5b looks as if it might give us the answer to the puzzle of the Fugue in C sharp major, *W.K.* I, which has been written out so contradictorily in various editions (Ex. 153). Yet, as we see from

Ex. 153. Fugue in C sharp major, *W.K.* I

Table II, 5c and d, Bach himself gives three different versions of this theme in the same piece.

The situation covered by Numbers 3a–f is equally embarrassing. In the Sinfonia in F minor Bach gives a slur to the first three notes (Ex. 154). Without this indication everyone would undoubtedly play the notes as shown in Example 155. However, a glance at Numbers 3b–f shows that

Ex. 154. Sinfonia in F minor   Ex. 155. The same

of five pieces built with the same pattern, only the examples from Cantatas 25 and 81, and the tenor aria "O Schmerz" from the *St. Matthew Passion*, show corresponding articulation. Cantatas 73 and 101 make use of the opposite possibility and illustrate the justification of having several solutions for certain themes. This should serve as a stern warning against making decisions too hastily.

Of even greater interest, in my opinion, are the examples on Tables III–VI, which try to tabulate some of the characteristic figures of Bach's general language. Again we are confronted by an overwhelming variety of solutions for related situations, as, for example, for the "mordent

figure" 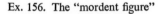, which is found in so many keyboard works (Ex. 156, and

Ex. 156. The "mordent figure"

all samples from Table III). In this respect the following two versions of the same piece, the first from Cantata 134, "Ein Herze, das seinen Jesum lebend weiss" (Ex. 157), the second from its secular sister, Cantata 134a,

Ex. 157. Cantata 134, No. 4

Ex. 158. Cantata 134a, No. 4

"Mit Gnaden bekröne der Himmel die Zeiten" (Ex. 158), are truly disturbing.

On the other hand, from all these different examples one very interesting conclusion can be drawn: the few slur marks that are found on rhythms like $\sqcap\sqcap$ or $\sqcap\sqcap$ occur only when the pieces are to be played at slow speeds (see the examples from Cantatas 92 and 106, Table III, 9 and 10); in *vivace* pieces these figures always appear unslurred. This supports our theory that the Fugue in G minor, *W.K.* I, should be taken faster than generally advised in printed editions, because Bach himself shows, in the last bar, that he reckons with nonlegato playing (Ex. 159).[28] The only possible fingering for the second part of the main

Ex. 159. Fugue in G minor, *W.K.* I, last bar

theme (upper voice on the lower staff) is continuous use of the thumb. Again one sees what minute details must sometimes be examined in order to find answers to basic problems.

For the characteristic figures of two to eight notes (Tables IV–VI), our tables show that there exists almost no combination of legato and nonlegato notes of which Bach does not make use. In many cases we even see that he took obvious delight in changing the articulation for repeated use of a given motive. This makes our task of prescribing articulation marks still more challenging.

However, the most important thing that we learn from this survey is concerned with Bach's general approach. We see that although the detail work in his articulation is of a variety and wealth beyond the ability of any person of lesser genius to reconstruct, his general attitude follows exactly the few basic rules reported by Quantz and C. P. E. Bach. Bach, too, follows the tradition of detached playing in brisk *allegros*, broad slurred playing in *adagios*, legato playing for close intervals, and detached or staccato playing for distant intervals. These rules are broken only for pictorial reasons, which always get priority when they serve Bach's musical purposes. All the exceptions that we placed on Table IX, the legato slurs over distant intervals, and also over chord figures that would normally be played nonlegato, are self-explanatory. In every case the symbol behind the notes is clear: in Number 6 from the *Christmas Oratorio* it is the "cradle" symbol; a similar figure, representing "inner

---

[28] See Tempo Table Ia, 19.

contentment," is used in Cantata 204 (No. 7; remember that "slurred intervals express the caressing"); a symbol for "embracing" is found in Number 5, from Cantata 186, for "clouds" (No. 3) in the famous example from the "Wedding" Cantata, 202, and for the "pleading gesture" (No. 8) in the bass line of the aria "Komm, lass mich nicht länger warten" (Come, let me no longer wait), from Cantata 172. It is interesting that although these words are set to a different melody, they could just as easily be sung with this instrumental line that symbolizes them. Logically, in the recitative "Der Heiland fällt vor seinem Vater nieder" (The Saviour falls before his Father), from the *St. Matthew Passion*, no legato slurs are found (No. 4); they would contradict the word "fällt." In contrast, the long slur in Number 1a, from Cantata 9, would never have been drawn by Bach's hand had it not been meant to represent the words "Wir waren schon zu tief gesunken" (We had sunk too deeply).

Two special rules, those concerned with dotted rhythms and upbeats, deserve special mention, as they are very little known and are verified by ample authentic slur material, especially in Bach's Suites for Unaccompanied Violin and Cello. The rhythm ♩. ♪ ♩. ♪ is always played ♩. ♪ ♩. ♪, never ♩. ♪ ♩. ♪ ♩. ♪ . Even if it occurs on a repeated note, the feeling for ♩. ♪ should be preserved. Equally fundamental is the rule governing the treatment of upbeats: an upbeat of *one* note is never connected by a slur to the next note. Keller advises playing the upbeats in the themes of the F major Fugue, *W.K.* I, and the B minor Fugue, *W.K.* II, legato (Ex. 160a, b), and comments that "without the slurs the themes would

Ex. 160a. Fugue in F major, *W.K.* I   Ex. 160b. Fugue in B minor, *W.K.* II

sound too unimportant." But those suggestions, as well as Czerny's articulation in the Gigue of the Sixth French Suite (Ex. 161a), are without any foundation from the hand of Bach, and all these should be played as in Example 161b. This rule also applies mostly to those cases in which a theme is begun on a weak beat in the middle of a bar. It is less valid when an upbeat contains several notes; see the examples on Table X where Bach's slurs stretch over the bar line.

A few remarks may also be added about articulation problems in dance pieces. Although authentic slur material is very small, restricted almost entirely to the French Suites, the Suites for Unaccompanied Violin

Ex. 161a. French Suite VI, Gigue   Ex. 161b. The same

and Violoncello provide material which can be put into good use, at least for general information. We do not feel it necessary to talk here about the basic rhythmical patterns of the various dance types, which are too well known to need special mention.[29] We have also abstained from including samples of this authentic slurring in our articulation tables, since these suites are readily available in *Urtext* editions and, partially, in facsimile reproductions. Yet the variety in the treatment of the characteristic patterns is so great that, at the end, nothing again is achieved in the direction of ultimate solutions. What we said above (p. 204) about the slurs in the D major and F minor Inventions—"it is disheartening that we have to admit the impossibility of ever having found them ourselves" —unfortunately also holds true here.

In regard to individual dances, the following observations can be made. The sixteenths prevalent in almost all allemandes are organized in groups of two, four, four, with the first or last detached, or in eighth notes (see especially the Allemande of the E flat major Suite for Violoncello, in which the variety of patterns is nearly at its greatest). For courantes (in 3/2 time), slurs over four notes are verified, among others, in that of the C minor Cello Suite. Correntes in 3/4 time with triplets of eighth notes show combinations of three, six, and nine notes linked by slurs (see the Corrente of the D minor Violin Suite). Correntes in 3/4 time, using mostly eighth notes, may be studied in the C major Cello Suite or the B minor Violin Suite; and those using mostly sixteenths in the D minor Cello Suite. In regard to sarabandes, the slur material of the D minor Violin Suite is especially rich in variety. The Gavotte of the C minor Cello Suite, as well as the Bourrée from the C major Cello Suite, proves that the groups of two eighths (before or after a quarter note) that are so characteristic of these dances can but need not be slurred. Little can be said about menuets because they are too diverse to be tabulated. We may be glad that we have authentic slurs for the Menuet of the Sixth French Suite. The chief patterns of the gigues are excellently represented in the

---

[29] For basic information consult the *Harvard Dictionary of Music.*

slurs from the solo suites, especially in those for the violoncello in G, C, and D major. Again, one will see that in groups of three notes Bach makes use of all varieties possible: three notes slurred, two notes slurred and the first or the last detached, and finally, all three nonlegato. The findings for these dances will be helpful for some pieces from the "Forty-eight" which are either real dance pieces, like the Fugues in F major, *W.K.* I, or B minor, *W.K.* II, or show similar rhythms like the Preludes in F major, A minor, *W.K.* I, and D major, *W.K.* II. Some other pieces among the Inventions (G major, A major) and the Sinfonias (C minor, A minor, B minor), which were not considered for slurs marks in the autograph, will this way at least be somewhat clarified.

One remaining source of information in regard to articulation and phrasing problems unfortunately does not yield any results in the case of Bach. In theory, authentic finger marks of the period could be helpful in giving illumination about connecting or separating certain groups of notes. Bach's position on fingering is, however, very peculiar. Contemporary reports praise the ingenuity of his fingering methods and stress that he was the first to give the thumb an important role, making this hitherto neglected finger a principal one.[30] Most regrettably, however, the few original fingerings that have come down to us reveal nothing about this new method, indeed, are rather old-fashioned. No binding conclusions can be drawn from them.[31] Since Forkel emphatically points out how far Bach's method of fingering was ahead of that of Couperin, from whose hand we possess quite a few thoroughly marked works, we are not allowed to apply to Bach's works any basic rules in regard to grouping of notes which we might be able to derive from this source.

CONCLUSIONS

The longer we meditate about the entire problem of articulation, the clearer it becomes that the remarks of Quantz and C. P. E. Bach, which agree so completely with each other and which at first seemed so vague and casual, represent not the minimum but the *maximum* of definite information that can be given on this subject. If we think them through thoroughly, if we take the true affect of each piece into due consideration, we can make sound decisions about the general manner of performance, "be it slurred, detached or what not"; it is true that we will not too often be able to

---

[30] His methods can be found in David and Mendel, *The Bach Reader*, pp. 223, 254, 258, 307ff. Although they are irrelevant here, their study is highly recommended.

[31] Fingerings are found in the *Applicatio* from the *Notebook for Friedemann Bach*, Prelude 11 from the Twelve Little Preludes, and in the Prelude and Fugue in C major, *W.K.* II, in its first version (Bach-Gesellschaft, vol. XXXVI, p. 224). This last work is discussed very well by Keller in his *Die Klavierwerke Bachs*, pp. 222ff.

come to *one* binding conclusion about the correct articulation of every minute detail in every piece, but we will not be wrong as long as we remain aware that "each piece may contain a great variety of mixtures of . . . pathetic, caressing, gay, splendid, or joking ideas. Therefore . . . one must be able to express a different affect—now sad, now gay, now serious; this is a very important tool for performance," and—as we can add now —for proper articulation.

From the results of our study we can formulate the following guide to articulation: in an *allegro* piece nonlegato to staccato playing is more probable; in an *adagio* piece a legato atmosphere generally prevails; in *moderato* the close intervals (the second and third, but the latter not without exceptions) are slurred, and the larger intervals are detached. That the distinction between small and large intervals is very often valid in *allegro* and even *presto* situations as well is proved by the slurs in the first and last movements of the Italian Concerto. In addition to these suggestions, there is a supplementary principle that takes into account the characteristic qualities of the harpsichord and clavichord. In the *allegro* and *moderato* categories, designation of a piece for the harpsichord increases the tendency toward nonlegato or staccato playing, and designation for the clavichord increases the chances of quasi legato to legato playing. *Adagio* implies basically a quasi legato performance on the harpsichord, molto legato on the clavichord.

CHAPTER 8

Symbolism

HISTORICAL REVIEW

The problems that we are going to discuss in this chapter do not have any immediate influence on the performance of Bach's keyboard works. To consider them of minor importance, however, would be most erroneous. On the contrary, we are now entering what we might justifiably call Bach's *sanctuarium*; we are getting some glimpses of the creative genius at work. More than ever, caution and discretion, reverence and awe, should guide us when we try to "read between the lines" for information about the nature of Bach's great spiritual concert "in praise of the Almighty's will and for my neighbor's greater skill."[1]

Of course, the element of symbolism cannot play as large a role in Bach's keyboard work as it does in his vocal music. Quite frequently, however, the presence of symbolic features is so obvious that it is impossible to deny their existence, unpleasant as this may be to those Bach lovers to whom his works represent the climax of *absolute* music. The greatest of these is, of course, Philipp Spitta, who feels rather uneasy whenever he can no longer ignore the presence of a symbolic device. If the master goes so far as to make an "escapade" into the fields of tone-painting—abhorred by Spitta, who was a partisan of Brahms in the famous intellectual fight between the adherents of "absolute music," and the defenders of Wagner's music of the future—Spitta hardly knows what words to use for explaining how Bach could show such a lack of good taste.[2]

---

[1] Dedication line of the *Orgelbüchlein:* "*Dem Höchsten Gott allein zu Ehren, dem Nechsten draus sich zu belehren.*" The English translation is from Hans David and Arthur Mendel, *The Bach Reader*, p. 75.

[2] Spitta, *Johann Sebastian Bach*, vol. II, p. 406.

Enormous progress has been made during the last fifty years in uncovering one secret after another of Bach's art of symbolism. It started with Schweitzer's doctrine, nearly revolutionary at its time, that there exists a kind of vocabulary for Bach's "poetic" language. The recent discoveries of Jansen,[3] Smend,[4] and others, about the role played by number symbols in many of Bach's most distinguished works, are equally startling. Friedrich Blume, in his excellent article on Bach in the new monumental encyclopedia, *Die Musik in Geschichte und Gegenwart*, states that discussion of these problems will be one of the foremost tasks for Bach research during the next generation, adding that above all, however, one should not overlook the fact that Bach, in spite of his many-sidedness (*Vielseitigkeit*), was not a frustrated minister or mathematician, but a musician.[5]

The merit of having awakened our generation to the enormous treasure of pictorial elements that form the nucleus of Bach's musical language is due irrevocably to Albert Schweitzer. His Bach book became the Bach Bible at the beginning of our century. It swept away the dryness of Bach interpretation that was customary at that time, when performers considered his works little more than highly respectable and most skillful products of a composer whose universal importance might have been easier to grasp had his strange contrapuntal idiom not prevented him from writing truly "human" music.[6] Who can blame Schweitzer for the fact that in his joy over having found the "true meaning" of the musical figures of Bach's language, he went too far in certain directions; unfortunately he formulated his findings in such a way that the musical layman could easily be misled into thinking that there exist "absolute" motives of joy, beatitude, pain, tumult, weakness, and so on. No doubt, the more cautious explanation of Bach's musical figures given by André Pirro[7] was done on a more "solid scholarly basis,"[8] especially since it was accompanied by evidence that Bach did not originate, but merely adapted musical material that had already been used by several generations of composers. But without the stirring enthusiasm of Schweitzer, the Bach missionary, we would never have advanced so quickly in understanding the timeless values of Bach's art.

---

[3] Martin Jansen, "Bach's Zahlensymbolik an seinen Passionen untersucht," *Bach-Jahrbuch* (1937), p. 96.

[4] See the list of essays by this great scholar in the Bibliography.

[5] Friedrich Blume, "Johann Sebastian Bach," *Die Musik in Geschichte und Gegenwart* (Kassel and Basel, 1949), vol. I, p. 1050.

[6] See Eugen D'Albert's statement in his edition of the *Welltempered Keyboard*, reprinted on p. 30.

[7] André Pirro, *L'Esthétique de Jean Sébastien Bach* (Paris, 1907).

[8] Manfred Bukofzer, *Music in the Baroque Era* (New York, 1947), p. 389. The entire paragraph dealing with Schweitzer's method is quoted on p. 226.

Among the more recent publications dealing with symbolism in music, especially in Bach's works, first place belongs to the articles of Arnold Schering, which after the death of their author were published in one book, entitled *Das Symbol in der Musik*.[9] Stressing the importance and necessity of having to intensify the research in the field of symbolism, his essays reach their climax with the demand that the study of "*Symbolkunde*" be acknowledged as a branch of musicology. Always stimulating, sometimes highly controversial, and arising from an insatiable thirst for widening our knowledge about the sources of creativity, Schering's ideas have already caused considerable discussion among the younger generation of continental musicologists.[10]

The chief merit of Schering's writings seems to be his proof of the extraordinary degree to which Bach's music is loaded with symbolic meanings. For example, he shows the simultaneous appearance of seven different symbols in the web of the first chorus of Cantata 77, "Du sollst Gott Deinen Herrn lieben."[11] He also stresses the fact that our present-day approach to the basic meaning of musical language differs markedly from that of Bach's time, and that this change in our attitude is responsible for the difficulties we have in getting a true picture of Bach's artistic intentions. The root of this difference lies in the definition of the word "genius."

It is in conformity with the baroque mentality not to make any ado about the "genius" of a great artist, but to see its essence in the gift for effortless discovery of similarities between things and in a good, perceptive memory. Nowhere, neither among writers on general subjects nor those on music, is anything to be found alluding to the conviction, which we owe to the Romantics, that a genius is a person specially selected, who has been bestowed with the divine gift of inspiration. In Bach's time one did not talk about the profoundness of sentiment, originality, personal idiom, or even the "*weltanschauliche*" confession, in a piece of music; these subjects were beyond consciousness and gave no foothold to the application of reason, which could not control them. We do not know what Bach might have considered decisive or unique in his artistic personality: certainly not technical or formal matters, which could be learned. More probably it would have been the awareness that he possessed a

---

[9] (Leipzig, 1941); see also the list of essays by Schering in the Bibliography.

[10] The most interesting publication after Schering's is the book by Arnold Schmitz, *Die Bildlichkeit der wortgebundenen Musik J. S. Bachs* (Mainz, 1950). Schmitz opposes the explanation of Bach's language by the help of symbolism, but turns to the art of rhetoric as a main source from which Bach drew inspiration. That Bach was fully familiar with the old doctrine of *Musikalische Oratorie* is well known (see Spitta, vol. II, p. 64); another rather important book is H. H. Unger's *Die Beziehungen zwischen Musik und Rhetorik im 16.–18. Jahrhundert* (Würzburg, 1941). Since both books deal primarily with the special problems of vocal music, we need not discuss the new viewpoints they offer.

[11] Bach-Gesellschaft, vol. XVIII, p. 235; for a discussion of symbolism in this cantata, see Schering, *Das Symbol*, pp. 39ff.

nearly inexhaustible, never-failing gift for creating symbols,[12] a thing that could never be acquired. This means nothing more than the ability to perceive the essence of things, to sense their secret and mysterious relationships and to express even the smallest reality in musical symbols of a related nature. This can only be achieved by "enlightenment," by the opening of inner fountains—an event always accompanied by the feeling of being blessed, and probably always accepted by Bach, too, as a gift from above: *Jesu juva! Soli Deo gloria.*[13]

In the lines just cited, Schering summarizes the essence of what Christian Wolff, pupil of Leibniz, says about symbolism in his *Psychologia empirica*,[14] a book that Schering thinks is most instrumental in helping us comprehend baroque thought more thoroughly. In the light of this analysis, we can better understand the validity of Bukofzer's criticism of Schweitzer's method:

It must be strongly emphasized that the musical figures were in themselves necessarily ambiguous, and took on a definite meaning only in a musical context and by means of a text or title. Since they did not "express" but merely "presented" or "signified" the affections, musically identical figures lent themselves to numerous and often highly divergent meanings. It is therefore misleading to isolate certain figures and classify them in a system of absolute meanings as motives of joy, steps, beatitude, and so forth. Nor should these procedures be misrepresented as emotional program music or as the psychological expression of feelings. The affections were non-psychological, static attitudes and were therefore peculiarly fitted for musical representation. Not by any means does the presence of metaphorical figures distinguish the music of Bach from that of other baroque composers, nor does it make any music automatically good. It is the masterly and highly refined integration of musical structure and metaphorical meaning that bestows on Bach's music its unique intensity.[15]

TONALITY PROBLEMS

Symbolic ideas first participate in the shaping of a piece of music and influence its general character when the composer selects the specific key in which a composition is going to be written. The question of whether or not individual keys actually have expressive qualities of their own has been debated for centuries; theorists have evolved highly convincing reasons

---

[12] "To write poetry means to be able to invent symbols. To understand poetry means to understand symbols. The real creative musician can only be understood by calling him a poet. He has the right to ask that one try to penetrate his world of symbols" (Schering, *Das Symbol*, p. 144).

[13] Schering, *Das Symbol*, pp. 85–86.

[14] (Frankfurt and Leipzig, 1733). Arnold Schmitz, however, severely questions the validity of Schering's reasonings (*Die Bildlichkeit*, p. 17).

[15] Bukofzer, *Music in the Baroque Era*, p. 389.

for negating the entire problem, whereas composers have nevertheless very often displayed greatest sensitivity to the selection of appropriate keys even for a short piece of music. The mere fact that pitch has varied during the centuries to a startling degree is sufficient to make any statement about the character of any key seem illusory. Yet it is undeniable that in the works of nearly all great composers, predilections for expressing certain moods in particular keys are so obvious that knowledge of this fact has become common property among music lovers: in this respect Mozart's key is G minor,[16] Beethoven's C minor,[17] and Chopin's A flat major.[18] Bach's preference, as is well known, is for B minor.

That no real aesthetic link but only "personal association" stands behind these selections of keys becomes evident when we realize that neither Bach's nor Mozart's "special keys" were ever used by Beethoven for any work of major proportions; except for a few sections of the Missa Solemnis and the Bagatelle, Op. 126, No. 4, the absence of B minor is nearly complete, which is even more surprising considering that Beethoven wrote so many works in D major. Furthermore, it would be futile to try to discover any significant similarities between Bach's works in G or C minor and those of Mozart and Beethoven. Any suspected resemblance between the *Grave, Adagio* of the Second Partita and the first bars of the Sonata Pathetique resides more on the paper than in the spirit of these pieces, and Mozart's Adagio in B minor for piano is perhaps the only work in the entire musical literature that measures up to the profundity of Bach's great manifestations in this key.

Yet never have the alleged characteristic features of various keys received wider discussion than during Bach's lifetime. The most detailed description of them is to be found in Mattheson's first major publication, *Das Neu-eröffnete Orchester*.[19] To give our readers at least an idea of

---

[16] Less well-known than Mozart's most famous works in this key (the symphony, the piano quartet, and the string quartet) is the fantastic modulation to G minor in the first movement of the Piano Concerto in C major (K.V. 457), which allows the piano to play a "vision" (never repeated in this piece) of the first theme of the Symphony in G minor, written years later.

[17] For example, Symphony No. 5; Third Piano Concerto; Piano Sonatas, Op. 10, No. 1, Op. 13, and Op. 111; Violin Sonata, Op. 30, and so on. In fact, nearly every key in Beethoven's works has such characteristic qualities in the hands of the master that his works are probably the main cause for the general attention given to this problem. It is no exaggeration to say that Beethoven's keys are as important for the understanding of his language as the little *Orgelbüchlein* is as a "Bach dictionary."

[18] Polonaise, Op. 53; Third Ballade; the great valses.

[19] (Hamburg, 1713); part III, section 2, deals with the characteristics of keys under the heading "Von der Musikalischen Töhne Eigenschafft und Würckung in Ausdrückung der Affecten." Only seventeen are described; C sharp, C sharp minor, D sharp minor, F sharp, A flat, G sharp minor, and B minor are omitted. The essence of Mattheson's "key portraits" is reprinted in the essay, "Tonartensymbolik zu Bach's Zeit," by Rudolph Wustmann, *Bach-Jahrbuch* (1911).

Mattheson's bizarre formulations (which nevertheless offer an interesting insight into baroque thought), we translate a few of them:

E major expresses desperate or deathly sorrow incredibly well; it is fitted for extremely amorous, helpless, and hopeless situations, and under certain circumstances it is so painful and piercing that it can only be compared to the fatal separation of body and soul. *F major* is capable of expressing the most beautiful sentiments in the world, be they magnanimity, perseverance, love, or whatever else is at the top of the register of virtues, and all this is done so naturally and with such incomparable facility that no help is needed to demonstrate it. Indeed, the courteousness and adroitness of this key cannot be better described than by comparing it to a good-looking person whose every gesture, even the smallest, fits his personality, and who, as the Frenchmen say, possesses *bonne grâce*.

F minor seems to represent a mild and composed, although profound, grave, and deathly anguish of the heart, combined with despair; it is immeasurably moving. It expresses beautifully a black, hopeless melancholy, and sometimes causes horror or shuddering to the listener.

G minor is almost the most beautiful key, because it not only mixes a slight seriousness (which it shared with G major) with a gay loveliness, but also has much grace and pleasantness; it is as well fit for tender and refreshing, longing and moderate laments as it is for temperate cheerfulness, and it is very flexible.

A major is very touching, in spite of some brilliancy; it is better for plaintive and sad passions than for divertissement; it is especially fit for composition for the violin.

B minor is bizarre, cheerless, and melancholy; it appears, therefore, only rarely.

Rudolf Wustmann succeeds in producing examples from Bach works that correspond accurately with Mattheson's descriptions. This, of course, convinces him that Bach was familiar with these writings. Nevertheless, he does not close his eyes to the fact that exceptions can be found in every case. Indeed, it is not difficult to see that each of these descriptions can be easily contradicted by abundant evidence from the works of Bach. Of all the pieces in the key of B minor, only one, the great Flute Sonata, can be called bizarre, cheerless (one has to take this word without a discriminating meaning), and melancholy; "bizarre," in fact, characterizes extremely well the incredibly bold dialogues between flute and harpsichord in the first movement, as well as the equally bold syncopations of the last.

In spite of Mattheson's notorious "eloquence"—or, more accurately, verbosity—it is certain that these descriptions are not the product of his brain exclusively, but that they express the general ideas prevalent during his time; otherwise they would not have been so often cited in the contemporary literature. Here and there he does hit upon characteristic features that we might easily have overlooked, such as the "mild and composed" elements of F minor. Without this hint the Prelude and Fugue in F minor from the second volume of the *Welltempered Keyboard*, and also the Invention in this key, could not be explained. On the other hand, the strange description of E major, which is supposed to represent "desperate or deathly sorrow," fails completely in regard to Bach, although it fits perfectly Handel's use of this key in Cleopatra's aria "Weep, lament," from *Julius Caesar*. Interestingly enough, Mattheson withdraws in later years from the position he took in 1713. In the *Grosse Generalbasschule* of 1731 we read: "A new and thoughtful French author [Crousaz, *Traité du Beau*, chap. IX, sect. VIII, p. 291] says wisely: 'I abstain from putting down all the modes in their order and from telling about the virtues and spirits attributed to each, because I do not consider them to be based on sufficiently good grounds.' This is my opinion also."[20]

Heinichen also denies the attribution of character to the keys: "If one wants to maintain that by nature the keys of D sharp minor, A sharp minor, and B major are much better suited for furious pieces [*furiose Sachen*] than A minor, E minor, and similar keys, which are more inclined to moderation, this, even if it were so, would not yet prove the *proprietates moderum*; the inclination of the composer is equally important. There exist very sad and tender pieces in D sharp minor, A sharp minor, B major, and C major [*sic!*], and strange and very brilliant pieces in A minor, E minor, and C minor by the most famous 'practitioners of the art of composing [*Practicis*].' "[21] To complete our citations from contemporary books, we will quote two paragraphs from Quantz's *Essay*:

The affect [of a piece] can be recognized by whether the keys are major or minor [*hart (Dur) oder weich (Moll)*]. Major is generally used to express the gay, the bold, the serious, and the sublime; minor for caressing, sadness, and tenderness.[22]

About special characteristic features of certain keys, whether major or minor, agreement does not exist. A minor, C minor, D sharp major [*sic*], and F minor express the sad affects more than other keys. . . . The other keys, major as well as minor, are used in pleasant, singing, *arioso* pieces.[23]

It would be worthless to tabulate Bach's works for the purpose of finding out whether generalizations about the use of keys can be made. Since he transposed not only single pieces[24] but also whole works when he wanted to have a certain scheme of keys complete (the French Overture, originally written in C minor, was transposed to B minor so that this key

---

[20] (Hamburg, 1731), p. 32.
[21] Johann David Heinichen, *Der Generalbass in der Komposition*, pp. 83ff.
[22] Quantz, *Versuch*, XI, paragraph 16.
[23] Quantz, *Versuch*, XIV, paragraph 6.
[24] The Fugue in A flat major, *W.K.* II, was originally written in F major.

could be represented in the *Klavierübung*), he could not have considered the choice of a key of any significance in regard to establishing a given mood. It is true that in the *Welltempered Keyboard* we find five hitherto unused keys; however, it is impossible to say that the moods expressed are also new ones. Here it is clear that Bach's sole purpose was completion of his premeditated scheme.[25] In spite of these facts, comparisons of pieces written in the same key will give us the opportunity to make unusually interesting observations in regard to the common sources to which, consciously or subconsciously, they owe their existence; therefore, it will prove highly rewarding to go into this subject in some detail.[26] To avoid creating any rank among the keys, we shall proceed in chromatic order.

C major

The "triumphant" element that distinguishes this key in the hands of Beethoven appears much more rarely in the works of Bach, who reserves D major for this purpose. Only the concertos for two and three harpsichords and two organ works, the preludes and fugues in 4/4 and 9/8 metres, possess this character. The prelude in 9/8 shows an unusually close relation to the first chorus of Cantata 65, "Sie werden aus Saba alle kommen." Otherwise this key displays a certain neutrality, which first drew the attention of Hermann Abert, who devoted an article to a discussion of Bach's themes in C major and A minor. He also stressed the prevalence of ascending scale-like motion in most of them.[27]

C minor

A general feeling of composure and imperturbability seems to be common to the second Invention and the Prelude and Fugue, *W.K.* II. One's interest is caught by the thematic similarity of the Air of the Second French Suite, the Capriccio of the Second Partita, and the final movements of the Fourth Harpsichord-Violin Sonata and the Concerto for Two Harpsichords, all of which are in 2/4 time except the Air, which is in ₵.[28] Appearances of the thematic material of the C minor Fugue, *W.K.* I, occur in the aria "Er kennt die rechten Freudenstunden" from Cantata 93 (Tonality Table, No. 1a). However, the most unusual phenomenon of this key is the construction of the violin part in the chorale "Ich bitte Dich, Herr Jesu Christ" from Cantata 166, which obviously combines elements of both fugues in C minor, *W.K.* I and II

---

[25] Kaspar Ferdinand Fischer's *Ariadne Musica* of 1700 uses only nineteen keys.

[26] Vocal and instrumental works will be mentioned only when helpful for comparison.

[27] Hermann Abert, "Tonart und Thema in Bach's Instrumentalfugen," in *P. Wagner-Festschrift*, ed. K. Weinmann (Leipzig, 1926), p. 1.

[28] See Tempo Tables (Appendix B).

(No. 1b). It is noteworthy that "composure and imperturbability" also characterize rather aptly the *Musical Offering*, whose "ghost" appears otherwise only in the strange fragment of the Fugue in C minor which originally belonged to the famous C minor Phantasy (reproduced in the Steingräber-Bischoff Edition, vol. VII, p. 152).

C sharp major and minor

C sharp major appears only in the *Welltempered Keyboard*, but C sharp minor is also used for the slow movement of the Violin Concerto in E major, the third movement of the Harpsichord-Violin Sonata in E major (both pieces show a passacaglia-like treatment of the bass line), and the slow movement of the Harpsichord Concerto in E major.

D major

Elements of French-overture style are obvious in the Fugue, *W.K.* I, as well as in the Prelude, *W.K.* II; the Fourth Partita opens with a real overture. Syncopation is found in the Aria of the Fourth Partita and in the opening chorus of Cantata 30, "Freue dich, erlöste Schar" (Tonality Table, Nos. 2 and 4). The aria "Gott ist unser Sonn' und Schild" from Cantata 79 is actually identical, as far as notes are concerned, with the Aria from the Partita (Nos. 2 and 3); moreover, the similarity between the Sarabande of this Partita and the Aria must also have been premeditated.[29] Finally, the beautiful "Little" Prelude in D major is a perfect example of the inner serenity that is common to all these pieces using syncopation.

D minor

The Prelude and Fugue, *W.K.* II, Toccata in D minor, Chromatic Phantasy and Fugue, Harpsichord Concerto, and Concerto for Two Violins all show a clear inner relation in regard to fire and temperament.[30] The Fugue of the Chromatic Phantasy and the last movements of the Harpsichord Concerto and the Concerto for Two Violins make abundant use of the rhythms ♩ ♫ and ♫ ♩. In the slower pieces, the Invention, the Sinfonia, the Prelude and Fugue, *W.K.* I, and the slow movement of the Toccata, a contemplative mood prevails. The *Art of the Fugue* is too great to be brought into direct relation with the pieces mentioned before. Yet it should not pass unnoticed that the Gigue of the

---

[29] Similar syncopated rhythms, all in 2/4 time, appear in three pieces of the *Christmas Oratorio*: No. 8, the aria "Grosser König"; No. 31, "Schliesse mein Herze"; and No. 51, the terzetto "Ach wann wird" (Tonality Table, Nos. 5–7).

[30] For comparison, see also the beginning of Cantata 90, "Es reifet Euch ein schrecklich Ende."

Sixth English Suite in D minor clearly contains in bars 20–21, 44–45, 52–53 germ material for Contrapuncti VIII and XI, and, moreover, in bars 42–43 a citation of B-A-C-H.

E flat major

This key, with its three flats, is frequently used by Bach to symbolize the Trinity, as in the famous Prelude and Triple Fugue for organ. Also linked with it is the use of the "fundamental" interval of the fourth (it establishes key consciousness by the step from dominant to tonic), which is amply demonstrated in the Prelude, *W.K.* I, and the Fugue, *W.K.* II. In addition, we find in this key some of the most wonderful demonstrations of "peace of mind," most notably in the Prelude, *W.K.* II, the Prelude for the Lute Keyboard (*Lautenclavicymbel*), the first movement of the Flute Sonata, and the second movement of the Oboe Sonata in G minor. The Prelude and Fugue in E flat major in the seventh volume of the Steingräber edition is a composition by Johann Christoph Bach.

E flat minor

E flat minor is used only in the *Welltempered Keyboard* and for the trio of the Menuet from the Suite in E flat major.

E major

As already mentioned, Bach's use of E major has not a single element in common with Mattheson's description of it. Inner serenity is the dominant feature of the Sixth Sinfonia, the Prelude, *W.K.* I, the Prelude and Fugue, *W.K.* II, and the beautiful "Little Prelude" in this key. Notice that the thirty-seconds in the Sixth Invention reappear in the final movement of the Violin Concerto in E major (both are in 3/8 time). Compare also the first movement of the Harpsichord-Violin Sonata in E major with the Prelude and Fugue in E major, *W.K.* II.

E minor

In spite of the eminence of some works in this key, such as the Partita, the Toccata, and another Organ Prelude and Fugue, the only significant feature that can be reported is that the Sinfonia in E minor breathes the same spirit of "passion" that also distinguishes the Organ Prelude in E minor. This is in keeping with the sizable role played by this key in the *St. Matthew Passion*.

F major

A "concertizing" style dominates the Italian Concerto and the Prelude of the Fourth English Suite, which sounds like a cousin to the first movement of Brandenburg Concerto No. 5. (Note that the first two Brandenburg Concertos are in F major.) Even the Invention in this key displays some concertizing elements *en miniature*, which erupt most energetically in the famous F major Toccata for Organ. The repetition of a sequence from the Prelude, *W.K.* II, in its companion fugue is quite remarkable (see Tonality Table, Nos. 11 and 12). In regard to this Fugue, it might not be impossible that Kuhnau's *Presto* (No. 9) played godfather to it. The same piece seems also to have been the "point of departure" for the Fugue of Bach's D major Toccata (No. 10).

F minor

The special role of F minor is so well known that we need not elaborate on it. The Sinfonia in this key and the Prelude and Fugue, *W.K.* I, exemplify Mattheson's description of "deathly anguish of the heart," an emotion that Bach also used for feigned sorrow in the "Lament" of the Departure Capriccio. Unfortunately, the obvious caricatural intention of the latter piece is often overlooked by interpreters. Other pieces in this key in which the expression of anguish is a predominant characteristic are the first movement of the Fifth Sonata for Harpsichord and Violin, the aria "Zerfliesse" from the *St. John Passion*, "O Schmerz" from the *St. Matthew Passion*, and the aria "Weh der Seele" from Cantata 102. No wonder that the "Crucifixus" of the B minor Mass, which uses the bass line of the Sinfonia in F minor, appears first in F minor (in Cantata 12, "Weinen, Klagen") before Bach transposed it to E minor, the other "Passion key." Looking at "Surely He hath borne our griefs" from *Messiah*, and a secular chorus, "Mourn ye muses," from *Acis and Galatea*, we see that Handel's use of F minor parallels Bach's completely. In regard to *allegro* movements in this key, the resemblance between the last movements of the Fifth Harpsichord-Violin Sonata and the Harpsichord Concerto in F minor cannot be overlooked.

F sharp major

This key appears only in the *Welltempered Keyboard*.

F sharp minor

With the exception of the Toccata in F sharp minor and the slow movements of the Harpsichord Concerto and Harpsichord-Violin Sonata in A major, the use of F sharp minor is restricted to the *Welltempered Keyboard*. The sadness, "more pensive and lovelorn than tragic and gloomy,"[31] which Mattheson associates with this key, depicts rather well

---

[31] Mattheson, *Das Neu-eröffnete Orchester*, p. 251; quoted here from the translation in Beekman C. Cannon's *Johann Mattheson, Spectator in Music* (New Haven, 1947), p. 127.

(if we forget the word "lovelorn") the Fugue, *W.K.* I, and Prelude, *W.K.* II, and, to some extent, the famous Canon from the Harpsichord-Violin Sonata in A major. But the magnificent Fugue, *W.K.* II, with three subjects, is certainly better described by the quotation from Goethe's *Faust* (Part II), cited in Busoni's edition: "I am too old to be merely playful, too young to be without desire" (*Ich bin zu alt, um blos zu spielen, zu jung, um ohne Wunsch zu sein*). The F sharp minor Toccata again uses the descending chromatic line that originated in the key of F minor; thus we see this motive used a half-tone higher, in contrast to its appearance a half-tone lower in the "Crucifixus" of the B minor Mass.

G major

The key of G major is richly endowed by Bach. In addition to its use in the Inventions, the Sinfonia, and the *Welltempered Keyboard*, it is found in the Fifth French Suite, the Fifth Partita, and the *Goldberg Variations*. One toccata, one duet, two Brandenburg Concertos, one violin sonata, the Sonata for Two Flutes, the Suite for Cello, and one Sonata for Viola da gamba also come to mind. The common bond of serenity is easily recognizable. Only here and there (in the Prelude, *W.K.* I, and the first movement of the Toccata) does this mood become one of almost exuberant joy. The last movement of the Toccata for Harpsichord and the Gigue of the Fifth Partita show decided similarities; on the other hand, the likeness in regard to metre and melodic pattern of the Fugue, *W.K.* II, and the first movement of the Fourth Brandenburg Concerto is probably too small to be considered significant.

G minor

Compared to the miracles wrought by Bach in the key of B minor, one cannot easily agree with Mattheson's enthusiasm for G minor, this "almost most beautiful key." Only one keyboard piece might seem to support such distinction, the famous Variation 25 of the *Goldberg Variations*, the "crown of thorns" of this incomparable work.[32] The other great manifestations of G minor appear in the *St. John Passion*, the famous Fantasia and Fugue for Organ, the Viola da gamba Sonata, and the Sonata for Violin Solo, whereas its use in keyboard works other than the collections is limited to the Third English Suite and one toccata.

The famous *parlando* style of the theme of the Fugue, *W.K.* II, which almost reminds one of the chorus "Lasset uns den nicht zerteilen" in the *St. John Passion*, recurs in the opening chorus of Cantata 78, also in G minor (see Articulation Table II, 15). The Fugue, *W.K.* I, has a counterpart in the aria "Ein unbarmherziges Gerichte" (A merciless judgment)

---

[32] If our memory is right, Wanda Landowska is the originator of this very fitting metaphor.

from Cantata 89 (Articulation Table II, 9); in the third bar of this D minor
piece Bach cites the principal theme (Ex. 162) in G minor, and the words

Ex. 162. Cantata 89, No. 3, aria "Ein unbarmherziges Gerichte," bar 3

of the aria seem to fit the dark character of the Fugue rather well. Let us
also add that the Prelude, *W.K.* I, uses a rhythmical pattern found in the
B flat Invention.

A flat major

It should not pass unnoticed that in three of the four A flat major
pieces of the *Welltempered Keyboard* (Prelude and Fugue, *W.K.* I, Prelude,
W.K. II), the triad provides the thematic material. The fourth piece, the
Fugue, *W.K.* II, has as its countersubject the descending chromatic phrase
used in the F minor pieces.

G sharp minor

The key of G sharp minor is found only in the *Welltempered Keyboard*. The singular beauty of the Prelude and Fugue of the second
volume has caused us to notice that for every key which he was introducing to musical literature, Bach wrote works of exceptional quality: it
would be hard to deny that the pieces written in these keys—C sharp
major, D sharp (E flat) minor, F sharp major, G sharp minor, and B flat
minor—are among the greatest of the collection.

A major

Seldom are pieces in the same key as strongly related to each other
as those in A major that are written in 9/8 and 12/8 time (the Prelude to
the First English Suite, the Fugue, *W.K.* I, and Prelude, *W.K.* II). Later
we will see that the symbolism in these pieces is also more easily discernible
than that in the majority of other cases. The first movement of the
Harpsichord-Violin Sonata in A major is the only piece in this key in
which the "touching" and "plaintive" elements of Mattheson's description
are traceable.

A minor

The unity of character of the A major pieces is still surpassed by that
found in the compositions in A minor. Indeed, nowhere else is the influence
of a chosen key on the affects of a piece as evident as here; nowhere else
do we find similar musical material used so frequently. To my knowledge,

the only piece in this key, at least among the instrumental compositions, that is without a related piece is the Sinfonia, with its bold syncopated rhythms. The group of "wild" pieces, in which the virtuoso element prevails, is particularly large: it includes the "Long" Fugue, which contains in its theme the rudiments of the great Organ Fugue in A minor, the Prelude of the Second English Suite, the Prelude and Fugue, *W.K.* I, the Fugue, *W.K.* II, the Prelude and Fugue in A minor which form the nucleus of the first and last movements of the Triple Concerto, and the "early" Prelude, also called "Fantasie," which starts with runs of thirty-seconds. To this group we can add the last movement of the First Partita for Solo Violin, the Allemande from the Sonata for Unaccompanied Flute, and the instrumental accompaniment of the chorale in Cantata 142, "Uns ist ein Kind geboren."

Among the cases of exact thematic relationship, a few merit our attention. The subject of the A minor Invention

appears both in the *Scherzo* of Partita III and in the Duet in A minor.

Ex. 163. Organ Fugue in A minor, bar 51

Ex. 164. Partita in A minor, Fantasia, bars 31–32

Ex. 165. Partita in A minor, Gigue, bars 13–14

The modulatory phrase of the Organ Fugue in A minor (Ex. 163) is found in the Fantasia of the Third Partita as well as in the Gigue of the same suite (Exs. 164 and 165).

The falling seventh 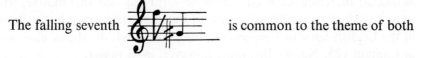 is common to the theme of both

fugues of the *Welltempered Keyboard*, and the descending chromatic line of the Organ Prelude in A minor reappears, with infinitely more boldness, in the Prelude, *W.K.* II.

B flat major

Moser has already pointed out that many of the themes in B flat major descend scalewise (for example, those of the Sinfonia, the bass part of the Prelude, *W.K.* I, the Prelude and Fugue, *W.K.* II).[33] But the most interesting occurrence in this key is the obvious relation between the Prelude to the Partita in B flat major and some of the material used in the aria "Ich traue seinen Gnaden" from Cantata 97 (Exs. 166 and 167).

Ex. 166. Partita in B flat major, Prelude, bar 1

Ex. 167. Cantata 97, "Ich traue seinen Gnaden," bar 15

Since the *largo* indication for the aria is autographic, we gain one more authentic tempo mark for a major keyboard work.[34]

B flat minor

This is another key found exclusively in the *Welltempered Keyboard*. What might have caused Bach to re-use the melodic line of the Prelude

---

[33] Moser, *Johann Sebastian Bach*, p. 149. See also his interesting comments on themes in C major, D major, F major, B minor, and A major.
[34] The main theme of this Prelude was used almost parodyingly by Johann Christian Bach in a sonata for harpsichord and violin (see Tonality Table, No. 13).

of volume I in the Prelude of the second volume will probably remain unexplained forever. The basic rhythm of the Prelude, *W.K.* I, obviously stems from a Prelude in F major in Fischer's *Musikalisches Blumen-büschlein*; therefore we need hardly be surprised that this motive, which must have had some special appeal to Bach, appears again in the Prelude of the English Suite in F major. On the other hand, the theme also occurs in Cantata 125, No. 4—this time, however, in G major.

B major

B major offers no special situations, appearing only in the *Well-tempered Keyboard* and in Passepied II of the French Overture.

B minor

The fame of B minor as Bach's "favorite" key has been firmly established by its use in a great quantity of compositions of the highest caliber. The B minor parts of the great Mass (which might almost better be called the "Mass in D major"), the aria "Es ist vollbracht" from the *St. John Passion*, the arias "Blute nur" and "Erbarme dich" and the chorus "Sind Blitze" from the *St. Matthew Passion*, the Organ Prelude and Fugue, the Flute Suite and Sonata, and the French Overture are only a few of the most important ones. Numerous crosslinks are in evidence. The dances in the Flute Suite share their spontaneity and "popular" character with those of the French Overture. The affect of weeping, symbolized by the descending second, is found in the Fugue, *W.K.* I, and the "Kyrie" of the Mass; it is also expressed in the appoggiaturas that play so large a role in all the arias of the Passions mentioned above.

The similarity of the themes of the fifteenth Invention and the fifteenth Sinfonia may, perhaps, be only accidental (Exs. 168 and 169).[35]

Ex. 168. Invention 15

Ex. 169. Sinfonia 15

---

[35] Notice, also the appearance of this theme in the same key in Cantata 136 (see Articulation Table II, 4b).

Yet, when we discover that relations can also be found between the last preludes and fugues of both volumes of the *Welltempered Keyboard*, we wonder whether this undeniable similarity was not also carefully planned by Bach.

It can only have been intentional that the fugues in B minor in both volumes begin with a descending minor triad: 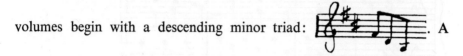. A rising minor triad appears in the corresponding preludes; it is concealed by passing notes in the Prelude of the first volume: , but is outspoken  in the second, where even the right hand starts with a triad figure: .

Most touching, however, is the way in which Bach not only exploits bar 24 of Prelude 24, *W.K.* I (Ex. 170), for the wonderful episode in its companion fugue (appearing first in bars 17–18, Ex. 171), but also gives

Ex. 170. Prelude 24, *W.K.* I, bar 24

Ex. 171. Fugue 24, *W.K.* I, bars 17–18

a kind of echo of these magnificent bars in Fugue 24 of the second volume, bars 87–89 (Ex. 172).

Ex. 172. Fugue 24, *W.K.* II, bars 87–89

What else could this citation mean than a "greeting" from volume I, emphasizing the unity of conception of both volumes? Certainly, the thematic similarities found in the Preludes in B flat minor of both volumes seem to confirm this idea.

Although these observations about the role of tonality in the creative process are not of decisive importance for our appreciation of the individual pieces, they doubtless enrich our knowledge of how Bach handles his language, and the aura of mystery that they carry makes them still dearer to us. Particularly interesting are the sometimes frequent shifts of material to keys a half tone higher or lower than the original. To the examples already given, we can add the theme of the first movement of the Harpsichord-Violin Sonata in C minor, which provides the material for the aria "Erbarme dich" from the *St. Matthew Passion*

Ex. 173. Harpsichord-Violin Sonata in C minor, Movement 1

Ex. 174. *St. Matthew Passion*, aria "Erbarme dich"

Ex. 176. Partita in E minor, Toccata

(Exs. 173 and 174),[36] and also the shift of the sighs in the Toccata of the Partita in E minor to the Prelude in F minor, *W.K.* II (Exs. 176 and 177).

Ex. 177. Prelude in F minor, *W.K.* II

ALLEGORY PROBLEMS

Our inquiry into the tonality problem has provided us primarily with information of a psychological nature; there was little to be learned about the "meaning" of any composition. Since the key to understanding Bach's vocal music almost always lies in grasping the meaning of the "pictorial" elements, it is not unjustifiable to search for similar devices in the keyboard music. Our desire to do this is heightened by the fact that pictorial elements appear with greatest clarity and frequency in the chorale preludes for the organ, from which Schweitzer got the inspiration for his "vocabulary" of Bach's motivic language. However, in their essential purpose, these chorale preludes still belong to the realm of vocal music. Bach wrote them with the wholly justified supposition that the organists as well as the congregation knew the words of the hymn and would appreciate the allegoric meaning of his music while listening. The keyboard music has, of course, no such specific ties, and since every piece was written either for pedagogical purposes or for "refreshing the spirit of the connoisseur," there was no real reason for the introduction of "material with hidden meaning." Yet the greater a person is, the more it becomes inevitable that whatever occupies his creative mind penetrates even the smallest utterances of his daily life. It is therefore not surprising that Bach's deep-felt religion, which is the basis of his entire personality, shapes the character of quite a few of his keyboard works and gives them an additional distinction.

Before we discuss the traces of symbolic language in Bach's keyboard works, it is very important to recall Heinichen's warning, cited on page

---

[36] This motive is also used in Cantata 82, "Ich habe genug" (Ex. 175).

Ex. 175. Cantata 82, "Ich habe genug," beginning of voice part

213, that the use of tone-painting can only help stir the artistic imagination. Equally important is the fact that the musical material used for symbolic purposes does not represent "tone poetry," as Schweitzer pretends, but is in itself "ambiguous and unemotional," deriving its "meaning" only through the *intervention of the intellect*." In the excellent essay, "Allegory in Baroque Music," from which this phrase is taken, Manfred Bukofzer points out that, strictly speaking, Bach's application of tone symbolism belongs to the classification of allegory.[37] To illustrate the ambiguity of Bach's "musical figures," he takes, among others, the case of widely spaced intervals, which are used for:

(1) describing the words "so far" (Ex. 178);[38]

Ex. 178

(2) allegorizing "anger" and "horror" (Ex. 179);[39]

Ex. 179

(3) expressing "my soul's ardent desire" (Ex. 180).[40]

Ex. 180

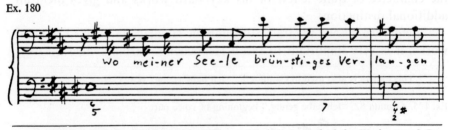

---

[37] Manfred Bukofzer, "Allegory in Baroque Music," *Journal of the Warburg and Cortauld Institutes*, vol. III (London, 1939–1940), 21.

[38] Bach-Gesellschaft, vol. VI, p. 222.

[39] Bach-Gesellschaft, vol. XII, p. 140.

[40] Bach-Gesellschaft, vol. XXXII, p. 64.

Even a musical figure of such expressive power as the famous chromatic progression represents three diverse ideas in the *St. John Passion* alone:

(1) weeping (Ex. 181);[41]

Ex. 181

(2) "malefactor" (Ex. 182);[42]

Ex. 182

(3) pushing (Ex. 183).[43]

Ex. 183

To these examples, also furnished by Bukofzer, we might add a few more. The essence of the motive remains the same, regardless of whether Kuhnau depicts the fall and death of Goliath, in the Biblical sonata "The Fight between David and Goliath" (Ex. 184), or Bach describes "Et sepultus est" in the "Crucifixus" of the B minor Mass (Ex. 185), or caricatures the sorrow of the friend of their beloved brother in the Departure Capriccio (Ex. 186).

---

[41] *St. John Passion*, Eulenburg's Miniature Score, p. 548.
[42] *St. John Passion*, p. 59.
[43] *St. John Passion*, p. 39.

Equally "neutral" is the musical symbol used to depict walking. Whether peasants are going, "step by step," to the old tavern in the "Peasant" Cantata (Ex. 187), or Christ hesitantly ascends the holy

Ex. 184. Kuhnau, "The Fight between David and Goliath"

Ex. 185. Mass in B minor, "Crucifixus"

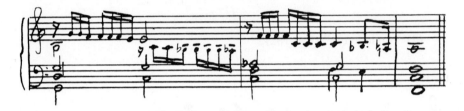

Ex. 186. Departure Capriccio

Ex. 187. "Peasant" Cantata

mountain in Cantata 159, "Sehet wir gehen hinauf gen Jerusalem" (Ex. 188), the figures are the same; thus they describe but have no emotional content per se.

Ex. 188. Cantata 159, "Sehet wir gehen hinauf gen Jerusalem"

CROSS SYMBOLS

Of all the musical figures, that which can be identified most easily in Bach's keyboard works is the sign of the cross. The symbol can be recognized from its use in the cantatas, where Bach tries, whenever possible, to give the word "*Kreuz*" (cross) to a note with a sharp, since in German the sharp is called "*Kreuz*" (Ex. 189). At these places the musical line is

Ex. 189. Cantata 56, "Ich will den Kreuzstab gerne tragen"

organized in such a way that a line drawn through the heads of the notes ascends and then descends, representing the arms of the cross. The most significant use of this symbol in the keyboard works appears in the final preludes and fugues of both volumes of the *Welltempered Keyboard*, which have already been shown to harbor other "secret messages." The cross is clear in all cases (Exs. 190a, b, and 191a, b), even in the Fugue of

Ex. 190a. Prelude in B minor, *W.K.* I, bars 42-43

Ex. 190b. Fugue in B minor, *W.K.* I, bars 1–2

the second volume, "secular" as this "passepied" is in comparison with its greater sister from the first volume.

17

That all these cross citations should be understood as symbolic offerings, musical settings of the famous initials "J. J." (*Jesu juva*) or "S. D. G." (*Soli Deo Gloria*) so often placed by Bach at the beginning or end of a composition respectively, is self-evident.

Ex. 191a. Prelude in B minor, *W.K.* II, bars 37–39

Ex. 191b. Fugue in B minor, *W.K.* II, bars 1–4

The sign of the cross in Fugue 12, *W.K.* I (Ex. 192), must certainly have been intended as the midway mark of this volume. It might perhaps

Ex. 192. Fugue in F minor, *W.K.* I

be far-fetched to detect the same midway symbolization in the Prelude in F minor of the second volume (Ex. 193); however, if we recollect

Ex. 193. Prelude in F minor, *W.K.* II

that Fugue 24, *W.K.* II, is a secular companion to Fugue 24, *W.K.* I, it is possible to consider the Prelude in F minor, *W.K.* II, a secular fantasy on the corresponding fugue from the first volume. At least the falling second is common to both. The most forceful underlining of the middle of a piece occurs in the *Goldberg Variations*. Not only is

Variation 16 the "overture" to the second half of the set, but Variation 15 also employs the lines of the cross (Ex. 194).

Ex. 194. *Goldberg Variations*, Variation 15

Actually, this example shows a simultaneous application of two allegoric devices, for the series of seconds in pairs are also the symbol of teardrops, used so effectively in the final chorus of the first part of the *St. Matthew Passion*.

The Sinfonia in F minor is outstanding for its use of the cross symbol in the two themes that appear in triple counterpoint with the famous chromatic line of the bass. We might almost call this piece "The Small Passion," borrowing the title that art historians have given to a famous series of woodcuts by Albrecht Dürer.

The theme of the Fugue in C sharp minor, *W.K.* I (Ex. 195), presents another opportunity for double interpretation. It represents not only the

Ex. 195. Fugue in C sharp minor, *W.K.* I

sign of the cross, but also a disguised allusion to the musical configuration of the name BACH, arrived at by following the German nomenclature of the keys (Ex. 196). For many years I have thought of how much delight

Ex. 196

and satisfaction Bach must have derived from the fact that his name inherently carried the symbol of the cross. However, recognition of this fact in the Bach literature has come only recently. In one of the best books of the Bach year, 1950, Fred Hamel writes: "So far nobody seems to have noticed that the four notes of the theme derived from Bach's name are more than a musical signature under the life work of the Master.

If one draws lines between the two middle notes, *A* and *C*, and the outer ones, *B* and *H*, the shape of the cross appears."[44]

THE FLIGHT OF ANGELS

The "flight of angels" is another religious symbol that has frequent appearances in Bach's keyboard works. Its identification is based on the chorale prelude "Vom Himmel kam der Engel Schar," the first of the canonic variations on the hymn "Vom Himmel hoch da komm ich her," the "Sanctus" of the B minor Mass, and numerous pictorial figures in the cantatas. Lines that go up and down with regularity are the characteristic feature of this symbol, which appears most frequently in 6/8, 9/8, and 12/8 time. In the keyboard works it is usually found in the keys of A major or E flat major, which is certainly not the result of chance, since the symbol of the Trinity is implied in the signatures of both keys.

The most obvious allusion to "angels' flight" occurs in the Prelude in A major, *W.K.* II, with the beautiful inversion of its principle motive (Ex. 197a, b). The marked relation between this piece and the Prelude in

Ex. 197a. Prelude in A major, *W.K.* II, bar 1

Ex. 197b. The same, bar 9

E flat major, *W.K.* II, the Prelude in the same key from the Prelude, Fugue, and Allegro for the Lautenklavier, and even the Prelude of the First English Suite, is rather fascinating, although we do not want to go so far as to claim a religious symbolism for the last-named piece, which would not be in accord with its gallant style. It should also be noted that the prominent use of the interval of the fourth in pieces in E flat major, which we have already linked with the symbolization of the Trinity,[45] is also reflected in the A major compositions, Prelude, *W.K.* II, and Fugue, *W.K.* I (Exs. 198 and 199).

---

[44] Fred Hamel, *Johann Sebastian Bach, Geistige Welt* (Göttingen, 1951), p. 223.
[45] See the discussion of E flat major on p. 232.

The 9/8 metre of the Sinfonia in E major, as well as the nature of its subject, which is used in alternation with its inverted form (Ex. 200a, b),

Ex. 198. Prelude in A major, *W.K.* II

Ex. 199. Fugue in A major, *W.K.* I

Ex. 200a. Sinfonia in E major, subject

Ex. 200b. The same, inversion

brings this piece, too, into a close inner relation with the group of pieces mentioned above, to which the Fugue in E major, *W.K.* II, may also be linked. Finally, we may dare to add to this group at least the Prelude and perhaps also the Fugue in F major, *W.K.* II. The Prelude, with its strange runs of eighth notes built into a web of five voices that never becomes truly polyphonic, looks so similar, on paper, to the organ prelude "Vom Himmel kam der Engel Schar," that such an assumption is hardly too far-fetched. The theme of the Fugue is pictorial in itself, suggesting a perfect "wing line" (Ex. 201). Indeed, we might interpret the entire piece

Ex. 201. Fugue in F major, *W.K.* II

as a game of hide-and-seek among three naughty little angels, so popular with baroque sculptors, were we not afraid of being criticized for an escapade into the territory of musical hermeneutics of a lower type.

SANCTUS AND CRADLE SYMBOLS

In Bach's vocal works, the appearance of the interval of the octave, preferably falling and in rather slow motion, symbolizes the word "Holy." Its most famous application occurs in the bass line of the "Sanctus" of the B minor Mass (Ex. 202). From the Passions we learn that this octave

Ex. 202. Mass in B minor, "Sanctus"

can be filled in with the notes of the major triad, which Bach always does when Jesus speaks "as a King" (Exs. 203 and 204).

Ex. 203. *St. John Passion*[46]

Ex. 204. *St. Matthew Passion*[47]

In the *Christmas Oratorio* we see that the same octave motive can also be used in a lighter way, especially in shorter note values (eighth

Ex. 205. *Christmas Oratorio*

---

[46] Bach-Gesellschaft, vol. XII, p. 53.
[47] Bach-Gesellschaft, vol. IV, p. 45 (a few bars later appear the words, "In my father's kingdom").

notes), to symbolize "cradle movement" in a lullaby, the aria "Schlafe, mein Liebster" (Ex. 205). The slurs are authentic and help distinguish the "cradle" interpretation from that of "Holy."

In Bach's keyboard music the octave symbol appears in all its majesty in the Prelude in D major, *W.K.* II, and in Variation 24 of the *Goldberg Variations*. The exuberant joy expressed in the Prelude in G major, *W.K.* I, which is given some dignity only by the octave figure in the bass (Ex. 206),

Ex. 206. Prelude in G major, *W.K.* I

makes this piece a kind of secular sister to the compositions just mentioned. The wonderful Prelude in A flat major, *W.K.* II, is another example of a deeply religious keyboard piece; the solemn falling octave is heard clearly above the notes placed in between (Ex. 207).

Ex. 207. Prelude in A flat major, *W.K.* II

The "lullaby" meaning of the falling and rising octave comes out most clearly in the E major Prelude, *W.K.* II. Its combination with the "flight of angels" in the Preludes in E flat major and A major, *W.K.* II, gives us three real Christmas pieces in this volume.

MISCELLANEOUS SYMBOLS

In addition to the symbolic features of Bach's keyboard works discussed above, there are a few whose appearances are less numerous but which nevertheless deserve to be mentioned. Two fugues in the second volume of the *Welltempered Keyboard* look and sound as if they were transcribed from vocal music: the Fugue in D major, called by Busoni a "*Christe eleison* fugue"; and that in E major, which is not too far removed from the idiom of the "Gratias agimus" of the Mass in B minor. The countersubject of the Fugue in F sharp minor, *W.K.* I, can be included in that group of themes which symbolizes teardrops.

Religious background is felt in the Sinfonias in E flat major and E minor, the Preludes and Fugues in B flat and E flat minor, *W.K.* I, the Prelude in B minor, *W.K.* I (which, as already noticed, uses the cross sign

at the end), and the Prelude in C sharp minor, *W.K.* II. In all these
pieces the interval of the fourth, a fundamental religious symbol, plays a
prominent role.

An aura of "Passion" is strongly felt in the Prelude and Fugue in G
minor, *W.K.* II. The vocal character of the Fugue has already caused us
to allude to its relation to the Chorus of the Roman Soldiers in the *St.
John Passion*, and the Prelude makes use of the rhythm of flagellation:

. It is of particular interest that the key of G minor

plays a very important role in the flagellation scenes of both Passions:
both flagellation recitatives end in this key, which is also used in the
chorus "Kreuzige" of the *St. John Passion*. Still farther afield, the second
movement of the Harpsichord Concerto in D minor, written in G minor
and later built into the chorus "Wir müssen durch viel Trübsal" of
Cantata 146, has a bar in common with the final chorus of the *St. Matthew
Passion* (Ex. 208).

Ex. 208. Harpsichord Concerto in D minor, Movement 2, bars 43–44

Two of Bach's most typical wave figures are combined in the Sinfonia
in B minor (Ex. 209). Water seems also to be pictured in the little figure
of the Fugue in F sharp major, *W.K.* I (Ex. 210). Other secular allegories

Ex. 209. Sinfonia in B minor

Ex. 210. Fugue in F sharp major, *W.K.* I, bar 7

can be found in the only composition by Bach that is real program music,
the Departure Capriccio. Among the symbols that help illustrate the

various scenes are those of the "flattery of the friends" (Ex. 211), the caricatural "ocean of tears" in the "Lament," the trumpet tune of the

Ex. 211. Departure Capriccio   Ex. 212. The same

coachman, and that of his whip (Ex. 212), which becomes the counter-subject of the fugue. Equally amusing is the imitation of hen and cuckoo in the early Sonata in D major.

Last but not least we come to the incredibly witty pun with which Bach announces the return of the Aria at the end of the *Goldberg Variations*. Who has not wondered about the quodlibet that ends the variations and the strange selection of folksongs? What is the meaning of these odd words:

Ich bin so lang nicht bei dir g'west	I've not been with you for so long
Ruck her, ruck her, ruck her.	Come closer, closer closer.
Kraut und Rüben haben mich vertrieben.	*Cabbage* and beets drove me far away.
Hätt mein Mutter Fleisch gekocht,	Had my mother cooked some meat,
So wär ich länger blieben.	Then I'd have stayed much longer.[48]

In 1934, Fritz Müller succeded in solving this enigma.[49] The folksongs announce the approaching return of the aria in the following way: "I" (the theme) have been away from "you" (the player) because cabbage and beets (the free variations) drove me away. If mother had cooked meat (if Bach had remained closer to the basic theme), I would have stayed. The return of the theme in its original form is the meat, so heartily longed for.[50] Readers who are familiar with Bach's method of using hymn melodies for symbolic purposes in his cantatas, will immediately grasp the similarity of procedure in the use of the folksongs in this quodlibet.

---

[48] With one minor exception, we follow Kirkpatrick's translation in the Preface to his edition of the *Goldberg Variations* (p. viii). To save my distinguished colleague Mr. Kirkpatrick from possible disappointment when dining in a German restaurant, we want to draw his attention to the proper translation of the word "Kraut," which is "cabbage" and not "spinach." It might also be better to translate "Rüben" as "turnips." A "beet" is only a "Rote Rübe."

[49] Fritz Müller, "Kraut und Rüben, einige Bemerkungen über die Schlussnummer in J. S. Bach's Goldberg Variationen," *Zeitschrift für Musik*, Jahrgang 101 (February 1934), p. 129. The melody "Ich bin so lang nicht bei Dir g'west" seems to have enjoyed popularity even outside of Germany. C. F. Kossmann reports in a very interesting article, "Ich bin so lang nicht bei Dir g'west," *Zeitschrift für Musikwissenschaft* (1925–1926), p. 295, that he found the melody mentioned in *Schelmuffsky, andrer Teil*, a "lie story" rather famous at its time, written by Christian Reutter (1665–?) and published anonymously in 1696. Therein the hero says that he heard this melody sung in Venice.

[50] Our description follows Moser's presentation in *Johann Sebastian Bach*, p. 151.

NUMBER SYMBOLISM

We have just seen that it took 190 years for the secret of the quodlibet to be unraveled. The rediscovery of the large and very important role that numbers play in so many of Bach's works is of equally recent date. The first random discoveries of a few cases, such as the ten citations of the subject in the pedal part of the chorale prelude "Dies sind die heiligen Zehn Gebot" (These are the Holy Ten Commandments),[51] and the eleven questions "Herr, bin ich's?" (Lord, is it I?) of Christ's disciples in the *St. Matthew Passion*,[52] gave rise to the opinion that these were "jokes" of the composer. Later, the numerous oddities and errors in Wilhelm Wercker's book *Studien über die Symmetrie im Bau der Fugen . . .*, which represents the first major publication in this field, brought the entire matter into such discredit that even the most recent discoveries, made primarily by Friedrich Smend, are still regarded with hesitancy and distrust, especially by his German colleagues.[53]

It would be very narrow-minded to take Bach's "number games" as jokes, and the reluctance of so many scholars to give any consideration to the problem reminds us vividly of the indignation aroused by the inquiries of Schweitzer and Pirro into the "meaning" of Bach's motive language. Although, as we have already stated, Friedrich Blume is right in emphasizing the fact that Bach was a musician and not a "frustrated minister or mathematician," the importance of this new branch of research for the clarification of Bach's "spiritual world" (*Hamel*) can never be

---

[51] It is interesting that when Bach writes another chorale prelude on this same hymn in the *Klavierübung*, part III, he gives it the form of a fughetta with ten entrances.

[52] By having the words sung only eleven times, Bach symbolizes the fact that Judas did not dare to ask the question at this moment.

[53] Hermann Keller says: "Smend has succeeded in proving that Bach knew 'games' with numbers (as we might call them). The only question is how essential or unessential they are to his music. Although it is to be expected that this aspect of Bach's music will be singled out for special attention during the coming decades, the limited results achieved so far seem to call for an attitude of utter reserve" (*Die Klavierwerke Bach's*, Leipzig, 1950, p. 129). Yet let it be noticed how carefully Smend himself formulates and limits the role of number symbolism in Bach research. "One should not make Bach the subject of arithmetic puzzles. Only in connection with other constructive factors should consideration be given to numbers in Bach's works" (*Luther und Bach*, Berlin, 1947, p. 19). How number research should *not* be done could best be learned from the article by Hans Nissen, "Der Sinn des Wohltemperierten Klaviers II. Teil," *Bach-Jahrbuch* (1951–1952), pp. 54ff. Nissen claims that Bach wanted to give in the *Welltempered Keyboard* a "musical picture of the Christian world-drama, starting with the Spirit of God and the Creation and ending with the Resurrection of the dead." Quite a few of Nissen's applications of number symbolism are based on faulty figures, reached by miscounting the bars of the pieces in question (almost unbelievable as this sounds). For example, the Fugue in C sharp minor has 71 bars, not 70; the Prelude in E flat major has 71, not 70; the Prelude in F major has 72, not 70; the Fugue in F major 99, *not* 84; that in F minor 85, not 84; the Fugue in B flat minor 101, not 100. Thus all of Nissen's conclusions, drawn from his "holy figures," collapse. One cannot understand why space was given to this article in the *Bach-Jahrbuch* without any rechecking.

overestimated. With discoveries being made at an ever-increasing pace, the immensity of Bach's greatness grows to such dimensions that we can hardly suppress a feeling of dizziness when we try to follow him on these paths of unsurpassed craftsmanship. That he could build the mathematical calculation of number symbolism into his designs without hindering the spontaneity and depths of expression is beyond understanding. The more we study his last and least-known masterpiece, the *Art of the Fugue*, the less able we are to comprehend how Bach could succeed in making the most complicated fugue in the collection, the four-part "Mirror Fugue," perhaps the most expressive, the most heartfelt piece of the entire fugue cycle.

Since many readers may not be familiar with the principles of number symbolism, a brief description is in order. The attribution of special meaning to various numbers is inherited from antiquity and has played a role in the fine arts and literature as well as in music.[54] Bach made use of certain figures connected with the Bible: "3" for the Trinity; "6" for the working days of the Creation; "7" for the Creator and Creation in general and also for the Holy Spirit, Evangelium, the Grace of God; "10" for the Ten Commandments; and "12" for the Church, Apostles, and Congregation. The days between the Resurrection and the Ascension are occasionally symbolized in his works, and even a few allusions to the numbers of the psalms seem to have been made.[55] Bach also used multiples of these figures, such as 3 times 7 (three times "Holy"), 7 times 7 (the forty-nine bars of the "Et incarnatus est" of the B minor Mass), and 7 times 12, which is exactly the number of measures in the "Patrem Omnipotentem" of the Mass. Smend's discovery that Bach actually marked the number "84" at the end of this chorus in the autograph[56] is highly significant as a proof that scholarly efforts to unearth the secrets of number symbols cannot be dismissed with a shrug of the shoulders and a comment about the foolishness of such inquiries.

It goes without saying that the great vocal works, the Mass in B minor and the Passions, are the principal compositions in which number symbols play a major role. Unfortunately, it is impossible for us to include here a report of the sometimes hair-raising discoveries that have already been made in regard to those pieces. In the keyboard works only a few

---

[54] Readers interested in more detailed information on the history of number symbolism are referred to J. J. Schmidt, *Der biblische Mathematicus* (1736), and F. C. Endres, *Mystik und Magie der Zahlen* (Zürich, 1951). A condensed review of the problems involved can be found in the excellent article by Fritz Feldmann, "Numerorum mysteria," *Archiv für Musikwissenschaft*, Jahrgang XIV, no. 2 (1957), p. 102.

[55] See Martin Jansen, "Bach's Zahlensymbolik."

[56] Cited by Friedrich Blume in "Johann Sebastian Bach," *Die Musik in Geschichte und Gegenwart*, p. 1030.

traces of number symbolism have been identified so far. Of course, whenever Bach put six pieces of the same kind together under one title, such as the Six English Suites, Six French Suites, and Six Partitas, he did so in order to pay homage to the six days in which the Lord created the universe. The same figure is also used for the Brandenburg Concertos, the Organ Trios, and the sonatas and suites for violin and cello. Some of Bach's predecessors also made such groupings; witness, for example, Johann Krieger's *Sechs Musikalische Partien*,[57] and Kuhnau's Six Biblical Sonatas.[58] Even Bach's son Carl Philipp Emanuel used sets of six for numerous publications, especially in his keyboard music, which includes Six Collections of Sonatas, Rondos, and Phantasies for connoisseurs and amateurs, Six Prussian Sonatas, Six Württemberg Sonatas, and so on. I am, alas, unable to tell why Bach chose "15" for the number of Inventions and Sinfonias. Since the *Goldberg Variations* consist of twice fifteen variations, this figure, too, may have symbolic meaning not yet explainable.

The figure "3" clearly played a role in the choice of key (three flats) of the E flat major Prelude, *W.K.* I, which is very closely related to the great Organ Prelude and Triple Fugue in E flat major from the *Klavierübung*, part III, in which the Trinity is the secret subject. In addition, the three "bows," as in bar 1 of the Prelude in A flat major, *W.K.* II,[59] are no doubt intended to signify "holy, holy, holy."

A special problem is offered by the number of notes found in the subjects of the opening and closing fugues of both volumes of the *Welltempered Keyboard*. Smend's investigations give sufficient evidence that Bach liked to play numerical "games" with his name.[60] If we give every letter of the alphabet a number: a = 1; b = 2; c = 3; and so on,[61] the sum of the letters of BACH is 14, of J. S. BACH, 41. Whether or not Bach put his "name seal" into the first volume of the *Welltempered Keyboard* by opening it with a fugue whose theme consists of fourteen notes is now being widely debated. That this is not a chance number seems to be proved by Bach's last composition, the hymn "Vor Deinen Thron tret' ich alhier" (I am appearing before Thy throne). The melody of this hymn is known by the name "Wenn wir in letzten Nöten sein," and the line cited above is the beginning of its last verse. Nothing is more moving than to see the dying composer select just this line as the title for this piece of unearthly beauty, which was his farewell to the world. To symbolize the "I," Bach used fourteen notes for the first line of the hymn, and forty-one

---

[57] (Nürnberg, 1697.)

[58] Johann Kuhnau, *Musikalische Vorstellung einiger Biblischer Historien. In 6 Sonaten* (Leipzig, 1700).

[59] See Example 207, above.

[60] F. Smend, *Bach, bei seinen Namen gerufen* (Kassel, 1950).

[61] I and j are 9; u and v are 20; z = 24 (see Smend, *Luther und Bach*, p. 18).

(J. S. Bach) for the entire *cantus firmus*.[62] In the light of this discovery, scholars have become inclined to acknowledge that the theme of fourteen notes at the beginning of the *Welltempered Keyboard* can hardly be considered an accidental affair.[63]

What is the situation in regard to the fugues in other prominent places of this collection? We discover that not only the theme of the twenty-fourth fugue of the first volume, but also the themes of Fugues 1, 24, and even 12 of the second volume, consist of twenty-one notes! The meaning of "21" is clear: 3 times 7 means "three times holy," which is a musical translation of the meaning of the letters "S. D. G." (*Soli Deo Gloria*) that Bach so often put at the end of a major work. This conscious indication of the midpoint of the second volume should not surprise us after our experience with the *Goldberg Variations*; but when we look for a similar structural symbol in the first volume, we find a theme with the unexpected number of eleven notes. Did Bach think that the middle of the work was underlined well enough by the use of a "Crucifixus" theme in Fugue 12?[64] Does the 11 have something to do with the eleven faithful disciples? This does not make much sense. More probably, the figure 11 here has a meaning which St. Augustine already attributed to it: "Transgressionem decalogi notat" (10 plus 1, trespass of the holy commandments).[65] Seen in this light, the "midway-fugue" in F minor would convey to us a deeply moving symbolic message: Crucifixus (the melodic line)—sinning mankind (the number 11)—Christ dying for the redemption of mankind.

This way of interpreting the meaning of Fugue 12 may help to solve the symbolic meaning of a still greater piece in the same key—the Sinfonia in F minor, admired all over the world as one of the most sublime manifestations of Bach's art. At first glance one can already decipher the symbols built into the lines of each of the three themes. Theme I is nothing else than the famous chromatic descending line which is linked by the "Crucifixus" of the B minor Mass with the death of Christ; themes II and III are clearly constructed as "cross" themes. When we look now into their number values, we discover to our amazement that we find for theme I again the figure 11, the same as in Fugue 12, *W.K.* I, symbolizing man the sinner. Theme II contains fourteen notes, the figure that represents Bach's name. Can this have any other meaning than that Bach identifies himself with man the sinner, that it is he who prostrates himself

[62] Smend, *Johann Sebastian Bachs Kirchenkantaten* (Berlin, 1947), vol. III, p. 20.

[63] The same holds, in our opinion, for the gigantic Gigue-Fugue which "seals" Bach's Opus I, the publication of the six partitas. Again, the theme consists of fourteen notes.

[64] This parallel with the *Goldberg Variations* is strengthened by the fact that Variation 15 also contains the cross symbol.

[65] See Fritz Feldmann, "Numerorum mysteria," p. 111.

before Christ? But now in theme III appear nineteen notes, an indivisible number and at the same time, the sum of 7 and 12, the holiest numbers, thus moving the earthly picture of the repenting Bach up to the throne of the Almighty. Has not everyone who has studied this incomparable piece instinctively felt that it seems to be one of the most personal ones of the composer? Now the mysterious numbers show that this piece gives us the most precious documentations of Bach's devotion and faith.

Much study will still be necessary to disclose the number mysteries that Bach has built into the *Art of the Fugue*. We cannot here go into details and must be satisfied with pointing out the all-important role which the figures 7 and 12, just mentioned, play here again. The main theme of the *Art of the Fugue* contains *twelve* notes, telling us that Bach is going to build a cathedral. The first theme of the unfinished quadruple fugue introduces a theme consisting of *seven* notes. What figure pyramids might Bach have erected, had he been allowed to finish this fugue of fugues? The pen fell out of his hand when he introduced his name theme, undisguised for the first time in his life, using it in all its glory as a personal seal.

CHAPTER 9

Final Remarks

The mysteries offered by the manuscripts of Bach's keyboard works, whose naked notes have become, by the verdict of fate, our chief source of information for giving these pieces an adequate performance, were the starting point of our investigations. The mysteries of number symbols mark the end of this long expedition into uncharted territory. Have we succeeded in contributing to a better knowledge of its topography?

In regard to the instrument question we have undoubtedly made progress. The viewpoints that musicology has held on this subject up to now cannot be characterized better than by two statements in Curt Sachs' book, *The Commonwealth of Art*. One says:

As late a work as Bach's *Wohltemperiertes Clavier* (whose arbitrary, too specific English title *Well-tempered Clavichord* fatally falsifies the intentional vagueness of the older German word *Clavier*) can be played on any adequate keyboard instrument including the organ, despite some modern attempts to determine from its style whether it was meant for harpsichord or for clavichord. Actually, it was hardly 'meant' for any one instrument because most of its music was abstract and did not depend on a particular kind of 'appearance.' Which, in turn, is not 'meant' to be a charter for those of our contemporaries who do not hesitate to murder the music of Bach with the full impact of some allegedly modern but in reality outworn-romantic 'appearance' hostile to its style and genius, its abstractness and impersonality.

Masters inclined to join the other side—like the English virginalists around 1600 with their broken chord passages or Domenico Scarlatti early in the eighteenth century or later Liszt and Chopin—on the contrary, created out of the spirit and the peculiar technical conditions of their instruments: one is tempted to say their own, individual instruments and nobody could mistake their works for organ music.[1]

---

[1] Curt Sachs, *The Commonwealth of Art* (New York, 1946), p. 277.

The other statement says:

While any painter has the sense to realize that Raphael's composition requires Raphael's colors and would be reduced *ad absurdum* by applying Cézanne's, musicians again and again exclaim: "If Bach had known the marvels of our modern pianos, organ skyscrapers, and mass orchestras!" However nonsensical all if-exclamations are, there is a simple answer to this antihistorical and antilogical question: Bach would either have rejected the modern marvels because they were due to a romantic attitude foreign and even hostile to him (just as the English harpsichordists of the seventeenth century ignored the timbre- and intensity-changing pedals that someone had invented against the trends of his time), or else he would have written *in a quite different style*, which again would have implied a quite different mind. In one sentence: he might have achieved great mastership, but would not have been Bach.[2]

These statements were no doubt meant only to represent a wizard's grandiose aerial view of centuries, where detailed observations matter no longer. Otherwise they would be incompatible. If Bach's music is abstract, if his keyboard music was played on harpsichord, clavichord, and organ interchangeably, then the piano "decently" treated of course may be acknowledged as the legitimate heir to his keyboard works without any major objections. But one hearing of, for example, the Prelude of the English Suite in G minor played successively on harpsichord, clavichord, organ, and piano would be sufficient to dispel this idea for good.

It is also no doubt true that the English virginalists were "virginal-minded," and that Scarlatti was as "harpsichord-minded" as Chopin and Liszt were "piano-minded." Why then should Bach, the greatest organ master of his time, the "devil at the organ" as contemporaries sometimes called him, have aspired to write only abstract music for the keyboard, without caring how it sounded? Could this possibly be true of the young Bach, the Bach of Weimar and Cöthen, who wrote so many pieces that demonstrate his obvious enjoyment of "showy" effects? Must the first volume of the *Welltempered Keyboard*, which is a product of Cöthen, be excluded from that category of Bach's work which tries to give not only enjoyment to the soul but also pleasure to the ear? Who could possibly want to hear the dazzling *perpetuum mobile* of the Prelude in D major, the pompousness of the overture-like Fugue that goes with it, the fierce Prelude in C minor, or the exuberantly joyful Prelude and Fugue in G major, on the tender clavichord? Who would enjoy hearing a plucked, even tone as the medium for the incredibly refined lines of the Preludes and Fugues in E flat minor and B minor, which are the true incarnation of the heart and soul of a clavichord? If all this were abstract music,

---

[2] Sachs, p. 336 (italics mine).

showing only accidentally traces of special fitness for the harpsichord here and there, how strange that wherever such traces are missing, eminent fitness for the clavichord immediately comes into the open.

We hope that our analysis of so many pieces has shown that Bach's ability to do justice to the keyboard instruments of his time has been underrated. Unified as all his works are by the indescribable substance "Bach," his keyboard pieces fully respect the possibilities and limitations as set by the individual mechanisms of harpsichord and clavichord, at least until that great moment arrives when the inspiration of a genius leaves the earth behind and turns to the unsayable, to the unplayable. No one was more aware of this privilege of the creative artist than Beethoven, who answered Schuppanzigh's complaint about the difficulty of certain passages for the violin by exclaiming: "Do you think that I have your miserable fiddle in mind when the spirit overcomes me?"

For the aging Bach, the gradual turn to abstract music is undeniable, and some pieces of the second volume of the "Forty-eight" clearly show traces of this tendency. However, it is obvious that for the greatest part of his keyboard music, consideration of the medium for which he wrote guided Bach's pen. When it comes to that acutely painful operation of transferring his keyboard pieces to the piano, knowledge of the original destination, of the "pedigree" of the piece in question, is the first and most decisive prerequisite. In this respect we hope to have brought our conceptions of "Bach style" a major step forward.

The problems of tempo, ornamentation, and articulation are not equally willing to yield to ultimate solutions. In these fields it was our goal to set a clear boundary between cases to which the traditional rules can be applied and those with which these rules are incompatible. This will at least provide a well-defined basis for future research, disturbing as it is that so much of the "grammar" of Bach's language is still veiled by uncertainty.

Yet is this uncertainty perhaps not the cause of that mysterious spell which we instinctively feel when we play Bach's works? Is it not just this remoteness and inaccessibility that preserve for us their singular value? If we in our time are still more "Bach amateurs" than "Bach connoisseurs," in contrast to his contemporaries who were more familiar with the subtleties of his language, we are yet blessed with the privilege of being able to sense better the uniqueness of this manifestation of the holy spirit of music which is symbolized for us in the name of BACH.

APPENDIX

Special Suggestions for the Interpretation of Bach's Keyboard Works

GENERAL REMARKS

The suggestions given here for the interpretation of Bach's keyboard works must, by necessity, be subjected to certain restrictions. To give a complete report on every detail of performance problems would be impossible without reprinting in full every single composition, and it is not our ambition to add one more "pedagogic" edition to the already existing ones. Even such an edition would be incomplete without a very detailed analysis of every work; otherwise no justification for the selection of the appropriate instrument and—for harpsichord pieces—of the appropriate registration could be given.

In order not to let this book grow to prohibitive size and yet to provide the Bach student with the opportunity to find in *one* place the essence of the result of our investigations, this Appendix contains, for every keyboard composition of major importance, the *basic* suggestions for the instrument to be used, dynamics, registration, tempo, articulation, and ornamentation. Observations of general interest, especially in regard to Bach's use of symbolism, will be added wherever they occur.

Problems of *dynamics* are basically solved as soon as one has decided which instrument one wants to use. In a work meant for clavichord, crescendo and diminuendo will conform with the increasing or decreasing density of the lines. In harpsichord works, the sonority of the terrace dynamics will depend on the quality of registers selected for the two keyboards.

Suggestions for *registration* are in general based on a harpsichord with hand registration and two keyboards: 8' and 16' (plus Theorbe) on the lower, 8" and 4" (plus lute stop for 8") on the upper keyboard. C means coupler, L means lute. An (l) added to a register—for example, 8'(l)—means "low," to be played one octave lower than written; an added (h) means "high," to be played one octave higher than written. The place to return to normal position will be indicated by the word "loco."[1]

It hardly needs to be said that for the vast majority of Bach's keyboard works the full wealth of the registration possibilities of so large an instrument should *not* be used. The highly debated 16′ register especially is suggested only when its use would measurably add to the beauty of interpretation. It goes also without saying that in pieces which are short enough to be played in *one* registration only (for example, many preludes of the "Forty-eight," dance pieces, sections of toccatas), various selections of tone color on one or two keyboards could be made with equally good justification. Purposely, we have abstained from suggesting any "exotic" registrations (see p. 36), much as we might have been tempted to do so. All our recommendations are based on the principle that they may correspond as closely as possible with the architecture of the piece in question. They are, of course, open to all possible changes which do not violate this precept.

For *tempo* we will not only give the appropriate metronome mark but also will add the number under which the piece can be found on the Tempo Tables. This will facilitate comparisons with "sister pieces."

Concerning the distressing *articulation* problem, for reasons just outlined we can give nothing more than suggestions for the interpretation of main themes. To indicate gradations between legato and staccato, we will use the following words: *legatissimo, molto legato, legato, quasi legato, tenuto, portato, nonlegato, leggiero, quasi staccato, staccato, staccatissimo.* This list may seem exaggerated, but sometimes the choice of just this and not that word will help to communicate some refined differentiations which, otherwise, could only be demonstrated at the instrument.

In regard to *ornamentation*, it is obviously impossible to list the correct execution of every ornament. Since for the vast majority of them the traditional rules can be applied, we will report only on those cases where special problems are involved.

THE INVENTIONS AND SINFONIAS

All the Inventions and Sinfonias are written with the clavichord in mind for their execution as manifested by the phrase in the original Preface, that they should be studied "to obtain a singing touch." Since the Landshoff edition contains complete information about articulation and ornamentation, we will mention only the few cases where strong reasons cause us to disagree with this most learned editor.

---

[1] Owners of harpsichords that lack the 16′ register but are equipped with 8′ and 4′ registers on the lower, 8′ on the upper keyboard, will have no difficulties in interpreting our registration suggestions if they follow the rule that on their instruments, 8″ and 4″ mean *lower*, 8′ means *upper* keyboard.

Invention 1 in C major

Tempo: ♩ = ± 80 (see Tempo Table Ia, 1)

Ornamentation: The ⟿ in the subject is a border case: Landshoff calls
it a "Praller" in contradiction to C. P. E. Bach's use of this term (see p.
163) and takes its execution as an "inverted mordent" so much for granted
(apparently on account of Krebs' testimonial; see pp. 165ff.) that he even
abstains from discussing the problem in his remarks on interpretation. We
are inclined to follow him, not completely excluding the possibility of a
four-note short trill, although we feel that the acoustic result—ccc d, ggg e
(victory theme!)—does not sound too Bachian. Four notes from above
should certainly be played for ⟿, not only in bar 6 but also in bar 14
(the latter again in contradiction to Landshoff).

Most noteworthy is the use Bach makes of the inversion of the theme (from
bar 3 on), accompanying it at the same time by the augmentation of the first
four notes which later (bar 19) appear in inverted form.

Invention 2 in C minor

Tempo: ♩ = ± 80 (see Tempo Table Ia, 2)

Ornamentation: The ⟿ in bar 3 and corresponding ones can be executed
only as "inverted mordents" (see Trill Table, 1).

Bars 1–9, right hand, are strictly canonically imitated in bars 3–11, left
hand. Then bars 11–19, left hand, give similar guidance to the right hand for
bars 13–21.

Invention 3 in D major

Tempo: ♩. = ± 60 (see Tempo Table Va, 1)

Ornamentation: The long notes in bars 26, 28, and 30 are meant to be trilled

Symbolism: A miniature "Gloria" (the motive of the falling octave)

Invention 4 in D minor

Tempo: ♩ = ± 60 (see Tempo Table Va, 2)

Ornamentation: A trill should be added in bars 17, 37, 51 to emphasize the
cadence.

Inversion of the theme is used in bars 22–25. The clash between f in the
left and f′ sharp in the right hand, bars 29–33, is noteworthy.

Invention 5 in E flat major

Tempo: ♩ = ± 80 (see Tempo Table Ia, 3)

This is the first invention to use a countersubject throughout.

Invention 6 in E major

Tempo: ♩. = ± 140 (♪ = 120; see Tempo Table Vb, 1)

Technically speaking, this is almost an "exercise for mordents," a remark
not meant to reflect on the artistic quality of this incomparable piece. One should
note the correspondence with the middle part of the last movement of the
Violin Concerto in the same key.

Invention 7 in E minor

Tempo: ♩ = ± 60 (see Tempo Table Ib, 1). The complicated ornaments make the indicated speed necessary. See also the very important variants in the copy made by Bach's pupil Gerber (Landshoff's *Revisionsbericht*, p. 69).

Invention 8 in F major

Tempo: ♩ = ± 100 (see Tempo Table IVa, 1). There is no inner reason to abuse this piece by superspeed.

Articulation: *Leggiero* for the eighths, *leggierissimo* for the sixteenths

Although this piece may be closer to harpsichord idiom than any other invention, *leggiero* and *leggierissimo* sound excellent on the clavichord, if done *con delicatezza*.

Invention 9 in F minor

Tempo: ♩ = ± 60 (see Tempo Table IVc, 1). This relatively slow speed is necessary to bring out the richness of Bach's original articulation (Czerny suggests ♩ = 116!).

Ornamentation: See p. 152, above, and also p. 71 of Landshoff's *Revisionsbericht* for the execution of the ornaments in bars 15–16.

The countersubject is obbligato.

Invention 10 in G major

Tempo: ♩ = ± 100 (see Tempo Table VIId, 1)

Articulation: The giguelike motive may be played *leggiero* throughout, or, probably better, two notes slurred, the third *staccato*. In figures where two seconds follow each other, three notes *quasi legato* are, however, preferable.

Invention 11 in G minor

Tempo: ♩ = ± 80 (see Tempo Table Ia, 4)

Articulation: As suggested by Landshoff, all eights and quarters in light *tenuto*

One more piece with obbligato countersubject. Notice the inversion of the latter, beginning at the end of bar 3.

Invention 12 in A major

Tempo: ♩. = ± 60 (see Tempo Table VIIIa, 1)

Articulation: Giguelike elements prevail again. The same suggestions for articulation may be applied which we gave for Invention 9.

Invention 13 in A minor

Tempo: ♩ = ± 80 (see Tempo Table Ia, 5); in contrast to Bischoff: ♩ = 116, who this time beats Czerny's ♩ = 104.

Articulation: *Leggiero* for sixteenths, *nonlegato* for the eighths.

Invention 14 in B flat major

Tempo: ♩ = ± 60 (see Tempo Table Ib, 2)

Articulation: All thirty-seconds *legato*, all sixteenths *nonlegato*, all eighths light *tenuto*, all quarters *tenuto*.

Invention 15 in B minor

Tempo: ♩ = ± 80 (see Tempo Table Ia, 6)

Ornamentation: The 〰 in the theme can only be played as an "inverted mordent" (see Trill Table, No. 4, which cites only the drastic case of bars 14–15. Yet already bar 2 reveals the same problem).

For a very interesting variant in bar 21 see *Revisionsbericht*, p. 77.

Sinfonia 1 in C major

It is impossible not to notice that there exist thematic links between Sinfonia 1 and Invention 1. The first four notes of the Sinfonia are a transposition of the Invention. Although they seem, at first glance, to be nothing else than four notes of a scale, the fact that they appear in inverted form at the end of the first bar proves that they are a "motif within the scale." They also appear, at the same time, in augmented form; Bach is doing here exactly what he does in the first Invention. When we notice that Sinfonia 15 and Invention 15 are thematically linked, too, the probability that all this signifies a hidden symbolic message between the Inventions and the Sinfonias is very great. When we also realize that the first four notes of the theme of the first Fugue in C major, *W.K.* I, are again the same ones, we can suspect that Bach inserted a kind of "greeting" from one collection to the other, a thought not out of line with other "Bach jokes." Yet, nothing more than a "pleased smile" is what such observations are able to give us. They should not be overrated, but they certainly add a kind of human touch to our conceptions of Bach's work. For interpretative purposes it is more important to notice that this game with four notes is immediately discontinued (in contrast to Invention 10) and reappears only sporadically in bar 12.

Tempo: ♩ = ± 80 (see Tempo Table Ia, 7)

Articulation: *Legato*

Ornamentation: The trills in bars 6 and 10 have to begin with a brief stop on the main note before trilling from above (see Trill Table, Nos. 10 and 11, and also the explanations on pp. 158ff.).

Let it be mentioned here that, in regard to architecture, the vast majority of the Sinfonias are close to "fugal setting." Only the support of the main theme by a bass part gives evidence that the Italian Trio Sonata also played a "godfather" role at their birth.

Sinfonia 2 in C minor

Tempo: ♩. = ± 80 (see Tempo Table VIIIb, 1)

Articulation: The "gigue formulas" should be respected

An admirable but almost enigmatic piece. The pensive, meditative elements seem to predominate over the giguelike ones, which are also present.

Sinfonia 3 in D major

Tempo: ♩ = ± 80 (see Tempo Table Ia, 8)

Articulation: The sixteenths *quasi legato*, the eighths *nonlegato* even for the intervals of seconds, as proved by the later addition of appoggiaturas.

Sinfonia 4 in D minor

Tempo: ♩ = ± 60 (see Tempo Table Ib, 3)
Articulation: The eighths *legato* except for the wide intervals in the subject;
    the sixteenths *quasi legato*.

Most noteworthy is the wonderful harmonization of the descending
chromatic scale in the two last bars.

Sinfonia 5 in E flat major

Tempo: ♩ = ± 60 (see Tempo Table IVc, 2; Czerny ♩ = 100!)
Ornamentation: Our reasons for disagreeing with Landshoff's solutions for the
    appoggiaturas are outlined on pp. 179ff.

This unique piece, a duet accompanied by a continuously repeated bass
figure, reveals its full beauty much more in the ornamented version.

Sinfonia 6 in E major

Tempo: ♩. = ± 80 (see Tempo Table VIIc, 1)
Articulation: *Legato* throughout, except, of course, for the skips in bar 38

Notice the wonderful clashes between the original and the inverted forms
of the subject, which appear first in bar 17 and climax in bar 35.

Sinfonia 7 in E minor

Tempo: ♩ = ± 60 (see Tempo Table IVc, 3)
Articulation: *Legato*, even *legatissimo* throughout, except for a few sixteenths
    in the countersubject, cited by Landshoff.
Ornamentation: Again, the ornamented version deserves preference by far. It
    is noteworthy that one more ornament (on f sharp) appears in bars 25 and
    27 of the ornamented version, but does not seem to be wanted in bar 37.
    Does this mean "added intensity" for the middle part and some relaxation
    toward the end? It goes without saying that the ornaments in the theme
    have to be added to every appearance of the subject.

The inner relation between this piece and the basic idiom of the Passions
is evident.

Sinfonia 8 in F major

Tempo: ♩ = ± 80 (see Tempo Table Ia, 9)
Articulation: As indicated by Landshoff
Ornamentation: The 〰 of the subject has to be played at its every
    reappearance. Trills have to be added at the dotted notes, bars 15 and 23,
    the final cadence.

Sinfonia 9 in F minor

Tempo: ♩ = ± 40 (see Tempo Table Ic, 1)

The ornamented version should by all means be thoroughly studied. To
achieve a clear rendering of the three subjects, prominence should be given to
the chromatic descending line. The deeply religious background is obvious; to
play this piece on a harpsichord almost has to be called a barbarian act.

Sinfonia 10 in G major

Tempo: ♩ = ± 80 (see Tempo Table IVb, 1)
Articulation: The quarters *tenuto*, the rest *quasi legato*

Sinfonia 11 in G minor

Tempo: ♩. = ± 40 (♪ = 120; see Tempo Table Vb, 2)
Articulation: The dash above the g″ in the subject which we owe to Gerber's
   copy is an indication that this note should always be separated from the
   following one.
   The grace of the melodic lines makes this piece almost a forerunner of
Schubert's "Ländler."

Sinfonia 12 in A major

Tempo: ♩ = ± 80 (see Tempo Table Ia, 10)
Ornamentation: A trill has to be added to the final cadence
   There is undeniably some inner relation to the Invention in A major.

Sinfonia 13 in A minor

Tempo: ♩. = ± 40 (see Tempo Table Vb, 3)
Articulation: The differentiation between the articulation of the subject (slight
   legato) and that of the countersubject (*leggiero* throughout), which appears
   first in bar 21, has to be underlined.
Ornamentation: The cadential note in the theme (b in bar 3) seems to ask for
   an added trill which appears, indeed, in the autograph in bar 35.

Sinfonia 14 in B flat major

Tempo: ♩ = ± 60 (see Tempo Table Ib, 4)
Articulation: The bass in the first and in the three last bars, which has the
   meaning of a continuo part, should be played in light *tenuto*; otherwise,
   the eighths are *nonlegato*, the sixteenths *quasi legato*.

Sinfonia 15 in B minor

Tempo: ♪. = ± 80 (see Tempo Table IXb, 1)
Articulation: Subject, two notes *legato*, the third *staccato*; countersubject,
   legato.
Symbolism: Both motives belong to Bach's favorite devices for "water." In the
   Romantic period, this piece might have been given the title "Little
   Barcarolle."
   The hand-crossings in bars 26ff. have been taken as a reason for assigning
this piece to a harpsichord with two keyboards. The dexterous way, however,
in which Bach uses in bar 28 the same key (d′) for both hands three times clearly
indicates that he planned a little technical stunt for *one* keyboard. No more
than slightly advanced finger technique is needed to let the hands pass each
other, especially with the help of the fingering we have in the Landshoff edition.
We also remind the reader of our general remarks about problems of hand-
crossing, pp. 43–44.

THE WELLTEMPERED KEYBOARD, volume I

Prelude in C major, W.K. I

Instrument: Clavichord
Tempo: ♩ = ± 80 (see Tempo Table Ia, 11)
Articulation: *Legato*, the bass line *molto tenuto*
For detailed discussion see pp. 60ff.

For comparison, see Johann Kuhnau, Prelude from Partie V, *Neue Klavierübung erster Teil* (Leipzig, 1689) (Ex. Al); and Johann Kaspar Ferdinand Fischer, Praeludium Harpeggiato from the "Clio" suite, printed in 1735 but apparently written before 1715, in *Musikalischer Parnassus* (Ex. A2).

Ex. A1

Ex. A2

Fugue in C major, W.K. I

Instrument: Clavichord
Tempo: ♩ = ± 60 (see Tempo Table Ib, 5)
Articulation: *Legato*; the intervals of the fourth and fifth *portato*
For detailed discussion see pp. 64ff.

Prelude and Fugue in C minor, W.K. I

Instrument: Harpsichord
Registration:

Prelude

	Right hand			Left hand
Bar 1–24	8″, 4″	Bar	1–24	8″, 4″
25–34⅛	8′, 16′, 8″, 4″		25–34¼	8′, 16′, 8″, 4″
34⁶⁄₃₂–38	8″, 4″		34¾–38	8″, 4″

Fugue

Bar			Bar		
$3\frac{3}{16}$–$9\frac{1}{8}$	8", 4"		1–$9\frac{1}{16}$	8", 4"	
$9\frac{2}{8}$–$11\frac{1}{8}$	8'		$9\frac{2}{16}$–$11\frac{5}{8}$	8'	
$11\frac{2}{8}$–$13\frac{1}{16}$	8", 4"		$11\frac{6}{8}$–$13\frac{1}{8}$	8", 4"	
$13\frac{2}{16}$–$15\frac{5}{8}$	8'		$13\frac{2}{8}$–$15\frac{1}{8}$	8'	
$15\frac{6}{8}$–$17\frac{1}{8}$	8", 4"		$15\frac{2}{8}$–$17\frac{1}{8}$	8", 4"	
$17\frac{2}{8}$–$20\frac{1}{8}$	8'		$17\frac{2}{8}$–$20\frac{5}{8}$	8'	
$20\frac{2}{8}$–$22\frac{1}{8}$	8", 4"		$20\frac{6}{8}$–$21\frac{8}{8}$	8", 4"	
$22\frac{2}{8}$–$25\frac{1}{8}$	8'		$22\frac{1}{8}$–$25\frac{1}{4}$	8'	
				+16'	
$25\frac{2}{8}$–$28\frac{6}{8}$	8", 4"		$25\frac{10}{16}$–$28\frac{3}{4}$	8", 4"	
		+C			
$28\frac{8}{8}$–31	8', 16', 8", 4"		$28\frac{8}{8}$–31	8', 16', 8", 4"	

Tempo: $\bm{\downarrow}$ = ± 80 (see Tempo Table Ia, 12)

Articulation: *Legato* for the "mordent figures"; *nonlegato* for the eighths; *legato* for the end of the theme.

For detailed discussion see pp. 55ff.

Prelude in C sharp major, W.K. I

Instrument: Clavichord

Tempo: $\bm{\downarrow}$. = ± 60 (see Tempo Table Va, 3). The tempo recommended here is considerably slower than that generally used, especially in concert performances on the piano. If, however, one takes the melody of the left hand as the leading part and compares the piece with all the other ones on Tempo Table Va, our reasons for the tempo indicated above will become evident.

Articulation: The sixteenths *leggiero*; the motive of the left hand always to be played with two notes slurred; the falling octave, as in bars 33, 35, etc., *staccato*; the first two sixteenths in bar 63 and corresponding ones slurred; all other sixteenths *leggiero*; the eighths in the left hand from bar 63 on light *portato*; the last chords *tenuto*.

Fugue in C sharp major, W.K. I

Instrument: Clavichord

Tempo: $\bm{\downarrow}$ = ± 80 (see Tempo Table Ia, 13)

Articulation: The first note *staccato*; the next five notes slurred; the same for the first four notes of bar 2; all the other notes *staccato*. See discussion of this subject on p. 216 and also Articulation Table II, 5a–d.

Prelude in C sharp minor, W.K. I

Instrument: Organ, harpsichord

Registration: One registration throughout: 8', 8', 16'; 4", 16'(C) equally recommended.

Tempo: $\bm{\downarrow}$. = ± 40 (see Tempo Table Xc, 1)

Articulation: *Molto legato*

Ornamentation: The many additional ornaments found in various contemporary copies deserve serious consideration. Even more than those mentioned by Bischoff may be played (for example, an appoggiatura before d sharp, bar 12, fourth quarter right hand, a trill on f sharp, bar 28, fourth quarter left hand). The length of the appoggiatura to the first note of bar 2 and in corresponding places should be that of a quarter.

Fugue in C sharp minor, W.K. I

Instrument: Organ, harpsichord. The monumental architecture and the many long sustained notes immediately suggest the organ as the most proper instrument. This choice is strengthened by closer examination of architectural details, since it then becomes apparent that Bach's writing method provides only very limited registration possibilities for a harpsichord with hand stops unless one makes use of a "helper."

Registration:

	Right hand				Left hand	
Bar	$1-35\frac{1}{4}$	8', 16', 8", 4"	Bar	$1-35\frac{1}{2}$	8', 16', 8", 4"	
	$35\frac{2}{4}-75\frac{8}{8}$	8", 4"		$35\frac{3}{4}-72\frac{8}{8}$	8", 4"	
	$76-94\frac{1}{4}$	8', 16', 8", 4"		$73-94\frac{1}{4}$	8', 16', 8", 4"	
	$94\frac{2}{4}-104\frac{4}{4}$	8", 4"		$94\frac{2}{4}-102\frac{1}{4}$	8", 4"	
	$105-115$	8', 16', 8", 4"		$102\frac{2}{4}-115$	8', 16', 8", 4"	

If one wants to rely on the cooperation of a helper, bars 1–35 could be played 8', 16', both hands, otherwise as before, and the helper would prepare the coupling of the keyboards between bars 35 and 72 when both hands are playing on the upper keyboard.

Tempo: $\downarrow = \pm 80$ (see Tempo Table IIa, 1)

Articulation: *Molto legato* for first theme and entire first part, *legato* for the other themes. The main theme is in all probability derived from "B-A-C-H."

Prelude in D major, W.K. I

Instrument: Harpsichord

Registration: 8", 4" or 4", 16'(C) for both hands until bar $33\frac{1}{4}$, then "full work" (8', 16', 8", 4") until the end.

Tempo: $\downarrow = \pm 120$ (see Tempo Table Ie, 2)

Articulation: *Leggiero* throughout

Fugue in D major, W.K. I

Instrument: Harpsichord

Registration: (see also discussion on p. 59)

	Right hand				Left hand	
Bar	$2\frac{2}{4}-6\frac{5}{32}$	8', 16', 8", 4"	Bar	$1-6\frac{1}{4}$	8', 16', 8", 4"	
	$6\frac{6}{32}-8\frac{1}{4}$	8", 4"		$6\frac{2}{4}-7\frac{1}{4}$	8", 4"	
	$8\frac{2}{4}-9\frac{1}{4}$	8', 16', 8", 4"		$7\frac{2}{4}-17\frac{1}{4}$	8', 16', 8", 4"	
	$9\frac{2}{4}-11\frac{1}{4}$	8", 4"		$17\frac{2}{4}-20\frac{1}{4}$	8", 4"	
	$11\frac{2}{4}-21\frac{1}{4}$	8', 16', 8", 4"		$20\frac{2}{4}-27$	8', 16', 8", 4"	
	$21\frac{2}{4}-22\frac{1}{4}$	8", 4"				
	$22\frac{2}{4}-27$	8', 16', 8", 4"				

Tempo: ♩ = ± 60 (see Tempo Table Ib, 6)
Articulation: *Marcato e quasi legato*

For reasons outlined on p. 192 we feel very hesitant to recommend the exaggerated "French dotting" suggested by Dolmetsch and used by the majority of harpsichordists.

Prelude in D minor, W.K. I

Instrument: Clavichord
Tempo: ♩ = ± 60 (see Tempo Table Ib, 7)
Articulation: Right hand *legato*, left hand *portato* until bar $20\frac{4}{8}$, then *legato*

It is nearly impossible to come to a final conclusion about how to phrase the line of the right hand. Groups of six and twelve notes are clearly distinguishable; toward the end (bar 24) even groups of three notes seem indicated. We do not want to deprive the student of the thrilling experience of searching for his own version.

Fugue in D minor, W.K. I

Instrument: Clavichord (see discussion on p. 71)
Tempo: ♩ = ± 80 (see Tempo Table IVb, 2)
Articulation: *Legato*; the autographic dash on the b' flat of the second bar should be understood as *molto portato*.
Ornamentation: As outlined on p. 158 (see also Trill Table, No. 12) the trill in the theme has to start with the main note. We recommend additional trills in bars 9, 10, 11, 23, 28, 29, 30, 31, 32 on the corresponding places and also a mordent on the d of bar 43 in the right hand.

Prelude in E flat major, W.K. I

Instrument: Organ, harpsichord
Registration: A satisfactory registration on the harpsichord without a helper is almost impossible and does not do justice to the splendor of the piece which only an organ can display.

Version 1 (not recommended)

	Right hand			Left hand	
Bar	$1–10\frac{1}{4}$	8'	Bar	$1–10\frac{1}{4}$	8'
	$10\frac{2}{4}–25\frac{1}{16}$	8", 4"		$10\frac{3}{4}–25\frac{1}{4}$	8", 4"
	$25\frac{2}{16}–35\frac{1}{4}$	8'		$25\frac{2}{4}–38\frac{9}{16}$	8'
	$35\frac{2}{4}–49\frac{9}{16}$	8", 4"		$38\frac{10}{16}–49\frac{3}{4}$	8", 4"
	$49\frac{10}{16}–64\frac{1}{4}$	8'		$49\frac{4}{4}–61\frac{8}{16}$	8'
	$64\frac{2}{4}–70$	8", 4"		$61\frac{3}{4}–70$	8", 4"

This version could be slightly improved by playing the part of the left hand, at bars $46–49\frac{3}{4}$, $61\frac{3}{4}–64\frac{2}{4}$, 66–70, one octave lower than written (8" plus 4" [l]), producing thus a pseudo-16' effect.

Version 2 (with helper)

	Right hand			*Left hand*	
Bar	1–$10\frac{1}{4}$	8', 16	Bar	1–9	8', 16'
	$-16'$				
	$11\frac{3}{4}$–$25\frac{1}{16}$	8", 4" (l *ad lib.*)		10–$25\frac{1}{4}$	8", 4" (l *ad lib.*)
	$25\frac{2}{16}$–$35\frac{1}{4}$	8'		$25\frac{2}{4}$–$38\frac{9}{16}$	8'
	$35\frac{2}{4}$–$45\frac{8}{8}$	8", 4"		$38\frac{10}{16}$–$45\frac{16}{16}$	8", 4"
	46–$49\frac{9}{16}$	8', 16', 8", 4"		46–$49\frac{3}{4}$	8', 16', 8", 4"
	$49\frac{10}{16}$–$64\frac{1}{4}$	8", 4"		$49\frac{4}{4}$–$61\frac{8}{16}$	8", 4"
	$64\frac{2}{4}$–70	8', 16', 8", 4"		$61\frac{3}{4}$–70	8', 16', 8", 4"

The helper couples the keyboards between bars 39–45 when both hands play on the upper one.

Tempo: ♩ = ± 80 (see Tempo Table Ia, 14)
Articulation: *Molto legato*

The recommendation to play this piece on the organ gains additional weight, since the key of E flat major as well as the motive of rising fourths are used by Bach several times for the symbol of the Trinity.

Fugue in E flat major, W.K. I

Instrument: Harpsichord, clavichord. The question of why Bach linked this elegant "secular" Fugue with the solemn Prelude, which contains a fugue in itself, will probably never be answered satisfactorily. Although, in our opinion, it sounds best on a clavichord, we give a discreet registration for the harpsichord for reasons of unity of interpretation.
Registration:

	Right hand			*Left hand*	
Bar	1–$17\frac{5}{8}$	8'	Bar	3–$17\frac{4}{8}$	8'
	$17\frac{6}{8}$–$25\frac{8}{16}$	8"		$17\frac{5}{8}$–$25\frac{7}{8}$	8"
	$25\frac{10}{16}$–$34\frac{6}{8}$	8'		$25\frac{8}{8}$–$34\frac{6}{8}$	8'
		+C			
	$34\frac{15}{16}$–37	8', 8"		$34\frac{14}{16}$–37	8', 8"

Tempo: ♩ = ± 80 (see Tempo Table Ia, 15)
Articulation: Same as Keller's version (Ex. A3)

Ex. A3. Fugue in E flat major, *W.K.* I. Keller's version

Ornamentation: The trill in the theme should certainly also be played in bars 12
   and 35. A trill on the last f of bar 36, which is reported by Altnikol, also
   makes good sense.

Prelude in E flat minor, W.K. I

Instrument: Clavichord
Tempo: ♩ = 50 (see Tempo Table Xa, 1)
Articulation: All larger intervals *molto portato*, otherwise *legato*

Fugue in E flat minor (D sharp minor), W.K. I

Instrument: Clavichord. No harpsichord registration for this fugue can be made
   that corresponds to its architecture. He who feels shocked about the
   designation for the clavichord may realize that the grandeur of this piece
   is not an exterior but an inner one. No majesty is displayed, but there is
   a wealth of feeling, and the complicated overlappings of the theme can only
   be made audible on the clavichord.
Tempo: ♩ = ± 80 (see Tempo Table Ia, 16)
Articulation: All larger intervals *portato*, otherwise *legato*

Prelude in E major, W.K. I

Instrument: Clavichord
Tempo: ♩. = ± 80 (see Tempo Table VIIIb, 2)
Articulation: *Molto legato*

Fugue in E major, W.K. I

Instrument: Clavichord
Tempo: ♩ = ± 100 (see Tempo Table Id, 1)
Articulation: The first eighth of the theme always *staccato*, the next note *tenuto*,
   the sixteenths *leggiero*. The "sighs" in the tenor, bars 13–16, and in the
   soprano, bars 22–25, should be emphasized.

Prelude in E minor, W.K. I

Instrument: Harpsichord, for reasons of unity only; the separation of melody
   and accompaniment and the expressiveness of the melodic line would
   come out much better on a clavichord.
Registration: First part, right hand 4″(l), left hand 8′; *Presto*, both hands 8′;
   or: First part, right hand 8′, left hand 8″; *Presto*, both hands 8′.
Tempo: First part ♩ = ± 60; *Presto* ♩ = ± 120 (see Tempo Tables Ib, 8, and
   Ie, 3).
Articulation: Right hand *molto legato* for the melody, *tenuto* for the eighths;
   left hand *quasi legato*; *Presto leggiero*.
Ornamentation: Note the authentic trills in bars 10 and 12

Fugue in E minor, W.K. I

Instrument: Harpsichord (see discussion on p. 75)
Registration:

	Right hand			Left hand	
Bar	1–$3\frac{2}{8}$	8", 4"	Bar	3–$5\frac{2}{8}$	8", 4"
	$3\frac{6}{16}$–$10\frac{12}{16}$	8'		$5\frac{6}{16}$–$12\frac{12}{16}$	8'
	11–$13\frac{2}{8}$	8", 4"		13–15	8", 4"
	$13\frac{6}{16}$–$15\frac{12}{16}$	8'		16	8'
	16	8", 4"		17	8", 4"
	17	8'		18	8'
	18–$20\frac{4}{16}$	8", 4"		19–$22\frac{2}{8}$	8", 4"
	$20\frac{6}{16}$–$21\frac{12}{16}$	8'		$22\frac{6}{16}$–$29\frac{12}{16}$	8'
	22–$24\frac{2}{8}$	8", 4"		30–$32\frac{2}{8}$	8", 4"
	$24\frac{6}{16}$–$31\frac{12}{16}$	8'			
	32–34	8", 4"		$32\frac{6}{16}$–$34\frac{12}{16}$	8'
	35	8'		35	8", 4"
	36	8", 4"		36	8'
	37	8'		37–42	8", 4"
	38–42	8", 4"			

Tempo: ♩ = ± 120 (see Tempo Table IVe, 1)
Articulation: *Leggiero*

Prelude in F major, W.K. I

Instrument: Clavichord
Tempo: ♩. = ± 60 (see Tempo Table VIIIa, 2)
Articulation: The first three sixteenths *legato*, the next three *leggiero* throughout the piece; in the left hand two eighths slurred, the third *staccato*. At the end, the last note of the left hand *tenuto*, the three sixteenths before *portamento*.
Ornamentation: All trills the traditional way

Fugue in F major, W.K. I

Instrument: Clavichord (see discussion on p. 83)
Tempo: ♩. = ± 60 (see Tempo Table Va, 4)
Articulation: The upbeat always *portato*, the first two eighths of the first bar slurred, the third eighth *staccato*; all the other notes *legato*.
Ornamentation: All 〰 as in bar 7 are long ones to be executed traditionally "from above" or with start and brief stop on main note.

Prelude in F minor, W.K. I

Instrument: Clavichord
Tempo: ♩ = ± 60 (see Tempo Table Ib, 9)
Articulation: *Molto legato*

Fugue in F minor, W.K. I

Instrument: Clavichord (see discussion on p. 73)

Tempo: ♩ = ± 60 (see Tempo Table Ib, 10)

Articulation: *Molto legato*

Ornamentation: The last note but one of the theme doubtless needs a trill, preferably with start and brief stop on main note.

Symbolism: The theme symbolizes the cross: the midpoint of the first volume has been reached. Note the same symbolization in Variation 15 of the *Goldberg Variations*.

Prelude in F sharp major, W.K. I

Instrument: Clavichord

Tempo: ♩. = ± 60 (see Tempo Table IXc, 1)

Articulation: *Quasi legato*, almost *leggiero*

Ornamentation: Every note of ♩. value should get a trill

Fugue in F sharp major, W.K. I

Instrument: Clavichord (see discussion on p. 79)

Tempo: ♩ = ± 80 (see Tempo Table Ia, 17)

Articulation: *Legato*; in the "wave figure," two notes slurred

Ornamentation: The trill in the theme may be executed either traditionally or with start and brief stop on main note. The latter version is supported by the situation in bar 12, second quarter, where the "Schwenke" copy explicitly has a trill.

Symbolism: "Water" figures

Prelude in F sharp minor, W.K. I

Instrument: Clavichord

Tempo: ♩ = ± 80 (see Tempo Table Ia, 18)

Articulation: *Legato* for sixteenths; not too light *staccato* for eighths

Fugue in F sharp minor, W.K. I

Instrument: Clavichord

Tempo: ♩. = ± 40 (see Tempo Table Xc, 2)

Articulation: *Legato*; in the countersubject first note light *portato*, the falling or rising seconds slurred in pairs, the rest *legato*.

Ornamentation: Always a trill on the penultimate note of the theme, preferably with start and brief stop on the main note.

Prelude in G major, W.K. I

Instrument: Harpsichord

Registration: Full work or 8″, 4″ throughout

Tempo: ♩. = ♩ = ± 60 (see Tempo Table IXd)

Articulation: All sixteenths *leggiero*, all eighths light *portato* except for the falling seconds, bars 11 and 12.

Symbolism: The falling octave = Praise the Lord

Fugue in G major, W.K. I

Instrument: Harpsichord
Registration:

Right hand			Left hand		
Bar	1–37	8″, 4″	Bar	5–38$\frac{1}{8}$	8″, 4″
	38–61$\frac{3}{8}$	8′		38$\frac{2}{8}$–60$\frac{3}{8}$	8′
	61$\frac{4}{8}$–86	8″, 4″		60$\frac{4}{8}$–86	8″, 4″

Tempo: ♩. = ± 60 (see Tempo Table VIa, 1)
Articulation: See Example A4. All runs of sixteenths *leggiero*

Ex. A4

Ornamentation: Trills in the inverted theme (bars 25, 26) to be added to bars
    29, 30, 44, 45, 71, 72, with start and brief stop on main note. For technical
    reasons, the trill, bar 69, has to stop on the fourth beat of bar 70.

Prelude in G minor, W.K. I

Instrument: Harpsichord, only for unity. If this piece had come to us as a
    single one, designation for the clavichord would be natural because of the
    similarity to the Invention in B flat major.
Registration:

Right hand			Left hand		
Bar	1–6	8′	Bar	1–6	8″
	7–15$\frac{3}{4}$	8″		7–14$\frac{1}{16}$	8′
	15$\frac{14}{16}$–19	8′		14$\frac{2}{16}$–15$\frac{9}{16}$	8″
				15$\frac{10}{16}$–19	8′

Tempo: ♩ = ± 60 (see Tempo Table Ib, 11)
Articulation: *Legato*
Ornamentation: A long appoggiatura may be added to the trill on the las tnote.

Fugue in G minor, W.K. I

Instrument: Harpsichord (see discussion on p. 57)
Registration:

For a large harpsichord

Right hand			Left hand		
Bar	2$\frac{6}{8}$–12$\frac{1}{8}$	8″, 4″	Bar	1–12$\frac{1}{4}$	8″, 4″
	12$\frac{2}{8}$–19$\frac{1}{8}$	8′		12$\frac{6}{8}$–19$\frac{1}{8}$	8′
	19$\frac{2}{8}$–19$\frac{5}{8}$	8″, 4″		19$\frac{2}{8}$–19$\frac{5}{8}$	8″, 4″
	19$\frac{6}{8}$–20$\frac{1}{8}$	8′		19$\frac{6}{8}$–20$\frac{1}{8}$	8′
	20$\frac{2}{8}$–24$\frac{9}{16}$	8″, 4″		20$\frac{2}{8}$–24$\frac{5}{8}$	8″, 4″
	24$\frac{10}{16}$–28$\frac{1}{8}$	8′		24$\frac{6}{8}$–28$\frac{1}{4}$	8′
	28$\frac{2}{8}$–34	8″, 4″		28$\frac{6}{8}$–34	8″, 4″

For a small harpsichord with one keyboard, and 8′, 8″ or 8′, 4′ registers

$$
\begin{array}{ll}
\text{Bar} \;\; 1–12\tfrac{1}{8} & 8', 8'' \text{ or } 8', 4' \\
& -8'' \text{ or } -4' \\
12\tfrac{2}{8}–28\tfrac{1}{8} & 8' \\
& +8'' \text{ or } +4' \\
28\tfrac{2}{8}–34 & 8', 8'' \text{ or } 8', 4'
\end{array}
$$

Tempo: ♩ = ± 80 (see Tempo Table Ia, 19)

Articulation: First two eighths *legato*, the two quarters *tenuto*, the sixteenths *leggiero* (the eighth between them, of course, *nonlegato*). The entire character of this fugue is *molto energico* and not *molto tranquillo* (see p. 218).

Prelude in A flat major, W.K. I

Instrument: Clavichord

Tempo: ♩ = ± 80 (see Tempo Table IVb, 3)

Articulation: Quarters *tenuto*, eighths *portato*; the "mordent" figures and sixteenths *legato*.

Fugue in A flat major, W.K. I

Instrument: Clavichord

Tempo: ♩ = ± 60 (see Tempo Table Ib, 12)

Articulation: The eighths *legato e portato*, the rest *legato*

Note the inner relation between Prelude and Fugue, symbolized by the notes of the A flat major triad.

Prelude in G sharp minor, W.K. I

Instrument: Clavichord

Tempo: ♩. = ± 60 (see Tempo Table VIa, 2)

Articulation: The six sixteenths of the subject of this veritable "sinfonia in three parts" may be subdivided into three *legato* and three *leggiero* notes. The rest are *legato*.

Fugue in G sharp minor, W.K. I

Instrument: Clavichord (see discussion on p. 71)

Tempo: ♩ = ± 60 (see Tempo Table Ib, 13)

Articulation: The first seven notes *legato*, the two next ones slurred, the rest of the theme slight *portato*.

Prelude in A major, W.K. I

Instrument: Clavichord

Tempo: ♩ = ± 80 (see Tempo Table Ia, 20)

Articulation: *Molto legato* throughout. Special attention must be given to the "declamation" of the sighs of the third theme of this "sinfonia with three obbligato subjects," a distant relative of the F minor Sinfonia. See also Articulation Table II, 14a–d.

Fugue in A major, W.K. I

Instrument: Clavichord
Tempo: $\downarrow$. = ± 60 (see Tempo Table VIIa, 1)
Articulation: The first note *tenuto, molto legato* for the eighths, *legato* for the sixteenths which may frequently be subdivided into three *legato* and three *leggiero* notes. A fine observation is Keller's suggestion that a comma be inserted after the eleventh note of the soprano part. The entire piece is *dolce e molto espressivo*. Czerny's *fortissimo* for the first note is probably the gravest mischief in his edition.

Prelude in A minor, W.K. I

Instrument: Harpsichord
Registration: Either full work or 8', 8", 4" or 8", 4". The following subdivision would also be correct:

	Right hand			Left hand
Bar 1–8	8', 8", 4" (16' *ad lib.*)	Bar	1–12	8', 8", 4" (16' *ad lib.*)
9–21	8", 4"		13–19	8", 4"
22–28	8', 8", 4" (16' *ad lib.*)		20–28	8', 8", 4" (16' *ad lib.*)

Tempo: $\downarrow$. = 60 (see Tempo Table VIIa, 2)
Articulation: *Nonlegato* throughout, all eighths *bien marqué*. The entire piece is almost *feroce*.

Fugue in A minor, W.K. I

Instrument: Pedal harpsichord
Registration:

	Right hand			Left hand
Bar	$4\frac{2}{8}$–$14\frac{5}{8}$ 8", 4"	Bar	1–$14\frac{5}{8}$ 8", 4"	
	$14\frac{6}{8}$–$27\frac{5}{8}$ 8'		$14\frac{6}{8}$–$27\frac{5}{8}$ 8'	
	$27\frac{6}{8}$–$35\frac{1}{8}$ 8", 4"		$27\frac{6}{8}$–$35\frac{1}{8}$ 8", 4"	
	$35\frac{2}{8}$–$43\frac{1}{16}$ 8'		$35\frac{2}{8}$–$43\frac{5}{8}$ 8'	
	$43\frac{2}{16}$–$48\frac{1}{8}$ 8", 4"		$43\frac{6}{8}$–$48\frac{1}{8}$ 8", 4"	
	$48\frac{2}{8}$–$53\frac{5}{8}$ 8'		$48\frac{2}{8}$–$53\frac{1}{8}$ 8'	
	$53\frac{6}{8}$–$65\frac{1}{8}$ 8", 4"		$53\frac{2}{8}$–$63\frac{3}{4}$ 8", 4"	
	$65\frac{2}{8}$–$73\frac{5}{8}$ 8', 16'		+16'	
	$73\frac{6}{8}$–$80\frac{1}{4}$ 8", 4"		$63\frac{7}{8}$–$64\frac{5}{8}$ 8", 4"	
			$64\frac{6}{8}$–$72\frac{8}{8}$ 8', 16'	
			$73\frac{2}{8}$–$80\frac{1}{4}$ 8", 4"	

+C

$80\frac{3}{4}$–87	8', 16', 8", 4"	$80\frac{3}{4}$–87	8', 16', 8", 4"

A helper may substitute for the pedal installation and play the A in the bass part at the end.

Tempo: ♩ = ± 80 (see Tempo Table Ia, 21)
Articulation: See Example A5. In general *nonlegato*; *più legato* only for the
    beautiful episode, bars 40–42.

Ex. A5

Prelude in B flat major, W.K. I

Instrument: Harpsichord
Registration:

	Both hands	
Bar	1–11$\frac{1}{8}$	8″, 4″
	11$\frac{2}{4}$–11$\frac{25}{32}$	8′, 16′, 8″, 4″
	11$\frac{26}{32}$–13$\frac{1}{8}$	8″, 4″
	13$\frac{2}{4}$–13$\frac{25}{32}$	8′, 16′, 8″, 4″
	13$\frac{26}{32}$–15$\frac{1}{8}$	8″, 4″
	15$\frac{2}{4}$–16$\frac{9}{32}$	8′, 16′, 8″, 4″
	16$\frac{10}{32}$–17$\frac{16}{32}$	8″, 4″
	17$\frac{3}{4}$–18$\frac{9}{32}$	8′, 16′, 8″, 4″
	18$\frac{10}{32}$–20	8″, 4″

Tempo: ♩ = ± 80 (see Tempo Table Ia, 22)
Articulation: The eighths *portato*, the thirty-seconds *leggiero*, the chords *molto
    tenuto*.

Fugue in B flat major, W.K. I

Instrument: Harpsichord (see discussion on p. 76)
Registration:

	Right hand			Left hand	
Bar	1–19$\frac{1}{16}$	8″, 4″	Bar	1–13$\frac{1}{8}$	8″, 4″
	19$\frac{2}{16}$–30$\frac{1}{8}$	8′		13$\frac{2}{8}$–19$\frac{1}{8}$	8′
				19$\frac{2}{8}$–22$\frac{1}{8}$	8″, 4″
				22$\frac{2}{8}$–26$\frac{1}{8}$	8′
				26$\frac{2}{8}$–30$\frac{1}{16}$	8″, 4″
	30$\frac{2}{8}$–33$\frac{1}{16}$	8″, 4″		30$\frac{2}{16}$–33$\frac{1}{8}$	8′
	33$\frac{2}{16}$–37$\frac{1}{8}$	8′		33$\frac{2}{8}$–35$\frac{1}{8}$	8″, 4″
				35$\frac{2}{8}$–41$\frac{1}{8}$	8′
	37$\frac{2}{8}$–48	8″, 4″		41–48	8″, 4″

Tempo: ♩ = ± 100 (see Tempo Table IVa, 2)
Articulation: *Nonlegato* for the eighths, except for the two falling seconds d–c
    and e flat–d, which should be slurred; the sixteenths *leggiero*.
Ornamentation: An additional trill on the penultimate note of the soprano
    seems justified.

Prelude in B flat minor, W.K. I

Instrument: Organ, harpsichord
Registration: 4″, 16′ or 8′, 16′ throughout (full work for the end after the fermata possible).
Tempo: ♩ = ± 40 (see Tempo Table Ic, 2)
Articulation: *Molto legato e tenuto*

Fugue in B flat minor, W.K. I

Instrument: Organ, harpsichord, but a helper is indispensable
Registration:

	Right hand			Left hand	
Bar	1–25¼	8″, 4″	Bar	3–25¼	8″, 4″
	25²⁄₄–37²⁄₄	8′		25²⁄₄–47⁸⁄₈	8′
	37³⁄₄–54⁴⁄₄	8″, 4″		48–54	8″, 4″
	55–63	8′, 8″, 4″		55–63	8′, 8″, 4″
	64–75	8′, 16′, 8″, 4″		64–75	8′, 16′, 8″, 4″

The helper prepares the coupling of the keyboards between bars 48–54 and adds the 16′ at the end of bar 63. Gliding from second keyboard to first in bar 25 and from first to second (right hand only) in bar 37 is technically not difficult. Without the helper, only the following registration could be applied:

	Both hands	
Bar	1–25¼	8′, 16′, 8″, 4″
	25²⁄₄–54	8″, 4″
	55–75	8′, 16′, 8″, 4″

This would, however, bring an acoustic result A–B–A which does not correspond with the majestic architecture of this fugue.
Tempo: ♩ = ± 60 (see Tempo Table IIb, 1)
Articulation: First two notes *molto tenuto*, the others *ben legato*

Prelude in B major, W.K. I

Instrument: Clavichord
Tempo: ♩ = ± 80 (see Tempo Table Ia, 23)
Articulation: *Dolce* throughout
Ornamentation: A trill on the penultimate note of the soprano may be added.

Fugue in B major, W.K. I

Instrument: Clavichord
Tempo: ♩ = ± 60 (see Tempo Table Ib, 14)
Articulation: *Legato* with slight *tenuto* for the last two eighths of the theme
Ornamentation: The trill of bar 2 (with start and brief stop on the main note) should be added to each appearance of the theme. This is not always easy but technically possible. The thematic relation between Prelude and Fugue is most obvious.

Prelude in B minor, W.K. I

Instrument: Clavichord

Tempo: *Andante* (autographic); ♩ = ± 80 (see Tempo Table Ia, 24). See also discussion on p. 124.

Articulation: *Legato*

Symbolism: Cross symbols in first bars and in bars 42–44

Fugue in B minor, W.K. I

Instrument: Clavichord

Tempo: *Largo* (autographic); ♩ = ± 40 (see Tempo Table Ic, 3)

Articulation: The first three notes *legato e portato*, the rest slurred in pairs (autographic). Notice the relation between bar 24 of the Prelude and bar 17 of the Fugue.

Symbolism: Cross symbol in the theme. Do not overlook the indescribably moving human touch of the two "false starts" of the theme in bars 19 (alto) and 28 (tenor). The voices seem to be so overwhelmed with mourning that they have to stop and do not find enough composure to sing out the entire theme before bars 21 (alto) and 30 (tenor), where they start on the same note as before.

THE WELLTEMPERED KEYBOARD, volume II

Prelude in C major, W.K. II

Instrument: Clavichord

Tempo: ♩ = ± 60 (see Tempo Table Ib, 15)

Articulation: *Molto legato*

Fugue in C major, W.K. II

Instrument: Clavichord

Tempo: ♩ = ± 100 (see Tempo Table IIIa, 1)

Articulation: The interval of the fifth *portato*, the rest *quasi legato*

Prelude in C minor, W.K. II

Instrument: Harpsichord; clavichord also possible

Registration:

	Right hand			Left hand	
Bar	1–12	8′	Bar	1–12	8′
	13–21$\frac{1}{8}$	8″		13–22$\frac{1}{8}$	8″
	21$\frac{2}{8}$–28	8′		22$\frac{2}{8}$–28	8′

Tempo: ♩ = ± 80 (see Tempo Table Ia, 25)

Articulation: The sixteenths *leggiero*, the eighths *nonlegato* except for bars 21 and 27 which are *più legato* in groups of four, starting on the second beat.

A relation in motives with the Prelude in C minor, *W.K.* I, is evident. While the Prelude of volume I was "stormy," here the storm has calmed.

Fugue in C minor, W.K. II

Instrument: Harpsichord, clavichord also possible
Registration:

	Right hand			Left hand	
Bar	$2\frac{1}{8}$–$14\frac{1}{8}$	8″, 4″	Bar	1–$16\frac{1}{16}$	8″, 4″
	$14\frac{2}{8}$–$21\frac{1}{4}$	8′		$16\frac{2}{16}$–$19\frac{1}{4}$	8′
	$21\frac{2}{4}$–$23\frac{5}{8}$	8″, 4″		$19\frac{2}{4}$–$23\frac{5}{8}$	8″, 4″
	$23\frac{6}{8}$–$27\frac{3}{4}$	8′, 8″, 4″		$24\frac{2}{8}$–$27\frac{1}{4}$	8′, 8″, 4″
	$27\frac{7}{8}$–28	8′, 16′, 8″, 4″		$27\frac{10}{16}$–28	8′, 16′, 8″, 4″

The keyboards can be coupled by a slight interruption after $23\frac{5}{8}$; the 16′ register can be drawn at $27\frac{3}{4}$. In spite of the registration just suggested, we cannot help feeling that both the Prelude and Fugue in C minor could be interpreted just as well and more modestly on a clavichord, especially on the larger pedal clavichord. The pedal would take over the bass part from bars $19\frac{2}{4}$ to $21\frac{3}{16}$ and from bars $26\frac{2}{8}$ to 28. This would give even better results than our harpsichord registration, which suffers from the impossibility of singling out the lines just mentioned. For the same reasons, even the organ could be included as a possible medium for this Prelude and Fugue.

Tempo: ♩ = ± 60 (see Tempo Table Ib, 16)

Articulation: *Legato*

Ornamentation: The ∿ on a, bar 2, last quarter, is a trill with start and brief stop at the main note. It should be added in bar 4 on the corresponding place.

Prelude in C sharp major, W.K. II

Instrument: Here we give preference to the clavichord because of the great resemblance to the Prelude in C major, *W.K.* I, with which it originally shared the key. A performance on the harpsichord is, however, also acceptable, by virtue of the overture character which would justify a broader interpretation. For this version, the registration 4″, 16′ (C) for the first part, and 8″, 4″ for the second part, might sound best.

Tempo: ♩ = ± 80 (see Tempo Table Ia, 26); *Allegro*: ♩. = ± 60 (see Table Va, 5).

Articulation: Left hand *portato*, right hand *legato*; second part: *legato* except for those eighths which form larger intervals.

Fugue in C sharp major, W.K. II

Instrument: Again the clavichord seems to be preferable, in order to bring out every detail of the very complicated texture. For a performance on the harpsichord, the following registration may be justified:

	Right hand				Left hand	
Bar	$1\frac{6}{8}-7\frac{1}{8}$	$8''$, $4''$		Bar	$1\frac{2}{8}-6\frac{8}{8}$	$8''$, $4''$
	$7\frac{6}{8}-11\frac{1}{8}$	$8'$			$7\frac{2}{8}-11\frac{3}{8}$	$8'$
	$11\frac{2}{8}-14\frac{5}{8}$	$8''$, $4''$			$11\frac{4}{8}-14\frac{5}{8}$	$8''$, $4''$
	$14\frac{8}{8}-25\frac{1}{8}$	$8'$			$14\frac{6}{8}-25\frac{1}{16}$	$8'$
	$25\frac{2}{8}-35$	$8''$, $4''$			$25\frac{2}{16}-35$	$8''$, $4''$

Tempo: ♩ = ± 60 (see Tempo Table Ib, 17)
Articulation: *Portato* for the eighths in the theme, *nonlegato* for diminution, *molto tenuto* for augmentation of the theme, the rest more *leggiero* than *quasi legato*.

Prelude in C sharp minor, W.K. II

Instrument: Clavichord
Tempo: ♩. = ± 40 (see Tempo Table VIIb, 1)
Articulation: *Molto portato* for all chord figures, otherwise *legato*
Ornamentation: All appoggiaturas before ♩. and ♩ notes need the length of an eighth; appoggiaturas before a dotted eighth (bar 8, seventh eighth note and corresponding places) need the length of a sixteenth. To prove this, see Appoggiatura Table, Nos. 7, 8, 14, 15.
This is a sinfonia in three parts of unique beauty.

Fugue in C sharp minor, W.K. II

Instrument: Clavichord
Tempo: ♩. = ± 60 (see Tempo Table IXc, 2)
Articulation: *Quasi legato*; larger intervals *leggiero* if sixteenths, *portato* if eighths.

Prelude in D major, W.K. II

Instrument: Harpsichord, organ also to be considered
Registration:

	Both hands	
Bar	1–16	$8'$, $16'$, $8''$, $4''$
	$17-30\frac{1}{8}$	$8''$, $4''$
	$30\frac{2}{8}-33\frac{1}{8}$	$8'$, $16'$, $8''$, $4''$
	$33\frac{2}{8}-40\frac{13}{16}$	$8''$, $4''$
	$40\frac{14}{16}-56$	$8'$, $16'$, $8''$, $4''$

Tempo: ♩. = ± 80 (see Tempo Table VIIIb, 3)
Articulation: The dotted rhythm *molto portato*, "chord fanfares" *nonlegato*, sixteenths *quasi legato*.
Symbolism: A majestic instrumental "Sanctus"

Fugue in D major, W.K. II

Instrument: Harpsichord, also organ
Registration:

	Right hand			Left hand	
Bar	$2\frac{6}{8}$–$10\frac{1}{8}$	8′	Bar	1–$20\frac{3}{4}$	8′
	$10\frac{2}{8}$–$16\frac{1}{8}$	8″, 4″		$20\frac{8}{8}$–$27\frac{5}{8}$	8″, 4″
	$16\frac{2}{8}$–$22\frac{1}{8}$	8′			
	$22\frac{2}{8}$–$27\frac{5}{8}$	8″, 4″			

+C

	$27\frac{8}{8}$–$33\frac{1}{8}$	8′, 8″, 4″		$27\frac{6}{8}$–$33\frac{1}{8}$	8′, 8″, 4″
		+16′			
	$33\frac{3}{8}$–$44\frac{5}{8}$	8″, 4″		$33\frac{2}{8}$–$40\frac{1}{8}$	8″, 4″
	$44\frac{6}{8}$–50	8′, 16′, 8″, 4″		$40\frac{2}{8}$–50	8′, 16′, 8″, 4″

The coupler can be applied with a brief interruption at $27\frac{5}{8}$. The 16′
register can be drawn during the rest of two eighths in bar 33.
Tempo: ♩ = ± 80 (see Tempo Table IId, 1 and remarks on p. 127)
Articulation: The quarters *tenuto*, the eighths *quasi legato*
    The character of this Fugue is described by Keller as one of "rebellious
humor," while Busoni calls it "dry, catholic," alluding to the vocal character
of the theme. I feel inclined to agree with Busoni.

Prelude in D minor, W.K. II

Instrument: Harpsichord
Registration:

	Right hand			Left hand	
Bar	1–$35\frac{1}{16}$	8″, 4″	Bar	1–17	8″, 4″
	$35\frac{2}{16}$–$43\frac{1}{8}$	8′		18–$26\frac{1}{4}$	8′
	$43\frac{2}{8}$–61	8″, 4″		$26\frac{6}{16}$–$34\frac{1}{16}$	8″, 4″
				$34\frac{2}{16}$–$42\frac{1}{8}$	8′
				$42\frac{2}{8}$–56	8″, 4″
				57–61	8′

Tempo: ♩ = ± 100 (see Tempo Table IVa, 3)
Articulation: The quarters *tenuto*, the eighths *nonlegato*, the sixteenths *leggiero*

Fugue in D minor, W.K. II

Instrument: Harpsichord
Registration: The entire piece "full work." In bar 20, the second and third
    quarter can and may be played on the upper keyboard (8″, 4″).
Tempo: ♩ = ± 80 (see Tempo Table Ia, 27)
Articulation: Triplets and sixteenths *quasi legato*, a "comma" after the fifth
    eighth, then *legato* for the descending line.

Prelude in E flat major, W.K. II

Instrument: Problems similar to those in the Prelude and Fugue in E flat major, *W.K.* I, are arising again. In volume I, we were inclined to assign the Prelude to the organ, the Fugue to the clavichord, and felt it nearly impossible to understand what made Bach link these pieces together. Here, in volume II, the opposite seems to be the best solution: clavichord for the Prelude, organ for the Fugue. Yet, this time, the religious character keeps both pieces well together: the Prelude makes use of the symbol for "flight of angels" and of the rhythm for "Sanctus." The Fugue makes frequent use of the interval of the fourth, so often linked with this "key of Trinity."

    If played on the harpsichord for reasons of unity, the entire Prelude should be played on the softest register, 8″, until bar 60, first eighth. There, one may shift to 8′ and play from bar 67 after the rest (which can be used for coupling) 8′, 8″ until the end.

Tempo: ♩ = ± 80 (see Tempo Table VIIc, 2)

Articulation: *Legato*; left hand on all places like bar 3 light *portato*; chord figures *nonlegato*; in the many groups of three notes, two notes slurred, the third *leggiero*.

Ornamentation: The appoggiatura in bar 2 may have the length of 3 eighths, following the rule mentioned on p. 178, but the length of 2 eighths may not be wrong, although Bischoff opposes this execution because of the "ugly parallel fourths." Such parallels, however, apparently did not sound ugly to Bach, who writes them frequently (e.g., Fugue in D sharp minor, *W.K.* II, bar 13).

Fugue in E flat major, W.K. II

Instrument: Organ, harpsichord
Registration:

	Right hand			*Left hand*	
Bar	7–30$\frac{1}{4}$	8′, 16′, 8″, 4″	Bar	1–30$\frac{2}{4}$	8′, 16′, 8″, 4″
	30$\frac{2}{4}$–55$\frac{1}{4}$	8″, 4″		30$\frac{3}{4}$ (shift) –53$\frac{2}{4}$	8″, 4″
	55$\frac{2}{4}$–70	8′, 16′, 8″, 4″		53$\frac{3}{4}$–70	8′, 16′, 8″, 4″

    This registration is perhaps somewhat pompous and could be made milder if 8″, 4″ is substituted for every "full work" and 8′ for every 8″, 4″.

Tempo: ♩ = ± 80 (see Tempo Table IIa, 2)

Articulation: *Tenuto e portato*, the eighths *legato*

Prelude in D sharp minor, W.K. II

Instrument: Clavichord
Tempo: ♩ = ± 80 (see Tempo Table Ia, 28)
Articulation: *Legato*

Fugue in D sharp minor, W.K. II

Instrument: Clavichord
Tempo: ♩ = ± 60 (see Tempo Table Ib, 18)
Articulation: See Example A6

Ex. A6

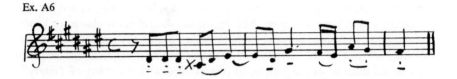

Although of less immediate appeal than the corresponding Prelude and Fugue of volume I, both pieces here are "gems for connoisseurs."

Prelude in E major, W.K. II

Instrument: Clavichord
Tempo: ♩ = ± 80 (see Tempo Table IVb, 4)
Articulation: The first eighth light *portato*, the rest *legato* except all eighths which belong to the "cradle" motive (see p. 251); they should be slurred in pairs.
Ornamentation: A mordent for the last note in the soprano may be added
Symbolism: "Cradle" motives in bars 18–23, 43–48

Fugue in E major, W.K. II

Instrument: Clavichord
Tempo: ♩ = ± 80 (see Tempo Table IIa, 3)
Articulation: *Molto legato*. Basically vocal in conception; the theme (which is by Kaspar Ferdinand Fischer; see p. 21) as well as the entire Fugue shows a close relation to "flights of angels" (see p. 249). One might not go wrong to call this Fugue a kind of instrumental "Et in terra pax." Seen in this spirit, Prelude and Fugue are ideal "Christmas pieces."

Prelude in E minor, W.K. II

Instrument: Harpsichord for reasons of unity; the piece is so close to the Two-Part Inventions that the clavichord would be preferable.
Registration:

	Right hand			Left hand	
Bar	1–48	8′	Bar	1–48	8′
	49–72	8″		49–71	8″
	73–108	8′		72–108	8′

Tempo: ♩. = ± 60 (see Tempo Table Va, 6)
Articulation: *Legato*, the eighths *portato*

Fugue in E minor, W.K. II

Instrument: Harpsichord
Registration: (for reasons of simplification we count 12 eighths)

	Right hand			Left hand	
Bar	1–$23\frac{10}{8}$	$8''$, $4''$	Bar	$6\frac{11}{8}$–23	$8''$, $4''$
	$23\frac{11}{8}$–$49\frac{10}{8}$	$8'$		24–$41\frac{10}{8}$	$8'$
	$49\frac{11}{8}$–$70\frac{2}{4}$	$8''$, $4''$		$41\frac{11}{8}$–$70\frac{2}{4}$	$8''$, $4''$
		$+C$			
	$71\frac{2}{8}$–$83\frac{8}{8}$	$8'$ $8''$, $4''$		$70\frac{8}{8}$–$83\frac{3}{4}$	$8'$, $8''$, $4''$
		$+16'$			
	$83\frac{9}{8}$–86	$8'$, $16'$, $8''$, $4''$		83 last $\frac{1}{16}$–86	$8'$, $16'$, $8''$, $4''$

Tempo: $\downarrow$ = ± 80 (see Tempo Table IIa, 4)
Articulation: *Nonlegato*, the prominent quarters in the theme *molto portato*
   Let us merely mention that the sixteenths after a dotted note have to be
played together with the last note of the triplets.

Prelude in F major, W.K. II

Instrument: Clavichord
Tempo: $\downarrow$ = ± 100 (see Tempo Table Xa, 2; see also discussion on p. 142)
Articulation: *Legatissimo*; the slurs over four notes found in reliable copies
   make good sense.

Fugue in F major, W.K. II

Instrument: Clavichord
Tempo: $\downarrow$. = ± 120 (see Tempo Table IXa, 1)
Articulation: *Leggiero*
Symbolism: Flight of angels, indubitably in the Prelude, perhaps also in the
   Fugue (see discussion on pp. 249ff.).

Prelude in F minor, W.K. II

Instrument: Clavichord
Tempo: $\downarrow$ = ± 80 (see Tempo Table IIIb, 1)
Articulation: The sighs slurred, of course; otherwise *quasi legato*; figures as in
   bar 20, second half, slurred in groups of four.
Ornamentation: The 〰 on the first note of the sigh must be played as
   an "inverted mordent"; see discussion on pp. 153ff., and Trill Table, No. 6.

Fugue in F minor, W.K. II

Instrument: Clavichord
Tempo: $\downarrow$ = ± 100 (see Tempo Table IIIa, 2)
Articulation: *Leggiero*, no slurring of the upbeat; the two last sixteenths of the
   first bar could be lightly slurred.

Ornamentation: A mordent on the first f of the theme seems highly desirable and is found in several reliable copies.

Prelude in F sharp major, W.K. II

Instrument: Clavichord

Tempo: ♩ = ± 80 (see Tempo Table IVb, 5)

Articulation: *Molto legato*. This piece is one of the very few where application of the "exaggerated French dotting" makes good sense (see discussion on p. 191).

Ornamentation: The appoggiatura in bar 1 and corresponding places needs the length of an eighth, that of bar 15, etc., the length of a sixteenth.

Fugue in F sharp major, W.K. II

Instrument: Clavichord. Here as well as in the Prelude, the constant fluctuation of the lines annihilates all attempts for a logical registration on the harpsichord, which otherwise would have been helpful to underline the brightness of both pieces.

Tempo: ♩ = ± 80 (see Tempo Table IIa, 5)

Articulation: Quarters *nonlegato*, eighths *legato*, the falling second of bar 4 and all corresponding places slurred.

Ornamentation: The trill with which the theme opens begins with the main note, stopping briefly on it. All $\mathcal{M}$ are inverted mordents (see discussion on pp. 166ff. and Trill Table, Nos. 7, 8).

Prelude in F sharp minor, W.K. II

Instrument: Harpsichord

Registration:

	Right hand			*Left hand*	
Bar	1–29$\frac{1}{4}$	8′	Bar	1–29$\frac{1}{4}$	8″
	30–43	8″, 4″		29$\frac{4}{8}$–30$\frac{1}{8}$	8″, 4″
				30$\frac{1}{8}$–40$\frac{1}{8}$	8′
				40$\frac{2}{8}$–43	8″, 4″

or:

Bar	1–29	8″, 4″	Bar	1–29$\frac{1}{4}$	8′
		+C, +16′ (*ad lib.*)			
	30–43	8′, (16′), 8″, 4″		29$\frac{4}{8}$–43	8″, 4″

Many other ways of registration are possible; for example, beginning: right hand 4″(l), left hand 16′(h); second part: 4″, 16″ with coupler, loco both hands, etc.

Tempo: ♩ = ± 60 (see Tempo Table IVc, 4)

Articulation: All large intervals *portato*, otherwise *molto legato*

This Prelude may be called an aria with two accompanying parts. Compare with the second movement of the Italian Concerto and also with Variations 13 and 25, *Goldberg Variations*.

Fugue in F sharp minor, W.K. II

Instrument: Harpsichord
Registration:

	Right hand			Left hand	
Bar	$4\frac{3}{8}$–$20\frac{3}{4}$	$8'$	Bar	1–$20\frac{5}{8}$	$8'$
	21–$37\frac{1}{4}$	$8''$, $4''$		$20\frac{6}{8}$–$38\frac{1}{16}$	$8''$, $4''$
	$37\frac{5}{8}$–$51\frac{1}{8}$	$8'$		$38\frac{2}{16}$–$53\frac{7}{8}$	$8'$
	$51\frac{2}{8}$–70	$8''$, $4''$		$53\frac{8}{8}$–$57\frac{9}{16}$	$8''$, $4''$
				$57\frac{10}{16}$–$60\frac{5}{16}$	$8'$
				$60\frac{6}{16}$–$63\frac{1}{16}$	$8''$, $4''$
				$63\frac{2}{16}$–$66\frac{1}{8}$	$8'$
				$66\frac{2}{8}$–70	$8''$, $4''$

Tempo: $\quarternote = \pm$ 80 (see Tempo Table Ia, 29)
Articulation: Theme I: all seconds *legato*, all other intervals *portato*. Theme II: *quasi legato*, the interval of the fourth *portato*. Theme III: all sixteenths *quasi legato*, the eighths *portato*.

Prelude in G major, W.K. II

Instrument: Clavichord
Tempo: $\quarternote = \pm$ 100 (see Tempo Table IVa, 4)
Articulation: The sixteenths *quasi legato*; all eighth notes with larger intervals than that of the second *portato*; the seconds *legato*.

Fugue in G major, W.K. II

Instrument: Clavichord
Tempo: $\dotted\quarternote = \pm$ 60 (see Tempo Table Va, 7)
Articulation: *Leggiero* for sixteenths; concerning the eighths, only intervals of a second *legato*, the others *nonlegato*.

Prelude in G minor, W.K. II

Instrument: Harpsichord
Registration: $8'$, $16'$ or $4''$, $16''$ + coupler throughout
Tempo: *Largo* $\quarternote = \pm$ 40 (see Tempo Table Ic, 4)
Articulation: *Molto marcato*. The dotting may certainly be played in the "exaggerated" form (*à la française*), but, in this case, the sixteenths after a dotted eighth (bars 3, 4, 8, 10, etc.) must be played equally fast (see discussion on p. 187).

20

Fugue in G minor, W.K. II

Instrument: Harpsichord
Registration:

	Right hand			Left hand	
Bar	$5-17\frac{1}{8}$	$8'', 4''$	Bar	$1-17\frac{5}{16}$	$8'', 4''$
	$17\frac{2}{8}-20\frac{7}{16}$	$8'$		$17\frac{6}{16}-20\frac{2}{8}$	$8'$
	$20\frac{8}{16}-24\frac{5}{16}$	$8'', 4''$		$20\frac{2}{4}-24\frac{1}{8}$	$8'', 4''$
	$24\frac{6}{16}-28\frac{4}{16}$	$8'$		$24\frac{1}{8}-28\frac{3}{8}$	$8'$
	$28\frac{5}{16}-40\frac{1}{8}$	$8'', 4''$		$28\frac{4}{8}-32\frac{1}{16}$	$8'', 4''$
	$40\frac{2}{8}-45\frac{1}{16}$	$8'$		$32\frac{2}{16}-36\frac{1}{16}$	$8'$
	$45\frac{2}{16}-59\frac{5}{16}$	$8'', 4''$		$36\frac{2}{16}-40\frac{5}{16}$	$8'', 4''$
	$59\frac{6}{16}-63\frac{1}{8}$	$8'$		$40\frac{6}{16}-45\frac{1}{4}$	$8'$
	$63\frac{2}{8}-67\frac{2}{8}$	$8'', 4''$		$45\frac{2}{4}-67\frac{1}{4}$	$8'', 4''$
			+C		
	$67\frac{6}{16}-73\frac{1}{4}$	$8', 8'', 4''$		$67\frac{2}{4}-73\frac{1}{4}$	$8', 8'', 4''$
			+16'		
	$73\frac{4}{8}-84$	$8', 16', 8'', 4''$		$73\frac{4}{8}-84$	$8', 16', 8'', 4''$

Tempo: ♩ = ± 80 (see Tempo Table IVb, 6)
Articulation: *Molto tenuto e portato*, the sixteenths *nonlegato*
General character: *Molto feroce*
Symbolism: Both Prelude and Fugue seem to represent a "Calvary" scene, the
  Prelude symbolizing flagellation (see p. 252), the Fugue a chorus of Roman
  soldiers (see pp. 234, 252).

Prelude in A flat major, W.K. II

Instrument: Harpsichord, clavichord also possible
Registration:

	Right hand			Left hand	
Bar	$1-7\frac{1}{16}$	$8'$	Bar	$1-7\frac{5}{32}$	$8'$
	$7\frac{2}{16}-16\frac{1}{16}$	$8''$		$7\frac{6}{32}-15\frac{1}{4}$	$8''$
	$16\frac{2}{16}-23\frac{1}{16}$	$8'$		$15\frac{14}{32}-23\frac{5}{32}$	$8'$
	$23\frac{2}{16}-33\frac{1}{32}$	$8''$		$23\frac{6}{32}-33\frac{5}{32}$	$8''$
	$33\frac{2}{32}-40\frac{1}{16}$	$8'$		$33\frac{6}{32}-40\frac{5}{32}$	$8'$
	$40\frac{2}{16}-49\frac{1}{16}$	$8''$		$40\frac{2}{32}-48\frac{1}{4}$	$8''$
	$49\frac{2}{16}-63\frac{3}{8}$	$8'$		$48\frac{14}{32}-64\frac{5}{32}$	$8'$
		+4			
	$64-75\frac{1}{4}$	$8'', 4''$		$64\frac{6}{32}-75\frac{1}{4}$	$8'', 4''$
		+C (+16' ad lib.)			
	$75\frac{8}{16}-77$	$8', (16'), 8'', 4''$		$75\frac{8}{16}-77$	$8', (16'), 8'', 4''$

Tempo: ♩ = ± 60 (see Tempo Table IVc, 5)
Articulation: The first motive of left hand always three notes slurred; *molto
  legato* throughout. Dolmetsch's suggestion to play the dotted rhythm
  exaggerated and with all thirty-seconds abbreviated in the French manner

has to be rejected by the evidence of bars 62, 63, 69, which hardly can be treated this way. Notice too that bar 43 of the G minor Fugue, *W.K.* II, completely corresponds in writing with this Prelude.

Fugue in A flat major, W.K. II

Instrument: Harpsichord, clavichord also possible
Registration:

	Right hand			Left hand	
Bar	$1–10\frac{1}{8}$	$8'', 4''$	Bar	$6–10\frac{1}{16}$	$8'', 4''$
	$10\frac{2}{8}–16\frac{5}{8}$	$8'$		$10\frac{2}{16}–13\frac{5}{8}$	$8'$
	$16\frac{6}{8}–27\frac{9}{16}$	$8'', 4''$		$13\frac{6}{8}–16\frac{9}{16}$	$8'', 4''$
	$27\frac{10}{16}–35\frac{1}{8}$	$8'$		$16\frac{10}{16}–18\frac{9}{16}$	$8'$
	$35\frac{2}{8}–46\frac{3}{4}$	$8'', 4''$		$18\frac{10}{16}–27\frac{5}{8}$	$8'', 4''$
				$27\frac{6}{8}–32\frac{1}{8}$	$8'$
				$32\frac{2}{8}–40\frac{3}{8}$	$8'', 4''$
					$+16'$
				$41\frac{2}{8}–46\frac{3}{4}$	$8', 16'$
		$+C$			
	$46\frac{14}{16}–50$	$8', 16', 8'', 4''$		$46\frac{14}{16}–50$	$8', 16', 8'', 4''$

Tempo: ♩ $= \pm 60$ (see Tempo Table Ib, 19)
Articulation: *Molto legato*

Just as we reject Dolmetsch's "French interpretation" of the Prelude, which would transform its deep religious feeling into "worldly pomp," we also feel that playing both Prelude and Fugue on the clavichord would intensify their religious background, which is underlined by Bach by the application of the Sanctus symbol (see p. 251). The complicated contrapuntal texture and the obvious *molto legato* for articulation are other factors favoring an interpretation on the clavichord.

Prelude in G sharp minor, W.K. II

Instrument: Harpsichord
Registration:

	Right hand			Left hand	
Bar	$1–2$	$8'$	Bar	$1–15\frac{5}{8}$	$8''$
	$3–4$	$8''$		$15\frac{14}{16}–24$	$8'$
	$5\frac{2}{8}–8\frac{1}{4}$	$8'$			
	$8\frac{6}{16}–16\frac{6}{8}$	$8''$			
	$17\frac{2}{8}–24$	$8'$			
	$25–31\frac{1}{8}$	$8''$		$25\frac{2}{8}–42\frac{16}{16}$	$8''$
	$31\frac{2}{8}–34\frac{1}{16}$	$8'$		$43–50$	$8'$
	$34\frac{2}{16}–40\frac{6}{8}$	$8''$			
	$41–42$	$8'$			
	$43\frac{2}{16}–43\frac{6}{8}$	$8''$			
	$44\frac{2}{8}–50$	$8'$			

Tempo: $\quad$ ♩ = ± 80 (see Tempo Table Ia, 30)

Articulation: All "appoggiatura sighs" slurred; sixteenths *quasi legato*, eighths *portato*.

Ornamentation: All appoggiaturas have, of course, the length of an eighth

Fugue in G sharp minor, W.K. II

Instrument: Harpsichord

Registration:

	Right hand			*Left hand*	
Bar	1–61$\frac{2}{8}$	8″	Bar	5–61$\frac{2}{8}$	8″
	61$\frac{3}{8}$–97$\frac{2}{8}$	8′		61$\frac{3}{8}$–96$\frac{6}{8}$	8′
	97$\frac{3}{8}$–143	8″, 4″		97–143	8″, 4″

The 4″ register has to be drawn by the left hand in bar 68. This registration corresponds exactly with the organization of this magnificent double fugue: fugue on the first theme, fugue on the second theme, fugue on both themes.

Tempo: $\quad$ ♩. = ± 80 (see Tempo Table VIb, 1)

Articulation: *Molto legato*; the interval of the fourth as in bar 24 and all larger intervals in interludes *nonlegato*. Keller makes the fine observation that the first three eighths in bars 1 and 3 of the theme should get a slight, almost inaudible intensification by being slurred within the general *legato*. The chromatic line of theme II is closely related to bars 27–28, Fugue in C sharp minor, *W.K.* II.

Prelude in A major, W.K. II

Instrument: Clavichord

Tempo: $\quad$ ♩. = ± 80 (see Tempo Table VIIIb, 4)

Articulation: *Legato*, but frequent application of the "gigue formula": two notes slurred, the third *staccato*; the rhythms of the left hand *portato*.

Symbolism: Flight of angels (see p. 248)

Fugue in A major, W.K. II

Instrument: Clavichord

Tempo: $\quad$ ♩ = ± 80 (see Tempo Table Ia, 31)

Articulation: *Quasi legato*; the notes d′ and e′ *nonlegato*, almost *staccato*

General character: Mild, certainly not *energico*, as recommended by Bischoff

Prelude in A minor, W.K. II

Instrument: Harpsichord

Registration: Many methods of registration are possible. We suggest 4″, 16″ coupled throughout.

Tempo: $\quad$ ♩ = ± 60 (see Tempo Table Ib, 20)

Articulation: *Legato*, except that octave leaps as in bars 6, 7, and corresponding places ought to be played *nonlegato*.

Fugue in A minor, W.K. II

Instrument: Harpsichord
Registration: "Full work" throughout
Tempo: $\quad \downarrow = \pm 80$ (see Tempo Table Ia, 32)
Articulation: *Molto marcato e tenuto*; all runs *quasi legato*

   One of the most "explosive" pieces ever written by Bach. The theme belongs to a long series of themes used by various seventeenth- and eighteenth-century composers as well as by Handel in *Messiah* and Mozart in the Requiem. Quite a few of them are listed in Seiffert-Weitzmann, *Geschichte des Klaviers*, pp. 206ff.

Prelude in B flat major, W.K. II

Instrument: Harpsichord
Registration: For easier playing we recommend the exchange of parts of right
   and left hand from bars $15\frac{4}{16}$ to $17\frac{3}{16}$ and from bars $39\frac{4}{16}$ to $41\frac{3}{16}$. Our
   indications for registration are based on this exchange.

Right hand			Left hand	
Bar	1–8	8″, 4″	Bar 1–$8\frac{10}{16}$	8″, 4″
	9–$17\frac{3}{16}$	8′	$8\frac{11}{16}$–$13\frac{3}{16}$	8′
	$17\frac{4}{16}$–32	8″, 4″	$13\frac{4}{16}$–32	8″, 4″
	33–$48\frac{7}{16}$	8′	33–$37\frac{3}{16}$	8′
	49–52	8″, 4″	$37\frac{4}{16}$–$41\frac{3}{16}$	8″, 4″
	53–$64\frac{11}{16}$	8′	$41\frac{4}{16}$–$48\frac{10}{16}$	8′
	$65\frac{2}{16}$–$76\frac{3}{16}$	8″, 4″	$48\frac{11}{16}$–$52\frac{10}{16}$	8″, 4″
			$52\frac{11}{16}$–$66\frac{1}{16}$	8′
			$66\frac{2}{16}$–$76\frac{3}{16}$	8″, 4″
		+C		
	$76\frac{8}{16}$–87	8′, 8″, 4″	$76\frac{8}{16}$–87	8′, 8″, 4″

Tempo: $\quad \downarrow. = \pm 60$ (see Tempo Table IXc, 3)
Articulation: *Legato*; from bars 9–$17\frac{3}{16}$ and, correspondingly, right hand, bars
   37–$41\frac{3}{16}$ and both hands, bars 53–56: *più leggiero* for sixteenths; the ♪. in
   the hand-crossing sections *portamento*.

Fugue in B flat major, W.K. II

Instrument: Harpsichord
Registration:

Right hand			Left hand	
Bar	5–$32\frac{1}{8}$	8″	Bar 1–$32\frac{1}{4}$	8″
	$32\frac{2}{8}$–$78\frac{1}{8}$	8′	$33\frac{2}{4}$–$69\frac{1}{8}$	8′
	$78\frac{2}{8}$–93	8″, 4″	$69\frac{2}{8}$–93	8″, 4″

   The 4″ register is drawn by the left hand in bar 32.
Tempo: $\quad \downarrow = \pm 100$ (see Tempo Table IVa, 5)

Articulation: *Legato* throughout; the falling seconds in bars 3 and 4 are slurred
  in pairs in all reliable copies and have to be treated this way through the
  entire piece. The subdivision of the first twelve notes of the theme into two
  groups of six notes, as recommended by Keller, seems to us too restless
  unless done with utter discretion.

Symbolism: "Flight of angels" in the Prelude, "cradle"–peace on earth (compare
  with the Mass in B minor, "Et in terra pax") in the Fugue make this
  Prelude and Fugue again a Christmas scene.

Prelude in B flat minor, W.K. II

Instrument: Harpsichord, organ
Registration:

	Right hand			Left hand	
Bar	1–$16\frac{5}{8}$	8", 4"	Bar	1–$16\frac{1}{8}$	8", 4"
	$16\frac{6}{8}$–$25\frac{1}{4}$	8'		$16\frac{2}{8}$–$24\frac{1}{8}$	8'
	$25\frac{3}{8}$–$42\frac{1}{8}$	8", 4"		$24\frac{2}{8}$–$41\frac{4}{4}$	8", 4"
	$42\frac{2}{8}$–$54\frac{3}{8}$	8'		42–54	8'
	55–83	8", 4"		$55\frac{3}{8}$–83	8", 4"

This registration is the closest to the architecture of this piece which we
are able to find, but it does not do justice enough to its grandeur, as we are
dealing here with the most majestic prelude and fugue from volume II.
For this reason we consider the organ a more proper medium.

With hesitancy we recommend using the chance offered in bar 67,
last quarter, to get the left hand free for drawing the 16' register and
playing left hand from bar 70 to the end 8', 16'. This makes playing *legato*
in bar 76 quite a problem. Still better would be to interrupt quickly at the
end of bar 69, couple the keyboards (we assume that the 16' has been
added in bar 67 as recommended before), and play "full work" until
the end.

Tempo: $\downarrow = \pm\, 60$ (see Tempo Table IIb, 2)
Articulation: *Legato e tenuto*

Fugue in B flat minor, W.K. II

Instrument: Harpsichord, organ
Registration:

	Right hand			Left hand	
Bar	1–$27\frac{2}{4}$	8', 16', 8", 4"	Bar	5–26	8', 16', 8", 4"
	$27\frac{3}{4}$–$42\frac{1}{4}$	8", 4"		27–41	8", 4"
	$42\frac{2}{4}$–$67\frac{2}{4}$	8', 16', 8", 4"		42–66	8', 16', 8", 4"
	$67\frac{3}{4}$–79	8", 4"		67–$80\frac{2}{4}$	8", 4"
	80–101	8', 16', 8", 4"		$80\frac{3}{4}$–101	8', 16', 8", 4"

Tempo: $\textbf{d} = \pm$ 80 (see Tempo Table Xa, 3)
Articulation: See Example A7. Only the slurs are *quasi legato*

Ex. A7

Prelude in B major, W.K. II

Instrument: Harpsichord
Registration:

	Right hand			Left hand	
Bar	1–$12\frac{1}{4}$	$8''$, $4''$	Bar	1–$12\frac{1}{16}$	$8'$
	$12\frac{6}{8}$–$17\frac{9}{16}$	$8'$		$12\frac{2}{16}$–$23\frac{1}{8}$	$8''$, $4''$
	$17\frac{10}{16}$–$23\frac{5}{16}$	$8''$, $4''$		$23\frac{6}{16}$–$29\frac{1}{8}$	$8'$
	$23\frac{6}{8}$–$28\frac{9}{16}$	$8'$		$29\frac{5}{16}$–32	$8''$, $4''$
	$28\frac{10}{16}$–46	$8''$, $4''$		33–$36\frac{9}{16}$	$8'$
				$36\frac{10}{16}$–46	$8''$, $4''$

Tempo: $\textbf{d} = \pm$ 100 (see Tempo Table Id, 2)
Articulation: *Quasi legato*; from bars $12\frac{6}{8}$ to $15\frac{5}{16}$ and from $23\frac{5}{8}$ to $28\frac{9}{16}$ *più legato* in the right hand. In bars 17, 18, 19, 20, 21, 22, 23, and 29, a "comma" after the fifth note of every bar. The inner organization of bars 30–32, however, can also be understood as six times eight sixteenths in a row.

Fugue in B major, W.K. II

Instrument: Harpsichord
Registration:

	Right hand			Left hand	
Bar	5–$27\frac{1}{2}$	$8''$, $4''$, $16'$ (C)	Bar	1–$27\frac{1}{2}$	$8''$, $4''$, $16'$
	$28\frac{2}{4}$–$48\frac{8}{8}$	$8''$, $4''$		$27\frac{3}{4}$–$47\frac{8}{8}$	$8''$, $4''$
	$49\frac{2}{4}$–$60\frac{1}{8}$	$8''$, $4''$, $16'$		48–$60\frac{1}{2}$	$8''$, $4''$, $16'$
	$60\frac{2}{8}$–$85\frac{8}{8}$	$8''$, $4''$		$60\frac{3}{4}$–$74\frac{8}{8}$	$8''$, $4''$
	86–104	$8''$, $4''$, $16'$		75–104	$8''$, $4''$, $16'$

In order not to overload this Fugue with sound volume and to show the lesser "height" of this piece compared with the Fugue in B flat minor, we suggest deducting the $8'$ register from the "full work."
Tempo: $\textbf{d} = \pm$ 80 (see Tempo Table IIa, 6)
Articulation: *Tenuto e quasi legato*

Prelude in B minor, W.K. II

Instrument: Clavichord
Tempo: $\textbf{d} = \pm$ 80 (see Tempo Table IIa, 7); *allegro*

Articulation: The eighths *legato*, the quarter notes *tenuto*; in the syncopated rhythms of bars 13–15, 37–40 and all later similar places the first eighth *staccato*. It is interesting to see "long sighs" written out in bars 26, 61, 62. The two chords of bar 64 are *molto tenuto*. The notation problems of this piece are discussed on p. 126.

Fugue in B minor, W.K. II

Instrument: Clavichord

Tempo: ♩. = ± 60 (see Tempo Table Va, 8)

Articulation: The upbeat eighth *staccato*; in the first bar, the first two notes slurred, the last eighth *staccato*; *staccato*, too, throughout bars 3 and 4 and first eighth of bar 5; all the rest *legato*.

Symbolism: On pp. 239 and 246 we discussed the links between this Prelude and Fugue and the corresponding pieces in volume I, and also the cross symbols found everywhere. Those who expect a glowing climax at the end of this gigantic volume might feel disappointed with this Fugue. We see, however, in it an *Ausklang* (this noble German word cannot easily be translated; "final sound" probably approaches it most closely) for the entire collection, quite as unassuming as the Prelude in C major of volume I, which is no more than a portal, an entrance gate. Seen in this light, we can only admire again Bach's superior wisdom that abhorred cheap effects.

THE SUITE COLLECTIONS

By linking six suites together for each of his three collections of suites—the English, the French, and the Partitas—Bach follows an old tradition among musicians to pay in such a way homage to the six working days of the Lord. Both the English and the French Suites were written in Cöthen around 1720–1722. A study by Wilhelm Fischer, "Zur Chronologie der Klaviersuiten J. S. Bachs," in *Bericht über den musikwissenschaftlichen Kongress in Basel* (Leipzig, 1925), questions rather convincingly the generally established belief that the French Suites were the first to be written. Yet Hermann Keller is not wrong when he points out that the priority problem has no great importance for pieces written during a period of so few years. In regard to the instrument question, the English Suites are clearly intended for harpsichord. The French Suites, however, are stylistically so different that, as in the case of the Inventions and Sinfonias, the clavichord seems to be the only instrument on which they can display all their beauty. This becomes even more evident by comparing them with the suites by Weckmann and Boehm, which are real prototypes of clavichord music. The title "Sex Sviten pur le Clavessin compossee par Mos. J. S. Bach" [*sic!*], which is found on an autograph of the first four French Suites, is *not* from Bach's hand. Keller's statements that the titles "Suite pour le clavecin" for the French Suites, and "Suites avec prelude" for the English Suites, stem from Bach's own hand (Keller, *Die Klavierwercke Bach's*, pp. 169, 180) get no verification in Schmieder's catalogue. The instrument problems found in the Partitas will be dealt with later.

We hardly need to mention that neither of the names "English" or "French" is authentic. Truly convincing explanations for these names have not yet been found, but it seems that they might have originated in the second half of the eighteenth century.

Since for reasons explained on p. 109 not every single dance has received a place on the Tempo Tables, we give for those dances not found there a notice, "Compare with . . .," to explain our choice of tempo. Also in regard to articulation, we do not think it necessary to give a detailed description for every dance. A reader who has worked through our guiding remarks concerning articulation for the "Forty-eight" will have seen that the basic general rule—*legato* for seconds; *tenuto, portato,* or even *nonlegato* for larger intervals—holds true for at least 90 per cent of all articulation cases. Unusual situations, wherever they arise, will, of course, be mentioned.

English Suite I in A major

Prelude

Registration: One registration throughout, either 8' or 8" or 8", 4" or 4", 16' (C)
Tempo: ♩. = ± 80 (see Tempo Table VIIIb, 5)
Articulation: *Legato*

Allemande

Registration: 8"
Tempo: ♩ = ± 80 (compare with Tempo Table IIe, 2)
Articulation: *Legato*

Courante I

Registration: 8'
Tempo: ♩ = ± 80 (see Tempo Table Xb, 2)
Articulation: *Quasi legato*

Courante II with two Doubles

Registration: Courante—8", 4"; Double I—8'; Double II—8", 4"
Tempo: ♩ = ± 80 (compare with Tempo Table Xb, 2)
Articulation: *Quasi legato*

In all courantes, the interpreter has to be watchful for changes between 3/2 and 6/4 time. Some interesting slurs are found in reliable copies. It should hardly be necessary to mention that it can never have been Bach's intention to have four courantes played one after the other. Enough documentary evidence exists to show that in such cases the composer left it to the player to make his own choice.

Sarabande

Registration: 4", 16' (+C)
Tempo: ♩ = ± 60 (compare with Tempo Table IVf, 1, 2)
Articulation: *Molto legato*

Bourrée I

Registration: 8″, 4″
Tempo: $\downarrow$ = ± 100 (compare with Tempo Table IIf, 11)
Articulation: *Leggiero* in general, but interesting slurs appear in reliable copies

Bourrée II

Registration: 8′ or 8′, 16′(l)
Tempo: Same as Bourrée I
Articulation: *Nonlegato*

Gigue

Registration: 8″, 4″ (possibly 8′ for bars 12–16, 36–40)
Tempo: $\downarrow$ = ± 60 (compare with Tempo Table IVc, 1)
Articulation: Upbeat *staccato*, in general *quasi legato*

English Suite II in A minor

Prelude

Registration:

	Right hand			Left hand	
Bar	$1–55\frac{1}{8}$	8″, 4″	Bar	$1–70\frac{1}{8}$	8″, 4″
	$55\frac{2}{8}–59\frac{2}{16}$	8′		$70\frac{2}{8}–82\frac{1}{8}$	8′
	$59\frac{2}{8}–62\frac{1}{8}$	8″, 4″		$82\frac{2}{8}–99\frac{1}{8}$	8″, 4″
	$62\frac{2}{8}–66\frac{1}{16}$	8′		$99\frac{2}{8}–107\frac{1}{4}$	8′
	$66\frac{2}{16}–95\frac{1}{8}$	8″, 4″		$107\frac{9}{16}–108\frac{2}{4}$	8″, 4″
	$95\frac{2}{8}–99\frac{1}{16}$	8′			
	$99\frac{2}{16}–108\frac{2}{4}$	8″, 4″			
			+C, +16′		
	$108\frac{6}{8}–110\frac{1}{8}$	8′, 16′, 8″, 4″		$108\frac{6}{8}–110\frac{1}{8}$	8′, 16′, 8″, 4″
	$110\frac{2}{8}–156\frac{1}{8}$	8″, 4″		$110\frac{2}{8}–156\frac{1}{4}$	8″, 4″
	$156\frac{2}{8}–164$	8′, 16′, 8″, 4″		$156\frac{4}{8}–164$	8′, 16′, 8″, 4″

Tempo: $\downarrow$ = ± 100 (see Tempo Table IVa, 6)
Articulation: *Nonlegato* for sixteenths, *portato* for eighths

Allemande

Registration: 8′
Tempo: $\downarrow$ = ± 80 (compare with Tempo Table IIe, 1)
Articulation: *Legato*

Courante

Registration: 8″, 4″
Tempo: $\downarrow$ = ± 80 (compare with Tempo Table Xb, 2)
Articulation: *Quasi legato*; most quarters in left hand *portato*
Ornamentation: Watch the interesting appoggiatura before the first half note of
bar 4, which seems clearly to ask for the length of a quarter.

Sarabande

Registration: 8', 16' or 4", 16' (C)

The "agréments de la même Sarabande" should be played substituting for the repeat of the Sarabande and not as a "second Sarabande" after the first. That this was the historical method is proved by Chambonnières' Sarabande "O beau jardin" (*Œuvres complètes de Chambonnières*, Paris, 1925, p. 119), where the last measure of each part of the Sarabande is printed at the beginning of the Double. That "harmony-filling" notes have to be added to the upper part of the *agréments* goes without saying.

Tempo: $\mathsf{J} = \pm 60$ (compare with Tempo Table IVf, 1)
Articulation: *Molto legato*

Bourrée I

Registration: 8", 4"
Tempo: $\mathsf{J} = \pm 100$ (see Tempo Table IIf, 11)
Articulation: *Nonlegato*

Bourrée II

Registration: Right hand 4" (1); left hand 8' or 16' (h)
Tempo: Same as Bourrée I
Articulation: *Più legato*

It is impossible to state with complete certainty that the tradition of repeating the first dance of a dance couple has always been strictly observed. Since the word *alternativement* is mostly missing, we do not want the player to feel that he is bound by law to do so.

Gigue

Registration: 8", 4"; *ad lib.* 8', 8", 4" or 8', 16', 8", 4" for repeats
Tempo: $\mathsf{J.} = \pm 120$ (see Tempo Table VIc, 5)
Articulation: *Nonlegato*

English Suite III in G minor

Prelude

Registration: (see discussion on pp. 45ff.)

	Right hand			Left hand	
Bar	$1-33\frac{1}{16}$	8", 4"	Bar	$2-33\frac{2}{8}$	8", 4"
	$33\frac{2}{16}-67\frac{1}{8}$	8'		$35\frac{2}{16}-67\frac{1}{8}$	8'
	$67\frac{2}{8}-99\frac{1}{16}$	8", 4"		$68\frac{2}{8}-101\frac{1}{16}$	8", 4"
	$99\frac{2}{16}-101\frac{1}{8}$	8'		$101\frac{2}{16}-103\frac{1}{8}$	8'
	$101\frac{2}{8}-103\frac{1}{16}$	8", 4"		$103\frac{2}{8}-105\frac{1}{16}$	8", 4"
	$103\frac{2}{16}-105\frac{1}{8}$	8'		$105\frac{2}{16}-109\frac{1}{8}$	8'
	$105\frac{2}{8}-125\frac{1}{16}$	8", 4"		$109\frac{2}{8}-125\frac{2}{8}$	8", 4"
	$125\frac{2}{16}-137\frac{1}{8}$	8'		$127\frac{2}{16}-184\frac{1}{8}$	8'
	$137\frac{2}{8}-139\frac{1}{16}$	8", 4"		$184\frac{2}{8}-213$	8", 4"
	$139\frac{2}{16}-147\frac{1}{8}$	8'			
	$147\frac{2}{8}-149\frac{1}{16}$	8", 4"			
	$149\frac{2}{16}-157\frac{1}{8}$	8'			
	$157\frac{2}{8}-161\frac{1}{8}$	8", 4"			
	$161\frac{2}{8}-180\frac{1}{8}$	8'			
	$180\frac{2}{8}-213$	8", 4"			

Tempo: $\downarrow$. = ± 60 (see Tempo Table Va, 9)

Articulation: *Portato* for eighths, *nonlegato* for sixteenths. Bars 31–32 and corresponding bars have to be played as one bar in 3/4 time, a well-known tradition.

Allemande

Registration: 8′

Tempo: $\downarrow$ = ± 80 (compare with Tempo Table IIf, 1)

Articulation: *Legato*

Courante

Registration: 8″, 4″

Tempo: $\downarrow$ = ± 80 (compare with Tempo Table Xb, 2)

Articulation: *Quasi legato*

Sarabande

Registration: 8′, 16′ or 4″, 16′ (C)

Tempo: $\downarrow$ = ± 60 (compare with Tempo Table IVf, 1)

Articulation: *Molto legato*

Gavotte I

Registration: 8″, 4″

Tempo: $\downarrow$ = ± 80 (see Tempo Table IIf, 8)

Articulation: *Nonlegato*

Gavotte II (*ou la Musette*)

Registration: 4″ Solo or right hand 4″ (l), left hand 16′ (h)

Tempo: Same as Gavotte I

Articulation: *Legato*

Gigue

Registration: 8″, 4″; *ad lib.* 8′, 8″, 4″ or 8′, 16′, 8″, 4″ at repeats

Tempo: $\downarrow$. = ± 120 (compare with Tempo Table VIc, 5)

Articulation: *Nonlegato*

English Suite IV in F major

Prelude

Registration:

Right hand		Left hand	
Bar 1–$27\frac{9}{16}$	8″, 4″	Bar 2–$20\frac{1}{8}$	8″, 4″
$27\frac{10}{16}$–$34\frac{3}{4}$	8′	$20\frac{3}{16}$–$24\frac{2}{8}$	8′
$34\frac{14}{16}$–$45\frac{9}{16}$	8″, 4″	$24\frac{4}{8}$–$27\frac{3}{4}$	8″, 4″
$45\frac{10}{16}$–$51\frac{3}{4}$	8′	$24\frac{13}{16}$–$39\frac{5}{8}$	8′
$52\frac{10}{16}$–$60\frac{1}{16}$	8″, 4″	$39\frac{6}{8}$–$60\frac{1}{4}$	8″, 4″
$60\frac{2}{16}$–$75\frac{9}{16}$	8′	$60\frac{4}{8}$–$70\frac{1}{16}$	8′
$75\frac{10}{16}$–$84\frac{3}{4}$	8″, 4″	$70\frac{2}{16}$–$75\frac{3}{4}$	8″, 4″
+16′		$75\frac{14}{16}$–$77\frac{9}{16}$	8′
$84\frac{8}{8}$–$87\frac{16}{16}$	8″, 4″	$77\frac{10}{16}$–$88\frac{5}{8}$	8″, 4″
		+C	
$88\frac{6}{8}$–$89\frac{1}{16}$	8′, 16′, 8″, 4″	$88\frac{6}{8}$–$89\frac{1}{16}$	8′, 16′, 8″, 4″
$89\frac{2}{16}$–$106\frac{1}{8}$	8″, 4″	$90\frac{2}{16}$–$106\frac{1}{4}$	8″, 4″
$106\frac{2}{8}$–108	8′, 16′, 8″, 4″	$106\frac{4}{8}$–108	8′, 16′, 8″, 4″

A brief interruption at bar 88⅝ to couple the keyboards (or the use of a helper for this job, which can be done any time between bars 78–88) seems to be the only way to underline the climactic importance of the cadence in bar 88. Yet in regard to the rest of the piece we do not pretend that our solution is the only possible one. It is most delightful to feel in this piece the "vicinity of conception" of the Fifth Brandenburg Concerto, and it is almost strange to meet in it a major version of the first phrase of the Prelude in B flat minor, *W.K.* I.

Tempo: ♩ = ± 100 (see Tempo Table Id, 3)

Articulation: *Quasi legato* in general, the eighths in bars 22–27 *portato*, in bars 46–51 light *portato*. The same holds true, of course, for all corresponding bars.

Allemande

Registration: 8′

Tempo: ♩ = ± 80 (compare with Tempo Table IIf, 1)

Articulation: *Legato*

Courante

Registration: 8″, 4″

Tempo: ♩ = ± 80 (compare with Tempo Table Xb, 2)

Articulation: *Quasi legato*

Sarabande

Registration: 8′, 16′ or 4″, 8″ (C)

Tempo: ♩ = ± 60 (compare with Tempo Table IVf, 1)

Articulation: *Legato*; the eighths in bar 3 and corresponding ones slurred in pairs. It is not only justified but desirable to improvise *agréments* for the repetition of both parts.

Menuet I

Registration: 8′

Tempo: ♩ = ± 120 (see Tempo Table IVf, 15)

Articulation: *Legato*

Menuet II

Registration: 8″

Tempo: Same as Menuet I

Articulation: Same as Menuet I

Gigue

Registration: 8″, 4″ (8′, 16′, 8″, 4″ for repeat *ad lib.*)

Tempo: ♩. = ± 120 (see Tempo Table VIIIc, 2)

Articulation: *Nonlegato*

English Suite V in E minor

Prelude

Registration:

	Right hand			Left hand	
Bar	1–40$\frac{1}{16}$	8", 4"	Bar	1–40$\frac{1}{8}$	8", 4"
	40$\frac{2}{16}$–52$\frac{1}{8}$	8'		40$\frac{5}{8}$–54$\frac{1}{8}$	8'
	52$\frac{2}{8}$–81$\frac{1}{8}$	8", 4"		54$\frac{2}{8}$–82$\frac{1}{8}$	8", 4"
	81$\frac{5}{8}$–92$\frac{1}{8}$	8'		82$\frac{2}{8}$–94$\frac{1}{8}$	8'
	92$\frac{2}{8}$–97$\frac{1}{8}$	8", 4"		94$\frac{2}{8}$–96$\frac{1}{8}$	8", 4"
	97$\frac{4}{16}$–117$\frac{1}{8}$	8'		96$\frac{4}{16}$–100$\frac{1}{8}$	8'
	117$\frac{2}{8}$–156	8", 4"		100$\frac{2}{8}$–105$\frac{1}{8}$	8", 4"
				105$\frac{2}{8}$–118$\frac{5}{8}$	8'
				119–156	8", 4"

Tempo: ♩. = ± 60 (see Tempo Table VIa, 3)

Articulation: *Quasi legato*, the eighths in bar 14 and corresponding ones *portato*, in bars 40–51 and 82–87 light *portato*.

Allemande

Registration: 8'

Tempo: ♩ = ± 80 (compare with Tempo Table IIf, 1)

Articulation: *Legato*

Courante

Registration: 8", 4"

Tempo: ♩ = ± 80 (compare with Tempo Table Xb, 2)

Articulation: *Quasi legato*

Ornamentation: Note that the appoggiatura at the beginning of the last but one bar can have only the length of an eighth (in contrast to the situation in bar 4 of the Courante of the A minor Suite).

Sarabande

Registration: 8', 16' or 4", 16' (C)

Tempo: ♩ = ± 60 (compare with Tempo Table IVf, 1)

Articulation: *Legato*

Passepied I en Rondeau

Registration: All main parts 8", 4", all "Interludes" 8'

Tempo: ♩. = ± 60 (see Tempo Table Vc, 1)

Articulation: *Quasi legato*, the eighths *portato*

Passepied II

Registration: 4" Solo or 4" (l) Solo

Tempo: Same as Passepied I

Articulation: *Più legato*; the eighths in bars 2, 6, 10, 18, 19, 20 *staccato*; in bars 7 and 23 the first two eighths slurred.

Gigue

Registration: 8", 4" (8', 16', 8", 4" *ad lib.* for repeats)
Tempo: $\downarrow. = \pm$ 80 (see Tempo Table Vc, 6)
Articulation: *Quasi legato* in general. For the two possible articulations of bar 2, either the first two or the second and third eighth can be slurred. We feel preference for the first version; the other one can, however, be defended too.

English Suite VI in D minor

Prelude

Registration:

Right hand		Left hand	
Bar 1–$38\frac{1}{16}$	8' (16' *ad lib.*)	Bar 1–$38\frac{1}{8}$	8' (16' *ad lib.*)
		$-16'$	
$38\frac{2}{16}$–$48\frac{2}{8}$	8", 4"	$39\frac{2}{16}$–$48\frac{1}{16}$	8", 4"
$48\frac{8}{16}$–$58\frac{7}{16}$	8'	$48\frac{2}{16}$–$58\frac{1}{16}$	8'
$58\frac{8}{16}$–$86\frac{1}{8}$	8", 4"	$58\frac{2}{16}$–$86\frac{3}{8}$	8", 4"
$86\frac{2}{8}$–$98\frac{3}{8}$	8'	$86\frac{6}{8}$–$93\frac{1}{16}$	8'
$98\frac{8}{16}$–$113\frac{1}{16}$	8", 4"	$93\frac{2}{16}$–$113\frac{1}{8}$	8", 4"
$113\frac{2}{16}$–$126\frac{7}{16}$	8'	$113\frac{2}{8}$–$125\frac{4}{8}$	8'
$126\frac{8}{16}$–$143\frac{1}{8}$	8", 4"	$125\frac{5}{8}$–$143\frac{3}{8}$	8", 4"
$143\frac{2}{8}$–$147\frac{1}{8}$	8'	$143\frac{6}{8}$–$147\frac{1}{8}$	8'
$147\frac{5}{16}$–$157\frac{2}{8}$	8", 4"	$147\frac{2}{16}$ (glide)–$157\frac{1}{8}$	8", 4"
$157\frac{8}{16}$–$166\frac{7}{16}$	8'	$157\frac{2}{16}$ (glide)–$166\frac{1}{16}$	8'
$166\frac{8}{16}$–195	8", 4"	$166\frac{2}{16}$–195	8", 4"
		or	
		$166\frac{2}{16}$–$194\frac{3}{8}$	8", 4"
		$+16'$	
		$194\frac{11}{16}$–195	8', 16'

The terraces in this gigantic piece are so clearly cut and so even that there is no place where it would be worthwhile to use a helper for coupling the keyboards to obtain more sound volume.

Tempo: $\downarrow. = \pm$ 60 (see Tempo Table VIIa, 3a and 3b); the *adagio* mark after bar 37 and the *allegro* at bar 38 are found in all reliable copies.

Articulation: The "introduction" *legato*, the *Allegro quasi legato* for sixteenths; the eighths in the theme *nonlegato*. All figures like the eighths in bar 61 have two notes slurred, the third *staccato*. We are inclined to give the same slurring to the seventh and eighth eighth notes in bars 86, 87 (left hand), 90, 91 (right hand), and corresponding places (117, 118, 166, 167, 169).

Allemande

Registration: 8'
Tempo: $\downarrow = \pm$ 80 (compare with Tempo Table IIf, 1)
Articulation: *Legato*

Courante

Registration: 8″, 4″

Tempo: ♩ = ± 80 (compare with Tempo Table Xb, 2)

Articulation: *Quasi legato*

Sarabande

Registration: 8′, 16′ for Sarabande, 4″, 16′ for Double. We consider the Double
to be nothing else than an *agrément*, written out as in Suites II and III,
and we play it instead of a mechanical repetition of the individual parts of
the Sarabande.

Tempo: ♩ = ± 60 (see Tempo Table Xb, 4a and b)

Articulation: *Molto legato*

Gavotte I

Registration: 8″, 4″

Tempo: ♩ = ± 80 (compare with Tempo Table IIa, 7 or 8)

Articulation: The two upbeat quarters *staccato*, otherwise *nonlegato*; the three
last chords in *tenuto*

Gavotte II

Registration: 4″ Solo

Tempo: Same as Gavotte I

Articulation: Left hand *un poco più legato*, right hand as in Gavotte I

Gigue

Registration: 8″, 4″ (for repetition *ad lib.* 8′, 16′, 8″, 4″)

Tempo: ♩. = ± 60 (see Tempo Table IXc, 7)

Articulation: *Nonlegato*, the eighths *molto portato*. This is the wildest gigue of
the entire literature. Do not bars 20–21, 44–45, 52–53 sound like ideas for
Contrapuncti VIII and XI of the *Art of the Fugue*? Moreover, bars 42–43
clearly cite B-A-C-H.

The Six So-called "French Suites"

From the external viewpoint, the French Suites offer much greater variety
than the English ones. They add airs, anglaises, polonaises, and loures to the
dance types represented in the "Suites avec prelude," as the English Suites are
sometimes called in contemporary copies. Yet, in regard to their content, the
unity of spirit is a perfect one, never going beyond the border-line of intimacy,
loveliness, and tenderness. This makes it unnecessary to discuss every dance of
every suite separately but allows us to discuss most problems in a more general
way. Once more let it be said that they all should by preference be played on
the clavichord. A harpsichord is excellent for series of pieces of widely different
character. Here, where everything leans to intimacy, it would by nature be out
of place. Our suggestions for tempo are as follows:

Allemandes ♩ = ± 80, except for those of Suites I and II, which because of
the frequent presence of thirty-seconds should be played at
the speed of ♩ = ± 60.

Correntes Suite II: ♩ = ± 140 (no sixteenths used)
Suites IV, V, VI: ♩ = ± 120

Courantes   Suite I: ♩ = ± 80 (3/2 is the basic time)
               Suite III: ♩ = ± 160 (6/4 is the basic time)
Sarabandes   All to be played at ♩ = ± 60
Menuets   Suites I, II, VI: ♩ = ± 120
               Suite III: ♩. = ± 60
               Suite IV: ♩ = ± 100
Gavottes   Suites IV, V, VI: ♩ = ± 80
Bourrées   Suites V and VI: ♩ = ± 100
Anglaise   Suite III: ♩ = ± 80
Loure   Suite V: ♩ = ± 120
Polonaise   Suite VI: ♩ = ± 100
Airs   Suite II: ♩ = ± 80 (¢)
               Suite IV: ♩ = ± 80 (C)
Gigues   Suite I: ♩ = ± 80 (C)
               Suites II and III: ♩. = ± 80 (3/8)
               Suites IV and VI: ♩. = ± 100 (6/8)
               Suite V: ♩. = ± 60 (12/16)

Authentic articulation marks are found in
               Suite II, Sarabande and Menuet
               Suite III, Sarabande
               Suite IV, Gavotte and Menuet
               Suite V, Sarabande and Loure (important dots to be played
                    nonlegato quasi portato).
               Suite VI, Menuet (important slurs over first and second quarters
                    of bars 2, 4, 6, and corresponding ones). The variety of
                    slurs in bars 7, 12, 13, 14, 21, is remarkable.

Dotted notes: For bar 5 of the Gigue, Suite I, see p. 188, note 14. The sixteenths
               following a dotted eighth in the Courante of Suite IV have
               to be played "à la C. P. E. Bach"; see Chapter 5, Example
               141.

Ornaments: Suite II, Gigue: All ∿ should be played as "inverted
               mordents" because of the parallel fifths which would arise
               in bar 42 at the collision of ∿ and ∿ if one
               would try to execute them as short trills of four notes.
               Suite V, Sarabande: All appoggiaturas at the length of an eighth.
               A trill should be played on the first note, right hand, in bars
               20 and 36. For bar 39, see Chapter 5, Example 59.
               Suite V, Loure: All appoggiaturas at the length of an eighth.
               Suite VI, Polonaise: The appoggiatura in the last bar needs the
               length of a quarter.
               Suite VI, Gigue: A trill may be added in bars 12 and 45, right
               hand. For all other ornaments, the traditional rules contain
               the necessary information.

THE *KLAVIERÜBUNG*, PART I

The Six Partitas: General Remarks

While both the English and the French Suites show almost complete uniformity in their organization, it is the diversity of constructive principles that distinguishes the third set of suites, the greatest of the three. Each partita has its own very definite character. The dances lose more and more connection with the standard dance types and become character pieces—we do not hesitate to say tone-poems—in which only the tempo reminds us of their point of origin. Bach himself is fully aware of this fact and instead of using the traditional dance titles, writes in the Fifth Partita, *Tempo di Minuetta*, in the Sixth Partita, *Tempo di Gavotta*. It is touching that Forkel, Bach's first biographer, is fully aware of the overwhelming grandeur of the partitas and expresses his admiration in the following words: "This work made in its time a great noise in the musical world. Such excellent compositions for the clavier had never been seen and heard before. Anyone who had learnt to perform well some pieces out of them could make his fortune in the world thereby; and even in our times, a young artist might gain acknowledgment by doing so, they are so brilliant, well-sounding, expressive, and always new."[2]

Partita I in B flat major

There can be no doubt that Partitas II–VI are clearly written for the harpsichord. An attempt to make an exception for the First Partita and to assign it to the clavichord has unavoidably to be met with disbelief or at least considerable distrust. Yet I must confess that every performance of this piece on the harpsichord which I have ever heard and every attempt which I made over many years to play it on this instrument left me deeply dissatisfied. Bach's writing style here is so different from that in the other partitas that the clavichord seems to me the only instrument which can reveal the unique beauty of this Partita.

May we be allowed to give our main arguments for our dissenting opinion? In the Prelude, the thematic material resembles very much that of the B flat major Invention (notice the likeness of key!), which is clearly meant for the clavichord. The contrapuntal technique is very close to that of the Three-Part Sinfonias. Toward the end, Bach increases the quantity of notes more than in any other piece and even writes octaves at the very end. Such sudden increases of tone volume have, however, nothing to do with virginal technique and are, as we can see from nearly every composition of C. P. E. Bach, the private domain of clavichord music. The octaves just mentioned would be a strong argument in favor of the harpsichord had they been written by Domenico Scarlatti, who uses this technique systematically—we might almost say "commercially"—to substitute for the 16' register which is in general missing on Italian harpsichords. But Bach uses this device too rarely for it to have any

---

[2] Our translation follows that of David and Mendel, *The Bach Reader*, pp. 337–338.

significance;[3] wherever octaves are needed, the registers of the harpsichord provide for them. In our particular case the importance of these octaves for assigning the Prelude to the harpsichord is invalidated by the authentic *forte* indication in the third bar before the end. At first glance, this *forte* seems again to indicate harpsichord designation. Which register could, however, take care of it? If *forte* is to be expressed by 8″ plus 4″, the addition of so many notes would mean an enormous and very ugly acoustic difference from the rest of the Prelude, at 8′. If Bach meant only 8′ for the end as against 8″ before, this small difference in sound volume would not justify special mention. Besides, one would be unable to understand why Bach omitted similar *forte* signs in innumerable similar cases. Strange as this *forte* sign is, it makes sense only if the Prelude is meant for clavichord.

Yet other and more convincing proofs that there is something wrong with the "harpsichord designation" are to be found in the following dances. The Allemande shows a strange and, for Bach, a very unusual shifting between polyphonic and homophonic setting. The first bars look so "modern" (from the viewpoint of the "Viennese Classics") that one thinks almost instantly of the piano (exploiting its pedal possibilities) for playing them with best results. This holds, as a matter of fact, still more for many bars of the Corrente. The bars 33–37 look and sound as if they stem from Schubert's Impromptu in E flat major, Op. 90. A very puzzling bar in the Allemande is bar 6. Let us confess that we feel unable to admire Bach's writing: something sounds wrong. Is the g in the bass meant as a secret pedal point, as are the bass notes in the first four bars? In this case, the harmony stands still in a very unconvincing way. If the f sharp of the ninth sixteenth is meant as a real "bass" note, the voice leading is ugly—we would have to say "un-Bachian." It can only be made milder by accentuating its importance. On the harpsichord, this can be done merely by a small agogic halt which, acoustically, is not enough. On the clavichord, one can, however, solve this acoustic problem easily by making a rather intensive crescendo and decrescendo. Also bar 17 requires in the first half prominence for the soprano, in the second prominence for the alto, which also only the clavichord can procure. We omit the acoustically "neutral" Corrente. New problems arise, however, in the Sarabande. This piece is very different from others of Bach and reveals in the scarcity of notes for the bass part a writing style which is most typical of C. P. E. Bach's clavichord pieces. On the harpsichord, such a bass sounds dull and meager, but it comes to wonderful life in a clavichord interpretation.

Not wanting to argue about clavichord features in the Menuets, we turn to the Gigue, which is again unique in Bach's work. The traditional registration:

---

[3] Other cases are: the end of the Gigue of the Fifth Partita, the end of the Fugue of the Chromatic Phantasy, the end of the second movement of the Harpsichord-Flute Sonata in B minor, and the end of the wild "harpsichord obbligato" accompaniment in the cantata "Amore traditore," second aria. It is most interesting to observe that, in the Fugue of the Chromatic Phantasy, Bach writes out the octaves in the fourth and third bars before the end and then stops doing so, since the fermata in the penultimate bar allows the drawing of the coupler and the 16′ register, which can now take care of producing octave sound.

8″, 4″ for the melody, 8′ for accompaniment, sounds simply miserable. We hardly know what is worse: the clocklike "tic-tic" of the accompaniment or the hacked mechanical repetition of sharp 8″, 4″ sounds for the wonderful melody which is much too beautiful and tender for such a treatment. That hand-crossing is by no means, as popularly believed, a typical feature of harpsichord music we have already proved (see pp. 43–44). One needs only to hear this incomparable Gigue on the clavichord to "let the lines speak for themselves."

Whatever may be the case of this Partita in regard to the choice of the right instrument, we felt it our duty to mention our severe objection to using the harpsichord. One will therefore understand and forgive us that we do not want to give here suggestions for a harpsichord registration which we feel unable to defend.

Prelude

Tempo: ♩ = ± 60 (see Tempo Table Ib, 21)

Articulation: *Molto legato*. The right phrasing is so obviously indicated by the melodious line that it cannot be misunderstood.

Allemande

Tempo: ♩ = ± 80 (see Tempo Table IIf, 3)

Articulation: *Legato*

Ornamentation: The ∿ in bars 12, 14, 15, etc., are obviously "inverted mordents."

Corrente

Tempo: ♩ = ± 120 (see Tempo Table IVf, 7)

Articulation: *Leggiero*. The sixteenths of the left hand may be played together with the third note of the triplet. It is, however, undeniable that in this piece the "overdotted" playing sounds extremely well (see discussion on p. 197).

Sarabande

Tempo: ♩ = ± 60 (compare with Tempo Table IVf, 1 or 2)

Articulation: *Molto legato*, left hand *molto tenuto*

Menuet I

Tempo: ♩ = ± 60 (see Tempo Table IVf, 18)

Articulation: Right hand *quasi legato*, left hand quarter notes *portamento*

Menuet II

Tempo: Same as Menuet I (see Tempo Table IVf, 20)

Articulation: *Molto legato*

Gigue

Tempo: ♩ = ± 140 (see Tempo Table IIf, 15, and discussion on p. 129)

Articulation: The melody *molto legato*, the triplets *leggiero*. A small but distinguishable accent should be given to the eleventh note of bars 15 and 47 to underline the "dominant" meaning of the harmony against the 6/4 meaning of the previous notes.

Partita II in C minor

Sinfonia

Registration: *Grave, Adagio* (bars 1–7): 8', 16', 8", 4"
  Andante:

	Right hand			Left hand	
Bar	8–15	8'	Bar	$8–25\frac{8}{8}$	8"
	$16\frac{2}{8}–19\frac{25}{32}$	8"		$26–28\frac{1}{4}$	8'
	$19\frac{26}{32}–23\frac{25}{32}$	8'			
	$23\frac{26}{32}–25\frac{25}{32}$	8"		$+4''$	
	$25\frac{26}{32}–28\frac{1}{8}$	8'			
	$28\frac{6}{32}–53\frac{5}{16}$	8", 4"		$28\frac{3}{4}–53\frac{2}{8}$	8", 4"
	$53\frac{6}{16}–54\frac{5}{16}$	8'		$53\frac{6}{16}–54\frac{2}{8}$	8'
	$54\frac{6}{16}–55\frac{5}{16}$	8", 4"		$54\frac{6}{16}–55\frac{2}{8}$	8", 4"
	$55\frac{6}{16}–56\frac{5}{16}$	8'		$55\frac{6}{16}–56\frac{2}{8}$	8'
	$56\frac{6}{16}–57\frac{5}{16}$	8", 4"		$56\frac{6}{16}–57\frac{2}{8}$	8", 4"
	$57\frac{6}{16}–58\frac{5}{16}$	8'		$57\frac{6}{16}–58\frac{2}{8}$	8'
	$58\frac{6}{16}–59\frac{5}{16}$	8", 4"		$58\frac{6}{16}–59\frac{2}{8}$	8", 4"
	$59\frac{6}{16}–60\frac{5}{16}$	8'		$59\frac{6}{16}–60\frac{2}{8}$	8'
	$60\frac{6}{16}–80\frac{5}{16}$	8", 4"		$60\frac{6}{16}–80\frac{2}{8}$	8", 4"
	$80\frac{6}{16}–81\frac{5}{16}$	8'		$80\frac{6}{16}–81\frac{2}{8}$	8'
	$81\frac{6}{16}–82\frac{5}{16}$	8", 4"		$81\frac{6}{16}–82\frac{2}{8}$	8", 4"
	$82\frac{6}{16}–83\frac{5}{16}$	8'		$82\frac{6}{16}–83\frac{2}{8}$	8'
	$83\frac{6}{16}–91$	8", 4"		$83\frac{6}{16}–91$	8", 4"

Tempo: *Grave, Adagio*, $\downarrow = \pm\,40$ (see Tempo Table IIe, 4)
  Andante, $\downarrow = \pm\,60$ (see Tempo Table Ib, 22)
  [Allegro], $\downarrow = \pm\,100$ (see Tempo Table IVa, 7)
Articulation: *Molto tenuto*; "overdotted" playing "à la française" (but see
  remarks on pp. 194 and 196).
  Andante: Right hand *molto legato*, left hand *quasi legato*
  Allegro: First three notes, first five notes of second bar and last four notes
    of third bar slurred, the rest *staccato* for eighths and *quasi legato* for
    the sixteenths.

Allemande

Registration: 8'
Tempo: $\downarrow = \pm\,80$ (compare with Tempo Table IIf, 1)
Articulation: *Legato*; the first notes of bars 13, 14, left hand, and corresponding,
  of course, *portato*.
Ornamentation: The third eighth in the final bar of both parts should get a
  trill.

Courante

Registration: 8", 4"
Tempo: $\downarrow = \pm\,80$ (see Tempo Table Xb, 3)
Articulation: *Quasi legato*

Sarabande

Registration: 8', 16' or 4", 16' (C)
Tempo: $\quad \downarrow = \pm\ 60$ (compare with Tempo Table IVf, 1)
Articulation: *Legato*, all larger intervals of eighth-note length *portato*
Ornamentation: The ∿ in bar 4 should get a connecting "*nachschla-gendes*" a before the g (for "*Nachschlag*" see p. 179).

Rondeau

Registration:

	Right hand			Left hand	
Bar	$1-17\frac{1}{16}$	8", 4"	Bar	$2-17\frac{2}{8}$	8", 4"
	$17\frac{2}{16}-32\frac{3}{8}$	8'		$18-32\frac{2}{8}$	8'
	$33-48\frac{2}{8}$	8", 4"		$32\frac{6}{16}-47$	8", 4"
	$49\frac{2}{16}-64\frac{3}{8}$	8'		$48-64\frac{2}{8}$	8'
	$65\frac{2}{16}-80$	8", 4"		$64\frac{6}{16}-81\frac{1}{8}$	8", 4"
	$81-97\frac{1}{16}$	8'		$81\frac{2}{8}-96\frac{1}{16}$	8'
	$97\frac{2}{16}-112$	8", 4"		$96\frac{2}{16}-112$	8", 4"

Tempo: $\quad \downarrow . = \pm\ 60$ (see Tempo Table Va, 10)
Articulation: The eighths *staccato*, the sixteenths *quasi legato*, a slur in bar 2 and corresponding ones.

Capriccio

Registration: The registration of this piece is not easy to determine. It is too long to be played in one registration throughout. We suggest, without being fully convinced of having found the only possible solution:

	Right hand			Left hand	
Bar	$1-22\frac{1}{4}$	8", 4"	Bar	$1-22\frac{1}{8}$	8", 4"
	$22\frac{2}{16}$ (glide)$-28\frac{1}{8}$	8'		$22\frac{2}{8}-28\frac{1}{8}$	8'
	$28\frac{2}{8}-48$	8", 4"		$28\frac{2}{16}$ (glide)-48	8", 4"
	$49\frac{2}{8}-70\frac{3}{8}$	8'		$49-72\frac{1}{8}$	8'
	$70\frac{2}{8}$ (glide)-96	8", 4"		$72\frac{2}{8}-96$	8", 4"

Tempo: $\quad \downarrow = \pm\ 100$ (see Tempo Table IIIa, 4)
Articulation: *Quasi legato* for sixteenths, *staccato* for all leaps of eighths, *portato* for seconds.

Partita III in A minor

Fantasia

Registration: Were this piece not the introduction to the powerful Third Partita, we would consider it to be a Two-Part Invention and play it on the clavichord. The best solution for registration might be *not* to give it a power which it does not possess and play it as follows:

Right hand			Left hand		
Bar	1–67$\frac{1}{16}$	8′	Bar	1–66$\frac{1}{16}$	8′
	67$\frac{2}{16}$–97$\frac{1}{16}$	8″		66$\frac{2}{16}$–97$\frac{1}{8}$	8″
	97$\frac{2}{16}$–120	8′		97$\frac{2}{8}$–120	8′

Tempo: ♩. = ± 60 (see Tempo Table Va, 11)

Articulation: *Legato* for all sixteenths, the eighths *portato*. Notice bars 31–32, which are to be found also in the Gigue (bars 13–14) and in the great Organ Fugue in A minor (bars 61–62).

Allemande

Registration: Since the 8′ register was already used for the Fantasia, it cannot be used again for the Allemande, as we have done so far with all Allemandes in the English Suites as well as in the Second Partita. For this Allemande, 4″, 16″ (C) throughout will be right; here we meet for the first time a dance so highly stylized that the original dance character shines through only a little.

Tempo: ♩ = ± 60 (see Tempo Table IIf, 4). The abundance of thirty-seconds enforces the lowering of the speed compared with the allemandes, which use sixteenths as the fastest notes and can therefore be played at ♩ = ± 80. "Overdotted" playing of sixteenths is necessary in bars 2, 5, 6, 7, 13, 16, where sixteenths and thirty-seconds collide.

Articulation: *Molto legato*

Corrente

Registration: 8″, 4″

Tempo: ♩ = ± 120 (see Tempo Table IVf, 5)

Articulation: *Quasi legato*. Bach's wildest Corrente, as stormy as the boldest gigues of the English Suites.

Sarabande

Registration: Again a unique piece which might be called a "Sarabande à la Polonaise." It deserves an unusual registration and we suggest: 8′, 16′, 4″ (full work minus 8″).

Tempo: ♩ = ± 60 (no piece for comparison exists)

Articulation: The triplets slurred, also the falling seconds in bar 2, etc.; all other eighths *portato*.

Ornamentation: Bischoff reports that the ornament on the second note of the Sarabande is unreadable. It may be played as an inverted mordent or, probably better, as a turn of three short notes and one long note. The collision between three and two sixteenths in bar 22 may be played "correctly" or with the two sixteenths of the right played so that the second falls together with the third note of the triplet.

Burlesca

Registration: 8″, 4″

Tempo: ♩ = ± 120 (no piece for comparison exists)

Articulation: *Quasi legato*, the quarters *portato*

Scherzo

Registration: 8', *ad lib.* 8", 4"
Tempo: ♩ = ± 100 (see Tempo Table IIIa, 5)
Articulation: *Nonlegato*

Gigue

Registration: 8", 4" (for repetition 8', 16', 8", 4" *ad lib.*)
Tempo: ♩. = ± 120 (compare with Tempo Table VIIIc, 1 or 2)
Articulation: *Nonlegato*

Partita IV in D major

Overture

Registration: The registration of this mighty piece is very problematic. It is not easy, indeed is nearly impossible, to get rid of the coupling of the keyboards at the end of the Overture without a helper, if one wants to play the introduction with "full work." To play the entire piece 8", 4" alone, alternating in the 9/8 section with 8', makes the introduction sound very shabby. The best compromise would be (in order not to overload the *Allegro* with sound masses) to use 16', 8", 4" coupled so that one can alternate between 16', 8", 4" and 8", 4" terraces. Personally, we prefer the idea of a helper and base our suggestions for registration on this assumption.
Introduction: 8', 16', 8", 4" at the speed of ♩ = ± 60 (see Tempo Table IIe, 1). Then (we begin counting the bars with the 9/8 time):

Right hand			*Left hand*		
Bar	$1-16\frac{1}{16}$	8", 4"	Bar	$3-16\frac{2}{8}$	8", 4"
	$16\frac{2}{16}-33\frac{1}{8}$	8'		$16\frac{4}{8}-30\frac{2}{8}$	8'
	$33\frac{2}{8}-55\frac{1}{8}$	8", 4"		$31\frac{2}{8}-55\frac{7}{16}$	8", 4"
	$55\frac{2}{8}-66\frac{1}{16}$	8'		$55\frac{8}{16}-62\frac{2}{8}$	8'
	$66\frac{2}{16}-70\frac{1}{16}$	8", 4"		$62\frac{4}{8}-70\frac{5}{8}$	8", 4"
	$70\frac{2}{16}-83\frac{2}{8}$	8'		$70\frac{7}{8}-80\frac{2}{8}$	8'
	$83\frac{8}{16}-93\frac{1}{8}$	8", 4"		$80\frac{4}{8}-87\frac{1}{8}$	8", 4"
	$93\frac{2}{8}-95$	8', 16', 8", 4"		$87\frac{2}{8}-95$	8', 16', 8", 4"

The helper draws the 16' and couples the keyboards between bars 84 and 86.
Tempo: ♩. = ± 60 (see Tempo Table VIIa, 4)
Articulation: *Quasi legato;* chord figures of eighths as well as large intervals *nonlegato;* quarters *tenuto;* the Overture with overdotted rhythms.

Allemande

Registration: The most beautiful and most stylized of all Bach's allemandes. The length of the piece requires more detailed registration. Our suggestion:

	Right hand			*Left hand*	
Bar	1–24$\frac{7}{8}$	8′	Bar	1–18$\frac{1}{4}$	8″
	24$\frac{8}{8}$–40$\frac{3}{4}$	8″		18$\frac{2}{16}$ (glide)–24$\frac{7}{8}$	8′
	40$\frac{14}{16}$–56	8′		25–40	8″
				41–56	8′

Tempo: ♩ = ± 60 (see Tempo Table IIf, 5)
Articulation: *Molto legato*

Courante

Registration: 8″, 4″
Tempo: ♩ = ± 120; the basic metre is more 6/4 than 3/2. No piece for comparison is available, since the Courante of the Third French Suite uses no sixteenths.
Articulation: *Quasi legato*
Ornamentation: The long appoggiaturas written out in bars 8, 29, 30 are remarkable. For reasons of similarity the appoggiatura in bar 6 should have the length of a quarter, as well as that of bar 4, where the danger of parallels also forbids a shorter length.

Aria

Registration: 8′ (8″ for repetitions but return to 8′ for the last four chords)
Tempo: ♩ = ± 80 (see Tempo Table IIIb, 3)
Articulation: Upbeat *portato*, syncopations *tenuto*, the falling seconds slurred, larger intervals of eighths *portato*, the rest *legato* except the last chords, which are *portato*.
Again a unique piece.

Sarabande

Registration: 4″, 16′ (C)
Tempo: ♩ = ± 60 (compare with Tempo Table IVf, 1)
Articulation: *Molto legato*
In spite of its beauty this Sarabande is to us a slight disappointment within this Partita, since Bach uses again the "aria-technique" (leading voice with accompaniment) as he had already done in the Allemande and the Aria.

Menuet

Registration: 8′ for right, 8″ for left hand; in the repetitions both hands 8″. If both hands would play on 8′, the chords of the left hand would get an ugly supremacy.
Tempo: ♩ = ± 120 (see Tempo Table IVf, 16)
Articulation: *Legato*, larger intervals *portato*. The sixteenths after the dotted eighths should be played together with the last note of the triplets; and in bar 14, the d in the left hand also should be played together with g sharp, right hand.

Gigue

Registration:

	Right hand			Left hand	
Bar	1–37$\frac{6}{16}$	8″, 4″	Bar	7–36	8″, 4″
	38–48	8′, 16′, 8″, 4″		37$\frac{5}{16}$–48	8′, 16′, 8″, 4″
	55–85$\frac{8}{16}$	8″, 4″		49–88	8″, 4″
	85$\frac{9}{16}$–96	8′, 16′, 8″, 4″		89–96	8′, 16′, 8″, 4″

Tempo: ♪. = 120 (see Tempo Table IXb, 2)
Articulation: *Quasi legato*

Partita V in G major

Praeambulum

Registration:

	Right hand			Left hand	
Bar	1–20	8″, 4″	Bar	1–20	8″, 4″
	21–25$\frac{2}{8}$	8′		21–29$\frac{1}{8}$	8′
	25$\frac{4}{8}$–37$\frac{1}{8}$	8″, 4″		29$\frac{2}{8}$–37$\frac{1}{8}$	8″, 4″
	37$\frac{2}{8}$–40$\frac{5}{8}$	8′		37$\frac{6}{8}$–41$\frac{1}{8}$	8′
	41–44	8″, 4″		41$\frac{5}{8}$–44	8″, 4″
	45$\frac{2}{16}$–49$\frac{1}{16}$	8′		45–52	8′
	49$\frac{2}{16}$–56$\frac{12}{16}$	8″, 4″		53–57$\frac{1}{8}$	8″, 4″
	57$\frac{2}{16}$–64$\frac{1}{16}$	8′		57$\frac{2}{8}$–63$\frac{1}{16}$	8′
	64$\frac{2}{16}$–68	8″, 4″		63$\frac{2}{16}$–68	8″, 4″
	69$\frac{2}{8}$–79$\frac{2}{8}$	8′		69–81$\frac{1}{8}$	8′
	79$\frac{4}{8}$–86$\frac{1}{4}$	8″, 4″		81$\frac{2}{8}$–86$\frac{1}{4}$	8″, 4″
		+C, +16′			
	86$\frac{6}{16}$–95	8′, 16′, 8″, 4″		87$\frac{2}{16}$–95	8′, 16′, 8″, 4″

Tempo: ♩ = ± 100 (see Tempo Table IVa, 8)
Articulation: In the "Motto" sixteenths *quasi legato*, chords *molto portato*; for the other parts sixteenths *più legato*, eighths *portato*.

Allemande

Registration: 8′
Tempo: ♩ = ± 80 (compare with Tempo Table IIf, 1)
Articulation: *Legato*
Ornamentation: In spite of the appoggiatura written out in eighths in bar 14, the length of the appoggiaturas in bars 2, 3, 16 can only be that of a sixteenth (notice the parallel octaves when executed as eighths, listed on Appoggiatura Table, No. 2).

Corrente

Registration: 8″, 4″
Tempo: ♩. = ± 60 (see Tempo Table Vc, 7)

Articulation: Sixteenths *quasi legato*, eighths *nonlegato* but *legato* for the
melodious lines in the second part; the upbeat to the second part and
corresponding places *staccato*. The eighths cb, ba, ag in bars 8–14 are
slurred in pairs, the other eighths, however, remain *nonlegato*.

Sarabande

Registration: 4″, 16′ (C)
Tempo: $\downarrow$ = ± 60 (compare with Tempo Table IVf, 1)
Articulation: *Legato e tenuto*
Ornamentation: See remarks on pp. 179 and 187. We suggest for the various
appoggiaturas the following values: in "upbeat bar" a sixteenth, same for
left hand in bar 2, for right hand: bar 2 an eighth, bar 4 a quarter (corresponding with bar 8). As outlined on p. 187, the fifth eighth in bar 4 must
be played as a sixteenth (corresponding with beginning). This holds, of
course, too for all corresponding places: bars 11, 20, 22.
Notice also the beautiful parallel fourth in bar 30.

Tempo di Minuetta

Registration: 8′ or 8″
Tempo: $\downarrow$. = ± 60 (see Tempo Table IVf, 19)
Articulation: *Leggiero*, the quarters *nonlegato*

Passepied

Registration: 8′, 8″ (C)
Tempo: $\downarrow$. = ± 60 (see Tempo Table Vc, 2)
Articulation: *Quasi legato*, upbeat *staccato*; all bars like 3: two eighths slurred,
the third *staccato*.
Ornamentation: The appoggiatura in bar 2 must be played as a sixteenth (see
Appoggiatura Table, No. 1).

Gigue

Registration:

	Right hand			*Left hand*	
Bar	1–32	8″, 4″	Bar	1–32	8″, 4″
	33–49$\frac{11}{16}$	8′		33–50$\frac{5}{8}$	8′
	49$\frac{12}{16}$–64	8″, 4″		51–64	8″, 4″

Tempo: $\downarrow$. = 60 (see Tempo Table VIc, 1)
Articulation: *Quasi legato*, upbeat *staccato*, larger intervals in eighths *nonlegato*.
In figures like that in the left hand, bars 4 (second half), and 5, 9–10$\frac{1}{2}$,
26–27, etc., it seems logical to play the first eighth *staccato*, the next two
slurred.

Partita VI in E minor

Toccata

Registration: (see discussion on pp. 48ff.)

Right hand		Left hand	
Bar 1–$8\frac{13}{16}$	8', 16', 8", 4"	Bar 1–8	8', 16', 8", 4"
$8\frac{14}{16}$–$12\frac{7}{8}$	8", 4"	9–12	8", 4"
13–$20\frac{13}{16}$	8', 16', 8", 4"	13–20	8', 16', 8", 4"
$20\frac{14}{16}$–$24\frac{7}{8}$	8", 4"	21–24	8", 4"
25–$26\frac{7}{8}$	8', 16', 8", 4"	25–$26\frac{7}{8}$	8', 16', 8", 4"
–C, –16', –4" (the 4" can be removed during bars 27–28)			
$26\frac{8}{8}$–$37\frac{1}{16}$	8'	$26\frac{8}{8}$–$37\frac{1}{8}$	8'
$37\frac{2}{16}$–$40\frac{5}{16}$	8"	$37\frac{2}{8}$–$40\frac{3}{8}$	8"
$40\frac{6}{16}$–$42\frac{16}{16}$	8'	$40\frac{4}{8}$–$44\frac{8}{16}$	8'
43–$44\frac{8}{16}$	8"	$44\frac{9}{16}$–$45\frac{16}{16}$	8"
$44\frac{9}{16}$–45	8'	46–$53\frac{2}{8}$	8'
$46\frac{1}{16}$–$46\frac{7}{16}$	8"		+4"
$46\frac{8}{16}$–$57\frac{9}{16}$	8'	$53\frac{4}{8}$–$56\frac{1}{8}$	8", 4"
$57\frac{10}{16}$–$67\frac{1}{16}$	8", 4"	$56\frac{2}{8}$–$57\frac{9}{16}$	8'
$67\frac{2}{16}$–$68\frac{7}{8}$	8'	$57\frac{10}{16}$–$67\frac{1}{8}$	8", 4"
$68\frac{8}{8}$–$71\frac{13}{16}$	8", 4"	$67\frac{2}{8}$–$81\frac{14}{16}$	8'
$71\frac{14}{16}$–$77\frac{7}{8}$	8'	$81\frac{8}{8}$–88	8", 4"
$77\frac{8}{8}$–88	8", 4"		

+C, +16'

89–108	8', 16', 8", 4"	89–108	8', 16', 8", 4"

Tempo: $\downarrow$ = ± 80 (see Tempo Table IIe, 5). Introduction and Fugue should probably be played at the same speed. Keller wants the Fugue to be played at half speed of the Toccata because of

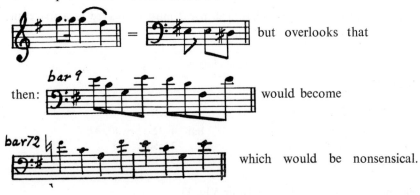

but overlooks that

then: would become

which would be nonsensical.

Sighs of a quarter's length can be found in Prelude 24 in B minor, *W.K.* II (at ₵ time!). See, however, pp. 127 and 132.

Articulation: *Legato* in general, all "sighs" slurred; bar 9 left hand and similar places: three eighths slurred, the fourth eighth *staccato*.

Ornamentation: The in the theme of the fugue ought to be executed as an inverted mordent (see discussion on pp. 153ff., 166ff.).

Allemande

Registration: 8′ (repetitions 8″)
Tempo: $\quad = \pm\ 60$ (see Tempo Table IIf, 6)
Articulation: *Legato*

Corrente

Registration: This, the longest of all correntes, shows clear evidence of terrace dynamics.

Right hand			Left hand	
Bar	$1-6\frac{2}{16}$	8″, 4″	Bar	$1-52\frac{1}{32}$	8′
	$6\frac{7}{32}-8\frac{2}{16}$	8′		$52\frac{2}{32}-54\frac{2}{8}$	8″, 4″
	$8\frac{7}{32}-9\frac{2}{16}$	8″, 4″	(a shift to 8″, 4″ can already	
	$9\frac{7}{32}-10\frac{2}{16}$	8′	start at bar 47 if preferred)	
	$10\frac{7}{32}-11\frac{2}{16}$	8″, 4″		
	$11\frac{7}{32}-12\frac{2}{16}$	8′		
	$12\frac{7}{32}-18\frac{2}{16}$	8″, 4″		
	$18\frac{4}{16}-28\frac{3}{16}$	8′		
	$28\frac{7}{32}-30\frac{8}{32}$	8″, 4″		
	$30\frac{9}{32}-32\frac{8}{32}$	8′		
	$32\frac{9}{32}-38\frac{1}{8}$	8″, 4″		
	$38\frac{7}{32}-40\frac{4}{32}$	8′		
	$40\frac{7}{32}-54\frac{2}{8}$	8″, 4″		
	$54\frac{6}{16}-60\frac{2}{16}$	8″, 4″		$55-113\frac{1}{32}$	8′
	$60\frac{7}{32}-62\frac{2}{16}$	8′		$113\frac{2}{32}-116$	8″, 4″
	$62\frac{7}{32}-66\frac{2}{16}$	8″, 4″	(again, a shift to 8″, 4″ can	
	$66\frac{7}{32}-67\frac{2}{16}$	8′	already start at 108)	
	$67\frac{7}{32}-74\frac{2}{16}$	8″, 4″		
	$74\frac{7}{32}-79\frac{1}{16}$	8′		
	$79\frac{2}{16}-82\frac{2}{16}$	8″, 4″		
	$82\frac{7}{32}-83\frac{2}{16}$	8′		
	$83\frac{7}{32}-84\frac{2}{16}$	8″, 4″		
	$84\frac{7}{32}-85\frac{2}{16}$	8′		
	$85\frac{7}{32}-91\frac{8}{32}$	8″, 4″		
	$91\frac{9}{32}-93\frac{8}{32}$	8′		
	$93\frac{9}{32}-99\frac{1}{8}$	8″, 4″		
	$99\frac{7}{32}-101\frac{2}{16}$	8′		
	$101\frac{7}{32}-116$	8″, 4″		

Tempo: $\quad = \pm\ 120$ (see Tempo Table Vc, 8)
Articulation: All syncopations of eighths *portato*; the other eighths *quasi legato*; the rest *legato*; the final cadences *molto portato*.

Air

Registration: 8′, repetitions 8″, the "petite reprise" (the last five bars) 8′
Tempo: $\quad = \pm\ 80$ (see Tempo Table IIa, 14)
Articulation: The eighths *legato*, the quarters *nonlegato*, the "chords" *portato*

Sarabande

Registration:

Right hand			Left hand		
Bar	1–12$\frac{2}{4}$	8', 16'	Bar	1–12$\frac{2}{4}$	8', 16'
	(repetition 8')			(repetition 8')	
		add 16' immediately again			
	12$\frac{3}{4}$–24$\frac{2}{4}$	8" (take over the		12$\frac{3}{4}$–23	8"
		a of left-hand			
		part in bar 24)			
	24$\frac{3}{4}$–28$\frac{16}{32}$	8', 16'		24$\frac{6}{32}$–28$\frac{1}{4}$	8', 16'

+C

+4" at rest of second quarter

28$\frac{3}{4}$–36   8', 16', 8", 4"   both hands

This most "baroque" of all sarabandes certainly deserves the greatest possible splendor of harpsichord registration.

Tempo: $\downarrow$ = ± 60 (see Tempo Table IVf, 3)

Articulation: *Molto legato e tenuto*

Ornamentation: The diagonal dashes between the notes of the first chord are "acciaccaturas": the diatonic notes between the notes printed have to be added in a general "arpeggio." Very noteworthy is the mordent, written out in notes, in bar 19 left hand. This is the only ornament in Bach's works to be played before the time of the main note. The same solution holds apparently also for bar 17 where Bach writes the ᴸᴸᴸ sign for the same purpose. Did Bach become aware, while writing this piece, that his intentions in bar 17 could be misunderstood and therefore wrote in bar 19 what he wanted to be played (remember Scheibe's criticism, cited on p. 148)?

Tempo di Gavotta

Registration: 8", 4"

Tempo: $\downarrow$ = ± 80 (see Table IIf, 9)

Articulation: *Quasi legato.* See comments on this piece on p. 197

Gigue

Registration:

Right hand			Left hand		
Bar	3–9$\frac{1}{4}$	8', 16', 8", 4"	Bar	1–9$\frac{1}{8}$	8', 16', 8", 4"
	9$\frac{2}{4}$–13$\frac{5}{4}$	8", 4"		9$\frac{2}{8}$–13$\frac{5}{4}$	8", 4"
	13$\frac{6}{4}$–15$\frac{5}{4}$	8', 16', 8", 4"		13$\frac{12}{8}$–15$\frac{9}{8}$	8', 16', 8", 4"
	15$\frac{6}{4}$–20$\frac{3}{8}$	8", 4"		15$\frac{10}{8}$–20$\frac{1}{8}$	8", 4"
	20$\frac{4}{8}$–33$\frac{1}{8}$	8', 16', 8", 4"		20$\frac{2}{8}$–33$\frac{3}{8}$	8', 16', 8", 4"
	33$\frac{2}{8}$–37$\frac{11}{8}$	8", 4"		33$\frac{4}{8}$–37$\frac{9}{8}$	8", 4"
	37$\frac{12}{8}$–41$\frac{9}{8}$	8', 16', 8", 4"		37$\frac{10}{8}$ (glide)–41$\frac{11}{8}$	8', 16', 8", 4"
	41$\frac{10}{8}$–45$\frac{1}{8}$	8", 4"		41$\frac{12}{8}$–45$\frac{1}{4}$	8", 4"
	45$\frac{2}{8}$–52	8', 16', 8", 4"		45$\frac{4}{8}$–52	8', 16', 8", 4"

Tempo: ♩ = ± 80 (see Table IIf, 14a and b)

Articulation: *Molto tenuto e maestoso*, the smaller values *quasi legato*

Ornamentation: The trill on the penultimate note of the theme should, of course, follow the recipe "start and brief stop on the main note."

The majestic climax of all gigues ever written.

THE *KLAVIERÜBUNG*, PART II

General Remarks

The great length at which we have studied the possibilities for registration for the Italian Concerto (pp. 33–40) and for the French Overture (pp. 40–43) makes it unnecessary to repeat here what has already been said. Since both these pieces are the only ones in which Bach himself gives detailed information on his registration methods, it is the duty of every serious Bach student to give them a very special study. From now on we will also change our methods of reporting on articulation problems. The reader who has followed our descriptions of and suggestions for articulation through the *Welltempered Keyboard* and the suite collections will already have discovered the constant repetition of a few basic rules outlined on pp. 221–222: the preference for *legato* for seconds and eventually thirds, the preference for *portato* or *nonlegato* for larger intervals. It can also be said that wherever note values of quarters and eighths or eighths and sixteenths appear at the same time the smaller value will need a more outspoken *legato* than the other one. For internal organization of a few notes, our samples on Articulation Tables III–VI give all the information obtainable from authentic sources. To avoid unnecessary repetitions therefore, we shall from now on report on articulation only if the danger of serious mistakes should arise.

The Italian Concerto

Instrument: Harpsichord

Registration: See pp. 33–40

Tempo: First movement, ♩ = ± 100 (see Tempo Table IIIa, 3)

       Second movement, ♩ = ± 40 (see Tempo Table IVd, 1)

       Third movement, ♩ = ± 100 (see Tempo Table IIc, 1)

Articulation: Notice and study the many authentic slurs

Ornamentation: For ∿ in bar 34, first movement, see Trill Table, No. 9. Also the many ornaments written out by Bach in full notes in the second movement deserve highest attention. See Example A8 for comparison.

Ex. A8. Georg Muffat, *Florilegium Musicum* (1695), Fasc. IV
Impatientia Symphonie (D.T.Ö., I, p. 76)

A "Sonate pour le Clavecin, dédié à qui la jouera le mieux" by Johann Mattheson, Hamburg, 1713, has also unquestionably influenced the first movement of the Italian Concerto.

The French Overture

Instrument: Harpsichord

Registration: See pp. 40–43

Tempo: Overture: first and third part, ♩ = ± 60 (see Tempo Table IIe, 2); middle part, ♩. = ± 60 (see Tempo Table VIa, 4).

    Courante: ♩ = ± 80 (compare with Tempo Table Xb, 1)

    Gavotte I and II: ♩ = ± 80 (compare with Tempo Table IIf, 7)

    Passepied I and II: ♩. = ± 60 (see Tempo Table Vc, 3)

    Sarabande: ♩ = ± 60 (compare with Tempo Table IVf, 1)

    Bourrée I and II: ♩ = ± 100 (see Tempo Table IIf, 12)

    Gigue: ♩. = ± 80 (see Tempo Table VIc, 3)

    Echo: ♩ = ± 100 (see Tempo Table IIIa, 6)

Articulation: Since Bach asks in bar 9 and many similar bars of the middle section of the Overture that the first eighth of the group of three should be held, it is obvious that the correct articulation of the eighths in the theme (after the *staccato* upbeat!) is two eighths slurred, the last *staccato*. Bischoff's suggestion of *staccato* throughout is not understandable.

Ornamentation: For the appoggiatura in bar 2 of the Overture we strongly recommend the length of an eighth. The same holds for the appoggiaturas in the Courante. In Bourrée II the length of the appoggiatura in bar 1 can also be that of a quarter. The appoggiatura rule mentioned on p. 178 sounds convincing at least when applied to the Gigue, but we do not dare to say that it ought to be the only solution permissible.

THE *KLAVIERÜBUNG*, PART III

The Duets

The mystery of the true meaning of the four Duets which are to be found in the third part of the *Klavierübung* is not yet solved. Although one has given up the thesis that they were printed only by a mistake of the publisher, as Schweitzer still thought,[4] it is not clear for which instrument they were meant. Stylistically they belong to the idiom of the Two-Part Inventions and lean therefore to the clavichord. They can, of course, be played on every other keyboard instrument, and, since all the other pieces of the *Klavierübung*, Part III, are written for the organ, nothing can be said against their execution on the same instrument. Moser agrees with W. Ehman that they might have been planned as "Verlängerungsmusik" for the Communion.[5] Heinrich Husmann emphasizes that the four duets stand in the *Klavierübung*, Part III, at the same place as do the

---

[4] *Bach*, p. 298.

[5] Moser, *Johann Sebastian Bach*, p. 152; W. Ehman, in *Musik und Kirche*, Jahrgang V, p. 2.

four canons in the *Art of the Fugue* and takes assignment to the organ for granted.[6] Klaus Ehricht constructs links between the Duet in A minor and the hymn "Christus unser Herr zum Jordan kam"; the Duet in F major and "Jesus Christus, unser Heiland"; the Duet in E minor and "Kyrie Gott Vater in Ewigkeit"; the Duet in G major and "Allein Gott in de Höh sei Ehr."[7] It is hard to deny similarities in the respective lines, but they appeal more to the eye than to the ear. Because of his findings, Ehricht assigns all the Duets to the organ and places them at the side of these choral preludes in the master plan of the *Klavierübung*, Part III.

In regard to their interpretation, there is no necessity for elaborate discussion. Our tempo suggestions are as follows:

Duet in E minor	♪ = ± 100 (see Tempo Table Vb, 4)
Duet in F major	♩ = ± 100 (see Tempo Table IIIa, 7)
Duet in G major	♩. = ± 60 (see Tempo Table VIIIa, 4)
Duet in A minor	♩ = ± 80 (see Tempo Table IId, 2)

THE *KLAVIERÜBUNG*, PART IV

The Goldberg Variations

The excellent edition made by Ralph Kirkpatrick (Schirmer, New York) gives complete information on all performance problems. This allows us to restrict our own report on this towering piece of harpsichord literature to tables for registration and tempo and to comments on those cases where, for pressing reasons, we felt it necessary to deviate from Kirkpatrick's suggestions (see also discussion on pp. 43–45).

In contrast to the great variety of tempi used by Kirkpatrick, we felt it advisable to underline the architectural unity of Variations 1, 5, 8, 14, 17, 20, 23; of Variations 10, 18, 22; and of Variations 13 and 25 by giving them the same speed. We also feel that Kirkpatrick asks too much from human tempo-consciousness when he advises us to play Variation 2 at the speed of ♩ = 94 instead of ♩ = 95, and Variation 21 at ♩ = 56 instead of ♩ = 55. Otherwise, his twofold set of metronome indications is a model of artistic conscientiousness.

In general, every suggestion for registration holds for the entire set of variations. Only for the following variations do we recommend some changes, mostly to facilitate the technical execution:

Variation 5:

	Right hand			*Left hand*	
Bar	1–8	8′	Bar	1–8⅛	8″
	9–16	8″		8²⁄₄–16	8′
	17–32	8′		18–32	8″

---

[6] "Die Kunst der Fuge als Klavierwerk," *Bach-Jahrbuch* (1938), p. 52.

[7] "Der zyklische Gehalt und die Aufführungsmöglichkeit des III. Teils der Klavierübung von J. S. Bach," *Bach-Jahrbuch* (1949–1950), p. 40.

The Goldberg Variations

Bach's Prescriptions	Registration	Time	Tempo
Aria	8'	3/4	♪ = ± 60 (see Tempo Table IVc, 6)
Var. 1 à 1 Clavier	8", 4"	3/4	♪ = ± 100 (see Tempo Table IVa, 17)
2 à 1 Clavier	8', 16'	2/4	♪ = ± 100 (see Tempo Table IIIa, 8)
3 à 1 Clavier	8'	12/8	♪. = ± 60 (see Tempo Table VIIIa, 3)
4 à 1 Clavier	4", 16', C	3/8	♪ = ± 60 (see Tempo Table Va, 12)
5 à 1 overo 2 Claviers	8', 8"	3/4	♪ = ± 100 (see Tempo Table IVa, 18)
6 à 1 Clavier	8", 4"	3/8	♪ = ± 60 (see Tempo Table Va, 13)
7 à 1 overo 2 Claviers	r.h.: 4" (1) l.h.: 8'	6/8	♩. = ± 80 (see Tempo Table VIb, 2)
8 à 2 Claviers	r.h.: 8", 4" l.h.: 8', 16'	3/4	♩ = ± 100 (see Tempo Table IVa, 19)
9 à 1 Clavier	4", 16', C	C	♩ = ± 80 (see Tempo Table Ia, 35)
10 à 1 Clavier	8', 4", 16', C	¢	𝅗𝅥 = ± 80 (see Tempo Table IIa, 8)
11 à 2 Claviers	r.h.: 8' l.h.: 8"	12/16	♩. = ± 60 (see Tempo Table IXc, 4)
12 no prescription given	8' (16' ad lib.)	3/4	♩ = ± 80 (see Tempo Table IVb, 7)
13 à 2 Claviers	r.h.: 4" (1) l.h.: 8'	3/4	♩ = ± 40 (see Tempo Table IVd, 2)
14 à 2 Claviers	r.h.: 8", 4", C l.h.: 8', 8", 4"	3/4	♩ = ± 100 (see Tempo Table IVa, 20)

15 à 1 Clavier	8'	2/4	♩ = ± 40 (see Tempo Table IIIc, 1)
16 à 1 Clavier	8', 16', 8", 4", C	¢, 3/8	♩ = ± 60 (see Tempo Table IIe, 3)
	2nd part 8", 4"		♩. = ± 60 (see Tempo Table Va, 14)
17 à 2 Claviers	r.h.: 8", 4"	3/4	♩ = ± 100 (see Tempo Table IVa, 21)
	l.h.: 8' (16')		
18 à 1 Clavier	8', 16', 4", C	¢	𝅗𝅥 = ± 80 (see Tempo Table IIa, 9)
19 à 1 Clavier	8' or 4"	3/8	♩. = ± 60 (see Tempo Table Va, 15)
	r.h.: 8'		
20 à 2 Claviers	l.h.: 8"	3/4	♩ = ± 100 (see Tempo Table IVa, 22)
21 no prescription given	8', 16'	C	♩ = ± 60 (see Tempo Table Ib, 23)
22 à 1 Clavier	8', 16', 4", C	¢ Alla breve	𝅗𝅥 = ± 80 (see Tempo Table IIa, 10)
	r.h.: 8", 4"		
23 à 2 Claviers	l.h.: 8', 8", 4", C	3/4	♩ = ± 100 (see Tempo Table IVa, 23)
24 à 1 Clavier	8', 16', 8", 4", C	9/8	♩. = ± 80 (see Tempo Table VIIc, 3)
	r.h.: 8'		
25 à 2 Claviers	l.h.: 8"	3/4	♩ = ± 40 (see Tempo Table IVd, 3)
	r.h.: 8'		
26 à 2 Claviers	l.h.: 8", 4"	3/4 (18/16)	♩ = ± 60 (see Tempo Table IVc, 7)
	r.h.: 8"		
27 à 2 Claviers	l.h.: 8'	6/8	♩. = ± 60 (see Tempo Table VIa, 7)
	r.h.: 8"		
28 à 2 Claviers	l.h.: 8'	3/4	♩ = ± 80 (see Tempo Table IVb, 8)
29 à 1 overo 2 Claviers	8', 16', 8", 4", C	3/4	♩ = ± 80 (see Tempo Table IVb, 9)
30 à 1 Clavier	8', 16', 4", C	C	♩ = ± 80 (see Tempo Table Ia, 36)

It is very practical to change the parts of right and left hands from bars $20\frac{6}{16}$ to $26\frac{4}{16}$, as Busoni recommends. If one wants to escape nearly all technical hazards in this difficult variation, one may play the left hand throughout with the registration 4″ (l), but the "fun of the show" is lost this way.

Variation 11: This variation also can, for the same reason, be played with the part of the left hand 4″ (l) instead of 8″. Since bar 16 would, in this case, go beyond the range of this register, one must play from bar $16\frac{5}{16}$ to the end of the bar on 8′.

Variation 14: It is advisable to play the part of the left hand from bars $9\frac{7}{32}$ to $15\frac{1}{16}$ and from $25\frac{3}{32}$ to $31\frac{1}{16}$ on II 8″, 4″ to secure uniform sound volume.

Variation 20: In this variation also the trick of playing the left hand 4″ (l) instead of 8″ can be applied; in that case, one must play the first five eighths of bar 17, left hand, on 8′.

Variation 23: Our recommendation to play the part of the left hand one degree louder than that of the right gets its justification in bars 27–31, where Bach writes eighths for the left and sixteenths for the right hand.

Variation 24: Our suggestion to play this variation in "grand style" with "full work" (all performers whom I ever heard apply only 8′) gets its full justification by the octave motive and the rhythm ♩ ♫♫ , so typical for the expression of triumph in the works of Bach (see pp. 139 and 250 and compare this variation with the Prelude in D major, *W.K.* II, the Organ Prelude in C major [9/8], and the opening chorus of Cantata 65: "Sie werden aus Saba Alle kommen").

Variation 25: It will not be overromantic if we play its most intimate part, bars $25–28\frac{1}{4}$, in the right hand also on 8″.

Variation 26: Our registration, right hand 8′, left hand 8″, 4″, holds only for the beginning. The following changes are necessary:

	Right hand			Left hand	
Bar	1–8	8′	Bar	1–8	8″, 4″
	9–16	8″, 4″		9–16	8′
	$17–25\frac{1}{8}$	8′		17–32	8″, 4″
	$25\frac{4}{16}–32$	8″, 4″			

Ornamentation: In a few cases, we deviated from Kirkpatrick's solutions and have already discussed them; for the theme, see p. 178, and for Variation 13, in which all appoggiaturas are *Nachschläge*, see p. 179.

We reproduce here (Ex. A9) a Ground by Henry Purcell (from the Complete Edition of the Purcell Society, vol. VI, p. 33), to be compared with the first bars of Variations 2, 3, and 6. One will notice that the bass of this Ground is completely identical with the bass line of the first eight bars of the theme of the *Goldberg Variations*; more amazing is the obvious relation between the first two bars of Variation 2 and the soprano of Bach's theme. Also a relation between Variation 3 (Purcell) and Variation 4 (Bach), even between Variation 6 (Purcell) and Variation 20 (Bach) is not too far-fetched. Does this Ground represent a "germ" for Bach's masterpiece?

Ex. A9. Purcell, Ground

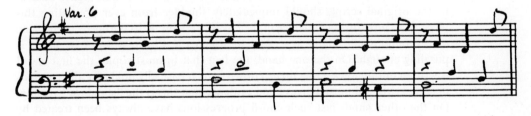

INDIVIDUAL PIECES

General Remarks

For the same reasons which caused us gradually to reduce the quantity of detailed information on interpretation the further our investigations advanced, the less we felt it necessary to include in our discussion every single piece which has come to us from Bach's hand. Without any qualms we decided not to discuss the toccatas at all, for it is precisely the most characteristic feature of all toccatas to allow the player all possible liberties. Toccatas are meant to be vehicles for the display of the player's virtuosity. To give, especially in regard to registration, one fixed prescription for their interpretation is an impossibility. Quite a few equally valid methods of registration could easily be found, and we do not want to deprive the Bach student of the pleasure of searching for them. The only parts of the toccatas where registration problems could arise would be their fugal sections.

Yet not a single problem arises anywhere which has not already been covered before: terrace dynamics are presented with such a clarity that mis-interpretation is impossible. We selected therefore for discussion here only a small group of pieces where we felt that either their unusual importance or other special reasons might make it desirable to go into details. This should not sound like discrimination against the pieces omitted. It may be noted that nearly all the toccatas were written in the earlier years of Bach's life; from the Leipzig period comes only the highly disciplined Toccata of the Sixth Partita. The mature Bach turned more and more away from the desire to shine and only because of a commission allowed it a smiling "comeback" in the fabulous *Goldberg Variations*.

The Chromatic Phantasy and Fugue

The Chromatic Phantasy and Fugue is not only Bach's most popular but also his most ill-fated and mistreated piece—ill-fated, since the autograph is lost and variants have come to us from more or less reliable copies. Hence a trustworthy reconstruction of Bach's original version is almost impossible. Mistreated, since the belief has almost unanimously been accepted that this piece lends itself more than all the other works of Bach to being played "as is" on the modern piano. For several generations, a standard piano recital almost always has started with it as the opening number. Unfortunately, if any piece does *not* lend itself to being played on the piano, it is just the Chromatic Phantasy. A thoughtful pianist who learns that the opening section should sound in at least two, better in three, octaves, and adds the lower and higher octaves to the original script, should immediately shudder from ever presenting this piece to an unknowing audience in the "as is" version. Also the correct rendering of the famous chromatic arpeggios to which the Phantasy owes its name is puzzling enough. On the one hand, the fact that in most copies the first chord is written out in notes going up *and* down (which basically holds for all arpeggios in early keyboard music) gives good evidence that this is the "standard" version. On the other hand, just such chord progressions have always been treated by players in an improvisatory way. The gigantic "cadenza" which is found in the great A minor Prelude (spiritual father of the first movement of the Triple Concerto in A minor) reveals how many auxiliary notes could be built in at "chord arpeggios." Yet the version given by Georg Mantel in his essay "Zur Ausführung der Arpeggien in J. S. Bachs 'Chromatischer Fantasie,' "[8] which owes much to this model, is only partially recommendable. We, too, like to improvise on these chords every time a little differently. Nothing testifies more to the liberties which contemporary players took in phantasies or toccatas than the well-known "second version" for the final bars of the Chromatic Phantasy, which is reprinted in nearly every edition of it.

We abstain from making prescriptions for tempo and registration of the Phantasy and want only to mention that the first section until bar 20 must certainly be played with all available registers of the harpsichord and that the Recitativo sounds excellent in 4", 16' (C). Some *piano* signs in this section, found in contemporary copies, do not sound too convincing to us, especially the one in the second bar of the piece which appears on the manuscript in Berlin, Staatsbibliothek No. 577, an otherwise rather reliable copy. In regard to notation, everybody should check to see that his edition reads b double flat and a flat in bar 50, 3rd and 4th eighths. Many editions print, erroneously, b flat and a.

For the Fugue we suggest the following registration:

	Right hand			Left hand	
Bar	$1-36\frac{1}{16}$	8", 4"	Bar	$9-36\frac{5}{16}$	8", 4"
	$36\frac{2}{16}$ (glide)–59	8'		$36\frac{6}{16}$ (glide)–$59\frac{1}{8}$	8'
	$60-83\frac{1}{8}$	8", 4"		$59\frac{2}{8}-83\frac{1}{4}$	8", 4"
	$83\frac{3}{16}-89$	8'		$83\frac{7}{16}-89$	8'
	90 (glide)–$97\frac{2}{4}$	8", 4"		$90-97\frac{1}{4}$	8", 4"
	$97\frac{2}{16}$ (glide)–106	8'		$97\frac{5}{16}-106\frac{1}{8}$	8'
	$107-126\frac{1}{8}$	8", 4"		$106\frac{2}{8}-126\frac{1}{16}$	8", 4"
	$126\frac{2}{8}$ (glide)–130	8'		$126\frac{2}{16}-130$	8'
	131 (glide)–$160\frac{1}{16}$	8", 4"		$131-160\frac{1}{16}$	8", 4"
		+C, +16'			
	$160\frac{2}{32}-161$	8', 16', 8", 4"		$160\frac{2}{32}-161$	8', 16', 8", 4"

The octaves written in bars $158-160\frac{1}{16}$ obviously compensate for the inability of the player to use the 16' and coupler earlier.

Tempo: $\downarrow = \pm 100$ (see Tempo Table IVa, 10)

Articulation: *Quasi legato*, the sixteenths in bar 8 and so on always *nonlegato*

Phantasy in C minor

This Phantasy is very popular with pianists because of its "Scarlattian" features. Originally a fugue belonged to it, of which only the beginning is preserved. The fragment shows that we should complain of the loss of an apparently very unusual and highly interesting piece.

---

[8] *Bach-Jahrbuch* (1929), pp. 142ff.

Registration:

	Right hand			*Left hand*	
Bar	1–8	8″, 4″	Bar	1–8	8″, 4″
	9 (part of the triplets)–$13\frac{5}{8}$	8′		9 (part of eighths)–24	8″, 4″
	$13\frac{6}{8}$–24	8″, 4″		25 (part of triplets)–26	8′
	25 (part of eighths)–26	8″, 4″		27 (part of eighths)–$28\frac{5}{8}$	8″, 4″
	27 (part of triplets)–$33\frac{1}{16}$	8′		$28\frac{7}{8}$–$33\frac{5}{8}$	8′
	$33\frac{2}{16}$–40	8″, 4″		$33\frac{20}{16}$–40	8″, 4″

We hope that our figures will make it clear that, for technical reasons, we change the parts for triplets and eighths in bar 27. The piece is so powerful that it can also be played "one terrace higher," alternating between 8′, 16′, 8″, 4″, and 8″, 4″. We do not advocate this too much, just because of the "Scarlattian elements."

Tempo: ♩ = ± 80 (see Tempo Table Ia, 33)

Articulation: *Quasi legato*; all falling seconds slurred, the other eighths *tenuto*

Phantasy and Fugue in A minor

The shortest Phantasy, only a series of arpeggiated chords, is linked here with Bach's longest Fugue. Although hardly an important Fugue, it is noticeable as the greatest document of youthful fire, not to say "storm and stress," from Bach's earlier years, a truly "Lisztian" piece. Of special interest is the undeniable fact that it is a preparatory piece for the great Organ Fugue in the same key. A second relation, that to the (also certainly later) Prelude of the Second English Suite, should, however, not be overlooked.

Registration: Phantasy: 8′, 16′, 8″, 4″. The chords are treated as in the Chromatic Phantasy, the first chord to be arpeggiated twice.

Fugue:

	Right hand			*Left hand*	
Bar	1–33	8″, 4″	Bar	7–33	8″, 4″
	34–53	8′		34–43	8′
	54–$59\frac{1}{16}$	8″, 4″		44–$49\frac{1}{16}$	8″, 4″
	$59\frac{2}{16}$–71	8′		$49\frac{2}{16}$–71	8′
	72 (glide)–$81\frac{1}{4}$	8″, 4″		72–$81\frac{1}{16}$	8″, 4″
	$81\frac{3}{4}$–92	8′		$81\frac{2}{16}$–101	8′
	93–121	8″, 4″		102–$121\frac{2}{4}$	8″, 4″
	122–137	8′		$121\frac{3}{4}$–155	8′
	138–$143\frac{1}{16}$	8″, 4″		156–198	8″, 4″
	$143\frac{2}{16}$–155	8′			
	156–198	8″, 4″			

A helper can prepare coupler and 16′ between bars 157–176 and "full work" could start at bar 177. Another possibility: draw 16′ with the left hand, bar 178 or 179, interrupt a moment at $191\frac{1}{16}$ for coupling, and play "full work" from there. Other, later possibilities for coupling could be found in bar 196 after the first sixteenth or at the end of the same bar.

Tempo: $\quad\downarrow = \pm\ 120$ (see Tempo Table IVe, 2). $\quad\downarrow = \pm\ 100$ would also be reasonable through likeness to the Prelude of the Second English Suite (see Tempo Table IVa, 6).

Phantasy and Fugue in A minor (Schmieder No. 904)

While the Chromatic Phantasy was definitely written in its first version at Cöthen, in its final one not later than 1730, this Phantasy shows all evidence of maturity and is, although it shuns any display of virtuosity, one of Bach's most majestic compositions. A serious question might even arise as to whether it is not meant for the organ. It asks from the harpsichord almost more than this instrument can give.

Phantasy
Registration:

	Right hand			Left hand	
Bar	$1–12\frac{1}{4}$	8′, 16′, 8″, 4″	Bar	1–12	8′, 16′, 8″, 4″
	12 (glide)–$31\frac{1}{4}$	8″, 4″		13–30	8″, 4″
	31 (glide)–$42\frac{1}{4}$	8′, 16′, 8″, 4″		$31–42\frac{1}{2}$	8′, 16′, 8″, 4″
	42 (glide)–$69\frac{1}{4}$	8″, 4″		$42\frac{5}{8}–68$	8″, 4″
	69 (glide)–$80\frac{1}{4}$	8′, 16′, 8″, 4″		$69–80\frac{1}{2}$	8′, 16′, 8″, 4″
	80 (glide)–99	8″, 4″		$80\frac{3}{4}–99$	8″, 4″
	100–111	8′, 16′, 8″, 4″		100–111	8′, 16′, 8″, 4″

Tempo: $\downarrow = \pm\ 80$ (see Tempo Table IIa, 11)
Articulation: *Molto legato*

Fugue
Registration:

	Right hand			Left hand	
Bar	$1–18\frac{5}{8}$	8″, 4″	Bar	$5–18\frac{9}{16}$	8″, 4″
	$18\frac{5}{8}–25\frac{9}{16}$	8′		$18\frac{10}{16}–22\frac{3}{4}$	8′
	$25\frac{5}{8}$ (glide)–$29\frac{1}{8}$	8″, 4″		$22\frac{5}{8}–29\frac{1}{8}$	8″, 4″
	$29\frac{2}{8}–33\frac{1}{16}$	8′		$29\frac{2}{16}$ (glide)–32	8′
	33 (glide)–$36\frac{3}{4}$	8″, 4″		$33–36\frac{5}{8}$	8″, 4″
			$+16', +C$		
	$37\frac{2}{4}–56\frac{13}{16}$	8″, 4″ (1)		$36\frac{4}{4}–54\frac{3}{4}$	8″, 4″ (1)
	$56\frac{4}{4}$ (glide)–$59\frac{1}{16}$	8′, 16′, 8″, 4″ loco		$54\frac{4}{4}–59\frac{3}{16}$	8′, 16′, 8″, 4″ loco
	$59\frac{2}{16}–62\frac{1}{4}$	8″, 4″		$59\frac{4}{16}–60$	8″, 4″
	$62\frac{2}{4}–71\frac{4}{4}$	8′, 16′, 8″, 4″		$61–71\frac{5}{8}$	8′, 16′, 8″, 4″
	$71\frac{3}{4}$ (glide)–$74\frac{8}{16}$	8″, 4″		$71\frac{3}{4}$ (glide)–$74\frac{2}{4}$	8″, 4″
	$74\frac{9}{16}–80$	8′, 16′, 8″, 4″		$74\frac{3}{4}–80$	8′, 16′, 8″, 4″

Tempo: $\downarrow = \pm\ 80$ (see Table Ia, 34)
Articulation: *Molto legato*; the two sixteenths on the first quarter of bar 39 and all corresponding places *nonlegato*, almost *staccato*

Prelude and Fugue in A minor (Schmieder No. 894)

This gigantic piece, which Bach later transformed into the first and last movement of the Triple Concerto in A minor, is now unduly neglected. It is true that its dimensions are tremendous and that playing it gives more joy to the player than to the listener, since two "color terraces" are not sufficient to maintain the continued interest of the ear. This was undoubtedly the reason which caused Bach to give it in the later version—which is far more than an arrangement—the additional colors of flute, violin, and string orchestra. Yet the full grandeur of the Triple Concerto can only be understood by a thorough study of the parental piece, and the tremendous challenge to finger dexterity makes its study extremely worthwhile.

Prelude

Registration:

Right hand		Left hand	
Bar $1-18\frac{1}{8}$	8″, 4″	Bar $1-18\frac{1}{4}$	8″, 4″
$18\frac{2}{8}-27\frac{1}{8}$	8′	$18\frac{5}{8}-27\frac{3}{8}$	8′
$27\frac{2}{8}-40\frac{1}{8}$	8″, 4″	$27\frac{6}{8}-40\frac{1}{8}$	8″, 4″
$40\frac{6}{8}-41\frac{1}{8}$	8′	$40\frac{2}{8}-41\frac{1}{8}$	8′
$41\frac{2}{8}-41\frac{5}{8}$	8″, 4″	$41\frac{2}{8}-41\frac{5}{8}$	8″, 4″
$41\frac{6}{8}-44\frac{5}{8}$	8′	$41\frac{6}{8}-45\frac{1}{8}$	8′
$44\frac{6}{8}-46\frac{1}{4}$	8″, 4″	$45\frac{2}{8}-46\frac{1}{4}$	8″, 4″
$46\frac{4}{8}-48\frac{5}{8}$	8′	$46\frac{2}{8}-48\frac{5}{8}$	8′
$48\frac{6}{8}-49\frac{5}{8}$	8″, 4″	$48\frac{2}{8}-49\frac{5}{8}$	8″, 4″
$49\frac{6}{8}-50\frac{5}{8}$	8′	$49\frac{6}{0}-50\frac{5}{8}$	8′
$50\frac{6}{8}-55\frac{1}{8}$	8″, 4″	$50\frac{6}{8}-55\frac{1}{8}$	8″, 4″
$55\frac{2}{8}-56\frac{1}{8}$	8′	$55\frac{6}{8}-56\frac{1}{8}$	8′
$56\frac{2}{8}-58\frac{1}{8}$	8″, 4″	$56\frac{2}{8}-58\frac{1}{8}$	8″, 4″
$58\frac{2}{8}-59\frac{1}{8}$	8′	$58\frac{6}{8}-59\frac{1}{8}$	8′
$59\frac{2}{8}-62$	8″, 4″	$59\frac{2}{8}-63\frac{1}{4}$	8″, 4″
$63\frac{2}{8}-66\frac{5}{8}$	8′	$63\frac{5}{8}-64\frac{8}{8}$	8′
$66\frac{6}{8}-77$	8″, 4″	$65-77$	8″, 4″
bars 78–83 both hands, first half 8′, second half 8″, 4″			
$84-85$	8″, 4″	$84-86\frac{1}{4}$	8″, 4″
	+C, +16′		
$86\frac{1}{8}-98$	8′, 16′, 8″, 4″	$86\frac{6}{8}-98$	8′, 16′, 8″, 4″

Tempo: ♩ = ± 80 (see Tempo Table Ia, 37)

Articulation: The sixteenths and thirty-seconds *quasi legato*, the eighths *portato*

Fugue

Registration:

Right hand		Left hand	
Bar $5-55\frac{3}{16}$	8′	Bar $1-53\frac{3}{16}$	8′
$55\frac{4}{16}-76\frac{2}{16}$	8″, 4″	$54-73\frac{8}{16}$	8″, 4″
$76\frac{4}{16}-117$	8′	$74-118\frac{11}{16}$	8′
$118-152\frac{5}{16}$	8″, 4″	$119-152\frac{7}{16}$	8″, 4″
	+C, +16′		
$152\frac{9}{16}-153$	8′, 16′, 8″, 4″	$152\frac{12}{16}-153$	8′, 16′, 8″, 4″

Tempo: $\quad$. $= \pm 60$ (see Tempo Table IXc, 5)
Articulation: *Quasi legato* for all triplets, eighths *portato*

Prelude in G major (*Schmieder No. 902*)

This heavenly piece was originally the Prelude to a Fughetta in G major, first version of the Fugue in G major now found in *W.K.* II. Here we meet with the rare case of a piece too good, too great to be linked with a "light-weight" fugue. It has remained virtually unknown, although Bischoff reprinted it in the appendix to his edition of *W.K.* II. It is strange to find here Bach overconscientious and dismissing a piece of rarest beauty (although its final substitute, the Prelude in *W.K.* II, is also a magnificent piece) while in the case of the Prelude and Fugue in E flat major, *W.K.* I, he remained indifferent to the apparent lack of balance between Prelude and Fugue.
Instrument: Clavichord
Tempo: $\quad = \pm 60$
Articulation: *Molto legato* except where larger skips occur

Adagio in G major (*Schmieder No. 968*)

Although this piece is only a transcription of the first movement of the Sonata in C major for Unaccompanied Violin, it should be studied by every Bach lover on account of its tremendous importance for the understanding of transcription problems. It shows that Bach's artistic vision of the harmonic background of an unaccompanied line is so bold and wide that no arranger could ever compete with it. It throws an interesting sidelight upon Busoni's daring arrangement of the Chaconne for Solo Violin for piano, which has so severely been criticized by "purists." It would be hard to deny that Bach goes much farther in "amplification" of the original piece than Busoni ever did. Bischoff finds the keyboard arrangement "unquestionably much more poetic than the original version." Keller says that this "meditation" dims the untouched purity of the violin prelude.[9] We are inclined to agree more with Bischoff and also cannot suppress the confession that instead of condemning Busoni's arrangement of the Chaconne, we admire the tactfulness and discretion with which this masterful transcription has been done. That our admiration for other transcriptions stops for the vast majority of the literature involved does not need, we hope, to be emphasized.
Instrument: Clavichord
Tempo: $\quad = \pm 80$

Capriccio in B flat major, sopra la lontananza del suo fratello diletissimo

This charming piece hardly needs a thorough discussion. The most interesting fact about it is to see Bach making fun of Johann Kuhnaus' serious

---

[9] *Bachs Klavierwerke*, p. 107.

approach to program music, since this Capriccio is clearly a parody on Kuhnaus' Biblical Sonatas. Otherwise it is still a very sketchy, immature piece, and it is really touching to see how Bach was, around 1704, still far away from being able to organize a fugue. Busoni's "rewriting" of the final fugue in his celebrated edition of the work, which has become a favorite among pianists, is a master demonstration of "how to correct a pupil's fugue."

No details for registration need to be given. For tempo we suggest:

No. 1 $\rfloor = \pm 40$ (see Table Ic, 5)

No. 2 $\rfloor = \pm 60$ (see Table Ib, 27)

No. 3 $\rfloor = \pm 60$ (no piece for comparison)

No. 4 $\rfloor = \pm 60$ (see Table Ib, 28)

No. 5 $\rfloor = \pm 80$ (no piece for comparison)

No. 6 $\rfloor = \pm 100$ (see Table Id, 16)

All ornaments in No. 2 should be played. They caricature the "dangerous journey" of the brother.

Ricercare in C minor (three parts) from the Musical Offering

This fugue cannot be omitted in our discussion, as it is, together with the B flat minor Fugue from *W.K.* II, the most important keyboard piece of the later years of Bach's life. Its very improvisatory character has certainly not been caused by limitations of the theme in regard to contrapuntal exploitation. The entire *Musical Offering* proves the contrary. We see in it a conscientious re-creation of that fugue which Bach improvised for Frederick II at his visit to Potsdam in 1747, an opinion also held by Spitta and by Hans T. David.[10] Although the reports on details of Bach's visit are not clear enough to draw definite conclusions, it seems highly probable that Bach improvised before Frederick on the historic night of May 7, 1747, not on a harpsichord, but on a "forte and piano." One could go so far (and David does not exclude this possibility[11]) to see in this loosely knitted fugue Bach's only keyboard composition which might be "meant" for the hammerklavier. Its style is, however, nowhere different from that of other harpsichord compositions. Since the harpsichord is, at least for Bach, certainly the instrument on which the thorough-bass part of the Trio Sonata was supposed to be played, it would be rather odd to add a piano to the instruments to be used for a complete performance of the *Musical Offering*. To give this fugue the full grandeur which it deserves, a helper for registration seems to be indispensable.

---

[10] Spitta, *Johann Sebastian Bach*, vol. II, p. 672; David, *J. S. Bach's Musical Offering* (New York, 1945), p. 110.

[11] *J. S. Bach's Musical Offering*, p. 45.

Registration:

	Right hand			*Left hand*	
Bar	1–31$\frac{1}{4}$	8′	Bar	10–31$\frac{1}{8}$	8′
	31$\frac{2}{4}$–38$\frac{1}{4}$	8″		31$\frac{2}{8}$–37	8″
	38$\frac{2}{4}$–46$\frac{1}{8}$	8′		38–45	8′
	46$\frac{2}{8}$–55$\frac{1}{4}$	8″, 4″		46–55$\frac{1}{4}$	8″, 4″
	55$\frac{2}{8}$ (glide)–71$\frac{5}{8}$	8′		55$\frac{2}{4}$–72$\frac{1}{8}$	8′
	71$\frac{6}{8}$–95$\frac{1}{8}$	8″, 4″		72$\frac{2}{8}$ (glide)–94	8″, 4″
	95$\frac{2}{8}$–122$\frac{3}{4}$	8′, 16′, 8″, 4″		95–122$\frac{3}{4}$	8′, 16′, 8″, 4″
	–16′				
	122$\frac{4}{4}$–140	8′, 8″, 4″		122$\frac{4}{4}$–142$\frac{1}{8}$	8′, 8″, 4″
	141–161$\frac{1}{4}$	8″, 4″ (1)		142$\frac{2}{8}$–147$\frac{1}{4}$	8″, 4″ (1)
				+16′	
	161$\frac{2}{4}$–168	8″, 4″ loco		147$\frac{4}{4}$–161$\frac{1}{8}$ (cont.)	8″, 4″ (1)
	169 (glide)–185	8′, 16′, 8″, 4″		161$\frac{2}{8}$–168	8″, 4″ loco
				169–185	8′, 16′, 8″, 4″

The only moment where the helper is absolutely necessary in the registration just recommended is between bars 142–168, where coupling of the keyboards has to be done while both hands are on the upper keyboard. We also assigned to the helper the addition of the 4″ register between bars 39–45, but even the player himself could do this by playing in bar 38 the last five notes of the upper part with the left hand and drawing the 4″ at this time with the right. Since we reckon with a helper, he may, of course, also spare the player the necessity of removing the 16′ in bar 122 during a two-quarter rest for the right hand (the last d′ can be played with the left hand, as can the first two eighths of the following bar), and, equally well, he may spare the player the task of adding the 16′ with the left hand during the rests in bar 147.

Tempo: ♩ = ± 80. Although the improvisatory character of the Fugue allows some freedom in regard to speed modification, we would not dare to go so far as Keller does, who recommends for the "Fantasia within the Fugue" (bars 109–141) a speed "almost twice as slow (*andante*), gradually resuming Tempo I."

Ricercare in Six Parts from the Musical Offering *and the* Art of the Fugue

The problems surrounding these last works are known to every Bach student. What did Bach have in mind when he had them printed in open score with a special staff for every voice? Did he want them to be considered as theoretical works demonstrating in practical examples what he could do with a single theme? Did he consider them as live music in which he left the choice of the instruments to the discretion of the players as did so many masters of the seventeenth century? ("Da sonare con ogni sorte di stromenti, da tasti ed altri" [For all sorts of instruments, keyboard or other ones], Frescobaldi prescribes for his *Fiori musicale*, also printed in open score; we know that Bach owned this work.) Or were all these pieces meant for a keyboard instrument, preferably the harpsichord, since their range goes beyond that of the organs of

Bach's time? For this latter possibility there seemed to be "proof material" available: the Six-Part Ricercare as well as the last, unfinished fugue from the *Art of the Fugue* have come to us not only in "open-score" print but also in autographic form written on two staves like normal keyboard music.

It was Wolfgang Graeser's arrangement of the *Art of the Fugue* for large orchestra, first performed in 1927 by Karl Straube in the Church of St. Thomas in Leipzig, which started renewed interest in the work, neglected for more than a century and a half. But even before this performance took place, the first article protesting its designation for orchestra was published in the *Bach-Jahrbuch* for 1926, the same periodical in which Graeser had outlined his arrangement of the work in the issue of 1924. In 1926 Professor Heinrich Rietsch[12] strongly repudiated Graeser's pretension that he had restored the original form and emphasized the fact that nowhere in the entire *Art of the Fugue* can a bar be found which is not playable on a keyboard instrument, especially on a harpsichord with pedal installation (the "mirror" fugues, of course, are played on two harpsichords). The years after 1927 saw the publication and performances of numerous other orchestrations, either for strings alone or for smaller or larger orchestra groups. On the other side, Tovey, Husmann, Leonhardt (for titles see Bibliography), and quite a few others came out with pleas for the keyboard version.

Although space is lacking for a detailed discussion of the pros and cons in the arguments of both parties, we think that the method we used for distinguishing between harpsichord and clavichord pieces gives the clue for the solution of this problem.

Not for one moment can there be any doubt that in the *Art of the Fugue* as well as in the Six-Part Ricercare of the *Musical Offering*, the notes which Bach used for his contrapuntal patterns were selected with the consideration that ten fingers (here and there supported by a pedal) would be able to bring them to life on a keyboard instrument. For example, bars 79 and 80 of the Ricercare, in which three voices are united in the second and first octave and the three others in the great and small octave, would never have been written in such a way had Bach not reckoned with a keyboard realization. The same holds for innumerable other situations, and Rietsch asks correctly how one could seriously believe that Bach would have written all these fugues in such a way that they could be played on a keyboard without his having had this keyboard in mind.[13] That Bach is not very consistent in regard to what he calls "playable" is true, especially in his attitude toward wide stretches. The examples which Leonhardt assembles[14] to show that Bach changed note values for the purpose of avoiding big stretches in the *Art of the Fugue* are by and large no more difficult than other places where Bach is less magnanimous (compare, for example, the events in the F minor Fugue, *W.K.* I: in bar 13, third beat, left hand, Bach gives the tenor the length of a sixteenth to go downward to E; in

[12] "Zur 'Kunst der Fuge' von J. S. Bach," *Bach-Jahrbuch* (1926), p. 1.
[13] "Zur 'Kunst der Fuge,'" p. 9.
[14] *The Art of the Fugue*, p. 14.

bar 14, third beat, left hand, the c′ of the alto has the length of an eighth making complete legato impossible for nearly everybody). But all this is beside the point.

There is only one serious mistake committed by those who attribute the *Art of the Fugue* and the Six-Part Ricercare to the harpsichord: the emphasis which they all put upon the word "meant" or "written for harpsichord," as most drastically demonstrated in Leonhardt's title, *The Art of the Fugue, Bach's Last Harpsichord Work: An Argument* (The Hague, 1952). These works *can* and *should be played* on the harpsichord, but they are not *written* for this instrument, since they are not written in such a style as to make a harpsichord sound well. Everyone who undertakes to play on the harpsichord first the Six-Part Ricercare and then, say, the Fugues in B flat minor and B major, *W.K.* II—pieces which are still "meant" for the harpsichord although they are already close to the borderline of what can be asked from this instrument—will even there find a world of difference in sound. Leonhardt's statement[15] "The Ricercare was *conceived* [my italics] for a keyboard instrument (the low B flat as well as the un-pedal-like bass voice excludes organ and, as a matter of fact, *every instrument except harpsichord and clavichord*) [italics by Leonhardt]; besides *it can be played without alteration on 1 keyboard with 2 hands* [my italics]" is untenable. We do not think that Leonhardt wanted to include the clavichord among the keyboard instruments for which this piece was "conceived." But to think that this Ricercare, one of the most majestic pieces of the literature, can and should be played on *one* keyboard is an offense to its grandeur. Even if one plays it with alternation of 8″ + 4″, and 8′ on two keyboards—which is technically possible—nothing is gained. The voice leading will never come out clearly, and no registration can help to produce a better oral enjoyment, aside from the fact that definite conclusions where the changes of tone color could be made are nearly impossible.

The truth is that playing the Ricercare on the harpsichord gives just a "report" on it, nothing more. The beauty of the piece or the craftsmanship built into it can be revealed only to the *eye*, not to the *ear* of the player, never to a listener.

Everything said about the Ricercare holds also for the entire *Art of the Fugue*. These greatest fugues of the music literature were not "conceived" as "pieces for harpsichord." Bach's real harpsichord pieces are, as we have shown in Chapter 2, constructed in a totally different manner, distinguishable from organ music as well as from those pieces which were "conceived" for the clavichord.

These last pieces of Bach's creative genius are the loftiest music ever written, a real music of the spheres. They are still much more remote from earthly sound than, for example, Beethoven's Great Fugue, Op. 133, which in actual sound leaves the medium of the string quartet far behind. Yet, in order to make this music accessible to those who are not blessed with the capability of *reading* it, Bach was magnanimous enough to curb his phantasy in such a way that ten human fingers could accompany him on this flight into the unheard.

---

[15] *The Art of the Fugue*, p. 9.

In such a spirit, understanding musicians should play this work on any keyboard, even on the modern piano, in their study, but heaven forbid that it be publicly performed as a "work *for* harpsichord." Although Heinrich Husmann still calls the *Art of the Fugue* a "Klavierwerk" which in its mixture of "manualiter" and "pedaliter" pieces easily is in line with the other keyboard pieces of Bach, he is fully right when he says that it belongs in the study of the understanding music lover or should be on the "*Pult des in sich gewandten Organisten*" (on the desk of an introspective organ player).[16]

Keller comes to the same conclusion; acknowledging that it can be played on a keyboard in a kind of "*Klavierauszug*" (piano-score) he warns against the wrong conclusion that it is a keyboard word.[17] The finest formulation of the meaning of the *Art of the Fugue* has been put down by Paul Hindemith:

If we are not experienced enough to have emotional images and intellectual coconstructions conjured up by the mere act of reading music, we may resort to an audible reproduction of the piece; but there is only one form of performance that is in the spirit of the work: to play it with the soloistic instruments at hand, essentially as an act of edification for the participants, and with no more than a handful of understanding listeners present, if any at all—never in large halls and never for an emotion-seeking audience. Don't say that this mode of performance would deprive many listeners of the enjoyment of hearing this composition. Why should every one have everything? Even with the most liberal and most democratic distribution of goods there will be many things that the average citizen will hardly ever have in sufficient quantities, such as diamonds, caviar, and Stradivarius violins. Should we not be glad to have certain pieces of music similarly kept away from the ordinary musical goings-on, if for no other reason than to give the ambitious seeker of higher musical truths an opportunity to grow? Since Bach did not grant us any access to his piece, we can merely try to understand it our own way, always knowing that we are only guessing and assuming: but we should not permit any arranger, even one with the best technique and the most honest intentions, to make any decisions for us. Consequence: the arranger is always wrong and particularly so in respect to the *Art of Fugue*.[18]

It is wonderful to see how Hindemith deals with one of the holiest problems of music in very down-to-earth language. Although we wholeheartedly agree with him in giving the *Art of the Fugue* a special place on the shelf of *musica reservata*, we feel a little more merciful with the arrangers and are less opposed to performing the work—although only here and there and most rarely—in a decent arrangement, especially through the medium of a small string orchestra which, at least, does not give it too much of additional romantic tone color. The result of such a performance will, it is true, not be much better than that so charmingly described by Moser: "Who lets himself becoming flooded [*berieselt*] with one hour and a half of D minor, sometimes slower, sometimes faster, and then pretends to have received unforgettable final insights and impressions, is certainly humbugging himself."[19] Yet it will not do any harm,

---

[16] "Die Kunst der Fuge als Klavierwerk," p. 61.
[17] *Bachs Klavierwerke*, p. 252.
[18] *A Composer's World* (Cambridge, Mass., 1952), pp. 141–142.
[19] *Bach*, p. 222.

and why should not the uninitiated music lover occasionally have the privilege
of hearing the holiest of the holy of our musical treasures? Do not also many
faiths on sacred days present to the believers holy relics of legendary times?
In such a spirit one should listen to a presentation of this unique work and, for
such occasions, we would even not condemn too heavily the idea of ending such
a performance with the playing of the hymn "Before Thy Throne, I am
appearing," which the editors of the first edition added to the work in order to
compensate the buyers for the disappointment of the unfinished last fugue. The
shock experienced when the music breaks off at the moment when it is just
starting to climb to hitherto unheard heights, is unbearable. Does it not seem
as if Fate itself gave, with the addition of the hymn, a hint for a satisfactory
end to a performance of Bach's *opus ultimum*? One should not consider playing
it as an attempt to introduce into the concert hall a sentimental scene, "Bach
on the Deathbed." The *Art of the Fugue* is Bach's testament to mankind. We
know now, thanks to Smend's research (see pp. 256–257) that this hymn twice
contains his name, following his system of applying number symbols. It seems
fully appropriate that Bach's testament, even unfinished, should get his
signature, his seal, at the very end.

APPENDIX B

LIST OF TABLES

ABBREVIATIONS

Used on Music Tables

L = Landshoff
Cz = Czerny
Ke = Keller
Bi = Bischoff
Ki = Kirkpatrick

Prel. = Prelude
Hps. = Harpsichord
Mvt. = Movement
Sug. = Suggested speed

Tempo Table Ia: Works in C Time; suggested speed: ♩ = ± 80

1. Invention 1: ♩ = 84L, 120Cz, 63Ke, 96Bi

2. Invention 2: ♩ = 63L, 108Cz, 52Ke, 69Bi

3. Invention 5: ♩ = 69L, 108Cz, 72Ke, 72Bi

4. Invention 11: ♩ = 69L, 108Cz, 58Ke, 80Bi

5. Invention 13: ♩ = 80L, 104Cz, 69Ke, 116Bi

6. Invention 15: ♩ = 84L, 104Cz, 92Ke, 96Bi

7. Sinfonia 1: ♩ = 80L, 96Cz, 69Ke, 96Bi

8. Sinfonia 3: ♩ = 76L, 92Cz, 76Ke, 76Bi

*9. Sinfonia 8: ♩ = 76L, 92Cz, 80Bi

10. Sinfonia 12: ♩ = 80L, 112Cz, 84Ke, 104Bi

11. *W.K.* I, Prel. 1: ♩ = 112Cz, 72Ke, 112Bi

12. *W.K.* I, Fugue 2: ♩ = 80Cz, 60Ke, 80Bi

13. *W.K.* I, Fugue 3: ♩ = 104Cz, 92Ke, 100Bi

14. *W.K.* I, Prel. 7: ♩ = 80Cz, 80Ke, 69Bi

15. *W.K.* I, Fugue 7: ♩ = 112Cz, 92Ke, 104Bi

16. *W.K.* I, Fugue 8: ♩ = 76Cz, 66Ke, 72Bi

*No speed given by Keller.

17. *W.K.* I, Fugue 13: ♩ = 88Cz, 63Ke, 76Bi

18. *W.K.* I, Prel. 14: ♩ = 100Cz, 80Ke, 108Bi

19. *W.K.* I, Fugue 16: ♩ = 80Cz, 56Ke, 60Bi

20. *W.K.* I, Prel. 19: ♩ = 80Cz, 66Ke, 84Bi

21. *W.K.* I, Fugue 20: ♩ = 72Cz, 66Ke, 66Bi

22. *W.K.* I, Prel. 21: ♩ = 84Cz, 66Ke, 76Bi

23. *W.K.* I, Prel. 23: ♩ = 76Cz, 58Ke, 80Bi

24. *W.K.* I, Prel. 24: ♩ = 80Cz, 56Ke, 69Bi

25. *W.K.* II, Prel. 2: ♩ = 132Cz, 84Ke, 120Bi

26. *W.K* II, Prel. 3: ♩ = 80Cz, 76Ke, 76Bi

27. *W.K.* II, Fugue 6: ♩ = 80Cz, 80Ke, 72Bi

28. *W.K.* II, Prel. 8: ♩ = 92Cz, 76Ke, 80Bi

29. *W.K.* II, Fugue 14: ♩ = 108Cz, 88Ke, 72Bi

30. W.K. II, Prel. 18: ♩ = 100Cz, 80Ke, 80Bi

31. *W.K.* II, Fugue 19: ♩ = 96Cz, 80Ke, 88Bi

*32. *W.K.* II, Fugue 20: ♩ = 66Cz, 60Bi

*No speed given by Keller.

33. Phantasy in C minor: ♪ = 126Ke, 66Bi

34. Fugue in A minor: ♩ = 80Ke, 84Bi

35. Goldberg Var. 9: ♩ = 80Cz, 84Bi, 58Ki

36. Goldberg Var. 30: ♩ = 88Cz, 96Bi, 80Ki

37. Prelude in A minor: ♩ = 76Bi

38. Toccata in E minor, pt. 2: ♩ = 76Bi

39. Concerto for 2 Hps. in C major, mvt. 3: ♩ = 96Ke

40. 12 Little Preludes, No. 1: ♩ = 96Bi, 63Ke

41. The same, No. 2: ♩ = 126Bi, 92Ke

42. The same, No. 4: ♩ = 88Bi, 66Ke

43. The same, No. 9: ♩ = 84Bi, 66Ke

44. 6 Little Preludes, No. 1: ♩ = 92Bi, ♩ = 132Ke

45. The same, No. 5: ♩ = 96Bi, 84Ke

Tempo Table Ib: Works in C Time; suggested speed: ♩ = ± 60

1. Invention 7: ♩ = 60L, 112Cz, 72Ke, 69Bi

2. Invention 14: ♩ = 69L, 88Cz, ♪ = 88Ke, ♩ = 69Bi

3. Sinfonia 4: ♩ = 66L, 84Cz, 54Ke, 56Bi

4. Sinfonia 14: ♩ = 58L, 66Cz, 54Ke, 76Bi

5. *W.K.* I, Fugue 1: ♪ = 116Cz, 108Ke, ♩ = 63Bi

6. *W.K.* I, Fugue 5: ♩ = 76Cz, 66Ke, 80Bi

7. *W.K.* I, Prel. 6: ♩ = 80Cz, ♪ = 104Ke, ♩ = 76Bi

8. *W.K.* I, Prel. 10: ♩ = 84Cz, 63Ke, 69Bi

9. *W.K.* I, Prel. 12: ♪ = 104Cz, ♩ = 48Ke, 56Bi

10. *W.K.* I, Fugue 12: ♩ = 63Cz, 58Ke, 66Bi

11. *W.K.* I, Prel. 16: ♩ = 69Cz, 44Ke, 56Bi

12. *W.K.* I, Fugue 17: ♩ = 60Cz, 42Ke, 60Bi

13. *W.K.* I, Fugue 18: ♪ = 108Cz, ♩ = 60Ke, 56Bi

14. *W.K.* I, Fugue 23: ♪ = 126Cz, ♩ = 58Ke, 60Bi

15. *W.K.* II, Prel. 1: ♪ = 108Cz, ♩ = 58Ke, 54Bi

16. *W.K.* II, Fugue 2: ♩ = 69Cz, 62Ke, 56Bi

17. *W.K.* II, Fugue 3: ♩ = 76Cz, 63Ke, 60Bi

18. *W.K.* II, Fugue 8: ♩ = 56Cz, 63Ke, 60Bi

19. *W.K.* II, Fugue 17: ♩ = 69Cz, 58Ke, 58Bi

20. *W.K.* II, Prel. 20: ♪ = 92Cz, 66Ke, ♩ = 60Bi

21. Partita I, Prel.: ♩ = 52Ke, 66Bi

22. Partita II, Sinfonia, pt. 2: ♪ = 80Ke, 108Bi

Andante

23. Goldberg Var. 21: ♩ = 66Cz, 56Bi, 56Ki

24. Toccata in D major, mid. part: ♩ = 60Bi

25. Toccata in G major: ♩ = 58Bi

Adagio

26. Toccata in C minor: ♩ = 56Bi

Adagio

27. Departure Capriccio, pt. 2: ♩ = 56Bi

28. The same, pt. 4: ♩ = 63Bi

29. 12 Little Preludes, No. 6: ♩ = 63Bi, 60Ke

Tempo Table Ic: Works in C Time; suggested speed: ♩ = ± 40

1. Sinfonia 9: ♩ = 48L, 69Cz, 46Ke, 50Bi

2. *W.K.* I, Prel. 22: ♪ = 92Cz, 56Ke, 92Bi

3. *W.K.* I, Fugue 24: ♪ = 92Cz, ♩ = 42Ke, 52Bi

4. *W.K.* II, Prel. 16: ♪ = 80Cz, 76Ke, ♩ = 48Bi

5. Departure Capriccio, pt. 1: ♪ = 96Bi

6. Toccata in D minor, pt. 3: ♪ = 80Bi

7. Partita II, Sinfonia: ♪ = 66Ke, 88Bi

8. Hps. Concerto in F minor, mvt. 2

Tempo Table Id: Works in C Time; suggested speed: ♩ = ± 100

1. *W.K.* I, Fugue 9: ♩ = 108Cz, 76Ke, 116Bi

2. *W.K.* II, Prel. 23: ♩ = 116Cz, 100Ke, 112Bi

3. English Suite IV, Prel.: ♩ = 96Ke, 108Bi

4. Toccata in C minor, Fugue: ♩ = 88Bi

5. Toccata in D major, pt. 2: ♩ = 96Bi

6. Toccata in G major, pt. 1: ♩ = 116Bi

7. Toccata in E minor, Fugue: ♩ = 108Bi

8. Toccata in F♯ minor, pt. 3: ♩ = 100Bi

9. Toccata in G minor, pt. 3: ♩ = 100Bi

10. Hps. Concerto in D minor, mvt. 1: ♩ = 92Ke, 88Bi

11. Hps. Concerto in E major, mvt. 1: ♩ = 92Ke

12. Hps. Concerto in A major, mvt. 1: ♩ = 100Ke

13. Concerto for 2 Hps. in C minor, mvt. 1: ♩ = 80Ke

14. Concerto for 2 Hps. in C major, mvt. 1: ♩ = 84Ke

15. Concerto for 3 Hps. in C major, mvt. 1: ♩ = 80Ke

16. Departure Capriccio, Fugue: ♩ = 100Bi

17. 12 Little Preludes, No. 8: ♩ = 116Bi, 88Ke

18. French Suite IV, Air: ♩ = 104Bi, 60Ke

For comparison

19. Brandenburg Concerto 1, mvt. 1

20. Brandenburg Concerto 2, mvt. 1

21. Brandenburg Concerto 3, mvt. 1

22. Brandenburg Concerto 5, mvt. 1

23. Brandenburg Concerto 6, mvt. 1

24. Violin Concerto in E major, mvt. 1

25. Concerto for 2 Violins in D minor, mvt. 1

26. Italian Concerto, mvt. 1

(C in version for two harpsichords)

27. Violin Concerto in A minor, mvt. 1

Tempo Table Ie: Works in C Time; suggested speed: ♩ = 120

1. *W.K.* I, Prel. 2: ♩ = 144Cz, 92Ke, 108Bi

2. *W.K.* I, Prel. 5: ♩ = 132Cz, 116Ke, 132Bi

3. *W.K.* I, Prel. 10, pt. 2: ♩ = 80Cz, ♩ = 126Ke, 120Bi

4. Toccata in G minor, Fugue: ♩ = 116Bi

Presto

5. Toccata in D minor, pt. 2: ♩ = 96Bi

Presto

Tempo Table IIa: Works in ℂ Time; suggested speed: ♩ = ± 80

1. *W.K.* I, Fugue 4: ♩ = 112Cz, ♩ = 58–63Ke,   2. *W.K.* II, Fugue 7: ♩ = 132Cz, ♩ = 80Ke, 63Bi
   ♩ = 100Bi

3. *W.K.* II, Fugue 9: ♩ = 60Cz, 52Ke, 60Bi   4. *W.K.* II, Fugue 10: ♩ = 80Cz, 72Ke,
                                                     ♩ = 132Bi

5. *W.K.* II, Fugue 13: ♩ = 58Cz, 80Ke, 69Bi   6. *W.K.* II, Fugue 23: ♩ = 60Cz, 52Ke, 63Bi

7. *W.K.* II, Prel. 24: ♩ = 80Cz, 60Ke, 66Bi   8. Goldberg Var. 10: ♩ = 84Cz, 76Bi, 80Ki

9. Goldberg Var. 18: ♩ = 92Cz, 80Bi, 66Ki   10. Goldberg Var. 22: ♩ = 96Cz, 92Bi, 76Ki

11. Phantasy in A minor: ♩ = 69Bi, 69Ke   12. Triple Concerto, last mvt.: ♩ = 76Ke

13. Concerto for 3 Hps. in C major, last mvt.:   14. Partita VI, Air: ♩ = 80Cz, ♩ = 66Ke, 80Bi
    ♩ = 84Ke

15. French Suite II, Air: ♩ = 80Cz, 76Ke, 80Bi

Tempo Table IIb: Works in ₵ Time; suggested speed: 𝅗𝅥 = ± 60

1. *W.K.* I, Fugue 22: 𝅗𝅥 = 60Cz, 48Ke,
   𝅘𝅥 = 104Bi

2. *W.K.* II, Prel. 22: 𝅗𝅥 = 60Cz, 52Ke, 58Bi

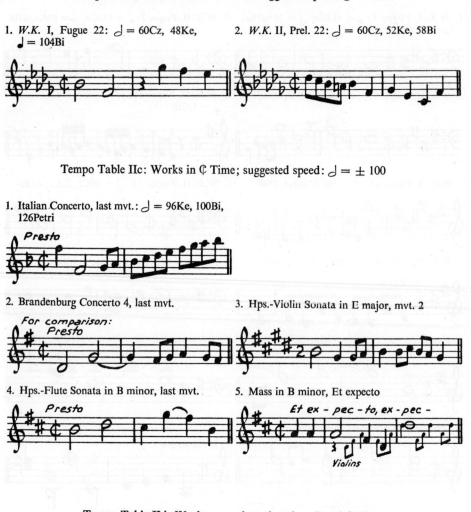

Tempo Table IIc: Works in ₵ Time; suggested speed: 𝅗𝅥 = ± 100

1. Italian Concerto, last mvt.: 𝅗𝅥 = 96Ke, 100Bi,
   126Petri

    Presto

2. Brandenburg Concerto 4, last mvt.

    For comparison:
      Presto

3. Hps.-Violin Sonata in E major, mvt. 2

4. Hps.-Flute Sonata in B minor, last mvt.

    Presto

5. Mass in B minor, Et expecto

    Et ex - pec - to, ex - pec -

    Violins

Tempo Table IId: Works wrongly assigned to C and ₵ Time

1. *W.K.* II, Fugue 5: 𝅘𝅥 = 80Cz, 𝅗𝅥 = 48–52Ke,
   𝅘𝅥 = 63Bi. Sug.: C, 𝅘𝅥 = ± 80

    (inner beat: quarter note)

2. Duet IV: 𝅗𝅥 = 88Ke, 𝅘𝅥 = 88Bi. Sug.: ₵,
   𝅗𝅥 = ± 80

    (inner beat: half note)

Tempo Table IIe: French Overtures (C and ₵ Time)

1. Partita IV: ♩ = 69Ke, 60Bi. Sug.: ♩ = ± 60   2. French Overture: ♩ = 63Ke, 69Bi. Sug.: ♩ = ± 60

3. Goldberg Var. 16: ♩ = 76Bi, 72Ki. Sug.: ♩ = ± 60

4. Partita II: ♪ = 66Ke, 88Bi. Sug.: ♩ = ± 40   5. Partita VI: ♩ = 76Ke, 66Bi. Sug.: ♩ = ± 80 (60?)

For comparison: Grave, Adagio

Tempo Table IIf: Dance Pieces in C and ₵ Time

1. French Suite I: ♩ = 72Cz, 60Ke, 72Bi. Sug.: ♩ = ± 80   2. English Suite I: ♩ = 72Ke, 72Bi. Sug.: ♩ = ± 80

Allemandes

3. Partita I: ♩ = 76Ke, 120Bi. Sug.: ♩ = ± 80   4. Partita III: ♪ = 104Ke, 108Bi. Sug.: ♩ = ± 60

5. Partita IV: ♩ = 63Ke, 69Bi. Sug.: ♩ = ± 60   6. Partita VI: ♩ = 54Ke, 60Bi. Sug.: ♩ = ± 60

7. French Suite V: ♩ = 88Cz, 80Ke, 80Bi. Sug.: ♩ = ± 80   8. English Suite III: ♩ = 88Ke, 92Bi. Sug.: ♩ = ± 80

Gavottes

9. Partita VI, Tempo di gavotta: ♩ = 52Ke,
  69Bi. Sug.: ♩ = ± 80

10. French Suite VI: ♩ = 112Cz, 88Ke, 100Bi.   11. English Suite II: ♩ = 96Ke, 100Bi. Sug.:
   Sug.: ♩ = ± 100   ♩ = ± 100

Bourrées

12. French Overture: ♩ = 96Ke, 96Bi. Sug.:
   ♩ = ± 100

13. French Suite I: ♩ = 104Cz, 80Ke, 100Bi.   14a. Partita VI, older version. Sug.: ♩ = ± 80
   Sug.: ♩ = ± 80

Gigues

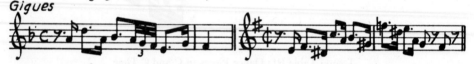

14b. Partita VI: ♩ = 76Ke, 80Bi. Sug.:   15. Partita I: ♩ = 144Ke, 138Bi. Sug.: ♩ = ± 140
   ♩ = ± 80

16. French Suite III: ♩ = 104Cz, 76Ke, 92Bi.
   Sug.: ♩ = ± 80

Anglaise

Tempo Table IIIa: Works in 2/4 Time; suggested speed: ♩ = ± 100

1. *W.K.* II, Fugue 1: ♩ = 120Cz, 100Ke, 112Bi . 2. *W.K.* II, Fugue 12: ♩ = 88Cz, 84Ke, 88Bi

3. Italian Concerto, mvt. 1: ♪ = 168Ke, ♩ = 104   4. Partita II, Capriccio: ♩ = 92Ke, 126Bi
Bi, 100–112Petri

5. Partita III, Scherzo: ♩ = 100Ke, 126Bi   6. French Overture, Echo: ♩ = 84Ke, 100Bi

7. Duet II: ♩ = 84Ke, 108Bi   8. Goldberg Var. 2: ♩ = 92Cz, 84Bi, 56Ki

9. Violin Concerto in A minor, mvt. 1   10. Concerto for 2 Violins, from mvt. 1

For comparison

11. Hps.-Violin Sonata 4, last mvt.   12. Suite for Flute in B minor, Badinerie

Tempo Table IIIb: Works in 2/4 Time; suggested speed: ♩ = ± 80

1. *W.K.* II, Prel. 12: ♩ = 80Cz, 56Ke, 80Bi   2. 6 Little Preludes, No. 4: ♩ = 92Bi, 76Ke

3. Partita IV, Aria: ♩ = 69Ke, 84Bi   4. Hps. Concerto in F minor: ♩ = 72Ke

Tempo Table IIIc: Work in 2/4 Time; suggested speed: ♩ = ± 40

Goldberg Var. 15: ♪ = 108Cz, 108Bi, 54Ki

Tempo Table IVa: Works in 3/4 Time; suggested speed: ♩ = ± 100

1. Invention 8: ♩ = 116L, 144Cz, 116–126Ke,   2. *W.K.* I, Fugue 21: ♩ = 116Cz, 96Ke, 120Bi
   126Bi

3. *W.K.* II, Prel. 6: ♩ = 126Cz, 112Ke, 120Bi   4. *W.K.* II, Prel. 15: ♩ = 132Cz, 96Ke, 132Bi

5. *W.K.* II, Fugue 21: ♩ = 108Cz, 120Ke, 126Bi   6. English Suite II, Prel.: ♩ = 108–116Ke, 120Bi

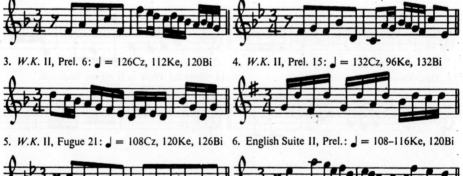

7. Partita II, pt. 1: ♩ = 108Ke, 112Bi   8. Partita V, Praeambulum: ♩ = 132Ke, 132Bi

9. Toccata in D minor, last pt.: ♩ = 104Bi   10. Chromatic Phantasy, Fugue: ♩ = 108Ke, 104Bi

11. 12 Little Preludes, No. 3: ♩ = 72Ke, 100Bi   12. The same, No. 5: ♩ = 116Ke, 132Bi

13. The same, No. 7: ♩ = 112Ke, 138Bi   14. The same, No. 10: ♩ = 92Ke, 116Bi

15. The same, No. 11: ♩ = 76Ke, 120Bi   16. 6 Little Preludes, No. 2: ♩ = 116Ke, ♩. = 58Bi

17. Goldberg Var. 1: ♩ = 108Cz, 100Bi, 94Ki   18. Goldberg Var. 5: ♩ = 126Cz, 120Bi, ♪ = 126Ki

19. Goldberg Var. 8: ♩ = 120Cz, 120Bi, 86Ki   20. Goldberg Var. 14: ♩ = 100Cz, 92Bi, 80Ki

21. Goldberg Var. 17: ♩ = 112Cz, 112Bi, 108Ki   22. Goldberg Var. 20: ♩ = 108Cz, 112Bi, 86Ki

23. Goldberg Var. 23: ♩ = 100Cz, 100Bi, 102Ki
24. Hps. Concerto in D minor, last mvt.:
♩ = 100Ke

25. Concerto for 2 Violins, last mvt.
26. Hps.-Violin Sonata 2, mvt. 2

For comparison

27. Sonata for 2 Flutes, mvt. 2
28. Magnificat

29. St. John Passion

Der Held aus Ju-da siegt mit Macht

Tempo Table IVb: Works in 3/4 Time; suggested speed: ♩ = ± 80

1. Sinfonia 10: ♩ = 88L, 100Cz, 96Ke, 100Bi
2. *W.K.* I, Fugue 6: ♩ = 66Cz, 72Ke, 72Bi

3. *W.K.* I, Prel. 17: ♩ = 96Cz, 72Ke, 108Bi
4. *W.K.* II, Prel. 9: ♩ = 80Cz, 58Ke, 76Bi

5. *W.K.* II, Prel. 13: ♩ = 92Cz, 84Ke, 88Bi
6. *W.K.* II, Fugue 16: ♩ = 84Cz, 72Ke, 72Bi

7. Goldberg Var. 12: ♩ = 84 Cz, 76Bi, 66Ki

8. Goldberg Var. 28: ♩ = 92Cz, 84Bi, 80Ki

9. Goldberg Var. 29: ♩ = 100Cz, 116Bi, 88Ki

10. St. John Passion

For comparison

Las- set uns den nicht zer - tei – – – – – – len

Tempo Table IVc: Works in 3/4 Time; suggested speed: ♩ = ± 60

1. Invention 9: ♩ = 58L, 116Cz, 46Ke, 60Bi

2. Sinfonia 5: ♩ = 50L, 100Cz, 48Ke, 52Bi

3. Sinfonia 7: ♩ = 60L, 88Cz, 56Ke, 56Bi

4. *W.K.* II, Prel. 14: ♪ = 116Cz, ♩ = 48Ke, 60Bi

5. *W.K.* II, Prel. 17: ♩ = 72Cz, 60Ke, 66Bi

6. Goldberg Var., Theme: ♩ = 72Cz, 76Bi, 56Ki

7. Goldberg Var. 26: ♩ = 100Cz, 92Bi, 84Ki

Tempo Table IVd: Works in 3/4 Time; suggested speed: ♩ = ± 40

1. Italian Concerto, mvt. 2: ♪ = 76Ke, 88Bi, 84Petri
2. Goldberg Var. 13: ♩ = 69Cz, 69Bi, 40Ki

3. Goldberg Var. 25: ♪ = 88Cz, 84Bi, 46Ki

Tempo Table IVe: Works in 3/4 Time; suggested speed: ♩ = ± 120

*1. *W.K.* I, Fugue 10: ♩ = 126Cz, 132Bi
2. Fugue in A minor: ♩ = 126Bi

*No speed given by Keller.

Tempo Table IVf: Dance Pieces in 3/4 Time

1. French Suite I: ♩ = 80Cz, 66Ke, 76Bi.   2. English Suite III: ♩ = 54Ke, 63Bi. Sug.:
   Sug.: ♩ = ± 60   ♩ = ± 60

3. Partita VI: ♩ = 54Ke, 60Bi. Sug.: ♩ = ± 60

4. French Suite V: ♩ = 132Cz, 104Ke, 120Bi. 5. Partita III: ♩ = 96Ke, 120Bi. Sug.: ♩ = ± 120
   Sug.: ♩ = ± 120

6. French Suite IV: ♩ = 138Cz, 112Ke, 120Bi. 7. Partita I: ♩ = 108Ke, 132Bi. Sug.: ♩ = ± 120
   Sug.: ♩ = ± 120

8. French Suite II: ♩. = 76Cz, ♩ = 144Ke,
   ♩. = 60Bi. Sug.: ♩ = ± 140

9. French Suite VI: ♩ = 100Cz, 96Ke, 100Bi.
   Sug.: ♩ = ± 100

10. Partita III: ♩ = 92Ke, 138Bi. Sug.:
    ♩ = ± 120

11. French Suite IV: ♩ = 108Cz, 104Ke, 120Bi. 12. No. 3 from Notebk. for W. F. Bach:
    Sug.: ♩ = ± 100   ♩ = 116Bi. Sug.: ♩ = ± 100

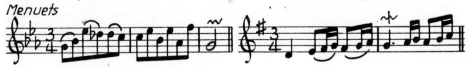

13. French Suite II: $\quarternote$ = 120Cz, 112Ke, 120Bi.
     Sug.: $\quarternote$ = ± 120

14. French Suite VI: $\quarternote$ = 120Cz, 96Ke, 120Bi.
     Sug.: $\quarternote$ = ± 120

15. English Suite IV: $\quarternote$ = 108Ke, 132Bi. Sug.:
     $\quarternote$ = ± 120

16. Partita IV: $\quarternote$ = 104Ke, 120Bi. Sug.:
     $\quarternote$ = ± 120

17. French Suite III: $\quarternote$ = 120Cz, 126Ke,
     $\dottedhalfnote$ = 60Bi. Sug.: $\dottedhalfnote$ = ± 60

18. Partita I, Menuet I: $\quarternote$ = 126Ke, $\dottedhalfnote$ = 60Bi.
     Sug.: $\dottedhalfnote$ = ± 60

19. Partita V: $\quarternote$ = 116Ke, 144Bi. Sug.: $\dottedhalfnote$ =
     ± 60

20. Partita I, Menuet II: $\quarternote$ = 126Ke, $\dottedhalfnote$ = 60Bi.
     Sug.: $\dottedhalfnote$ = ± 60

Tempo Table Va: Works in 3/8 Time; suggested speed: $\dottedquarternote$ = ± 60

1. Invention 3: $\eighthnote$ = 152L, $\dottedquarternote$ = 80Cz,
    $\eighthnote$ = 138Ke, $\dottedquarternote$ = 60Bi

2. Invention 4: $\eighthnote$ = 144L, $\dottedquarternote$ = 72Cz, 60Ke,
    76Bi

3. W.K. I, Prel. 3: $\dottedquarternote$ = 92Cz, 84Ke, 84Bi

4. W.K. I, Fugue 11: $\dottedquarternote$ = 66Cz, $\eighthnote$ = 152Ke,
    $\dottedquarternote$ = 60Bi

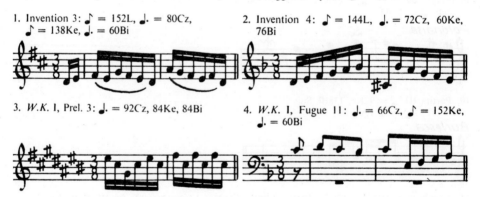

5. *W.K.* II, Prel. 3, 2nd half: ♩. = 63Cz,
   ♪ = 160Ke, ♩. = 60Bi

6. *W.K.* II, Prel. 10: ♩. = 66Cz, ♪ = 168Ke,
   ♩. = 76Bi

7. *W.K.* II, Fugue 15: ♩. = 76Cz, 48Ke, 76Bi

8. *W.K.* II, Fugue 24: ♩. = 76Cz, 58Ke, 54Bi

9. English Suite III, Prel.: ♩. = 63Ke, 84Bi

10. Partita II, Rondeau: ♩. = 76Ke, 84Bi

11. Partita III, Fantasia: ♪ = 138Ke, ♩. = 69Bi

12. Goldberg Var. 4: ♩. = 60Cz, 54Bi,
    ♪ = 156Ki

13. Goldberg Var. 6: ♩. = 60Cz, ♪ = 132Bi,
    132Ki

14. Goldberg Var. 16, 2nd half: ♩. = 76Cz, 76Bi,
    60Ki

15. Goldberg Var. 19: ♩. = 72Cz, 60Bi,
    ♪ = 152Ki

16. 6 Little Preludes, No. 3: ♩. = 60Ke, 72Bi

17. The same, No. 6: ♪ = 132Ke, ♩. = 69Bi

18. Hps. Concerto in F minor, Presto: ♩. = 63Ke

19. Brandenburg Concerto 4, mvt. 1

For comparison

20. Violin Concerto in E major, last mvt.

21. Organ Toccata in F major   22. Mass in B minor, Gloria

23. Mass in B minor, Osanna   24. St. Matthew Passion

Tempo Table Vb: Works in 3/8 Time; suggested speed: ♩. = ± 40 (♪ = ± 120)

1. Invention 6: ♪ = 104L, 144Cz, 96Ke, 138Bi   2. Sinfonia 11: ♪ = 126L, 60Cz, ♩. = 44Ke, 46Bi

3. Sinfonia 13: ♪ = 120L, 108Ke, 108Bi,
   ♩. = 60Cz

4. Duet 1: ♪ = 92Ke, 96Bi (♪ = 100 perhaps
   preferable)

Tempo Table Vc: Dance Pieces in 3/8 Time

1. English Suite V: ♪ = 152Ke, ♩. = 76Bi.   2. Partita V: ♪ = 152Ke, ♩. = 60Bi. Sug.:
Sug.: ♩. = ± 60   ♩. = ± 60

Passepieds

3. French Overture: ♪ = 152Ke, ♩. = 63Bi,
66Petri. Sug.: ♩. = ± 60

4. French Suite II: ♩. = 88Cz, 96Ke, 96Bi. Sug.:   5. French Suite III: ♩. = 84Cz, 76–84Ke, 80Bi.
♩. = ± 80   Sug.: ♩. = ± 80

Gigues

6. English Suite V: ♩. = 76Ke, 76Bi. Sug.:
♩. = ± 80

7. Partita V: ♩. = 63Ke, 80Bi. Sug.: ♩. = ± 60   8. Partita VI: ♪ = 112Ke, 132Bi. Sug.:
♩. = ± 40 (♪ = 120)

Correntes

Tempo Table VIa: Works in 6/8 Time; suggested speed: ♩. = ± 60

1. *W.K.* I, Fugue 15: ♩. = 80Cz, 76Ke, 76Bi   2. *W.K.* I, Prel. 18: ♪ = 126Cz, 96Ke, 132Bi

3. English Suite V, Prel: ♩. = 60Ke, 80Bi   4. French Overture: ♩. = 66Ke, 76Bi, 88Petri

5. Toccata in F♯ minor, last pt.: ♩. = 48Bi   6. Toccata in G major, last pt.: ♩. = 80Bi

7. Goldberg Var. 27: ♩. = 88Cz, 72Bi, 60Ki

Tempo Table VIb: Works in 6/8 Time; suggested speed: ♩. = ± 80

1. *W.K.* II, Fugue 18: ♩. = 56Cz, 69Ke, 76Bi   2. Goldberg Var. 7: ♩. = 84Cz, 88Bi, 72Ki

Tempo Table VIc: Dance Pieces in 6/8 Time

1. Partita V, Gigue: ♩. = 69Ke, 60Bi. Sug.: ♩. = ± 60

2. French Suite VI, Gigue: ♩. = 104Cz, 76Ke, 92Bi. Sug.: ♩. = ± 80   3. French Overture, Gigue: ♩. = 100Ke, 92Bi. Sug.: ♩. = ± 80

4. French Suite IV, Gigue: ♩. = 120Cz, 104Ke, 112Bi. Sug.: ♩. = ± 100   5. English Suite II, Gigue: ♩. = 126Ke, 120Bi. Sug.: ♩. = ±120

Tempo Table VIIa: Works in 9/8 Time; suggested speed: ♩. = ± 60

1. *W.K.* I, Fugue 19: ♩. = 69Cz, 60Ke, 66Bi   2. *W.K.* I, Prel. 20: ♩. = 84Cz, 72Ke, 80Bi

3a. English Suite VI, Prel., pt. 1: ♩. = 50Ke, 66Bi   3b. The same, pt. 2: ♩. = 72Ke, 76Bi

4. Partita IV, Overture, pt. 2: ♩. = 76Ke, 80Bi

Tempo Table VIIb: Work in 9/8 Time; suggested speed: ♩. = ± 40

W.K. II, Prel. 4: ♩. = 58Cz, 48Ke, 50Bi

Tempo Table VIIc: Works in 9/8 Time; suggested speed: ♩. = ± 80

1. Sinfonia 6: ♩. = 96L, 84Cz, 84Ke, 104Bi   2. *W.K.* II, Prel. 7: ♩. = 84Cz, 76Ke, 84Bi

3. Goldberg Var. 24: ♩. = 84Cz, 76Bi, 56Ki

Tempo Table VIId: Work in 9/8 Time; suggested speed: ♩. = ± 100

Invention 10: ♩. = 112L, 152Cz, 108Ke, 100Bi

Tempo Table VIIIa: Works in 12/8 Time; suggested speed: ♩. = ± 60

1. Invention 12: ♪ = 168L, ♩. = 84Cz, 72Ke,   2. *W.K.* I, Prel. 11: ♩. = 88Cz, 66Ke, 80Bi
   76Bi

3. Goldberg Var. 3: ♩. = 60Cz, 60Bi, 40Ki   4. Duet III: ♪ = 132–144, "not ♩. = 69" Ke,
                                  ♩. = 66Bi

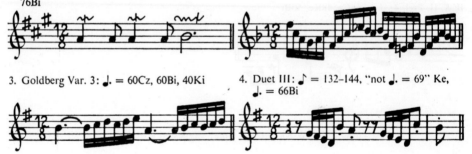

Tempo Table VIIIb: Works in 12/8 Time; suggested speed: ♩. = ± 80

1. Sinfonia 2: ♪ = 184L, ♩. = 100Cz, 63Ke,   2. *W.K.* I, Prel. 9: ♩. = 84Cz, 66Ke, 92Bi
  60Bi

3. *W.K.* II, Prel. 5: ♩. = 96Cz, 88Ke, 84Bi   4. *W.K.* II, Prel. 19: ♩. = 88Cz, 72Ke, 92Bi

5. English Suite I, Prel.: ♩. = 84Ke, 69Bi   6. Prel. for Lute or Hps.: ♩. = 108Bi

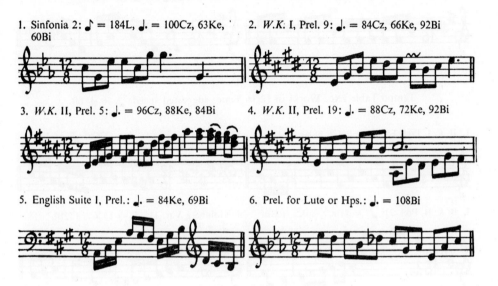

Tempo Table VIIIc: Dance Pieces in 12/8 Time

1. English Suite III, Gigue: ♩. = 116Ke, 138Bi.   2. English Suite IV, Gigue: ♩. = 120Ke, 132Bi.
  Sug.: ♩. = ± 120   Sug.: ♩. = ± 120

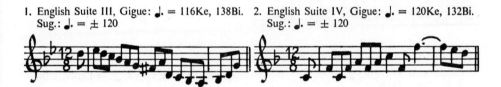

Tempo Table IXa: Works in 6/16 Time; suggested speed: ♪. = ± 120

1. *W.K.* II, Fugue 11: ♪. = 112Cz, 96Ke, 116Bi   2. Toccata in D major, last pt.: ♪. = 108Bi

Tempo Table IXb: Works in 9/16 Time

1. Sinfonia 15: ♪. = 80L, 112Cz, 72Ke, 100Bi.
   Sug.: ♪. = ± 80

2. Dance Piece: Partita IV, Gigue: ♪. = 152Ke,
   144Bi. Sug.: ♪. = ± 120

Tempo Table IXc: Works in 12/16 Time; suggested speed: ♩. = ± 60

1. *W.K.* I, Prel. 13: ♪. = 96Cz, 88Ke, 104Bi

2. *W.K.* II, Fugue 4: ♩. = 72Cz, ♪. = 108‑
   116Ke, 126Bi

3. *W.K.* II, Prel. 21: ♪. = 116Cz, 80Ke, 108Bi

4. Goldberg Var. 11: ♪. = 152Cz, 152Bi,
   ♩. = 72Ki

5. Fugue in A minor (later last mvt., Triple Con‑
   certo in A minor): ♩. = 76Bi

Dance pieces:

6. French Suite V, Gigue: ♩. = 76Cz,
   ♪. = 138Ke, 132Bi

7. English Suite VI, Gigue: ♪. = 120Ke, 120Bi

Tempo Table IXd: Work in 24/16 Time; suggested speed: ♩. = ± 60

W.K. I, Prel. 15: ♩. = 100Cz, 80Ke, 96Bi

Tempo Table Xa: Works in 3/2 Time

1. *W.K.* I, Prel. 8: ♩ = 100Cz, 𝅗𝅥 = 44Ke, 50Bi.
   Sug.: 𝅗𝅥 = ± 50

2. *W.K.* II, Prel. 11: ♩ = 104Cz, 𝅗𝅥 = 60Ke,
   60Bi. Sug.: 𝅗𝅥 = ± 100

3. *W.K.* II, Fugue 22: ♩ = 104Cz, 𝅗𝅥 = 72Ke,
   69Bi. Sug.: 𝅗𝅥 = ± 80

Tempo Table Xb: Dance Pieces in 3/2 Time

Courantes: suggested speed: 𝅗𝅥 = ± 80

1. French Suite I: 𝅗𝅥 = 80Cz, ♩ = 152Ke, 168Bi   2. English Suite I: ♩ = 160Ke, 160Bi

3. Partita II: ♩ = 132Ke, 120Bi   4a. English Suite VI, Sarabande: 𝅗𝅥 = 54Ke,
                                        63Bi. Sug.: 𝅗𝅥 = ± 60

4b. The same, Double

Tempo Table Xc: Works in 6/4 Time; suggested speed: ♩. = ± 40

1. *W.K.* I, Prel. 4: ♩ = 92Cz, ♩. = 36–40Ke,
   ♩ = 92Bi

2. *W.K.* I, Fugue 14: ♩ = 88Cz, 88Ke, 100Bi

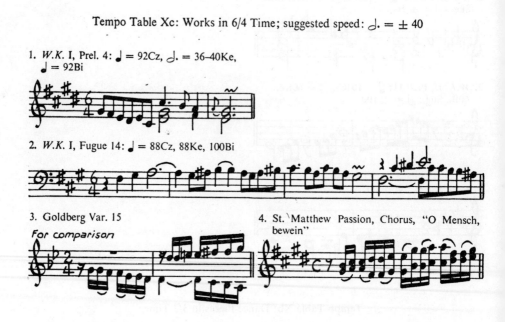

3. Goldberg Var. 15

For comparison

4. St. Matthew Passion, Chorus, "O Mensch, bewein"

Tempo Table Xd: Dance Pieces in 6/4 Time

1. French Suite III, Courante: ♩ = 160Ke,
   ♩. = 60Bi. Sug.: ♩ = ± 160

2. French Suite V, Loure: ♩ = 72Ke, 120Bi.
   Sug.: ♩ = ± 120

Trill Table

1. Invention 2, bar 3   **2. Invention 2, bar 13**   **3. Invention 7, bars 20–21**

4. Invention 15, bars 14–15   **5. Concerto for 2 Hps. in C major, last mvt., bars 42–43**

6. *W.K.* II, Prel. 12, bars 12–16

7. *W.K.* II, Fugue 13, bars 23–24   **8.** The same, bars 73–75

9. Italian Concerto, mvt. 1, bars 33–34

10. Sinfonia 1, bar 6   11. The same, bar 10

12. *W.K.* I, Fugue 6, bar 12   13. French Suite I, Menuet II,   14. *W.K.* II, Fugue 24, bar 13
                                            bar 18

15. Capriccio in E major, bar 12   16. The same, bar 31   17. The same,
                                                                                    bar 114

For comparison:

18. Choral Prelude: Nun danket alle Gott,
    B.G. XXV, p. 108

19. Choral Prelude: Liebster Jesu,
    B.G. XL, p. 76, bar 7

20. Choral Prelude: Christ lag in Todesbanden,
    B.G. XL, p. 11, last bar

21. Canonic Variations: Vom Himmel hoch,
    Var. 4, bars 38–39

22. Organ Toccata in C major, last part, bars
    71–72

23. Organ Trio in D minor, B.G. XXXVIII,
    p. 143, bar 3

24. The same, bar 12 from end

Appoggiatura Table

1. Partita V, Passepied, bar 2

2. Partita V, Allemande, bar 2

3. English Suite V, Courante, bar 27

4. French Suite V, Sarabande, bar 2

5. The same, bar 3

6. The same, pt. 2, bar 13

7. *W.K.* II, Prel. 4, bar 59

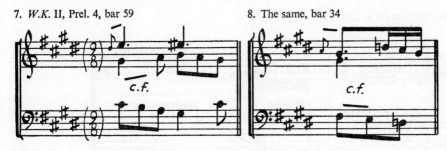

8. The same, bar 34

9. Partita V, Sarabande, bar 10

10. French Overture, Courante, bar 4

11a. "Wedding" Cantata 210, No. 2, Aria, bars 7–8   11b. Cantata 176, No. 3, Aria, bars 3–4

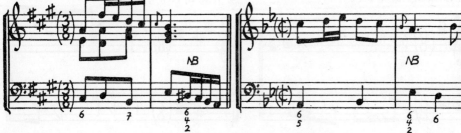

12a. Hps.-Violin Sonata 6, Largo, bars 1–2   12b. The same, bars 5–6

12c. Hps.-Violin Sonata 6, Largo, bars 16–17

13. Goldberg Var. 7, bar 8

14. *W.K.* II, Prel. 4, bar 20

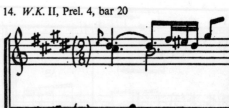

15. The same, bar 6

16a. Hps.-Viola da gamba Sonata, last mvt.,   16b. The same, bars 87 -88
     bars 69-70

17. Hps.-Violin Sonata 4, mvt. 1, bars 31-33

25A

Articulation Table Ia: Voice and Instruments in Complete Agreement

1a. Cantata 28, No. 1, Aria, bars 1–3

1b. The same, bars 21–23

2a. Cantata 92, No. 8, Aria, bars 1–2

2b. The same, bars 13–14

3a. Cantata 105, No. 3, Aria, bars 1–2

3b. The same, bars 17–19

4a. Cantata 11, No. 4, Aria, bars 1–2

4b. The same, bars 9–10

5a. Cantata 205, No. 5, Aria, bars 1–4

5b. The same, bars 17–20

6a. Cantata 80, No. 4, Aria, bars 1–2

6b. The same, bars 3–4

7a. Cantata 98, No. 3, Aria, bars 1–4

7b. The same, bars 17–20

8a. Cantata 144, No. 5, Aria, bars 1–2

8b. The same, bars 7–8

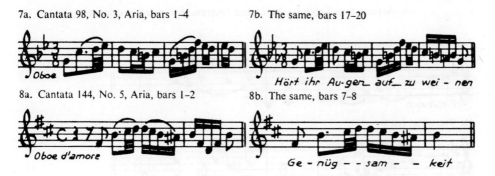

Articulation Table 1b: Voice and Instruments in Partial Agreement

1a. Cantata 114, No. 5, Aria, bars 1–2

1b. The same, bars 9–10

2a. Cantata 166, No. 2, Aria, bars 1–2

2b. The same, bars 7–8

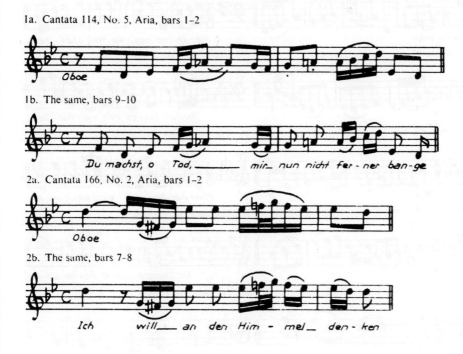

Articulation Table Ic: Voice and Instruments in Disagreement

1a. Cantata 132, No. 5, Aria, bar 1

1b. The same, bar 9

2a. Cantata 32, No. 3, Aria, bars 1–4   2b. The same, bars 17–20

3a. Cantata 47, No. 4, Aria, bars 1–2   3b. The same, bars 13–14

4a. Cantata 93, No. 3, Aria, bars 1–4   4b. The same, bars 17–20

5a. Cantata 167, No. 1, Aria, bars 1–2   5b. The same, bars 13–14

6a. Cantata 166, No. 5, Aria, bars 1–2   6b. The same, bars 9–10

7a. Cantata 41, No. 2, Aria, bars 1–2   7b. The same, bars 15–17

8a. Cantata 88, No. 5, Duetto, bar 1

8b. The same, bar 11

9a. Cantata 126, No. 2, Aria, bars 1–2

9b. The same, bars 7–8

10a. Cantata 151, No. 3, Aria, bars 1–2

10b. The same, bars 9–10

11a. Cantata 159, No. 2, Aria, bars 1–2

11b. The same, bars 8–10

12a. Cantata 176, No. 5, Aria, bars 1–2

12b. The same, bars 12–14

Articulation Table II: Examples of Relations between Keyboard, Vocal, and Instrumental Music

1a. Invention 4

1b. The same, bars 22–23

1c. Invention 3

1d. Cantata 57, No. 1, Aria, bars 13–14

1e. The same, bars 8–9

2a. Invention 13

2b. Cantata 206, No. 5, Aria

3a. Sinfonia 9

3b. St. Matthew Passion, No. 25, Recitativo

3c. Cantata 81, No. 1, Aria

3d. Cantata 25, No. 1, Chorus

3e. Cantata 101, No. 1, Chorus

3f. Cantata 73, No. 4, Aria, bars 13–17

4a. Sinfonia 15

4b. Cantata 136, No. 5, Duetto, bars 1–2

5a. *W.K.* I, Fugue 3

5b. Cantata 72, No. 4, Aria, bars 1–3
Oboe

5c. The same, bars 17–18
Mein Je- su will es tun

5d. The same, violin part (4 times)
Violin

6a. *W.K.* I, Prel. 5

6b. Cantata 110, No. 2, Aria, bars 1–2
Fl. I
Bassoon

6c. The same, bar 6
(sic!)

7a. *W.K.* I, Prel. 6

7b. Cantata 147, No. 5, Aria, bars 1–3

8a. *W.K.* I, Prel. 14

8b. Cantata 113, No. 4, Recitativo

9a. *W.K.* I, Fugue 16

9b. Cantata 89, No. 3, Aria, bar 1

9c. The same, bars 3–4

10a. *W.K.* I, Prel. 17

10b. Cantata 2, No. 3, Aria

11a. *W.K.* I, Prel. 18

11b. Cantata 1, No. 5, Aria

12a. *W.K.* II, Prel. 6

12b. Cantata 188, No. 1, Aria, bars 83–84

13a. *W.K.* II, Fugue 13, bars 24–26

13b. Cantata 32, No. 5, Duetto

13c. Cantata 154, No. 7, Duetto, bars 14–16

14a. *W.K.* I, Prel. 19

14b. The same, bars 14–16

14c. Cantata 3, No. 1, Chorus, bars 4–5

14d. The same, bars 7–9

15a. *W.K.* II, Fugue 16

15b. Cantata 78, No. 1, Chorus, bars 103–105

16a. English Suite IV, Prel., bars 3–4

16b. Cantata 125, No. 4, Duetto, bars 3–4

17a. English Suite V, Sarabande

17b. Cantata 188, No. 1, Aria

17c. The same, bars 15–16

18a. Departure Capriccio, pt. 1, bars 10–11

18b. Cantata 106, No. 2, Chorus, bars 31–32

19a. Duet II

19b. Cantata 58, No. 5, Duetto, bars 1–3

20a. Duet III

20b. Cantata 64, No. 7, Aria, bars 1–2

Articulation Table III: Mordent Figures

1. Cantata 1, No. 3, Aria

2. Cantata 2, No. 3, Aria

3. Cantata 2, No. 5, Aria

4. Cantata 102, No. 4, Arioso

5. Violin Concerto in E major, mvt. 1, bar 13   **6.** The same, bar 32

7. Cantata 134, No. 4, Duetto   **8.** Cantata 134a, No. 4, Duetto

9. Cantata 92, No. 2, Recitativo   **10.** Cantata 106, No. 1, Sonatina

Articulation Table IV: Groups of Two Notes

1. *W.K.* I, Fugue 24   **2.** Hps.-Flute Sonata in B minor, mvt. 1, bar 12

3a. The same, bars 14–15   3b. The same, bars 12–13

3c. The same, bars 96–97   4. The same, mvt. 3

5. Cantata 58, No. 3, Aria, bars 6–7   6. Cantata 6, No. 5, Aria

7. Cantata 60, No. 3, Duetto   8a. Cantata 58, No. 1, Duetto   8b. The same, bars 18–19

9. Solo Violin Sonata 3, mvt. 1

some more samples
see table „caressing"

Articulation Table V: Groups of Three Notes

1. Cantata 88, No. 1, Aria   2. Cantata 13, No. 1, Aria

3a. Cantata 104, No. 1, Chorus   3b. The same, bars 5–6

3c. The same, bars 18–20   4a. Hps. Overture in F major, Gigue

4b. The same, bars 7–11

5. Cantata 137, No. 2, Aria, bars 13–16

6. Hps.-Violin Sonata in C minor, last mvt., bars   **7a. Italian Concerto, mvt. 1, bar 15**
    104–105

7b. Cantata 151, No. 3, Aria   **8a. Italian Concerto, last mvt., bars 9–10**

8b. Cantata 74, No. 5, Aria   **9. Cantata 101, No. 2, Aria**

Articulation Table VI: Groups of Four and More Notes

1. Suite for Keyboard in E flat major (B.G. XXXVI, p. 8), Allemande

2. "Coffee" Cantata, No. 10, bars 6–9

3. Cantata 5, No. 3, Aria   **4. Invention 3**

5. Cantata 57, No. 1, Aria, bars 34–37

6a. The same, No. 3, Aria, bars 1–4   6b. The same, bars 9–11

7. Cantata 47, No. 2, Aria

8a. Cantata 137, No. 2, Aria   8b. The same, bar 5   8c. The same, bar 9

9a. Cantata 117, No. 1, Chorus   9b. The same, bar 67

10. Mass in A major, No. 5, Aria

11. Cantata 101, No. 4, Aria

Articulation Table VII: "Caressing"

1. *W.K.* II, Fugue 21

2. Christmas Oratorio, No. 3, Recitativo   3. The same, No. 10, Sinfonia

4. Cantata 71, No. 4, Arioso   5. Cantata 6, No. 1, Chorus

Articulation Table VIII: "Gay, bold"

1. *W.K.* II, Fugue 20

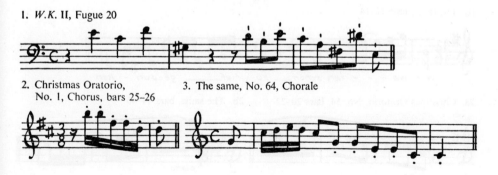

2. Christmas Oratorio,   3. The same, No. 64, Chorale
   No. 1, Chorus, bars 25–26

4. Cantata 136, No. 1, Chorus

5. Violin Concerto in E major, mvt. 1

6. Cantata 32, No. 1, Aria

7. St. Matthew Passion, No. 33, Chorus

8. Cantata 14, No. 2, Aria

9. Cantata 9, No. 1, Chorus

10. Cantata 5, No. 1, Chorus

Articulation Table IX: Special Cases

1a. Cantata 9, No. 3, Aria

1b. The same, bars 12–14

2a. Christmas Oratorio, No. 54, bars 20–22

2b. The same, bars 44–46

3. Cantata 202, No. 1, Aria

4. St. Matthew Passion, No. 28, Recitativo

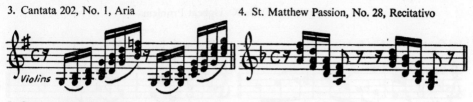

5. Cantata 186, No. 8, Aria

6. Christmas Oratorio, No. 19, Aria

7. Cantata 204, No. 2, Aria

8. Cantata 172, No. 5, Duett

Articulation Table X: Upbeat Problems

1a. Cantata 176, No. 5, Aria

1b. The same, bars 12–13

2a. Cantata 207, No. 4, Aria

2b. The same, bars 9–10

3a. Cantata 215, No. 1, Chorus

3b. Mass in B minor, No. 21, Chorus

4. Fugue from Prelude, Fugue, and Allegro for Lute or Hps.

Tonality Table

1a. Cantata 93, No. 4, Duetto

1b. Cantata 166, No. 3, Chorale

2. Partita IV, Aria

3. Cantata 79, No. 2, Aria, bars 13–14

4. Cantata 30, No. 1, Chorus

5. Christmas Oratorio, No. 8, Aria

6. The same, No. 31, Aria

7. The same, No. 51, Terzetto

8. *W.K.* II, Fugue 11

9. Johann Kuhnau, Sonata No. 3 from "Frische Klavierfrüchte"

10. Toccata in D major, Fugue

11. *W.K.* II, Prel. 11, bars 41–44

12. *W.K.* II, Fugue 11, bars 38–42

13. Johann Christian Bach, Sonata in B flat major for Violin and Hps., Op. X, No. 5

Selective Bibliography

Abert, Hermann. "Tonart und Thema in Bach's Instrumentalfugen," in *Peter Wagner-Festschrift*, ed. K. Weinmann, Leipzig, 1926, p. 1.

Adlung, Jacob. *Musica mechanica organoedi.* 2 vols. Berlin, [1768]. Reprint: Kassel, 1931.

Aldrich, Putnam. "The Principal Agréments of the Seventeenth and Eighteenth Centuries: A Study in Ornamentation." Unpublished dissertation, Harvard University, 1942.

——— "Bach's Technique of Transcription and Improvised Ornamentation," *Musical Quarterly*, vol. XXXV, no. 1 (January 1949), p. 26.

——— *Ornamentation in J. S. Bach's Organ Works.* New York, 1950.

Apel, Willi. *The Notation of Polyphonic Music 900–1600.* Cambridge, Mass., 1942.

——— *Harvard Dictionary of Music.* Cambridge, Mass., 1944.

——— *Masters of the Keyboard.* Cambridge, Mass., 1947.

Arger, Madame Jane. *Les Agréments et le rhythme.* Paris, [1917].

Auerbach, Cornelia. *Die deutsche Clavichordkunst des 18. Jahrhunderts.* Kassel, 1930.

Bach, Carl Philipp Emanuel. *Versuch über die wahre Art, das Klavier zu spielen.* Berlin, 1759, 1762. English edition: *Essay on the True Art of Playing Keyboard Instruments.* Trans. William J. Mitchell. New York, 1949.

Bach, Johann Sebastian. *Complete Works.* Bach-Gesellschaft, 1850–1897.

Bach-Gedenkschrift, 1950. Comp. International Bach Society. Ed. Karl Matthei. Zürich, 1950.

Bach-Jahrbuch. Publ. Neue Bach-Gesellschaft. Leipzig, 1904—.

Bedos de Celles, F. *L'Art du facteur d'orgues.* Paris, 1766–1778. Reprint: Kassel, 1934–1936.

Bernhard, Christoph. *Kompositionsschule*, 1648. Published under the title, *Die Kompositionslehre Heinrich Schützens in der Fassung seines Schülers Christoph Bernhard,* by Josef Müller-Blattau, Leipzig, 1926.

Besch, Hans. *Johann Seb. Bach. Frömmigkeit und Glaube.* Kassel and Basel, 1950.

Bessaraboff, Nicholas. *Ancient European Music Instruments.* Cambridge, 1941.

Beyschlag, Adolf. *Die Ornamentik der Musik.* Leipzig, 1908.

Bitter, Carl Hermann. *Johann Sebastian Bach.* Berlin, 1865.

Blume, Friedrich. "Johann Sebastian Bach," *Die Musik in Geschichte und Gegenwart.* Kassel and Basel, 1949, vol. I, p. 1031.

——— *Johann Sebastian Bach im Wandel der Geschichte.* Kassel, 1947. English edition: *Two Centuries of Bach.* London, New York, Toronto, 1950.

Boadella, Ricard, and Eta Harich-Schneider. "Zum Klavichordspiel bei Tomas de Santa Maria," *Archiv für Musikforschung*, vol. II, no. 2 (1937), p. 243.

Boalch, Donald. *Makers of the Harpsichord and Clavichord, 1440–1840.* New York, 1956.

Bodky, Erwin. *Der Vortrag alter Klaviermusik.* Berlin, 1932.

Bodky, *Das Characterstück*. Berlin, 1932.
—— "New Contributions to the Problem of the Interpretation of Bach's Keyboard Works," in *Kongressbericht, Internationale Gesellschaft für Musikwissenschaft*, Utrecht, 1952, p. 73.
Boehm, Georg. *Sämtliche Werke*. Wiesbaden, 1952—.
Borrel, E. "Les Notes inégales dans l'ancienne musique française," *Revue de Musicologie*, vol. XV, no. 40 (November 1931), p. 278.
Boughton, Rutland. *John Sebastian Bach*. New York, 1930.
Brandts Buys, Hans. *Het Welltemperierte Clavir van J. S. Bach*. Arnhem, 1944.
Brown, Mrs. John Crosby. *Catalogue of the Crosby Brown Collection*. New York: Metropolitan Museum of Art, 1901.
Brunold, Paul. *Traité des agréments et des signes*. Lyon, 1935.
Bruyck, Carl van. *Technische und aesthetische Analysen des Wohltemperierten Claviers*. Leipzig, 1867.
Buchmayer, Richard. "Cembalo oder Pianoforte," *Bach-Jahrbuch* (1908), p. 64.
Bukofzer, Manfred. "Allegory in Baroque Music," *Journal of the Warburg and Cortauld Institutes*, vol. III (London, 1939–1940), p. 1.
—— *Music in the Baroque Era*. New York, 1947.

Cannon, Beekman C. *Johann Mattheson, Spectator in Music*. New Haven, 1947.
Cart, William. *Johann Sebastian Bach*. Lausanne, 1946.
Chambonnières, Jacques Champion de. *Les pièces de clavecin*. Paris, 1670.
Cherbulicz, Antoine E. *Johann Sebastian Bach*. Olten, 1946.
Chiapusso, Jan. "Bach for Purists," *Proceedings*, M.T.N.A., ser. 35 (1940), p. 380.
—— "Editions of the Piano Works of J. S. Bach," *Proceedings*, M.T.N.A., ser. 38 (1944), p. 349.
Ching, James. "On the Playing of Bach's Clavier-Music," *Musical Times*, vol. 91, no. 1290 (August 1950), p. 299.
Closson, Ernest. *History of the Piano*. London, 1947.
Coon, Leland. "The Distinction between Clavichord and Harpsichord Music," *PAMS* (1936), p. 78.
Couperin, François. *L'Art de toucher le clavecin*. Paris, 1716. Complete edition, Paris, 1933.
—— *Pièces de Clavecin*. 1713, 1717, 1722, 1730.

D'Acquin, Louis Claude. *Premier Livre de pièces de Clavecin*. 1735.
Dandrieu, Jean François. *Livres de Clavecin*. 1705, 1724, 1728, 1734, 1739.
D'Anglebert, Jean Henri. *Pièces de Clavecin*. 1689.
Dannreuther, Edward. *Musical Ornamentation*. London, 1893–1895.
Dart, Thurston. *The Interpretation of Music*. London, [1954].
David, Hans T. "Die Gestalt von Bach's Chromatischer Fantasie," *Bach-Jahrbuch* (1926), p. 23.
—— *J. S. Bach's Musical Offering*. New York, 1945.
David, Hans, and Arthur Mendel. *The Bach Reader*. New York, 1945.
Davison, Archibald. *Bach and Handel*. Cambridge, Mass., 1951.
Davison, Archibald, and Willi Apel. *Historical Anthology of Music*. 2 vols. Cambridge, Mass., 1946, 1950.
Dehnert, Max. *Das Weltbild Johann Sebastian Bachs*. Leipzig, 1948.
Dieupart, Charles. *Six Suites de clavecin*. 1710. Reprint: Paris, 1934.
Diruta, Girolamo. *Il Transilvano*. Venice, 1593.
Dolmetsch, Arnold. *The Interpretation of the Music of the Seventeenth and Eighteenth Centuries*. London, 1915, 1946.
Dorian, Frederick. *The History of Music in Performance*. New York, 1942.
Dufourcq, Norbert. *Jean Sébastien Bach*. Paris, 1947.

Ehricht, Klaus. "Der zyklische Gehalt und die Aufführungsmöglichkeit des III. Teils der Klavierübung von J. S. Bach," *Bach-Jahrbuch* (1949–1950), p. 40.

Emery, Walter. "An Introduction to the Textual History of Bach's Clavierübung, Part II," *Musical Times*, vol. 92, nos. 1299 and 1300 (May and June 1951), pp. 205, 260.

—— "Bach's Keyboard Partitas: A Set of Composers' Corrections," *Musical Times*, vol. 93, no. 1317 (November 1952), p. 495.

—— *Bach's Ornaments*. London, 1953.

—— "A Rationale of Bach's Symbolism," *Musical Times*, vol. 95, nos. 1340 and 1341 (October and November 1954), pp. 533, 597.

—— "Bach's Symbolic Language," *Music and Letters*, vol. 30, no. 4 (October 1949), p. 345.

Endres, F. C. *Mystik und Magie der Zahlen*. Zürich, 1951.

Engel, Hans. *Johann Sebastian Bach*. Berlin, 1950.

Ernst, Friedrich. *Der Flügel Johann Sebastian Bachs*. Frankfurt, 1955.

Feldmann, Fritz. "Numerorum mysteria," *Archiv für Musikwissenschaft*, Jahrgang XIV, no. 2 (1957), p. 102.

Fischer, Edwin. *Johann Sebastian Bach*. Potsdam, n.d.

Fischer, Jacob. *Erläuterungen zur Interpunktiunsausgabe*. Vienna, 1926.

Fischer, Johann Kaspar Ferdinand. *Sämtliche Werke für Klavier und Orgel*. Leipzig, 1901.

Fischer, Wilhelm. "Zur Chronologie der Klaviersuiten J. S. Bachs," in *Bericht über den musikwissenschaftlichen Kongress in Basel*. Leipzig, 1925, p. 127.

Fleischer, Oskar. "Das Bach'sche Clavecymbel und seine Neukonstruktion," *Zeitschrift der Internationalen Musikgesellschaft*, Jahrgang 1 (1899), p. 161.

Florand, François. *Jean Séb. Bach*. Paris, 1947.

Forkel, Johann Nikolaus. *Musikalischer Almanach*. 1782.

—— *Über Johann Sebastian Bach's Leben, Kunst und Kunstwerke*. Leipzig, 1802. First English edition: London, 1820.

Frotscher, Georg. "Die Affektenlehre als geistige Grundlage der Themenbildung J. S. Bach's," *Bach-Jahrbuch* (1926), p. 90.

Fuller-Maitland, J. A. *The "48", Bach's Wohltemperirtes Clavier*. London, 1925.

Gabrieli, Andrea and Giovanni. *Ricercari composti et tabulati per ogni sorte di stromenti da tasti*. Venice, 1585.

Gelpin, Francis William. *Old English Instruments of Music*. Chicago, 1911.

Geiringer, Karl. *Musical Instruments*. London, 1943.

—— *The Bach Family*. New York, 1954.

Goehlinger, Franz August. *Geschichte des Klavichords*. Basel, 1910.

Grew, Eva Mary, and Sidney. *Bach*. London, 1947.

Gurlitt, Willibald. *Johann Sebastian Bach*. Kassel, 1947.

Haas, Robert. *Die Musik des Barocks*. Handbuch der Musikwissenschaft, vol. III. Potsdam, 1931.

—— *Aufführungspraxis der Musik*. Handbuch der Musikwissenschaft, vol. VIII. Potsdam, 1931.

Hamel, Fred. *Johann Sebastian Bach. Geistige Welt*. Göttingen, 1951.

Harding, Rosamond. *Origins of Musical Time and Expression*. London, 1938.

Harich-Schneider, Eta. *Die Kunst des Cembalospiels*. Kassel, 1939.

—— *The Harpsichord*. Kassel, St. Louis, 1954.

Heinichen, Johann David. *Der Generalbass in der Komposition*. Dresden, 1728.

Hennig, Hans. "Die Dynamik in J. S. Bachs Klaviermusik," *Bach-Jahrbuch* (1949–1950), p. 65.

Herz, Gerhard. *Bach im Zeitalter des Rationalismus und der Frühromantik*. Bern, 1936.
———— "Bach's Religion," *Journal of Renaissance and Baroque Music*, vol. I, no. 2 (June 1946), p. 124.
Hilgenfeldt, C. L. *Joh. Seb. Bach's Leben, Wirken und Werke*. Leipzig, 1850.
Hindemith, Paul. *A Composer's World*. Cambridge, Mass., 1952.
———— *Johann Sebastian Bach: Heritage and Obligation*. New Haven, 1952.
Hipkins, Alfred James. *Musical Instruments*. Edinburgh, 1888.
Husmann, Heinrich. "Die Kunst der Fuge als Klavierwerk," *Bach-Jahrbuch* (1938), p. 1.

Jansen, Martin. "Bach's Zahlensymbolik an seinen Passionen untersucht," *Bach-Jahrbuch* (1937), p. 96.

Kastner, Macario Santiago. "Portugiesische und spanische Clavichorde des 18. Jahrhunderts," *Acta Musicologica*, vol. XXIV, fasc. I–II (1952), p. 52.
Keller, Hermann. *Die musikalische Artikulation, insbesondre bei Joh. Seb. Bach.* Stuttgart, 1926.
———— *Die Klavierwerke Bachs*. Leipzig, 1950.
Kellner, Daniel. *Treulicher Unterricht im Generalbass*. Hamburg, 1732.
Kinkeldey, Otto. *Orgel und Klavier in der Musik des 16. Jahrhunderts*. Leipzig, 1910.
Kinsky, Georg. *Katalog des Musikhistorischen Museums von Wilhelm Heyer in Cöln*. Cologne, 1910.
———— "Zur Echtheitsfrage des Berliner Bachflügels," *Bach-Jahrbuch* (1924), p. 124.
———— "Pedalklavier oder Orgel," *Acta Musicologica*, vol. VIII, fasc. III–IV (1936), p. 158.
Kirkpatrick, Ralph. "Eighteenth Century Metronomic Indications," *PAMS* (1938), p. 30.
———— Preface to his (Schirmer) edition of the *Goldberg Variations*. New York, 1938.
Kirnberger, Johann Philipp. *Recueil d'airs de danses characteristiques*. Berlin, 1771.
———— *Die Kunst des reinen Satzes in der Musik*. Berlin and Königsberg, 1774–1779.
Krebs, Carl. "Die besaiteten Klavierinstrumente bis zum Anfang des 17. Jahrhunderts," *Vierteljahrsschrift für Musikwissenschaft*, vol. VIII (1892), pp. 91, 288.
Kuhnau, Johann. *Der musikalische Quacksalber*. 1700. New edition: ed. Curt Berndorf, 1900.
———— *Texte zur Leipziger Kirchenmusik*. 1710.

Landowska, Wanda. "Bach et l'interpretation des œuvres de clavecin de J. S. Bach," *Mercure de France*, November 15, 1905.
———— *La musique ancienne*. Paris, 1909.
———— "Bericht über die Tagung der Neuen Bach-Gesellschaft in Duisburg," *Bach-Jahrbuch* (1910).
———— "En vue de quel instrument Bach a-t-il composé son Wohltemperiertes Klavier?" *La Revue musicale*, vol. IX, no. 2 (December 1, 1927), p. 123.
Landshoff, Ludwig. *Revisionsbericht zur Urtextausgabe von Joh. Seb. Bach's Inventionen und Sinfonien*. Leipzig, 1933.
Lang, Paul Henry. *Music in Western Civilization*. New York, 1941.
Leonhardt, Gustav M. *The Art of Fugue: Bach's Last Harpsichord Work. An Argument.* The Hague, 1952.
Luciani, Sebastiani Artuor. "Clavicorde ou clavecin?" *Revue musicale*, vol. XV, no. 146 (May 1934), p. 146.
Lussy, Mathis. *Traité de l'expression musicale*. Paris, 1874.

Mantel, Georg. "Zur Ausführung der Arpeggien in J. S. Bachs 'Chromatischer Fantasie,' " *Bach-Jahrbuch* (1929), p. 142.

Marpurg, Friedrich Wilhelm. *Die Kunst das Clavier zu spielen*. Berlin, 1750, 1756.

—— *Historisch-kritische Beiträge*. Berlin, 1754–1762.

—— *Anleitung zum Clavierspielen*. Berlin, 1755.

—— *Kritische briefe über die Tonkunst*. Berlin, 1759–1763.

Mattheson, Johann. *Das Neu-eröffnete Orchester*. Hamburg, 1713.

—— *Das beschützte Orchester*. 2 vols. Hamburg, 1717.

—— *Critica Musica*. Hamburg, 1722–1725.

—— *Grosse Generalbassschule*. Hamburg, 1731.

—— *Kern melodischer Wissenschaft*. Hamburg, 1737.

—— *Der vollkommenen Kapellmeister*. Hamburg, 1739.

Mellers, Wilfrid. *François Couperin and the French Classic Tradition*. London, [1949].

Mendel, Arthur. See David, H. T.

Mersenne, Marin. *Harmonie universelle*. 1636.

Mies, Paul. "Zur Frage des Mathematischen bei Bach," *Bach-Jahrbuch* (1939), p. 43.

Milan, Luis de. *El Maistro*. 1535. Modern edition by Leo Schrade in *Publikationen älterer Musik*, vol. II (1927).

Moser, Hans Joachim. *Johann Sebastian Bach*. Berlin, 1935.

—— "Zu Frage der Ausführung der Ornamente bei Seb. Bach," *Bach-Jahrbuch* (1916), p. 8.

Mozart, Leopold. *Versuch einer gründlichen Violinschule*. Augsburg, 1756. New edition: Vienna, 1922. English edition: *A Treatise on the Fundamental Principles of Violin Playing*. Trans. Editha Knocker. London, New York, Toronto, 1948.

Muffat, Georg. *Apparatus musico-organisticus*. 1690.

Muffat, Gottlieb. *Componimenti Musicali per il Cembalo*. No date [1735–1739?]

Müller, Fritz. " 'Kraut und Rüben.' Einige Bemerkungen über die Schlussnummer von J. S. Bachs 'Goldberg-Variationen,' " *Zeitschrift für Musik*, Jahrgang 101 (1934), p. 129.

Nef, Karl. "Clavecymbel und Clavichord," *Jahrbuch der Musikbibliothek Peters*, Jahrgang 10 (1903), p. 15.

—— "Bachs Verhältnis zur Klaviermusik," *Bach-Jahrbuch* (1909), p. 12.

Neidhardt, Johann Georg. *Vorrede zu die beste und leichteste Temperatur des Monochordi*. [1706].

Neupert, Hanns. *Das Cembalo*. Kassel, 1933.

—— *Das Klavichord*. Kassel, 1948.

Niedt, Friedrich Erhardt. *Musikalische Handleitung*. 3 vols. [1700, 1706, 1717].

—— *Musikalisches A B C*. Hamburg, [1708].

Parrish, Carl Georg. "The Early Piano and Its Influence on Keyboard Technique and Composition in the Eighteenth Century." Unpublished dissertation, Harvard University, 1939.

Parry, C. H. H. *Johann Seb. Bach*. New York, 1909.

Paumgartner, Bernhard. *Johann Sebastian Bach*. Vol. I. Zürich, 1950.

Pessl, Yella. "French Patterns and Their Readings in Bach's Secular Music," *PAMS* (1941), p. 8.

—— "Scope and Possibilities of Harpsichord Music," *Proceedings*, M.T.N.A., ser. 36 (1941), p. 204.

Pirro, Andre. *L'Esthetique de Jean Sébastien Bach*. Paris, 1907.

Plamenac, Dragan. "Keyboard Music of the 14th Century," *JAMS*, vol. IV, no. 3 (1951), p. 179.

—— "New Light on Codex Faenza 117," *Kongressbericht, Internationale Gesellschaft für Musikwissenschaft*, Utrecht, 1952, p. 310.

Ponte, Joseph. "Problems in the Performance of J. S. Bach's Clavierübung, part I." Unpublished honor thesis, Harvard University, 1952.

Praetorius, Michael. *Syntagma Musicum*. 3 vols. 1615–1629.
Purcell, Henry. *A Choice of Lessons for the Harpsichord or Spinet*. London, 1696.

Quantz, Johann Joachim. *Versuch einer Anweisung die Flöte traversière zu spielen*. Berlin, 1752. Reprint: Ed. Arnold Schering. Leipzig, 1906. Facsimile reprint: *Documenta Musicologica, Erste Reihe*. Druckschriften-Facsimiles, II. Kassel and Basel, 1953.

Reinken, Adam. *Hortus Musicus*, 1687. Reprinted in *Publicaties van de Vereeniging voor Noord-Nederlandsch Muziekgeschiedenis*, vol. XIV (1886).
Rietsch, Henrich. "Zur 'Kunst der Fuge' von J. S. Bach," *Bach-Jahrbuch* (1926), p. 1.
Roethlisberger, Edmond. *Le Clavecin dans l'œuvre de J. S. Bach*. Geneva, 1920.
Rosenwald, Hans. "Changes in the Approach to Bach," *Proceedings*, M.T.N.A., ser. 34 (1939), p. 215.
Rothschild, Fritz. *The Lost Tradition in Music*. New York, 1953.
Rousseau, Jean Jacques. *Dictionnaire de Musique*. 1767.
——— *Methode . . . pour apprendre à chanter*. 1788.

Sachs, Curt. *Real Lexicon der Musikinstrumente*. Berlin, 1913.
——— *Katalog der Sammlung alter Musikinstrumente bei der Staatlichen Hochschule für Musik zu Berlin*. Berlin, 1922.
——— *Das Klavier*. Berlin, 1923.
——— *The History of Musical Instruments*. New York, 1940.
——— *The Commonwealth of Art*. New York, 1946.
——— *Rhythm and Tempo*. New York, 1953.
Saint-Lambert, Michel de. *Les principes du clavecin*. Paris, 1697.
Salazar, Adolfo. *Juan Sebastián Bach*. Mexico, [1951].
Scheibe, Johann Adolf. *Der Critischer Musikus*. Leipzig, 1737–1740.
Schenker, Heinrich. *Brahms Oktaven, Quinten u.a.* Vienna, 1953.
Schering, Arnold. Review of Hugo Goldschmidts, *Die Musikaesthetik des 18. Jahrhunderts, Zeitschrift für Musikwissenschaft*, vol. I, no. 5 (February 1919), p. 298.
——— "Bach und das Symbol," *Bach-Jahrbuch* (1928), p. 119.
——— *Aufführungspraxis der Musik*. Leipzig, 1931.
——— *Das Symbol in der Musik*. Leipzig, 1941.
Schloezer, Boris de. *Introduction à J. S. Bach*. Paris, 1947.
Schmieder, Wolfgang. *Thematisch-systematisches Verzeichnis der musikalischen Werke J. S. Bachs*. Leipzig, 1950.
Schmidt, J. J. *Der biblische Mathematicus*. 1736.
Schmitz, Arnold. *Die Bildlichkeit der wortgebundenen Musik J. S. Bachs*. Mainz, 1950.
Schneider, Max F. *Beiträge zu einer Anleitung Clavichord und Cembalo zu spielen*. Sammlung musikwissenschaftlicher Abhandlungen unter Leitung von Karl Nef, vol. XVI. Strasbourg, 1934.
Schreyer, Johann. *Beiträge zur Bach-Kritik*. Leipzig, 1911–12. *Allgemeine Musikzeitung* (1914).
Schünemann, Georg. "Die Musikinstrumente der 24 Alten," *Archiv für Musikforschung*, Jahrgang 1 (1936), Heft 1, p. 42.
Schweitzer, Albert. *Johann Seb. Bach, le musicien-poète*. Leipzig, 1905. German edition: Leipzig, 1908. English edition: Leipzig, 1911.
Seiffert, Max. *Geschichte der Klaviermusik: Umarbeitung der Geschichte des Klavierspiels und der Klavierliteratur von C. F. Weitzmann*. Leipzig, 1899.
Serauky, Walter. *Die musikalische Nachahmungsaesthetik im Zeitraum von 1700–1850*. Münster, 1929.
——— "Die meuzeitliche Bachforschung und Hans Kaysers Harmonik," *Bach-Jahrbuch* (1949–1950), p. 7.

Simpson, Christoph. *The Principles of Practicle Music*. London, [1665].
Skinner, William, compiler. *The Belle Skinner Collection of Old Musical Instruments*. Holyoke, Mass., 1933.
Smend, Friedrich. *Johann Sebastian Bachs Kirchenkantaten*. 6 small vols. Berlin, 1947.
——— *Luther und Bach*. Berlin, 1947.
——— *Bach, bei seinem Namen gerufen*. Kassel, 1950.
——— *Bach in Köthen*. Berlin, 1951.
Spitta, Philipp. *Johann Sebastian Bach*. 2 vols. Leipzig, 1873–1880.
——— *Musikgeschichtliche Aufsätze*. Berlin, 1892, 1894.
Steglich, Rudolf. *Wege zu Bach*. Regensburg, [1949].
Steinert, Morris. *The Morris Steinert Collection of Keyed and Stringed Instruments*. New York, 1893.
Stellfeld, Dr. J. A. "Bronnen tot de Geschiedenis der Antwerpsche clavecymbel- en orgelbouwers in de XVIe en XVIIe eeuwen," *Vlaamsch Jaarboek voor Muziekgeschiedenis*, Antwerp, 1942, p. 3.
Stratten, Frank B. "The Clavichord Then and Now," *Proceedings*, M.T.N.A., ser. 36 (1941), p. 198.
Strunk, Oliver. *Source Readings in Music History*. New York, 1950.
Sutherland, Gordon. "The Schweitzer Heresy," *Music and Letters*, vol. XXIII, no. 4 (October 1942), p. 265.

Terry, Charles Sanford. *J. S. Bach*. London, 1928.
——— *Bach, The Historical Approach*. New York, 1930.
Tosi, Pierfrancesco. *Opinioni de' cantori antichi e moderni o sieno osservazioni sopra il canto figurato*. Bologna, 1723.
Tovey, Donald Francis. *Essays in Musical Analysis*. London, 1944.
——— *A Companion to "The Art of Fugue."* London, 1931.
Türk, Daniel Gottlob. *Klavierschule*. Leipzig, 1789.

Unger, H. H. *Die Beziehungen zwischen Musik und Rhetorik im 16.–18. Jahrhundert*. Würzburg, 1941.

Vetter, Walther. *Der Kapellmeister Bach*. Potsdam, 1950.
Villanis, Luigi Alberti. *L'arte del Clavicembalo*. Torino, 1901.
Virdung, Sebastian. *Musica getutscht und ausgezogen*. 1511.

Walther, Johann Gottfried. *Musikalisches Lexicon*. Leipzig, 1732. Fascimile reprint: Kassel, 1953.
Weitzmann, C. F. *Geschichte der Klaviermusik*. See Seiffert, Max.
Wercker, Wilhelm. *Studien über die Symmetrie im Bau der Fugen und die Motivische Zusammengehörigkeit der Präludien und Fugen des "Wohltemperierten Klaviers" von Johann Sebastian Bach*. Leipzig, 1922.
Werckmeister, Andreas. *Der edlen Musickunst Würde, Gebrauch und Missbrauch*. Frankfurt, 1691.
Wesley, Samuel. *Letters to Mr. Jacobs relating to the introduction into this country of the works of J. S. Bach*. London, 1875.
Wolff, Christian. *Psychologia empirica*. Frankfurt and Leipzig, 1733.
Wölfflin, Heinrich. *Kunstgeschichtliche Grundbegriffe*. Munich, 1915.
Wolfrum, Philipp. *Johann Sebastian Bach*. Leipzig, 1910.
Wörsching, Joseph. *Die historischen Saiten-Klaviere und der moderne Clavichord und Cembalo Bau*. Mainz, 1946.
Wustmann, Rudolf. "Tonartensymbolik zu Bach's Zeit," *Bach-Jahrbuch* (1911), p. 60.

Index

Abert, H., 230

Acciaccatura, 182

Accent: with trillo, 150, 156, 160; with mordent, 157

Adagio tempo groups, 120, 131, 144

Adagio in G major, 101, 335

Affect: and tempo, 102, 106n, 112, 116, 118, 123–124, 125, 145; and ornamentation, 168, 180; and Couperin's "Tempo Marks," 207–208; and articulation, 208–213, 221–222; of keys, 228–229, 235, 238

Affektenlehre, 116, 211, 213. *See also* Affect

Agricola, 148

Aldrich, Putnam, 149n, 151n; on trills, 162, 163, 164, 169, 171, 172

Alla breve, 121–122, 125–127, 139

Alla sicilianas, 138–139

Allegory, 241–245

Allegro tempo groups, 120–121, 124, 126, 128, 130, 133, 135–136, 144

"Allein Gott in de Höh sei Ehr," hymn, 325

Allemandes, 108n, 115, 128–129, 220. *See also* Dance forms

Altnikol, 126, 277

Anapaest rhythm, 117, 119, 126

Andante tempo groups, 119, 124, 126, 128–129, 130, 131, 136, 138, 144

Angels, flight of, symbol, 248–250

Anglaises, 129. *See also* Dance forms

Appoggiatura, 148, 151, 152, 154, 155n, 163, 173–182, 238; and trill, 150; and sigh, 168

Aria variata in A minor, 110

Arpeggio, 182

Articulation, 18, 266; in Fugue 13, *W.K.* I, 80–81; in Invention 9, 131; authentic slurs, 142, 202–204, 213–221; and inequality, 185–186; and phrasing, 202;

meaning of slur, 204–208; Couperin's "Tempo Marks," 207–208; and affect, 208–213, 221–222; basic rules, 218, 222. *See also* Appendix A, *passim*

Art of the Fugue, 78, 118, 126n, 325, 337–341; number symbolism in, 255, 258; "Augmentation Canon," 176n; Fugue VI, 196; Contrapuncti VIII and XI, 231–232, 308

Auerbach, Cornelia, 18

Bach, Carl Philipp Emanuel, 10, 13, 29, 86n, 310; on tempo, 42n, 108, 117, 120; on ornaments, 147–148, 149n, 150, 151, 152, 154, 163–164, 165, 166–168, 173–174, 176, 177, 178, 179, 267, 309; on triplets, 197; on affect and articulation, 208, 211, 213, 221; use of number 6, 256; Fifth Sonata in *Probestücke*, 44n

Bach, J. Christian, 29n; Sarabande with Variations, 109n; Sonata in B flat major for Violin and Harpsichord, 237, 400

Bach, J. Christoph: Prelude and Fugue in E flat major, 232

Bach, Johann Sebastian: lack of performance information, 1–2; guiding marks 3; debate over instrument preferences, 27–29; specifications of musical instruments, 29n; as romantic, 90; concept of unity of language, 214–215; name theme, 232, 248, 256–257, 258, 308, 341

Bach Festival of *1910*, 29

Bach Flügel (harpsichord), 7–8, 31, 36n, 37n, 60

Banchieri, Adriano, 103

Baroque music, 9n, 11, 93; traditional rules, 1–2, 3, 18–20; ornamentation, 146–147, 148–149; articulation, 201–202, 207; Schering on, 225

Bebung, 10, 90, 91